To Burma and Back

The War Diaries of
Colin Dunford Wood
1939-46

The North-West Frontier, India, Iraq, Egypt,
Burma, China, UK, Germany, Holland

Edited by

James Dunford Wood

Published by
Kensington Square

First published in Great Britain in 2023
by Kensington Square.

ISBN 978-1-7392668-6-8

For Colin's grandchildren.

Colin Dunford Wood on the day he passed out from Sandhurst, 1938.

Contents

Contents

Contents

VIII

Introduction

MY FATHER, COLIN DUNFORD WOOD, kept his diary continuously from early 1939 to the time of his return to the Indian Army in 1946.

After graduating from Sandhurst in 1938, he arrived in India to join the Leicestershire Regiment on the North-West Frontier in Waziristan. It was here that he got his first taste of action, fighting against the Fakir of Ipi, the Osama bin Laden of his day.

Nine months after arriving, war broke out in Europe, and he was posted to the 13th Frontier Force Rifles in Madras. However, he soon grew frustrated. His brother Hugh was flying Blenheim bombers in England, while here he was, as he saw it, stuck in an Indian Army backwater. So in mid-1940 he started to take flying lessons and volunteered to join the RAF.

But there was a problem: his eyesight was less than perfect and he had to fly with specially adapted goggles. However, as he recounts in these pages, he managed to cheat on the eye test and got himself accepted for the 4th Intermediate Flying Training School at RAF Habbaniya, Iraq. As he was later to say - 'from the frying pan into the fire.'

Although RAF Habbaniya was considered a quiet posting, far from the war, it very soon became the front line after Rashid Ali's coup in Baghdad in April 1941. Suddenly Britain's oil supply, and its lines of communication, were in peril, and all that stood between the Iraqis, and their German sponsors, were the 39 trainee pilots and their instructors of 4 IFTS. My father was one of them. The story he tells in these pages is astonishing, and provides the basis for my companion book, 'The Big Little War.'

Of the three Indian army officers who transferred to the RAF alongside Colin, only one would survive the battle. Chapters 1-4 of these diaries cover the period up until be end of the battle, after which Colin graduates as an operational pilot.

Chapters 5-11 cover his time in the RAF in India, from where he is soon posted to support the army against the Japanese advance in Burma. During the chaotic British withdrawal in early 1942, the rapidly depleted RAF units were forced to retreat from one makeshift landing ground to another under constant harassment from Japanese Zeros and Navy 'O's. Colin flies Lysanders and Hurricanes.

In February 1942 he is shot down by friendly fire from the 17th Indian Division, and crash lands into a crocodile-infested river; in April, he is the 'last man in to bat', tasked with flying the last Hurricane out of Burma; in early 1943 he returns with a detachment of Hurricanes in support of the disastrous Arakan Campaign; and in September 1943, after completing over 100 operations, he is awarded the DFC.

Chapters 12-17 cover the period after repatriation to England in 1944. There, an uncertain future awaits him, as it is not at all clear that the RAF will want to keep Indian Army volunteers like him after the war is over.

Meanwhile, it still has a way to run. On arrival back in the UK, Colin is posted to an advanced training unit in Hawarden where he learns how to fly the latest Spitfires. Then, towards the end of 1944, he gets his final operational posting, to 2 Squadron based on Holland. Their role is photo reconnaissance, in support of the Allied advance into Germany across the Rhine in Operation Varsity. It proves every bit as dangerous as his previous flying in Burma. For a while, he doubts he will survive until the end. In fact losses of planes and pilots are so great, that at one point in April 1945 the squadron's low level photo-recces have to be abandoned. Finally, when the end of the war comes, it is something of an anti-climax, as anxious thoughts turn to what the future holds. Will he be sent back to India?

On 8th May 1945 he is in London for VE Day, where 'Two strange women insist on me kissing them in Piccadilly Circus', and he is presented to the King at an investiture.

There follows a scramble for jobs as operational units are wound down. In June he gets himself a posting as Air Movements Officer in The Hague, responsible for organising military flights to and from the Continent. How much work gets done is debatable, as life in Holland immediately after the war is wild, party following party, the alcohol free-flowing.

However, everything comes to a shuddering halt in September. Having survived the entire war without a scratch, Colin drives his jeep into the back of a stationary captured German tank on the autobahn in fog while returning from a party. As it turns out, the editor has that tank to thank for his existence, because repatriated to the UK, Colin spends three months in hospital, where he meets a very pretty young physiotherapist - the editor's mother. Within three months of meeting, they are married.

But just a week before his wedding his worst fears are confirmed - the RAF no longer needs his services, and he is returned to the Indian Army. At the time; this at a time when India is on the verge of Partition.

As Colin notes in an entry in March 1946, he started the war as an 2nd Lieutenant and now finds himself back in the same position, while 'wandering around with as many medals as a Lt Col at least...' It's as if he was never away...

He consoles himself with the knowledge that he will have a wife to keep him company. Except he won't - she immediately gets pregnant, and they are told that she will now need to wait a year before joining him. The diaries end on their tearful parting at a London underground station in April 1946, just three months after meeting, and six weeks after marrying.

I have included as a postscript to this story, an account written by my mother of the voyage she takes with her new baby to join her new husband in India a year later, in March 1947.

These diaries, then, are a vivid portrait of war across several continents and campaigns. Rather than follow the ordered chronology of the tidy historian, who has points to make and theories to prove, the narrative follows the haphazard progress of war on the ground and in the air – encompassing fear, boredom, incompetence, luck, romance, and horror – all interlaced with a self-deprecating humour that kept the man sane.

What's also revealing about them is how his outlook on life changes as he grows up against the background of war. From a naive 20-year-old on the North West Frontier in 1939, raring to go and desperate for action but still unsure of himself, he rapidly gains confidence in the social whirl of Madras, acquiring an irreverent attitude to authority that will stand him in good stead in adventures to come.

Over the course of these pages he meets and gets to know a variety of fascinating characters, including society hostess and Zionist campaigner 'Baffy' Dugdale, SAS hero Major Henry Druce, beautiful MI6 operative Iris Peake, Battle of Britain ace David Crook, Chindit commander and future Governor General of New Zealand Bernard Fergusson, and two Churchills - Winston's brother Jack and his daughter Mary.

He also takes dozens of photographs, including a number of images of Bergen-Belsen a month after its liberation in April 1945. Diaries of this sort are relatively rare, not least because it was forbidden for soldiers and airmen on the front line to record what they saw.

They are full of military expressions, slang and abbreviations, strange place names (occasionally transcribed inaccurately by me and often spelt wrong in the first place by my father), and on occasion snippets of Hindi, Urdu and Pashto. To decipher these, I have added a glossary at the end. Where I have made errors I would be delighted to be corrected!

I hope the reader will enjoy these largely unedited pages for what they are - a unique and unvarnished record of the often chaotic highs and lows of fighting and loving across three continents.

James Dunford Wood, London, September 2023

1

January - September 1939

1st Battalion
Leicestershire Regiment

Razmak / Razani
North-West Frontier

January 2nd 1939

Razani

WE MARCH DOWN TO RAZANI TODAY, TWELVE MILES. We head the column, which includes some other units including the 2/4 Gurkha Rifles We have two picquets to put out, below the Nazri on the left. A snowstorm comes on, and chaps put on their jerkins, but I have not brought mine. I am wearing full pack and haversack, and it strains the shoulders.

At Greenwood's Corner, the Battalion takes a shortcut down the Kud, which is tricky going for the mules. At the bottom of the road there's an icy surface, and one mule is down and unable to get up, the others queuing up behind. We pass on and eventually reach Razani. There's a full stand-to until the C.O. comes round and everything is settled.

Razani is a Battalion camp with a stone perimeter, with six numbered picquets on the surrounding hills, and one up near Melozai. Wana huts are the quarters, and most are dug down, some especially for officers, to head level. This is for protection against snipers.

The 3/14 Punjabis have very kindly moved out into the Brigade camp, ordinarily holes and mule lines, which is now full up, including the 2/4 Gurkha Rifles. The 3/14 and 2/4 are going on to Dandil on the 3rd to take part in a Khaisora column. We have to put up another tent as an anteroom - there's not enough room in the mess for fifteen officers, as well as feed.

Gunga Din[1] unpacks. I have a camp bed, a lilo, and four blankets. I forgot a pillow, so use a pair of greyers. The bed is near the door, and I freeze all night.

---

[1] Colin's nickname for his bearer. 'Gunga Din' is one of Rudyard Kipling's best-known poems. It features two characters, the speaker who is a British soldier fighting in India, and Gunga Din, an Indian water carrier.

Razani camp

January 3rd 1939

RECCE PATROL DOWN TO KHAISORA CROSSING, to let the Brigade through to Dandil. I am wearing chaplis[1] for a first tryout. My platoon picquets Lower Tambre Obo, an old built-up camp picquet, with the remains of a perimeter camp below it, overlooking the head of the Khaisora. A pretty dangerous-looking place, surrounded by nullahs (dry riverbed, ravine) whose beds are out of sight. In front is another platoon on Upper Tambre Obo, overlooking the village. The Green Howards had seven casualties on the Maidan on our left, whilst going up to Mamha Roga. Captain Ainsley was killed up there too. Clarke arrives up, as officer commanding D company, with a bottle of beer. I have just got it open when I get caught with returning fire. However, the platoon scrambles down, under cover of the VB[2] which I sent down to the old campsite, across the Khaisora and up a precipitous bank on the other side.

3

I reckon chaplis beat boots any day, except perhaps in snow. Recce patrol in future is done by gashts *(Urdu: promenade/ inspection patrol or survey on foot - see the Glossary at the end of the book).* Patrols of three or four platoons go out and leapfrog from hill to hill, parallel to the road, hoping to catch a Dushman (local word for an enemy). There's Khasadar picquet, Morton's Bump (after a lad in 3/14), 72, 71, and Knife Edge. Up the other way, it's more dangerous, with two villages, Razani and Zargaran.

We did a wonderful gasht up there to reconnoitre Zorgat Algad and it looks pretty grim, with a ruined village. I was holding a shale crest and took a section down the side of Zargaran to hold a position looking up towards Zorgat Algad, to cover a platoon. I needed a bodyguard with fixed bayonets as protection from fierce dogs, but the threat of a stone seemed quite sufficient.

Life in Razani when there's no patrolling is pretty dull, but we have a seven-a-side football league in which I play. The Gunners win that. Officers vs Sergeants on a Sunday morning and beer afterwards. Most enjoyable. Dick Forsythe is one of the gunners, Captain Guy Lambert is the other officer. Dick arrived in India last Easter, went to Hyderabad and Sind, and has been here eight weeks. Brigade HQ is at Nowshara, and has a section at Dandil. He goes off to Mir Ali after a bit, with all the rest of the gunners, and I take over Sally, a labrador belonging to the Adjutant of 3/14. I have her for about two weeks and am charged R7/12, for 1lb meat per diem @ 4 annas. I wrote to Captain Harvey about it.

I took up a squad and built a cookhouse up at No 4 picquet and did general repairs. Then the main well fell in on the cookhouse and the cook claims he was there, which I don't believe. In excavations, we find two unbroken eggs. Eventually Clarke has to revet with 16ft angle irons and corrugated iron, or the whole post would collapse.

I am pretty ill for three days, following a cold, with a chill on the liver and violent indigestion. Eventually I go up in a staff car on 29th January and roll down to the hospital to find I have catarrhal jaundice. I go back to my quarters and arrange a change of bearers.

Gunga Din gets my goat, always looking as though he had just had his pants kicked. Major Brain 6/13 got me the brother of his, one Attam Khan, a Pathan from near Peshawar. He arrives down at Razani with blankets around him like a tribesman, and I stammer Urdu at him and send him back up, as I am going to Razmak the next day. The handover is completed, and I move into the hospital.

[1] *An Indian kind of sandal or slipper.*
[2] *Viven-Bessières rifle grenade.*

February 10th 1939

RAZMAK

I AM PRONOUNCED BILE FREE AND ADVISED TO GET UP, as I'll soon be discharged. This is the thirteenth day in hospital and I'm about fed up. It was a nice rest at first, between sheets after four weeks in Razani, but a fat-free diet is very monotonous - soup and jelly predominant. The only thing I got my teeth into was toast and jam. Later comes promotion to boiled chicken and mutton and fruit salad. Breakfast is grape nuts, Force and two boiled eggs.

There's a very pleasant Assistant Surgeon here, Irving, and a Major looking just like something off the stage. I move in with Field for a bit who has been evacuated with some sort of flu. He goes out pretty soon. Captain Fowler, who succeeded Murray as the Doctor at Razani, looks in and says that a gang of Badmashes with a gun were reported between Khaisora and Razani.

Much shooting in Razani the other day, but only two villagers chasing a duck. Whilst I was there we had no shooting, the last being about Christmas, but they usually snipe when the Brigade is in camp there.

The picquets got windy one night and blew off all sorts of coloured Very lights at about 7.30 pm in the rain. Someone heard a noise in Nullah picquet, which guards a well. Nullah 685 all let off.

And our No 3 post too, thinking they saw someone just outside the wall. But only an Indian at the latrines.

They sacked 100 Khasadars up at Razmak Narai. The orderlies are pretty idle here, being the King's, up from Peshawar to relieve ours, as we are short of men. We have been up here three months without a shot fired at us; save two or three which landed on my platoon's sangars (sangar: an observation post) on patrol. Of course, I was in Nowshara, dammit.

A column went out Makin way just before Christmas, I had a platoon up Gibralter to cover them. A colossal battle they have at Tandi China corner. I hear guns, VBs and MGs. They come home with about twenty casualties. Two men are shot dead in Shora picquet, by the red fort. Whilst we are down in Razani, they shoot up some recce troops in Razmak.

There is the famous occasion in early December when the lad near Bakkoke picquet lets off thirty or forty shots at gunners mules returning from patrol. They lose two mules, and lots of artillery open on him. No good. Later that evening he moves around and puts a few into the camp - 6/13 lines and 2/7 Rajputs. One of the perimeter posts has V.B. trained on where he is believed to have been. They didn't open up as they were not risking punishment. Bloody fools.

Maybe it's the old custom of watching a new unit, watching it first keen, then going slack (familiarity breeds contempt) and eventually someone buys it. I hope it won't be me.

The 2nd Brigade including the Royal Ulster Rifles has moved up to Bannu, but it may only be normal relief of 1st Brigade. Rumour has it that they go to the lower end of Khaisora, and the 1st Brigade, who are now back in Dandil, take the upper end. It's also rumoured the Leicesters remain in Razani until 2/12 come as relief of 3/14 on March 15th. The 6/13 hung their shield last night and the first casualty comes down this morning - a Major Allan RIASC, who got hit by a bottle or some'at and broke his "eye film".

I have trouble getting books from the Club babu. I sent for his catalogue, and he swore he hadn't one, eventually relenting and letting me have it two days later, when I'd asked Fowler to call in and order it. I chose some books, got 'em, but next time he claimed they were all out. I'll sort him when I get up there.

Intelligence reports that Ipi is trying for a Holy War, when his pals have returned from the Plains. Also rumours of declaring operations, and Brain says they are giving a medal for 1938 and that we shall be eligible. Had a letter from Biddy Benbow, wanting a photo of me, and one from Bill[1] having taken six days only. I thought it took that to Karachi alone. He has no opinion of Arabs, "Oozlebats" or Jews, but hasn't had a battle yet. Nor have I for that matter. The troops reckon the Green Howards were pulling their legs. They got pitched straight into war when they arrived, whilst we have had three months calm, for training. I heard that the bushman who shot up the gate so long ago was ambushed by two Gurkhas and they chopped his hands off. Maybe. I also hear they got the chap who sniped Razmak, whilst we have been away, over by HMS Nelson, a factory chimney and incinerator. His fate I suppose will be six months jug, and when he's let out I believe they give him 50 chips to start life anew. It's so damn silly, he should be charged with attempted murder, or treason, as I believe he was a Khasadar *(local militia)*.

[1] *Colin's best friend Bill Robinson, based in Palestine.*

February 11th 1939

Razmak

I am up and walking about for two days now. Captain Fowler comes up and says he is treating a Khasadar who got shot in the Razani shooting the other day. On the second attempt, he got a bullet out of the Khasadar's foot, also some gravel and small stones, so reckons it must have been a ricochet. Pallot, who is acting adjutant up here, tells me there passed through his hands a request from 1/12 for a report on me. Lt Col Lockhart actually. I had thought that was a dead letter now. However, Quien Sabe? Major Allan got hit by a jerry whilst playing rugger in the club, and I believe there were one or two other casualties too.

First day on a normal diet of fats. Saw Tundan[1] in the bazaar. He was seen in Razani with an armband with BF on it; when questioned, so the story goes, he said "Brigade Photographer". He says he can't publish photos in the press, without getting Brigade's sanction which, he says, takes a month, by which time the photos no longer have any news value. Small hopes for me; there might be court-martials and all. I reckon I'm not yet bile-free, as there are deposits about midday. There is much rain lately, especially at night, so perhaps the snow is over, although Irving says it isn't warm here until April. District HQ moves up here, because in D.I.Khan it goes up to 120 degrees. The wind here is known colloquially as the "Sting of Death" and it certainly lives up to its reputation.

I'm sick of the picture, framed, squatting on the mantelpiece - "The man who missed on the first tee at St Andrews".

[1] *A local photographer.(B.R. Tundan was a civilian photographer on the North West frontier, whose images were widely printed for use by British troops).*

February 13th 1939

RAZMAK

A STRANGE INCIDENT LAST NIGHT. At about 11.45 pm there is a noise of someone letting off his rifle continuously, pretty close, and gradually getting further away, as though he were running off down the road. At first I thought it was in the compound, and eventually I dismissed it as some lad letting off fireworks to celebrate. But no, Irving swears it was shooting and that some of the shots hit the MO's mess and officer's quarters. It beats me.

THE MAN WHO MISSED THE BALL ON THE FIRST TEE AT ST. ANDREWS

Today I visit the dentist for a stopping. I see in the Statesman that on the night of February 5th/6th a Madda Khel lashkar[1] let off fifteen shots from 800 feet with a gun at Datta Khel fort. Two penetrated the walls, and eventually an aeroplane from Miramshah dispersed the gang at 2.45 am by moonlight.

One Assistant Surgeon here, an Anglo-Indian, had his own private practice at Razani, amongst the tribesmen, whom he treated in return for chicken and eggs. That's a regular occurrence, apparently, except with a British MO.

[1] Lashkars were rebel tribesmen, this one of the Madda Khel tribe.

February 15th 1939

RAZMAK

THIS MORNING DAWNS WITH SIX INCHES OF SNOW, and it is continually a steady downpour. I have had two teeth stopped and go today for a final polish. I hear the 1st Brigade went out yesterday, down the Khaisora. To join the 2nd Brigade I suppose.

The Faqir of Ipi

Ghazi Mirzali Khan Wazir, commonly known as the Faqir of Ipi, was a Pashtun tribal leader and holy man from Waziristan, an area bordering the North West Frontier province of British India and the non-administered tribal territory straddling the border with Afghanistan. This was, and remains, one of the most remote and anarchic places on earth, whose inhabitants have long cherished a fierce independence from any form of 'civilised' government. Ipi, a 1930's Osama Bin Laden, waged guerrilla warfare against the British Empire from 1936 until the British left in 1947, and, unlike Bin Laden, remained undefeated. Initially based in the village of Ipi, he subsequently relocated to caves near Gurwek, a remote village in North Waziristan on the border with Afghanistan. It was here that he declared an independent state - Pashtunistan - in 1937.

The initial cause of his rebellion was the interference of a British Indian court in the forced marriage and conversion to Islam of a Hindu girl in Bannu. The verdict in her favour enraged the Pashtuns, and Ipi succeeded in uniting the local Wazir tribes and raise a rebellion of 10,000 in the Khaisora Valley. The Pashtun rebels, including women as well as men, blocked roads, overran outposts, attacked picquets and ambushed convoys. In November 1936, the British sent two columns to the Khaisora valley to crush the rebellion, but suffered heavy casualties. Following this, they brought up two squadrons of aircraft, and pursued a campaign of scorched earth from the air, burning villages with petrol bombs and killing cattle with strafing attacks. On New Year's Eve 1936, the RAF bombed one of his remote hideaways in Arsal Kot while an infantry brigade, about 3,000 strong with light tanks, pushed up the virtually impassable valleys under constant sniper fire.

But after storming the lair they found eight caves, grouped on either side of a deep gorge, untouched from the fighting - and empty. It was said that Ipi slipped through a cordon of Frontier Scouts with his head wrapped in a sheet.

Unsurprisingly, the Fakir of Ipi quickly gained a mystical reputation in India - it was said his religious powers would protect his followers from bombs and bullets. The British estimated he could call on over 100,000 fighting men, and that his effective fighting force never dipped below 10,000 lashkars, with access to over 20,000 modern rifles, many manufactured by small gun factories set up in the villages of the tribal lands. Indeed, he was feted by the British themselves, who nicknamed him the 'Scarlet Pimpernel of Waziristan' - "They sought him here, they sought him there, those columns sought him everywhere."

The Waziristan insurgency was the only place throughout the Empire in the late 1930s where British officers could gain combat experience, and it got a reputation as a place of high adventure, much prized as a first posting by officers, such as Colin, graduating from Sandhurst.

Having failed to capture Ipi or bomb him into submission with their expeditionary forces and air campaigns, the British decided in 1937 to permanently garrison the area, in a new 'Forward Frontier' policy. 40,000 British-Indian troops, mostly Sikhs from the Punjab led by British officers, were based in Razmak, Bannu and Wanu. In response to an ambush by Waziristani tribesmen in which they killed over fifty British soldiers (including fifteen officers) - the Shahur Tangi ambush (see p. 29 for a description) - the British attempted to subdue the area through columns launched from their cantonments and picqueting on the hills, but they failed to quell the uprising and, with a constant stream of casualties, they eventually retreated to camp, concentrating instead on imposing fines and destroying the houses of the rebel leaders. This retreat was seized upon by the rebels as a great victory for Ipi, whose reputation soared, and he was soon being courted by the Italian and German legations in Kabul, who saw a way to destabilise the British. They offered him money and guns, some of which got through, but fortunately for the British, Ipi was disinclined to make an alliance with any foreign power, and he continued on his singular but highly effective guerilla campaign, at his own pace.

11

Finallly, tired of their inability to capture him, the British offered him a pardon and ceasefire in 1938, but he rejected it. He continued harassing the British, tying up valuable Indian divisions, throughout the war, and once the British left in 1947, he continued his struggle for independence against the newly created state of Pakistan.

He died peacefully in his bed in 1960, and his obituary in the Times described him as a "doughty and honourable opponent, a man of principle and saintliness, a redoubtable organiser of tribal warfare."

The Brigadier came in yesterday, after presenting Irving with his L.S. and G.C. medal. Andrews's "Challenge of the North West Frontier" puts forward some interesting opinions. Russia is no longer a menace, being occupied with her own undeveloped Asiatic territory, and faced with a German-Japan axis. India pays for the British troops out here, has no say in their employment, takes orders from Britain in the League of Nations, so we obtain two votes and seats there. He reckons there's no justification for keeping such a large army on the frontier. It's an Imperial reserve, no doubt, paid for by India, but our Waziristan policy seems a failure, and so many troops only irritate the tribesmen. He advocates a withdrawal, and the establishment of medical centres, as a beginning of peaceful administration. Air bombing, even with warning, seems to be just as barbarous in the actual results obtained, driving the homeless tribesmen to the rifle as a means of subsistence.

But they are responsible for raids on the plains or into Afghanistan - surely adequate border patrols and posts would keep the Plains safe? Maybe the Chatfield commission will have far-reaching developments and suggestions to put forward in their report. But Peter Fleming's account of Russian activities in Sinkiang seems to bear out the old bogey.[1]

[1] *News From Tartary, published 1936.*

February 16th 1939

RAZMAK

ABOUT FOURTEEN INCHES OF SNOW. They say that that gun was tried out on Datta Khel again, a few days ago, and blew up, taking three dushmen with it.

Had a talk with Major Allan. Razcol last year had 32 killed and 97 wounded, on what were 'Peace' columns. The Green Howards were asked why they used field dressings on peace columns. They replied that they had some casualties and were then, so he says, asked to state their authority for having casualties on peace columns!

The new well behind Somme lines was found by an RIASC officer, a water diviner. He used a twig, or a piece of wire. Major Allan was shown how to use it, and got a distinct tremor over a small burn. He came up with the original occupation troops in 1923, and was horrified at my description of the troops getting browned off, saying it was the old, old story, and we should buy it sooner or later.

Lord Chatfield was shown some mountain howitzers at Dandil, and asked how they were transported. When told on a mule, he exclaimed "But you can't get that on a mule!" He never realised that they were taken to pieces! After all his service, even though a naval officer. I am due for discharge tomorrow, being the 20th day of incarceration.

February 19th 1939

RAZMAK

I SEE THE BACK INTELLIGENCE REPORTS TODAY. Datta Khel seems to have been besieged for about a week. The gun that blew up was a 2.75" of local make, firing explosive shells. Mirali also seems to have been sniped pretty frequently, and all that upper Tochi area seems to be in a turmoil. Ipi is trying to get help from both sides of the border, and is receiving cash from the sale of animal skins, slaughtered for Id. All the recent sniping of Razmak and patrols is put down to the dismissed Tori Khel Khasadars. I think they were dismissed because their section of the Tori Khel failed to turn in the local outlaws who they were harbouring.

I play squash with Major James, then we go down to say goodbye to the 6/13. Brain is there and a lot of the 5/11. The proofs of my photographs are not very good, so I will go down tomorrow and get them done again.

Officer's lines at Razmak camp in winter.

February 20th 1939

THERE HAS BEEN NO MAIL FOR TWO DAYS, but it has stopped snowing today, and they are snow clearing, so it ought to get up today. My sea boots are a godsend. There's absolutely nothing to do up here. Saw Wallace Beery in "The Bad Man of Brimstone" the other night, which I missed seeing at home. It was on in Chester, when I changed there on my way to stay with Jonah.

Attam Khan (Colin's bearer) is doing pretty well, and my room looks as though it has been done up when I return from hospital. Feeding in the Club is very good and all for Rs 3/- a day. There are a few RIASC majors who mess there, and the Padre, two RCs, a Veterinary officer and an engineer too. Azarrepo has just come back from down the Jandola road. There is a scout post of 300 at Sarroga, and they apparently have fifteen "hostages" there. These are near relations of local badmashes, and they are in a sort of concentration camp receiving eight annas a day. If the badmashes

15

Khasadars, Lashkars and Khels

Before the British arrived, the hill-based frontier tribes survived by raiding the fertile valleys in summer. Their own stony hillsides were barren, and apart from some sheep, did not yield much of a living. So in order to keep them quiet, and to persuade them to cease raiding across the border into the administered areas, the British paid the tribal chiefs a stipend to keep the peace and 'render services' such as guard roads and camps. This cash grant amounted to one million rupees in 1939. In return, the tribal chiefs supplied manpower to undertake these tasks, called khasadars. (See opposite - the photograph was taken either by Colin or Arora, the local Army photographer, and a print bought by Colin.).

Cleverly, though, the chieftains tended to supply young boys and elderly men, all pre- or post fighting age, which meant that they retained a fighting force of fit young men should the need arise. These khasadars were often fairly useless. Whenever the Faqir of Ipi launched a raid, or when they were launched by the tribes (contrary to the agreement), these khasadars tended to melt away.

A lashkar refers to a rebel tribesman or a group of them - the young men of fighting age who remained to carry on what they had always done: fighting and scrapping with their neighbours, and with any outside power that attempted to subdue them. The tribal clans and villages they belonged to were called Khels.

misbehave, the "hostages" are put in the jug, receiving only three annas. All this seems damn silly, but I can't fathom the policy of the political administrator here. The hostages smuggled in with them two small boys to provide light entertainment.

That gun that blew up at Datta Khel was found by a scouting patrol. At least, they found the barrel and breech block, a large pool of blood and a man's ear. The site was also well marked by MG fire from the post, so they weren't far out. Letters from Uncle George and Mrs Robinson.

February 26th 1939
Razmak

Continuous snow on and off, for the whole week practically now. The mountain tops look rather grim when you see them outlined in a gap in the smokey grey mist which swirls about their base. They seem to sort of loom out of the mist, especially with the sun behind them. I met a Sikh, clad in a pair of pants, outside his barrack room, giving himself a bath with the aid of soap and cold water in an oil tin, the whole thing swept by an icy snow-laden wind.

The political administrator said the sniper was caught at HMS Nelson, was a small boy, with a rifle about the length of your arm, who said he was potting pigeons. The Masudha brought him in, and he is to be tried by a Jirga. *(An assembly of elders.)*

February 27th 1939
Razmak

I got orders to rejoin Razani yesterday. That's a bit of a blow, as I had intended visiting the 5/13 on March 3rd. However, it snowed a foot or so in the night so I am snowbound up here today.

Waziris at a tribal jirga, image by Arora.

February 28th 1939

RAZMAK

STILL SNOWING. RAZANI POSTPONED until Friday for some reason. I pay Attam Khan today, and when it is all settled he takes a look at it and asks what he is going to get next month. I tell him the same, and then he breaks out about the Major sahib giving him 35/- and 10/- for the contract. I say all very well but I'm not a Major sahib yet, nor drawing a Major sahib's pay, but when I transfer to the Indian army I will give him a rise. He has to be content with that.

I took a walk around the wall yesterday, at least I waded round and at the 2/1 G. lines I came upon a snow fight. I potted Seaward, was ambushed, and then joined in. The enemy were Sikh gunners living opposite. I broke one window and tried to hit some spectators at open windows but no good. I received one right down the throat, almost choking over it.

It's a queer site to look along one of the roads with an exit gate at its end, especially if slightly uphill. The white nothingness at the end gives the impression of it being a sort of pier head. Reminiscent

19

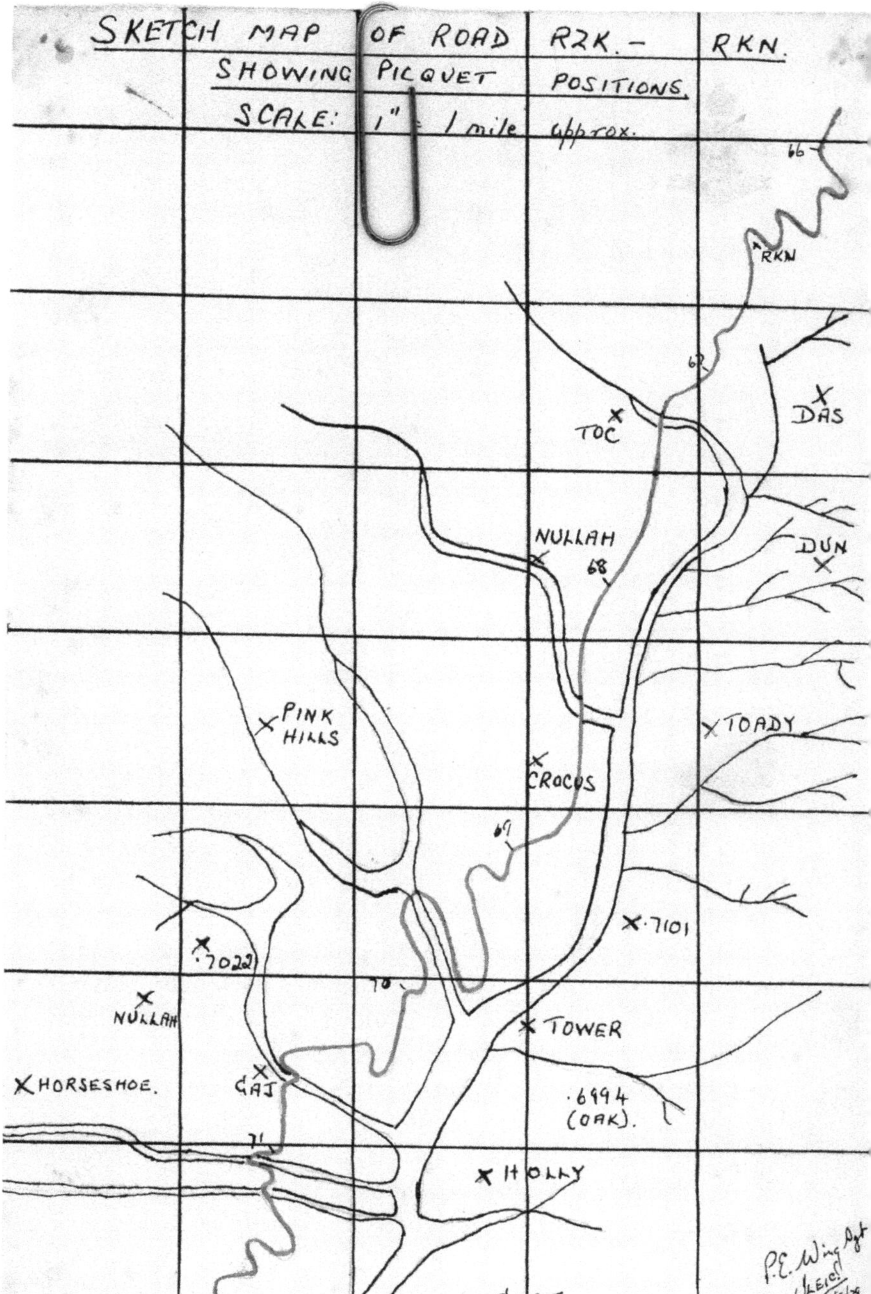

SKETCH MAP OF ROAD R2K. - RKN.
SHOWING PICQUET POSITIONS.
SCALE: 1" = 1 mile approx.

66

RKN

67

TOC

DAS

NULLAH
68

DUN

PINK
HILLS

TOADY

CROCUS

67

.7101

.7022

70

NULLAH

TOWER

HORSESHOE.

GAJ

.6994
(OAK).

71

HOLLY

GOAT

P.E. Wing Sgt
1/K.E.(O)
14/9/09

of Tiree. I see in the intelligence of India that all Pathan militiamen in the 4/2 have been discharged, as their services could no longer be relied upon. The Pathan quarter guard did nothing about the incident, and it was a Pathan who shot up the British officers. One Royal Ulster Regiment lad wounded the other day in Khaisora.

March 2nd 1939

Razmak

I GO OUT DOG SHOOTING with the Provost Sergeant, and Carey as well, and we shoot four pie dogs. Three in the 5/11 Officers lines, which won't go down too well, as we left the bodies lying there by the side of the path. Whilst out on the Jandola road, outside No 2. gate, I slip in my sea boots on the icy surface and break the stock of my gun and also the spectacle lens in my hip pocket. A damn silly thing to do. The Provost Sergeant said that about three weeks ago two 6/11 Jawas, carting out refuse just beyond HMS Razmak, were caught and stripped of everything, being sent back starko with their mules.

He also said some Chinamen operated a gambling den in the skating rink and several chaps lost up to Rs 200/-. One sportsman decided to take his revenge, as when he had returned to ask for Rs 10/- or so back for fags, he was thrown out. One night, whilst going to shut the bazaar, the Provost Sergeant saw a match striking close to the ground by the skating rink walls. He leapt over the wire, and the fellow got away but he found the walls petrol-soaked, breast-high.

March 5th 1939

Razani

HAD A LAST EVENING'S DOG SHOOT before coming down here on the 3rd. Badly hit one pie behind the abattoir, and I blew up another one in Borretts Park, but not much game out. James drove us down and we had a look at his well in the nullah.

Yesterday I went on a gasht and it rained with occasional snow, but I had a ground sheet which kept most of it off. The route was 72, 72 forward, Peacock Tree, and then Miller and I were ordered up to Zawata Manza ridge. This is "ungashted" country, and a bloody place to get up. About four or five nullahs seem to converge at the foot of a knife edge, and we could have been enfiladed out of sight of the MG covering fire. A Tochi scout picquet was at the top - keen-looking fellows squatting motionless with their rifles behind rocks. How different from the British soldier! They never moved, and hardly spoke.

One of the machine gunners on guard last night shot himself in the thigh with his revolver. He saw a bit of rust on the hammer and cocked it to clean it off. It went off and then exploded. It also must have been a dud charge, as the bullet broke the bone and is lodged in the leg. No marks of burning either. He was a Grimsby man, and claims he was so excited about Grimsby Town winning their cup match, that the accident happened.[1]

[1] *They beat Chelsea 1-0 in the 6th round of the FA Cup on March 4th, then went on to lose the FA Cup semi-finals to Wolves on March 25th.*

March 7th 1939

RAZANI

YESTERDAY I'M CAUGHT WITH THE "GENERAL ALARM" at 1 am, and get as far as the M.I. room on my way to the lines, in rubber boots and overcoat, before I realise what a bloody fool I am.

On a gasht yesterday. No. 7 picquet, along 70 ridge, Gardai camp, No. 72 and home. It is very pleasant down by Gardai camp, having crossed the nullah. A sound of a small burn in the nullah bed, an up convoy crossing the Khaisora, sounding like the roar of the sea.

I fancy I hear a sheep bleat, and I am back in Tiree. All very pleasant. Several loose camels can be seen grazing behind a flock of goats.

March 8th 1939

Razani

GOOD GASHT TODAY – No. 7, No. 74, Gardai, and then searched the ground overlooking Shini Alghad, where it joins the Khairsora. There was a Khasadar on No. 72 with a naik's stripes (Indian army corporal), who said he could arrange shooting up and down for Chakor (a bird) and Khargosh (rabbit), which latter were "so high", he said, putting his hand to the ground and sticking his fingers out from his ears like an elf. This is a rare opportunity, though I can't say I have ever seen one there. There is much aerial bombing, on and off for a week or so, and loud sounds from Mami Rohga way.

March 10th 1939

Bannu

AN RIASC CAPTAIN IS DETAINED at Razani with his convoy. He gives me a lift to Bannu on a lorry, the remainder knocking off at Mir Ali. It was an open sort of lorry, no windscreen, only a bit of tarpaulin to cover your knees. The rain came in, hit the back of the cab, and formed a large puddle which soaked my arse to the skin. I had understood it was essential to leave Bannu by 12.15, so I curse the driver to get me there in time and to go faster - but to no avail.

There is water in the nullah, and green stuff springing up in fields on the banks, a welcome sight. We reach Bagai Bannu depot at about 12.25 but they don't mind, and say the road is open until 4 pm. I seem to remember threatening a tonga wallah with my revolver, to make him get off the road quicker, as I was in such a bloody hurry. Bagai had a beautiful Oldsmobile ready, and off we go to Kohat. That stretch – Bannu-Kohat – is pretty desolate, a salt range looking like sandstone. No vegetation, all this bare red earth. We pass a few police posts, but no sign of R.P. troops or sangars or picquets.

There is a fellow here, Heard of 3/12. He was in Wanu during the Shahur Tangi show[1], and lost one subaltern of about six months service. About six British Officers were killed and nine wounded. A convoy with Wanu pay, and scouts, had passed through the gorge the day before, and they saw all these birds, like vultures, lining the Tangi. They said they were just sitting there watching, beady-eyed. In the Club, some wit said they were bagging who would get who, for future reference. Quite true.

Next day the convoy was told by Khasadars at Manzani that it would be suicide to go on. In the official report, the blame was put on the political agent - "Consequent on the political strategy..." – so off the convoy went and the Tangi wasn't picketed. They were well and truly ambushed. Fire poured in all along the line. A company of Punjabis, as local protection, took to the hills overlooking the Tangi, and did their best. The armoured cars did theirs. After they had finished the slaughter, the tribesmen raided the lorries, took what they wanted (about the only arms were British Officers' revolvers), and left the next morning.

Scouts had arrived the evening before, but could only close picquet the column, so that anyone coming near them went to hell, but could loot the convoy at his leisure. The convoy eventually reached Wana, with whole lorries full of dead, shot in the first volley. The bloody shame was that everyone knew it would happen, yet the convoy was allowed through.

Heard had also seen cheetah hunting – a disgraceful sport. The cheetah is sent after a herd of buck in the manner of a falcon. If well-trained, it tracks down a good stag and holds it down, without breaking its skin. Then the tribesmen slit its belly, having first castrated it, whilst it is still alive, and give the cheetah some blood

'Through the gate: returning to camp'.

from the bowels, apparently the only way to make the cheetah let go.

Went drinking to the Ekins with Hearn. Colonel Ekin seems to think the Bagai and the Mashud contractors pay out half their earnings to the Badmashes to keep the pot boiling. He reckons Razmak, being made up of regular troops instead of scouts, is the wrong principle for Waziristan, and the worst blunder we ever made. He recommends withdrawing to the administrative border, and building a sort of "Taggarts Wall"[2], with troops behind it, and possibly scouts inside the area.

Kohat is rather like Bannu, only smaller, and with magnificent flowers just now. A rather nice bazaar too, natural, and not like Razmak's pseudo-Bond Street.

[1] *An infamous ambush of the Royal Corps of Signals in the Shahur Tangi gorge in 1937.*
[2] *A barbed wire fence erected by the British in Palestine in 1938, to keep militants from infiltrating from Syria to the North. Charles Tegart was an advisor on the suppression of terrorism.*

Indian Army Infantry Regiments, 1938

Throughout the diaries there are references to units such as 6/13, 2/12, 3/14 etc. The first number denotes the Battalion (regiments typically had 3-5 Battalions), while the second corresponds to the regiment denominator as below. G.R. is normally added where the text refers to a Gurkha regiment.

1st Punjab Regiment
2nd Punjab Regiment
3rd Madras Regiment
4th Bombay Grenadiers
5th Mahratta Light Infantry
6th Rajputana Rifles
7th Rajput Regiment
8th Punjab Regiment
9th Jat Regiment
10th Baluch Regiment
11th Sikh Regiment
12th Frontier Force Regiment
13th Frontier Force Rifles
14th Punjab Regiment
15th Punjab Regiment
16th Punjab Regiment
17th Dogra Regiment
18th Royal Garhwal Rifles
19th Hyderabad Regiment
20th Burma Rifles
1st King George V's Gurkha Rifles
2nd King Edward's Gurkha Rifles
3rd Queen Alexandra's Gurkha Rifles
4th Prince of Wales's Gurkha Rifles
5th Royal Gurkha Rifles
6th Gurkha Rifles
7th Gurkha Rifles
8th Gurkha Rifles
9th Gurkha Rifles
10th Gurkha Rifles

Regiments and detachments based in Waziristan

Waziristan District: HQ Dera Ismail Khan
Detachment, 2/11th Sikh Regiment
Razmak Brigade: HQ Razmak
11th Light Tank Company, RTR
B Squadron, The Scinde Horse
1st Leicestershire Regiment
2/7th Rajput Regiment
3/10th Baluch Regiment
5/11th Sikh Regiment
2/1st Gurkha Rifles
1/8th Gurkha Rifles
25th Mountain Regiment
Bannu Brigade: HQ Bannu
Skinner's Horse
1 Troop, A Squadron, The Scinde Horse
C Squadron, The Scinde Horse
5/1st Punjab Regiment
1/12th Frontier Force Regiment
1/14th Punjab Regiment
The Tochi Scouts (at Miranshah)
2/12th Frontier Force Regiment (at Mir Ali)
1/4th Gurkha Rifles (at Dandil)
Wana Brigade: HQ Wana
A Squadron, The Scinde Horse (at Manzai)
1 Troop, A Squadron, The Scinde Horse (at Wana)
2/2nd Punjab Regiment (at Manzai)
3/8th Punjab Regiment
1/18th Royal Garhwal Rifles
2/3rd Gurkha Rifles
2/8th Gurkha Rifles
The South Waziristan Scouts (at Jandola)

March 13th 1939

Razani

I return to Razani today. Hired a car from Modern Motor Works for 45/-. There is a fellow wanting to go Bannu way, so he buys the contract for RS 5/- so that I might have hired him straight for 40/-. He is a Pathan and a wag. He offers me hard-boiled eggs, purchased on the roadside. I try to get the Khasadar to sit on the luggage grid, there being insufficient room in the back seat, and this causes much 'bat' and merriment. It is then explained to me that he may fall off, and anyhow the dushmen will not see him in the car, and may open fire. I think he is a bit windy of being exposed to a chance bullet.

March 17th 1939

Razani

Went on a gasht yesterday. Sugarloaf, Greenwood's Corner, Camel Hump, No. 78, Shoulder and home. There's quite a lot of snow still up there, which soaked my feet in my chapplies (Indian army sandals). Rumour seems to have it that we shall return to Razmak about the 26th, and go out on a column shortly afterwards. The home trooping draft has been postponed again until May. A deck tennis court has been rigged up here, and my "City of Venice" "all in" games stand me in good stead here.

We have a concert the other night. The troops spend most of the evenings singing, and you hear a surprising number of hymns. This country must surely be as far from the imagined India as possible. The hills are all covered in short bushy scrub, and at present, there is not a blade of grass anywhere. It is pleasant to sit up a hill on a warm day and watch the lower heights and nullahs. Traffic on the road, or another picquet going up below you, are like so many ants, although their movements are easily distinguishable.

'Convoy halt at Dandil'. Image by the photographer Tundan, Colin in shorts.

One can easily imagine a dushman lying behind a rock and taking careful aim at one.

I have my confidential report sent down from Razmak. I am 'tactful with Indians, strictly temperate, and rather abrupt.'

March 19th 1939

RAZANI

INTELLIGENCE REPORTS THAT DURING AN ACTION on the 16th in Khaisora, when the 1st Brigade was trying to evict some enemy from caves where they were lurking, (a very difficult and dangerous job by all accounts, as they have no mortars up there), Lt Beale from 3/17 was killed with ten Indian other ranks, along with two British officers wounded, one Indian officer and ten Indian other ranks. The enemy was reported to have 15 dead, 7 expected dead, and 20 were estimated as being wounded.

There are some gunners here, on their way down from Razmak. Apparently the R.U.R. (Royal Ulster Rifles) are a bloodthirsty lot, baying for dead tribesmen. A section was out doing something or other when they observed 15 armed men or so. After some loud discussion, they decided they were "blankety scouts". Just then three shots rang out, the section commander (Cooley, MM) fell with a bullet through the neck, and two others received holes in their Topees. Then they lay down and opened fire, killing six dushmen, the rest presumably fleeing. Not a bad effort.

There is much talk of us returning to Razmak in a few days, and more talk of the concentration of Razcol, so as to go out in April sometime. I only hope to God they do.

March 22nd 1939

RAZANI

THE 3/17 C.O. WAS STABBED IN THE ARM, and Simon was wounded by a bullet. Those were the two British officers wounded when Lt Beale was killed.

Gasht to Upper Tambre Obo yesterday, by lorry there and back. Had a long talk with my Khasadar, one Halim Khan. He says there will be a war round here in the warm weather, and mentioned a Holy War led by the Tori Khel. He has met Ipi, and says he is a young man with not much beard, who sits in one place all the time and dictates orders to others to do the work. His rifle cost him Rs 100/-, and he showed me a bullet wound between his toes which he got whilst defending a lorry attacked by dushmen in the nullah here. He was a sentry there and claims to have hit two dushmen. They gave us tea on No. 72 and I fox a few Khasadars with the three-card trick.

Talking of cards, one night in Razmak the C.O. was playing bridge and called "Two spades". The bearer who had brought in the drinks said "bahnt achcha" and left, to return with a toothpick. Now every bearer gets a toothpick on the command "Two spades".

March 27th 1939

Razani

Did a gasht down to Lower Tambre Obo in lorries. Nothing of note, though I fell down a steep slope and skinned my arm. Next day a long gasht up to No. 78 and No. 80. There I met the major (Moriarty) in command of the company of Baluchis in Alexandra picquet. He had not seen anybody for a week, and invited me up for a beer, but there wasn't time.

Some gunners and RIASC came up with several hundred mules, spending the night here on the way. They are with 2 Brigade in the Shaktu. Dushmen in caves were apparently dug in under an overhang, and so could not be got at. Beale, the 3/17 adjutant, crawled along the overhang and peered over, hoping to shoot someone with his revolver. But there were a few more enemy up the nullah, a little further on, and they shot him in the head. The P.A. eventually induced the 12 or so remaining to come out of their cave, saying their lives would be spared. They did, but suddenly one of them stabbed the C.O. in the arm. The Dogras then went in with the bayonet, and massacred the lot.

The Royal Ulsters take over from us on the 30th, when we march back to Razmak. They and 2/1 G.R. have to sit in the old camp for the night, which will be bloody awful as it has rained on and off now for three days. The section commander of the R.U.R. who got the bullet in the neck has just got the M.M. I relieve Ghari picquet today, and the tents up there are pretty flooded.

April 1st 1939

Razani

I come under fire for the first time today. I was up at 7022 Picquet which has been shot up before, and on which my platoon was shot up when I was in Nowshera. Well, Barlow's

Crossley armoured cars negotiating Greenwood's Corner.

platoon relieves me at about 12 o'clock so that I can get lunch at Company HQ. I cover his platoon off with two rifle sections lining the nullah bank, and the V.B. on Gaj Ridge. They start to move off the top, and his V.B. gunner stands up to prepare to move from his sangar, on the forward slope of the hill. About eight shots come over him, apparently from the usual place, the graveyard – about 1300 yards from Gaj Ridge. Well, they all get down again, and eventually withdraw two or three at a time, without loss. The MGs open up along with the artillery, and my two rifle sections. During spasmodic shooting, three or four shots whistle over my head on Gaj, and I quickly get down behind the V.B.'s sangar. One hits the bank in front of me, and another by the signaller behind me.

The Royal Ulsters relieved us at Razani, and we marched out without incident, although one of my chapplies was nearly sucked off in the wind on Greenwood's Corner shortcut. The R.U.R. have a wonderful reputation for letting off their rifles. They shoot up anyone who is not wearing a topee or a Gurkha hat. The scouts refused to operate unless given shorts to distinguish them. They shot up the Bombay Grenadiers, who were not having any of it, and replied.

Met Fregard, one of the Ulias *(Unattached list, Indian Army)* for the Garhwal Rifles. The Shaktu incident was apparently as follows: The political agent promised safe conduct to the tribesmen in the cave. They came out and were hustled by the bayonets of the Dogras. Then, thinking that they were to die anyway, they turned on the Dogras, including the C.O., and were all slaughtered. The P.A. had to be hustled out of Waziristan and down to the Plains. Bad luck for him, but his life would have been in danger any longer up here.

April 6th 1939

Razani

WHILE OUT HOLDING SHURAGAI, next to Gibraltar, I picked up the jagged base of an exploded Mills grenade on the way home. Letter from Mhairi last night, and Toby is on his way out to Ahomanygen. Manbray is on his way to plant tea in Assam, so I may see him there yet. I hear that Hugh (Colin's elder brother, serving in the RAF) has had his first crash (motor smash) and broke his arm, being now (then, at time of writing) in Cranwell Hospital.

There is a type of crow or shite hawk here that always cries "Hang on, Hang on".

April 11th 1939

Razani

A BIT OF SNIPING SOME TWO DAYS AGO on R.P. troops returning to camps, and also during the relief on Conical picquet. On the night of the 9th/10th someone lit a fire in the supply depot. The long row of lorry sheds opposite Bagai's office was burnt down. It must have been sabotage, as the fire started all along the line of sheds simultaneously. Also, several witnesses say that they saw torches flashing inside, and then someone running away. Anyway, it was a damn good fire, though I missed it being in bed, but the next day at about 1.00 pm there was still a flame licking out of a window. Eight or nine vehicles were destroyed, including a few three-ton lorries, reputed to cost Rs 20,000/- each.

April 13th 1939

Razani

A lot of the staff college are up here on a tour. Willie Armstrong and Abbott of 2/13, and Maloney of 1/12 were amongst them. Nelson of 1/8 G.R. is here too, also Seaward, 2/1 G.R. and Harvey-Kelly, 3/10. Beale, Bellamy and one or two others from Harvey-Kelly's school (Bedford Modern) have been killed in recent years, so we wonder how long he will last.

Armstrong says he will see what he can do for me.

A Gurkha in Bakkohi picquet got cut with stone chips, disturbed by a bullet which came into their foxhole from behind him. They were standing to, to help shepherd in R.P. troops.

A lot of shooting yesterday morning, at a couple of picquets or so down the road. Earlier than usual on an R.P. day. Much rain just recently. Brigade commander's inspection today and I handle a sword for the first time in nine months. I have had some of Tundan's and Arora's photographs enlarged to hang on the wall as pictures, and they are not bad at all.[1]

I hear the Staff College contingent got sniped at Dosalli, where they stopped for a demonstration. Willie Armstrong has the lowdown on the Chatfield report. It won't be published, the report that is, only the results thereof. All battalions will gradually be mechanised, except when up on the Frontier, and 16 battalions, including four Gurkha ones, will be given to the War Office. If they don't want them they will be disbanded. Much more likely

'M.G. in action on R.P.' - clearly posed, most likely taken by Tundan or Arora, and the pnt bought by Colin to illustrate his diary.

they will send them to Singapore or Hong Kong to relieve regular British Battalions.

[1] *B R Tundan & Co Ltd and Arora were both professional civilian photographers on the North West frontier, whose images were widely printed for use by British troops.*

April 15th 1939

RAZANI

THE ARTILLERY ARE PRACTISING TODAY, grouping fairly well on their targets, spurs and hilltops. Yesterday we saw Bakshi picquet relieved by 1/8 GR, and they were sniped and there was intermittent sniping for over an hour. The guns lobbed over three or four shells eventually. The only casualty, so the Khasadars told me, was a Kashmiri from the coolie camp who was cutting wood and put his leg in the way of a bullet.

Summer lightning, thunder and rain today. For the past few days there has been a regular hailstorm just after lunch. I go up to Goat picquet today. We send out a Khasadar picquet with a flag to the next ridge. They do a bit of shooting, and then one gabbles in a high-pitched voice to another back home in the Khasadar hut. He then comes and tells me in Pashtu that they have spotted a lashkar moving towards me, and mentions something about machine guns, so I suppose he wants me to get a gun and slaughter the lot. However, the Khasadars let off a few more shots, more come our way, and we get away safely. Holly picquet, next door, has a few shots over them.

An early start today, rising at 5.30 am. I bought Wittington's Smith and Wesson the other day, giving him mine, which he sold to the Doctor, Fowler, for 20 chips.

April 17th 1939

Razani

The Royal Ulters have been sniped a bit at Razani, and when withdrawing from No. 71 they received a volley; two receiving bullets through their fore and aft, and another with one on the puttee.

Had a party in the Club the other night. Nick and I met a couple of Rajputs, had supper and went to the cinema, and put away a good bit of booze. Talks of a column on the 28th – the Munshi[1] says it's rumoured in the bazaar.

Intelligence reports that the 1/8 GR were opposed by about twenty enemy the other day, and says laconically "two enemy hoped hit".

[1] *Secretary/language teacher.*

36

April 21st 1939

Razani

Went to the Dun today, out and home by lorry, so it wasn't much of a strain. No shooting, but a few shots let off at Toady while withdrawing with 1/8 GR. A gang of about thirty is reported to be lurking around the "RZK area". An R.U.R. was shot in the stomach in Ghari picquet the other day. He was killed, and another got three in the left arm and one in the right. Seems a bit odd to be shot in the stomach behind a breastwork.

I dined with Donald Gordon (2/7) the other night, and took as much as I could hold. I was doing alright until "one for the road" was insisted on, and as I sank that, I could just feel that one more would kill me. The night air wasn't too bracing either, but I made it back safely. We could see Tambre Obo Upper from Dun, which I hadn't noticed the last time I was up there.

April 25th 1939

Razani

Went out to Chapao (raid) on the night of the 21st – two platoons went out, and one lined the wall, standing to. We lay out for about two hours, 8.15-10.15 pm, and saw two jackals in the light of Rifleman Towers' searchlight. Some Gurkhas also went out all night up towards Green Dome, to see if they could catch anything. Went down and talked to some Rajput Indian officers yesterday, but I haven't yet the gift of the gab in Urdu, as have Donald and Mac. I could understand most of what was being said, but could not roll my thoughts out so fluently.

Yesterday I received a bill for Rs 16/- from the "Piffer Mess".[1]

Out collecting detail for a demonstration today, for when the Suffolk's tactical party comes up here. "D" company do three ways of picketing a hill from a column. The first is bloody awful, and we shall all be killed, the second is a bit better, but the chaps have grown "familiar through contempt". The third is the correct way, and no one is killed. An awful lot of bloody rain just now, and a thunderstorm is overhead. I am attached to the Quartermaster for a week, and it's quite an interesting job.

[1] *Mess of the Frontier Force Rifles.*

April 28th 1939

RAZANI

A COUPLE OF DAYS AGO THE LAD who lives between Buckshee and Conical picquets kept up intermittent firing between 1.30 and 4 pm. One shot hit a mule just inside No. 1 gate, and then badly wounded a surveyor Babu. The policeman said he dared not go into his sentry box if it rained, as it wasn't bulletproof.

Yesterday afternoon they saw some snipers lying out in the open, Horseshoe way, and No 2 post sprayed them ineffectively with a V.B. Had a letter from Bill (Bill Robinson, later his best man) today, enjoying himself, but expecting a war in Europe any time, and being rushed to Egypt in case that happens. Went up to Conical on an artillery shoot today. Conical commands a wonderful view, nullahs and reverse slopes innumerable. We controlled the fire by clock code methods, and we were surprisingly accurate. During one lull, an immense boar came ambling out of a clearing and waddled up a nullah out of site. An immense beast he was, and quite out of place up here.

The Rajput Indian officers tried out the skating rink last night and they were damn funny, being old and fairly stout.

Well, today is the day of the supposed column but no reliable news of one yet. Some lads can prove conclusively that there will be one soon, or between such and such dates, with first-hand evidence. Others similarly can prove there will be no column until the so and so'th. I wrote to Colonel Ekin last night to see if I can get any news.

May 1st 1939

RAZANI

WENT OUT ON R.P., ATTACHED TO 2/7 as the reserve platoon. They do themselves well. They gave me another breakfast. The C.O. brought out his lilo, and they usually take out darts and a pack of cards. 7101 was fired on, going up, and coming down about a hundred shots were let off at it and the HQ. I missed all that. There were supposed to have been three hundred dushmen reported by Alexandra picquet the day before. I go out on rifleman's range today – I put up some tins by the nullah bank and let off my revolver at them. I am surprisingly accurate. A letter from Bill the other day, and his photo in battle dress.

May 6th 1939

RAZANI

THE RAJPUTS HAVE A COCKTAIL PARTY on the 3rd. I go down at about 8.00 pm and manage to leave at 9. Old Bill Cummyns (3/10) is in good form, and Harvey-Kelly had to be carried back. R.P. next day. Up 7101, very pleasant and a wonderful view from up there. No shooting that day. Next day we have a demonstration rehearsal which isn't too good. I balls up my orders to start with, being accustomed to giving brief directions out on R.P. Yesterday I heard from Colonel Ekin, advising me to write to Major Smyth, the 2nd in command of 2/13 *(2nd Battalion, Frontier Force Rifles, the Indian army unit where CDW eventually transferred)*. Col Freeland returns on the 18th this month, so I can but wait and hope. Letter from Reggie Malone. He is due for 3/11 FFR.

May 8th 1939

D COY PLAY THE C.I.M.H. AT ICE HOCKEY yesterday. We get ten goals to their five, but a good time is had by all. I have passed the lower Urdu – 127/200 for the oral, and 84/100 for the written. I also have a letter from Niven saying they cannot promise a vacancy, but expect to get one, and will apply to the M.S. for me if I put them down as first choice. Willie Armstrong got onto that for me I think.

May 11th 1939

Razani

ON A WEAPON TRAINING CADRE under Cpl Clarricoates. Had a spot more ice hockey, and beat up C Coy yesterday. It's just beginning to get hot now, and all the badmashes seem to have left the district. I don't think there has been any shooting for about a fortnight. Drank a few beers in the Club last night, and then saw Donald back to bed. Murray has a wonderful accent, which I could sit and listen to for some time.

May 14th 1939

Razani

WENT UP TO HORSE SHOE ON 12TH. It is very pleasant up there, sitting in the sun for eight hours. All quiet save for the buzzing of flies and the odd bee. I try to learn a little Urdu while I am up there. Two horses graze down below. The silence is broken from the ranges under Bakhshi picquet. I take out a short gasht to examine the neighbouring nullahs, and we put up a partridge and a hare. I suddenly realise we have gone a bit too far, and that I should be for the high jump if we caught it. The badmash near Bakhshi puts in a bit of "tachdung-ing". There is a heavy sweet smell from the scrub, and the yellow mossy flowers. Whilst I am having lunch, there is a mighty rushing of wind behind me. On looking round, I see a narrow tornado, about ten yards wide, sweeping up the hillside. One end hits me, and whips off my topee and glasses.

Before the Red Flag appears (to call them in), I spend half an hour watching 7022 cemetery. I see nothing there, but sure enough, later on, the gang opens up. We put a couple of bursts from the V.B. into the cemetery, but I don't believe anyone was really there. The guns put a nice piece of shrapnel just beyond the qabristan (Urdu: cemetery).

District bigwigs are all up here now. I encounter the Intelligence Officer. He says the Brigadier sent 'Bakhshi Joe' a chitthi *(Urdu: epistle or letter, origin of the English word chit)* saying that if he didn't cut it out, he would get his house blown up. 'Bakhshi Joe' has stopped, but another has taken his place. He said that all these chaps wanted was to be such a nuisance to the Sirkar (Urdu: political agent), that we'll say "you ought to be on our side – come and be a Khasadar @ Rs 20/-" All except Ipi, who is honestly thinking of his religion.

Steward of 2/13 is up here on a Mountain warfare course, and is staying in the mess here.

May 17th 1939

Razani

YESTERDAY WE HAD OUR FIRST CASUALTY. We are all out watching the final of the British company brigade football. Suddenly bullets come over from Horseshoe way, and land on the pitch. The course soon clears, except for the Brigadier, who sits there as if he didn't know what the matter was. Chaps line the ditch and take cover. Then 'Bakhshi Joe' starts up an enfilade. He hits a man in C Coy in the chest, just coming out of his bungalow. The

41

man dies in hospital shortly afterwards, the doctors saying he never had a chance. We are all damn lucky out there not to cop it, as I see two or three which, with a slight alteration of the Dushman's aim, would have found marks.

An awful lot of flies come out here now. They wake me up between 6.00 am and 7.00 am by buzzing around my head and settling on my face. There is an O.H. *(Old Harrovian, like CDW)* up here, the district ordnance officer, M.W. Scott, from D.I.K. (Dera Ismail Khan). Mickey Wardle gives me the 'lowdown' on Palestine, and from what he says it seems there is some truth in the atrocity stories which the German press gets hold of. He hasn't much of an opinion of the Royal Scots, a pretty bloodthirsty lot apparently.

Went up to Das picquet on the 15th. A very steep climb, one of the steepest I think. On the top, a sangar or two, and a knife edge, overlooking Shimi village. I hold the knife edge, and we get a wonderful view from there.

May 20th 1939

RAZANI

I GO UP A RIDGE BETWEEN DAS AND DUN again two days ago, part of a brigade scheme for this mountain warfare course. We found a 'sniper's lair' up there. Some rock on the knife edge has been slightly built up to form a sanger covering Dun and the getaway, via Dun picquet. Behind was a tree to give shadow cover, with a few extra branches to help. Suspicious.

I am not on this column on Monday to the Narai. Only fifteen officers are to go, by brigade order. The Ulsters cop it today I believe. They hold No. 72, Knife Edge, M.G., 7 Camp picquet and Khaisora crossing. They had a draft coming out from Palestine. Well, just opposite No. 71 or so, fire was opened on the lorries and on the two sections of M.G. Five men and one British officer were wounded, but it just shows that these chaps can think up a scheme

'Camp rifle inspection'. Image by 'Arora'.

of some sort. They are fired at from Tambre Obo ridge too, which I have picketed many a time.

May 26th 1939

Razani

An Ulster B.O. – Lt Dowlea MC – got hit by a small piece of stone or bullet in the cavity just below the eye. The column went out on the 22nd and back on the 23rd. A few shots were fired on the way out. About midnight a volley of twenty-five or so fired into camp, but with no effect. Out on a Brigade recce show yesterday on Ghariom road, I got up to near the Postman's Daughter on the ridge up there. The Baluchis (3/10) had quite a battle on the right flank, and I saw the tanks returning from their recce, amid a hail of bullets from quite a short range. One RTC got "splashed" on the ear and a few tanks came home with bullet holes.

The Derby was won by Blue Peter (24th May). It costs me six beers as I divide the runners with Mickey Wardle, eight each, and he gets 1st, 2nd and even 3rd.

Letter from Ma and photo of June's wedding. Also from Pop Jacobs, who is planting nasturtiums on top of his air raid shelter for camouflage, and grows mushrooms inside - so long as the peace lasts, that is. Also heard from Toby, who is with the Camerons in Ahmednagar. I took some very fine pictures of Shini village, and neighbouring hills, from up Das the other day.

An interesting lecture by the Resident on 'policy,' but he didn't really say what the policy is, or why we can't retire to Bannu and build a 'Tegart's Wall.' *(See March 10th).*

June 1st 1939

RAZANI

DID A CHAPAO THE OTHER NIGHT. Mickey Wardle sat at Old Reservoir picquet, and I went on to a spur halfway on the wallah between Riflemans' and Landing Ground picquets. There was a bit of a shooting at about 10.30, and one Baluchi was wounded on the perimeter. We just sat there, and listened to the dogs and fellows shouting to each other in the villages. Of course it was bright moonlight, and I could easily have read a book out there. The Coy is now on weapon training, and bloody boring too. Bannu got fired on the other day, with one Indian other ranks being killed. We now have "Whitbread's" beer in the mess, bottled at home, and it's damn good.

June 5th 1939

RAZANI

TONY WARD ROLLS INTO MY ROOM THE OTHER DAY. He is up from the Devons in Murree to be vetted by the 1/8 GR. We have a few beers in the Club with Nelson and Mickey Wardle. He says Macpherson has gone mad, and is now in a loony bin. I see a very nice trip for £37 on P&O - 2nd class, Bombay, Colombo,

Penang, Singapore, Hong Kong, Shanghai, Kobe, and 10 days in Yokohama. Bombay to Bombay in just under 2 months.

The C.O. turned up to inspect the draft the other day with his topee on back to front, and then capped it all by asking a man "why's your flask on the wrong side?". Then there was the one about Cpl Bunell in Razani, who went up to Reggie Cox and said, "The manager of the Tocky Scouts is here to see you, Sir."

The Gunners gave a pretty wild party on Saturday evening. Many were pierced with darts, hit with billiard balls, and Major Marsden, C.O. of 3/10, was pitched through the window inside. Withington looked a bit battered with his arm in a sling. He tried to jump a sofa I believe, but couldn't see it.

June 9th 1939

Razani

WARD RETURNED. He is only up here for four days, but he seemed to have been a bit shaken by it.

I'm in the ranges under Bakhshi picquet for a few days from 12-4:30 pm. Damn hot down there when there is no wind blowing. The General (Quinan) comes round today; he shakes hands with the officers.

June 12th 1939

Razani

DAVID CAREY'S PLATOON GETS SHOT UP on Dun on R.P. on the 10th. His forward right-hand section is withdrawing from their sangar, and receives a volley from that wooded spar about 40 feet away across the nullah on the right of the Khasadar Hut. One man is killed, having been hit about six or seven times. Two others are wounded (including Farry M.M.), and one who receives a couple but manages to get down and fire his rifle. He claims to have got

45

off five rounds and shot a man whom he saw exposed above his cover to fire. He then was hit again, and has his right arm broken in two places, and one in this arse. Before the shooting, the Khasadars reported forty-eight enemy in sight behind Dun.

Lindsey-Young sent up a couple of platoons onto Das, but they had been withdrawn by the time Dun got the R.T.R. I am in 7101, and see a lot of suspicious movement round the Khasadar flag picquet from Dun. In the end a shell lands a few hundred years below them, which shakes them a bit.

June 13th 1939

Razani

THE TRUE VERSION OF THE DUN AFFAIR is that a couple of shots were fired from Dun and attracted everybody's attention. One section then withdrew from their sangars and down the razorback to Khasadar hut. The enemy then occupied their sangars, and blew up the other section, withdrawing from their sangars. It wasn't far away at the wooded nullah lip.

June 17th 1939

Razani

I TURNED OUT TO PLAY FOOTBALL THE OTHER DAY, and find four teams, including the R.A., in possession of the field. An R.A. officer comes up to me and we sort out the tangle. Then he says, "Are you Hugh D.W?" *(CDW's brother)*. I say, "No," and then it turns out he is Godfrey Pearse, up here after three years in Singapore. I went down Thursday night and had a few beers on him.

There are a lot of dust devils going about just now. We had a lot on the range, and one got into the butts whilst the small figure targets were up, and spun them all around. Bakhshi Joe started up again today, whilst we are on P.T. There seems to be another

'Football against R.A.' Image by the photographer Tundan. Colin is fourth from the right, with a V.

gang around here just now, sniping R.P. troops and being a bloody nuisance.

A platoon on our range covering troops got sniped on Goat yesterday. Shots were hitting their sangars, and they said they saw two of the Dushmen moving in the hillside. And all they did was let them have twenty-one shots from the V.B.

I have brought a pair of soccer boots in the bazaar for Rs14, made at home, and they are a great improvement to my game. We played Pearse and his gunners today, and it was a bloody awful exhibition. They took about 5-1 off us, but their troops know less about the game than I do. They won't kick it, they dribble round and then lose it, and above all, they won't mark their opposite numbers.

Extract from Battalion Orders of yesterday. "All officers below field rank, and all PSMs, will write an essay on the following subject in its relation to the defence of the Empire: "A marked failure to appreciate the factor of TIME on the part of the great democracies is the greatest military danger of the day." It took me the time of two cups of tea before I understood its meaning at all.

The sappers and miners bell has just rung 8, so I must go and drink my troubles away. I'm orderly officer tomorrow again.

June 23rd 1939

Razani

The Brigadier drove out to the Narai the other day when we were on R.P. He found a bomb there, and so told the Khasadars to destroy it when the troops had left. They had a few shots, and, thinking it a waste of ammunition, brought it in and laid it on the Brigade verandah. The sappers and miners then took it out and blew it up, with the devil of a bang.

A bomb exploded in the R.A. mule lines in Crocus yesterday, wounding two Indian other ranks. I always thought that was a pretty safe spot there. They also shot up the Tower from the heights above, Khasadars or no Khasadars.

I was out covering the range the other day, up a spur near Bakhshi. Suddenly there was a shot, just in front of that picquet, and movement was observed in the bushes. Then a Ghurka appeared, doubling back to Bakhshi picquet, in shorts and vest. In his left hand was a rifle and in his right a long fat hare.

Went out on chapao last night, from 1:30 until 5:30 am. My platoon lined the wall and slept, by No. 4 gate, and Wardle's went out, under Conical near the nullah, to try and catch the dawn snipers, who pot at mules being exercised. They wounded two Indian other ranks in their lats *(latrines)* a couple of days previously, like this. Nothing was seen, of course, save dawn breaking in Waziristan.

I see Geoffrey Holt in 'Picture Post' in the role of "a day in the life of an undergraduate." The cinema here is getting bloody awful films just now. The sort of type you get as runners-up in a provincial cinema, only rather longer.

Donald Gordon has returned from his course, and I met him where he will always be found, in the Club. R.P. tomorrow, and there seems to be a lot of lead flying round here these days.

Tribesmen broke into the British cemetery the other day, hacked trees about, and generally made a nuisance of themselves. I'm told they like the lead in the coffins, to make ammunition. Ipi is reported to be very short of the stuff, but the Dushmen round here seem to have plenty to spare.

June 25th 1939

RAZANI

I WIN THE OFFICERS AND SERGEANTS under thirty cross-country race. The C.O. says he will give Rs10 to the winner, and I just pip Lonsdale for it. I'm up Dun on R.P. yesterday. Practically every picquet was shot up except Das, Dun, Nullah and Goat. 7101 was in action the whole day. About 2000 rounds were fired, and no known enemy casualties. One gunner, an Indian, was wounded on Crocus. You just hold the Khasadar Hut on Dun now. The roof is sandbagged, with a loophole or two, and you sit up there all day.

I sat on a chair in the shade down below, talking to the Khasadars and eating freshly made chapatis. They even shot up Toq. A ricochet from down below bounced over us on Dun. I come running down Dun, just fail to make the Red Flag on a hill, miss it down below in a nullah, and eventually scramble up Crocus to report in. Harvey, the adjutant says, "What are you doing?"

I say, "Reporting in."

"Well," he says, in a nasty voice, "You're taking your time about it, aren't you!"

Willingly I would have shot him, me on my last legs and all. I heard nothing myself, but the air was pretty thick with lead, all down the road. The staff captain reckons the policy is to sit and wait until the locals get fed up with the Badmashes sniping every day, and when they have killed a Khasadar or two, perhaps the Waziris themselves will take action against them.

I had halted, coming back, between a couple of M.G. sections and a V.B. or two, and never have I heard such a noise.

49

June 29th 1939

OUT ON GAJ YESTERDAY. We leave at 5 am, and back by 2.30 pm. As I was about to withdraw from Ridge, a few shots are let off from a few ridges ahead. I don't know where they go, but Nelson said a few hit the bank on Gaj. It is raining by this time, and the shots sound more like cracks than 'tak-dungs.'

We get in absolutely soaked. A Signals British other ranks got hit in the leg in their canteen the other night. He was rushed to hospital, and the bullet taken out, but he was full of beer and was sick a few times. Since then gangrene has set in, and he has had the leg amputated.

July 4th 1939

RAZANI

HAD LUNCH IN THE MEDICAL MESS ON SUNDAY, at Dunkerton's invitation. A few beers first in the Club, and then we adjourn, Donald as well, at about 2.15. It is just like a breath of bonnie Scotland again, and I discover that Valentine lives in Edinburgh. We then go on to billiards and more beer, and at 4.00 pm I take my leave and go and play soccer. The rest stay until 5.00 pm and later we foregather on the skating rink, even Major James, G.E, as well, for ice hockey.

I take the Higher Urdu exam yesterday, and pass the oral. The second lad in brought out his paper and handed it round, but I was inside, and so missed this bit of "straight from the horse's mouth." The Munshi forecasts that I have passed the written exam as well. I hope so.

A letter from Niven (2/13), that the C.O. says I should go down and visit them in Madras, as it would then be better for all concerned. The C.O. here sends me off to work out the cost, which,

'Rifleman's Tower'

with a warrant and bearer, is Rs150, excluding 5 days' food. Total for the journey I suppose will be about Rs300, a bit much I think.

Lindsey Young then pens a letter to Ellin of 5/13, presumably to ask what it's all about. I personally think that someone else has applied, with strong claims, and they want to have a look at me to see who is the better man. That sounds like 'fall out Dunford Wood.' R.P. tomorrow and today, which they have shot up recently. Still, I am unlucky in these affairs, and I won't even hear a bullet in the air, I bet.

July 7th 1939

Razani

R.P. THE OTHER DAY AND TODAY. I win my bet, but it is a very tricky place to hold, and the Khasadars seemed unusually unfriendly. Two shots are fired from somewhere unseen within 300 feet of me, and go whistling over the heads of the rearguard down on the road.

I can't do anything about that though. Forty eight camels are stolen in broad daylight from outside Mirali. I see they have been offered back, 'on payment.' A chit from Brigade comes round saying a great bomb outrage is expected on the Razmak-Bannu road, on the lines of Shahur Tanji I suppose.

I attend an Indian court-martial yesterday and find I can understand all the interpreting. It is at the 2/7 school, and they give us lunch afterwards. I then return and have my first Pashtu hour with old Keroz Khan. Also go to the sergeants mess to watch company billiards with RIASC. Have a few beers and it's a damn good show, in bed by midnight.

Letter from Ma and Uncle George, enclosing Rs 30 for my 21st. Ma's includes messages from Alec and Johnny Graham etc to "Mr Colin, away among those heathens."

July 13th 1939

RAZANI

WE HAVE A BEANO IN THE CORPORAL'S CLUB on the 8th, and Munday confides to me that he was a cracksman before he joined the army. My 21st is on the 9th and I managed to get hold of a few beers in the Club before lunch. I do a bit of Pashti, then a moon about, and finally go down to the skating rink, where there is a party on, as Harry Rickets is going on his leave the day after. I join him and a few sergeants, and then do a bit of alcoholic skating about 9 pm. And so to bed - a letter and Rs30 from Uncle George.

A bomb bounces off Rifleman's Tower the next night, and they put a couple of bursts into some fleeting figures on the 30 feet range. The court-martial is pretty bloody awful, but we are off it for Brigade Day tomorrow.

The 2/7 give us lunch and a few beers, the Munshi reminding me very forcibly of a dog, and I'm sure old Chico Romilly must surely be the 'technical advisor.'

A 'daring holdup' on MS.60 yesterday just below the Narai, and to all intents and purposes unprotected. A Parsot lorry is held up by having its tires shot, four Hindus wounded, shot and stabbed, and about seven kidnapped. At first I thought Attam Khan was on it, as he comes back today, but he rolls in on the Dak Lorry, having had his wife die on him. Two companies of the 1/8 G.R. then did a surprise gasht from Alexandra picquet back along the top. They surprised about thirty enemy on Bare Patch, and I believe gave them a volley at about thirty yards. The enemy made off, apparently more the worse, and one British officer got hit in the arm. That, I fear, will keep them quiet tomorrow.

Colonel Ellin replied to Lindsey Young that I shouldn't spend £25 going to Madras, and he is writing to Freeland. I write to Niven, and say sorry but the C.O. thinks I will be too long away (three weeks). My application form goes in, in sextuplet, to 2/13, 5/13 and 12th[1], so I hope I come out of that alive and with something worthwhile. Wrote to Stephen King Hall for £1 of letters, so I hope it improves my knowledge. Everyone else's essay except mine seems to have come in, so think it must be so bloody awful, it's gone up for review.

Lindsey Young wants to sprinkle Wooded Ridge Tower with pepper, as an anti-sniping measure. The ridicule would be sufficient. He also proposed those old wicker tubes in toy conjuring sets that you put on your finger, and the harder you pull the tighter they become. You have to push into release I think. He would join all Khasadars up in pairs "finger to finger" and have the whole country laughing.

[1] *Colin was applying to the 2nd and 5th battalions of the 13th Frontier Force Rifles, and the 12th Frontier Force Rifles.*

July 16th 1939

A SNORTER OF A BRIGADE DAY ON THE 14TH. We went up Zargal Algad to False Narai, Green Dome, and onto Bare Patch. Out from 6.00 am until 6.00 pm. Quite a bit of shooting on the top of that ridge. I had to occupy a sangar position, and whilst rushing towards it through the bushes, about 200 feet away, I saw M.G.s kicking up dust all round it. Peter Withington I believe was screaming his head off, lest I get shot by the M.G.s. Eventually, on another sangar, shooting starts off pretty close judging by the noise. One of the M.G. mule drivers claims to see where it comes from, a bush about 500 feet away. I hold his mule and he opens up with his rifle on it, of course with no apparent result. This is too much for the remaining mule drivers, who hook their reins over the crook of their elbows and start blasting the countryside. I have to put a stop to that, as the mules attempt to bolt.

Eventually reach Bare Patch and find two empty (Dushmen's) rounds. The Ghurkhas apparently surprised the enemy there, drew their kukris and put the enemy to flight, as the tribesmen didn't wait. I also found dried blood, from his arm, which was smashed by a bullet. There was a hell of a lot of it, in a dried pool. Also the cover of his field dressing.

Peter Withington and I were sitting having lunch up there, and a couple of bullets passed over. We reckoned they came from Holly, aimed at another picquet lower down, and were 'overs'. I get lost on the way back and have to carry a rifle home from Bare Patch. A real good wind and rain, sweeping like Tiree. Ian Mitchell is very rude when I reach him, and ask him to point me to D Company HQ. Pretty bloody wet, but enjoyed it on the whole.

Next day we are on covering range on Goat. Corporal Atkinson finds a sentry reading "Spicy Adventure Stories", confiscates it, and when he has read a few, I pass a couple of pleasant hours reading it.

Harrow won at Lords, the first time since 1908, and a free fight took place. How I wish I was there, to bash in a few toppers. R.P. tomorrow, advanced guard – and my heel is bruised through playing ice hockey.

July 18th 1939

RAZANI

A NICE BIT OF SHOOTING YESTERDAY. 7022, Oak, 7021 opposite, and Nik on Das has a bit of shooting too. But the enemy does not hold the forward edge. I sit up to the left of Narai Serai. Suddenly a couple of shots ring out, from a ridge about 300 feet away. One NCO says he sees a man raise himself over the sangar to fire, and that the bullet hits the wall just in front of him. Well, two VBs and MGs open up on this sangar and neighbouring ones, and the most glorious waste of ammunition takes place. Now they start up the other side, below Alexandra picquet, and the Ulsters can be heard having a battle further down the road. Much ado about nothing!

It rains like hell on the way back, a sort of hail, and lucky I have a groundsheet. I pass three reasonable-looking Pathan women. I am shown my report on the attachment, and it's not too bad. I am retiring and inclined to be offhand at first sight, as it were, but apart from that I have the official favour, and "a good knowledge of frontier tactics".

July 21st 1939

RAZANI

THERE'S A REALLY GLORIOUS STORM ON JUST NOW. 2 pm, the usual time for rain, but this time it has got a real good wind at its back. This produces pukka-driven spray such as I haven't seen since I left Tiree. You can see it hurtling along in sort of belts, and the noise on my tin roof, combined with the wind in the eaves and edges, is reminiscent of Island House. Only the wind doesn't whine like it used to. A mighty torrent, breast high in places, rushes down the Nullah under Bakhshi picquet, and catches the range covering troops just as they are being withdrawn. Of course, three fools go and drop their rifles in the waters which whip them away. We all go out in the evening until 7.30 looking for them, and one is found. Two cows were seen, borne capsized past the picquets. Also huge boulders, and as Mitchell said, "I never saw anything like it, it would have been called a cloud burst at home!"

Shades of Tiree – try walking round that corner of the Lodge in January!

R.P. yesterday. I walk out to Gaj and back. The sods don't tell me lunch has arrived, so I would have got none but for Walsh who produced his, and two tins of beer.

July 22nd 1939

Razani

I spend all morning looking for those bloody rifles. I dig up the nullah bed, but no go. Mac has taken over the Company, so I must watch my step, I believe. I give the Khasadars this morning a few "daltah rashas" (come here) and "sahib sara larshaks" which seem to sink home, but they will answer in Urdu. Just as well actually, as I would not be able to understand it if they answered in Pashtu. Dicky Lonsdale tells the RSM (regimental sergeant major) "you know nothing about mountain warfare anyway" as a parting shot after an argument. I reckon he has to apologise, as RSM is insulted to the utmost degree.

Must write to Bill tomorrow, but I suppose I shall be out turning stones for rifles. A boil on my chin, blast it. But it's not going too badly. Last night, whilst beckoning sleep on my bed, I look down and see a glow-worm on the blanket, so I knocked him to the floor and put his glow out, just to be on the safe side, of course.

Doulea of R.U.R. got the MC the other day, down in Razani. The day their draft got shot up, he was MG officer down by Khaisora crossing. His guns had to be unloaded and got into action under fire, and apparently one lad got hit and rolled down into the nullah. Doulea hopped down, under fire, and whipped him up again. He was then hit once more and rolled down the khud, so that Doulea had to bring him up a second time.

July 26th 1939

Razani

THE RIFLES HAVE APPARENTLY BEEN GIVEN UP as lost, and as we are duty battalion, I spend the morning clearing scrub from round the 2/8 lines, from which they snipe the camp at night. Did so yesterday to a chorus of all types of firing from the R.P. troops. Dunkerton says it was the hottest day that they have ever had. 2/7 and 3/10 were out, and they brought in a few Khasadars as prisoners. The ground picquet protecting me opened up, Bakhshi way, at movement they are so good at spotting in head-high scrub at 1300 yards. On the way back I met the Gurkhas going out to picquet Bakhshi range. One of their NCOs salutes me, and twenty minutes later is dead with a bullet between his eyes, next door to Nelson.

About 6 pm, whilst I'm sitting in the Mess reading "Khyber Courtship" by Maud Diver[1], the orderly corporal brings the general 'stand-to' round. Out I double, to find everyone in a flap, and only A & C Coys to stand to. They go out with 1/8 to try and catch some 80-150 enemy located at Gaj. They never succeed of course, but manage to open fire at 600 feet or so, on parties seen making off. They just get in by dark, at about 8.15 pm. Stories come in though. Some lad in the Gurkhas had his company HQ and MG mules in the old Serai at Gaj. Every time he tries to get out the door, a swarm of bullets come over from Oak. He eventually sees a few men taking cover up there, so he lets rip with the MGs, and bugger the Khasadars up there. Three of them, wounded, roll into camp later, complaining bitterly.

Undy's HQ had a signal lamp, pointing outwards towards the forward troops, and this drew fire every time it was used. R.P. troops reckoned they had 1000 rounds fired at them, a couple of hundred in half an hour or so. This is supposed to be given to them by Ipi, and they are blowing it.

A tremendous roar a few nights ago, I never heard it, but they blew up a culvert, though without much effect. Lindsay Young says they are trying to hold up R.P. troops, draw more out of camp, and then hop down and "raid a post, and capture a rifle or two". How the bloody hell, I can't think.

Thursday – tomorrow – and I have to dig a bloody garden.

[1] *In the Cornhill Magazine, July 1939*

July 29th 1939

Razani

R.P. as far as Crocus, to cover a perimeter camp being built there for a scout post. D Coy provides the advance guard, with my platoon on the right. A couple of shots near the tower, but the range was too far and we did nothing about it. Then I am sent up to picquet a hill on Narai side of Toady. It has a village on it, with a large tower. We occupy the hilltop, and put up a bit of cover. In the meantime Toady is being shot up from our front. I and two others are squatting behind a brushwood and barbed wire fence, trying to locate this firing. Suddenly a bullet explodes not two yards in front of us, and we are spattered in stones, and then hear the shot. The other two have had blood drawn by stones or something, and when I get home I pick a bit of lead out of my forearm.

Well, the bullets rain down, they strike our sangar, and I see one chip a piece out of the tower. We nip off in two's, back off the hilltop, and as I am leaping the barbed wire I hear a shot, and the chaps say it whistled over my head. We line the backward slopes, and one man says he saw a rifle barrel poke out of the tower and fire at us. I don't believe it, as if this had been so he could hardly have missed at 50 feet. Still, we put a few shots into the tower. One man has left his pack and mug behind that exposed sangar. He says it's not worth risking a life to get it. Then like a fool (I must have been wishing to show off) I hop the wire and rush out there and get it. As I get to the sangar he takes a shot at me and I apparently groan and take cover, as Pierce comes charging over with putties flying shouting "Are ye hit sir, are ye hit?

He helps me up and we run back. I drop my stick and pointer staff, I pick up the pointer but he urges me not to go back for the stick, so it is "abandoned to the enemy". I try to get a man from the village to get it, but they are all so snug I cannot make contact with anyone. They pot us from time to time and we eventually retire, by dribbling off, and as the last sections go, there comes two parting presents, the first ones I hear that whine.

We get back to Crocus, and I am sent on to a spur of Toady to cover it down. Then I discover I left my pipe and field glasses up on that picquet too. Rearguard home, and when just above 70 milestone nullah, Mike Wardle's platoon gets shot at, doing rearguard over Pink hills. Private Tew gets hit in the calf. I locate the firing, and open up with V.B., and then take two sections up under cover of Pink hills to see if I can help. Can't help, so return. We continue to withdraw under a few bullets, and then make Gaj. Here Micky and I cover eighteen troops back from the ridge in front, as they retreat through us. They get over, and are nipping across the flat behind Gaj, when there is 'crack!' – they all fall to the ground and Private Newberry is hit in the arm. Chaps shout for stretcher bearers "This way! That! Medic wanted!" etc. So I leave the shelter of the Gaj Khasadar post and nip down to him. His

59

arm is already bandaged, but he is almost 'out' with the shock and pain so Smith, an NCO, and I hustle him along to a hole by the road. There is a 'crack' and a spurt just as we get there but we make it safely. I then run back up Gaj, and an armoured car comes and takes him away. We are all then pinned to Gaj – three platoons - by two or three men! I thought there was only one man, as we never heard two shots one after the other. All three VBs open up, and two of my men spend the next half hour taking periodic pots at the top of 7022, where of course they "see" movement.

The Red Flag is nearly in the barracks, but Mac signals back and they send out MG and artillery to extricate us. The platoon on the ground gets off creepy crawly Indian fashion by twos and threes, and after half an hour's shooting I get the RTR (military parlance 'ready to return'). Off by sections and run like hell down to the road where there is cover. Mickey Wardle doesn't get the order (he is on the 7022 end) and is left behind for twenty minutes as his signaller is "taking cover". He gets the shock of his life when he finds that I have left him there alone, but that's Mac's fault. There must surely be questions asked as to why Mickey was doing rearguard out as far as Pink Hills. Mac's to blame for that.

They reckon they inflicted seven or eight casualties on that evening show the other day. Last Thursday I am sent on Brigade garden fatigue (labour). There the Sanitary Inspector shows me the Brigade letter that says the fatigue will not be done Thursdays and Sundays. Dick Harvey of course never saw the letter. Blast his eyes.

July 31st 1939

RAZANI

I FIND TWO MORE PIECES OF LEAD, on my chest and forearm, making three in all. I hear all the guns are going to open up at 7.00 pm tonight, suddenly, on the Sidar Alghad, at a range of 4500 feet. It sounds rather grotesque. R.P. tomorrow, but I don't expect I shall even smell a bullet.

August 4th 1939

THE GUNS NEVER OPEN UP. It was that gunner Langford, with the head like a latrine bucket, who started it.

I smelt a couple of bullets on the R.P. yesterday. A new system of Company areas and local gashts was tried. Tanks cooperated, and it all seemed fairly successful. One man got his rifle hit on the fore end on Crocus.

I run 11/20 in the inter-company mile team race. It nearly kills me. Clarke has returned from an attachment to the RAF in Peshawar. That madman P.M. Bond is there, presumably on a short service commission. Intelligence reports three killed and eight wounded on the 25th, mostly during the evening sortie

August 7th 1939

Razani

THE 5/11 WENT OUT AT MIDNIGHT the other night and lay up round Green Dome and Bare Patch. Then 3 Bn Brigade went out the next morning, but no one was caught. One British other ranks shot in the stomach out on R.P., not a pleasant wound I believe. The sergeants came into the Mess for tea and tennis at 5.00 pm. After tea comes beer, and they left at 8.45 after much darts and billiards. A 'tippet' school started, but the RSM breaks it up by saying it's time to push off. R.P. at Dun tomorrow.

A good cartoon in C&M – an armoured car on a broken bridge, signed 'To Waziristan', with its nose in the river, and the tank wallah sitting on the roof with his head in his hands and a cigarette dangling from his lips. A lot of wild-looking tribesmen are rushing down to get him, firing their rifles in the air and waving swords. He says "And they call this peaceful penetration".

August 11th 1939

UP DUN THE OTHER DAY, BUT NO SHOOTING. I chat with the locals in Pashtu and Urdu fairly successfully. Colonel May was shot in his car yesterday evening, outside Bannu on the Mari Indus road. He dined here about ten days ago, with District HQ staff. The Frenchman is staying with us now and Major Callander (2nd in command of the Leicesters) is very amusing about him. A French Canadian comes into the Mess last guest night, and gets as pissed as an owl – and aggressive too.

A letter from Johnny Benbow, who reckons on going to 4/15 in Landi Kotal. I hear from Tony Ward, and under section 143(1) I get the Indian Army allowance from the date of passing Higher Urdu. Therefore on September's pay bill I ought to collect just under 800 chips.

August 13th 1939

DID ADVANCE GUARD TO NARAI and sat on Duncan's picquet. A bit of sniping from the slopes behind Toady, and the Scouts did a gasht in the hills west of Pink Hills. They had a good battle, and most of the day we saw shells bursting over there. I went up to Alexandra picquet in a staff car and had a beer with Donald Gordon. Inside it looks as though it might have stepped out of some film of the frontier, or Beau Geste. A wooden, railed platform all round the top of the wall, for stand-to, gives this impression. A very interesting log book is shown me, with some bloody funny entries in it. The Scouts did a gasht up that way, and were fired on. Some of the garrison are reputed to have heard them say "Don't shoot, we are Scouts", and the shooting stopped.

The Sappers blew up a bomb on the road a couple of furlongs from the Narai, and I see half a culvert that has been blown in, a night or two previously. I also saw some fragments of this bomb, which certainly looked tough enough. They reckon Alex is the highest permanent picquet in the Empire – but I don't know about that.

The Brigadier is reputed to have said that Ipi (now in Khame, so why the hell don't they blow him out of it) is sending up a gun or two to the Razmak front. It is almost a proscribed area up here now, as all the locals have orders to stay indoors on R.P. days, so that anyone out, if not a Khasadar, is liable to get shot. Though I'll be damned if I have ever seen a man yet who might be enemy. You hear the shot, or the bullet arrives, and God bless the Duke where it comes from.

A letter from Clapham today. *(Where his brother Hugh's new wife lived, pregnant with their first child).*

This munshi, Feroz Khan, is very bad mannered. Whilst your attention is fixed on "Hagha Dagha" *(Pashtu: this and that)* or "Khwab o'khial", or whatever it be, he slides a hand up his shirt, rummages about for a little, as though searching for tin tacks in the bottom of a bed, and then produces a long white hair, plucked from the shrubbery on his chest. He then holds it and contemplates it, almost regretfully, finally depositing it on your best Persian carpet. He cast a great many with Mickey Wardle but I, duly warned, used to watch him carefully when he was fiddling about, trying to unbutton his shirt, and stare so hard that he gave it up. Alas, the other day I looked up from the book and saw his hand come out like a snake from his bosom, and the deed was done. When he had gone, there shone a long, thin white hair on the floor.

Corporal Farry has the Military Medal for his effort on Dun on April 10th. He was badly wounded, but continued to fire back, and I reckon he killed the leader of the gang. Some say he was hit in the right shoulder and then turned over and fired from his left shoulder, but I wouldn't know about that. The 2/7 are hanging their shield on August 23rd, and Donald expects to come down from Alex for that. I must get into training as there are only ten days left.

August 15th 1939

Razani

HAD AN INTER-COY FOOTBALL GAME on Sunderland ground today. Some time before halftime, the bullets started to come over, about half a dozen I should think, and a few landed on the pitch. We all ran like bloody cheetahs and got off with no casualties. No 2 post V.B. opened up on a sangar on Horseshoe ridge, where they were supposed to be.

The whole Brigade is going out tonight. Three battalions at 24h00 to surround the villages opposite Dun, on the other side of the road, Mir Khan Khel and Spanam Khel. Anyone out of doors to be treated as enemy. We go out at 02h00 and picquet up to Toady to cover the troops coming home. I have Toady, and need to get up at 01h15.

August 17th 1939

Razani

I MANAGE TO GET TO BED AT 10.30 PM after listening to Mac's detail. However, what with Clarke's wireless, and sort of thinking of the morrow, I get no sleep, and get up at 1.00 am to a cup of tea and half a dozen biscuits. Well, we set off at about 2.00 am and take about half an hour to cross the aerodrome and get onto the road. From there it's all Plain, on the road all the way, and I don't care a damn if they do hear the noise we make with our boots, and open up.

I am sent on to Crocus where I halt, at about 4am, and wait for dawn. I hear two lads come shuffling down the road, so I hop out

The 'post gun' at Razani, fired at dusk to alert the patrols to return to camp.

with my revolver and hold them up. One complains in English that they are Baluchis, and looking for transport. At first light I send up a Khasadar, though he seems goofy and unable to understand my pashtu, and then we follow him onto Toady. The very devil of a noise starts on the other side, and goes on the whole day. There is a bit of shooting on the 7101 side, and we open up from the roof with the V.B. On coming off, we open up (Corporal Webb and his five rounds rapid) to keep their heads down, but I don't think they were really firing at us.

A couple come over on the way home, but I get in at 1.00 pm, shave, bathe, tiffin and am in bed at 2.00 pm to sleep like a snapdragon until 7.00 pm. Up at 7.30, bathe, and Pearse comes in. Afterwards over beer everyone discusses the day's operation.

The Scouts rounded up 58, who are in a "cage" down by the Treasury, guarded by 5/11 and surrounded by a speculative audience of all races. Some got away into the hills, and shot up picquets at 200 feet. A few got in between the outer and inner picquets of 2/1. They shot up the inner ones and then gathered their cloaks and themselves and went into a huddle, for a council of war. One of the outer picquets then got them in the rear with a VB.

2/1 met a party suddenly round a nullah, at ten yards range, and claim to have shot five out of seven of them. 58 prisoners were taken out of the village, and nine enemy estimated killed, but only three bodies recovered to date, and one rifle. The tanks fired an immense quantity of ammunition, and one gurkha got hit in the arse and the other in the knee, the bullet travelling up to near his ribs. All the village dogs started off about half an hour before dawn, and I heard cocks crowing as well. The prisoners were mostly locals from those two villages, with a few badmashes as well, and are to be interrogated about that hold-up below the narai on July 12th.

August 18th 1939
Razani

ROAD OPEN TODAY, and the 6-inchers open up from camp during lunchtime. At least everyone says they are 6 inchers. Had a meeting on the Roller Skating Hockey last night, down in the rink, and I hope to get the show starting sometime next week.

The Intelligence Reports say that Toady was continually shot up on 16th. The first I knew of it. Had arranged to continue that football match today, which was broken up by snipers on 15th, but the troops refuse to play, blast their cowardly souls. Still, it's just as well to give it a rest I suppose. Lt Col May had powder marks on his body and had been shot with a shotgun. A log was placed across the road, but he must have had his revolver unloaded, or under the seat I think, or he would not have been shot at such close range.

Mickey Wardle came off 7101 too soon the other day, owing to the signaller's mistake. Mac, of course, says "When the signaller said to you RTR, did you ask him 'Did HQ say to you No 7 picquet RTR?'" Like hell he did! Mac has never been up a picquet, the bloody fool. God help the Coy on a column with him as OC.

August 19th 1939

RAZANI

IT WAS THE POST GUNS YESTERDAY AFTERNOON, but at about 7.30 pm the 6-inchers went out onto the aerodrome and opened up. They took some time, as they forgot the rangefinder, and had to send back for it. Some locals apparently came in and said that parties of hostiles were in their area, and would we open up? Anyway, they had two targets, and put four six-inch shells on each, and they made some noise too. The RA have to stand-to most of the time to cover the Tochi Scouts camp on Crocus.

August 22nd 1939

RAZANI

WE WERE PLAYING A GAME OF ICE HOCKEY with the C.I.M.H. (military hospital) when at about half time the referee blew the whistle to halt play and a police corporal came and saluted and said "All Leicesters to return to barracks, sir!" That starts another night show, from which half a dozen chaps do not return. We are on the right flank, guarding the Green Dome area, 2/1 G.R. are left flank guard, and 5/11 and 3/10 are going via Bare Patch to surround a gang at Bandiza, together with the Scouts. I hop into bed from 10 to 11 pm and then we set out at midnight. I am to picquet Conical, the rest of Coy to picquet Cliff. We pass a drunken gunner in the cells shouting "I want to see a medical officer – I want to see etc etc" like a gramophone record that has stuck on one groove.

I am in front with Callander (2nd in command of the Leicesters) and Lonsdale for the night march, and it's damn funny. Callander with stick out, searching for wire or nullahs, and I hop gaily down the nullahs, which I can see, and get warned off for going too fast. I lead off, and we go up by the butts, hoping to strike a path for the M.G. mules. We do, and lose it twice, but arrive under the tower at 1.30 pm. We halt there until dawn, and then take up positions on the ridge. Bloody cold till dawn, the sweat of climbing the hill freezing in my shirt. I manage to get a groundsheet, but it's still bloody! We get tea from the tower and a charpoy, onto which some good Sikh brings out some bedding. There we stay until 7 pm.

A lot of shooting, Bare Patch way, and I see a hut go up on Horseshoe. The main body gets up OK, but Callander is told by villagers below Prospect Corner to be careful, as the place is crawling with enemy. He has to lead the whole Battalion expecting a volley at any minute.

"C" Coy have a picquet to the right of Postman's Daughter. It's on a forward slope, with a ridge in front of it, so I understand. A party of twelve armed men is seen on the road. It's not an R.P. day, so they cannot be fired on. The Khasadars shout "who are you?" and they nip off the road into the bushes. They could have been wiped out. C Coy's picquet is then fired on, the forward section being obliterated, and the remainder of the section running back. Then, under cover from the overlooking ridge, a knife party comes up, and two bodies and rifles are lost. What happens then I don't know, but eventually Nick goes forward with three men to look for the bodies. He sees eight dushmen at fifty yards running off, and after some trouble, gets out his revolver and gets off three rounds at them without success. The bodies are not found, though several attempts are made.

A lot of gallant deeds are done in rescuing chaps lying out in the open, and Walsh (R.A). is hit in the arm at 2 pm. He carries on directing the guns until 7 pm, so I expect he will collect an M.C. Six men are killed and six wounded, from C Coy and the M.G. section. Hundreds of guns open up from camp, and a short one lands on Postman's Daughter. A couple of snipers are under here on my side, but they don't do much damage. An aeroplane arrives, and bombs and machine guns enemy, as C Coy put out a 'T' – Flight Lt Gilbert gets a DFC for this. Two companies from 2/8

G.R. arrive on Conical from camp and send two picquets onto Prospect Corner Ridge. An ambulance arrives for the bodies, goes round the bottom corner by Prospect Corner, and is fired on from Skyline Ridge. I open up with M.G.s but it seems pretty useless so we knock off. The bodies can be seen coming down the hill on stretchers, the dead covered with a groundsheet, and the living with their heads left out. The aeroplane covers the Battalion down, ridge by ridge. I get R.T.R. about seven, and we are back by 7.30. Everyone lines the road to see us come in – a funny sight.

Khasadars later find the equipment of one body, less rifle, bayonet and ammunition, on Green Dome, and send it home.

Thirteen enemy are killed, including Khan Gul, one of Ipi's commissioned officers. The Brigade must have had twenty casualties. It seems the scheme was a balls-up. The Scouts were two hours late, and only half the village was surrounded. The Brigadier must have been so elated by his first night operation, and has taken a backhander from the enemy on this one. I wish I had been up on Postman's Daughter. I never smelt a bullet even. That makes the score eight killed, and ten wounded. The retreat is followed up with shooting all night long, near Rifleman's Tower. A raid is expected in Bannu just now. Officers go about in pairs, after dark, and armed.

August 25th 1939

RAZANI

THE TWO BODIES BROUGHT IN BY KHASADARS are untouched by mutilation. Four rifles have been lost, and eight enemy are known to have been killed, and Gagu's brother seriously wounded. The political administrator, Major Bacon, says there were four hundred enemy in that area that day, so we were damned lucky.

Rumour now has it that Ipi is out to get a British officer of this regiment in revenge for Khan Gul. I don't know about this, but I expect it will become rather dangerous round here during the next fortnight.

Signs of a war in Europe. All British citizens have been ordered to leave Germany, which I reckon is a bad sign. All officers passing through Bannu, by road or rail, have to report to Bannu Brigade, so a notice in the Club says. All leave stopped, in and ex-India.

August 30th 1939

Razani

Did advance guard to Crocus the other day. Nick on Pink Hills observed three men come out of a house and sit sunning themselves. He immediately opened up with his V.B., under the "Proscription Act", and saw one fall, which pleased him greatly. I was nearby, with Mickey, and whilst on Crocus, in the rain, we saw some chaps on the road about 1200 feet back who were coming out of a village. Also a man and a woman walked across Nullah picquet. We discuss whether to open up or not. I maintain that the road is closed behind us, and that therefore we have no excuse to murder them. Eventually Wardle compromises by taking a shot with a rifle at the woman on Nullah at about 900 feet and missing her. The adjutant later says that my opinion was correct, but that if they are observed armed, then by all means open fire.

Mickey, Pat Burder and myself bought a bottle of whiskey and went down to call on Walshe in hospital. Nick and Godfrey Pearse then arrived with another bottle, and we had a party. I had four stengahs (whiskey and soda over ice) and found that that was quite sufficient – "One more and I die".

Intelligence reports say that Ipi has gone into conference, and intends to make big trouble in ten or fifteen days time (about Sept 5th). I hope so, as I have got the job of A.P.M. *(Assistant provost marshal)* in this month's Razcol, through knowing Urdu, and Burder, a Company commander. A letter from Bill, on two months leave at home, and Daphne.

September 3rd 1939

Razani

WENT AND DINED WITH PEARSE IN THE R.A. MESS. The nicest mess in Razmak. Captain Findlay (O.H.) with one arm was there. On his artificial arm he had a hand which he could unscrew and, in its place, insert a hammer and screw it up. Damn funny it looked. Champagne, madeira, white ladys and beer, so I was bloody lucky to be in bed by 1am. I think Godfrey thought I was a bit of a wet going off so soon, but what of it!? Shaw, new Ulia, said that, at R.M.C. (Sandhurst), when French reserve officers came down to inspect, during one interminable salute one laddie took his right hand down and surreptitiously slipped up his left in its place, to give it a rest – Shayad! (Urdu: perhaps).

War about to start any minute now, so I am putting in a bit of packing, in case I get ordered to the "something-th" regiment by "next R.P. day". I want to sell those Persian carpets, but no one in the bazaar will take them. I have now given them to a Bagai agent, who is also a licensed government auctioneer.

Blimey seems to be on the wagon (almost) after his leave in Kashmir. I remember one guest night how he had to help his port glass up to his mouth with his left hand, during toasting the King, as the other was shaking so much that it couldn't make it.

War declared today – celebrated in true fashion.

September 5th 1939

Razani

CAME BACK FROM FOOTBALL ABOUT 4.30 PM on Sunday and we could just hear Chamberlain saying that a state of war existed with Germany. This was on Ian Mitchell's wireless, and we had to put our heads almost up to the machine to hear. Went into the Sergeants Mess at about 10.00 pm – Jack Greasly, Jackson, Burder, Miller,

Wardle and self. Pat Miller had to be taken back at about 10.15 pm, being too full of champagne, which he had sunk at dinner. Mickey took him, and apart from falling in a drain on the way, he arrived safely. Pat Burder very drunk, and slurring his words. The RSM in great form, and made a speech or two as did everyone else. I rendered "a portly Roman Senator", which shook some of them.

Yesterday was the 2/7 shield hanging party. I had a beer or two, and some lime juice, and then left the Club at about 9.00 pm, as was feeling a bit weak in the legs after football and the night before in the Sergeants Mess.

Mickey Wardle was brought home about 11.00 pm, having passed out cold when he got outside the Club. His door was shut, so Clive Pearson (1/12) broke through his fly proof window to open up. He then woke up in the morning feeling on top of his form, but with a bed full of sickness beside him. What a lad!

News yesterday morning of "Athenia" being torpedoed off Scotland. In about two hours the rumour was round it had been torpedoed with the Royal Scots on board. Never understood how it got like that!

September 11th 1939

Razani

POSTINGS ARE OUT, and I have the 2/13 *(2nd battalion, 13 Frontier Force Rifles)*. The awards also received for the Bodhari Sar show. Walshe has an M.C., Sgt Blake a DSM – he led search parties out several times looking for the bodies, and L/Cpl Rawson an M.M. He is a machine-gunner, but I don't quite know what he did. These are immediate awards, and others may have been sent home and recommended.

Got shot up on the range for the first time in this "war". I had been scoring in butts, and was returning along the Maidan, outside Coolie Camp, when a dushman between Bump and Bakhshi opened up. He had the range too long, and they sang over our heads well out of reach. I was due to bring down the covering troops, and am halfway through this operation, when of course Mac needs to get out of bed and do it himself, damn it.

A mixed platoon of "D" Company is on R.P. tomorrow, commanded by Burder. I go to the Adjutant and say that it is my platoon and what a disgrace the whole show is. He says yes, and you command it. So I have wangled a last R.P. tomorrow, and here's hoping, though as Ossy is commanding the detachment, I doubt they will allow us anywhere dangerous if it can be helped.

Holly tomorrow, the only picquet I have never been up, so that means a peaceful day, as nothing can ever happen up there.

September 14th 1939

Razani

I GO UP OAK EVENTUALLY. There is a bit of shooting on several picquets. Some sniping comes from the sangar, Bare Patch way, just above me, however they fire on everyone but us. Two shells arrive up there, so I put in two bursts of V.B. fire to sort of keep the pot boiling. This has the desired effect, and no more shooting from up there. "C" company on Horseshoe were shot up, Private Woodward being killed, and one other getting hit in the arse. I don't believe these buckshot stories. It's broken bullets or stones.

That night Pat Miller, Nick, and myself give a party in the Club lounge. We invite the Mess, Purcell, Nelson, Pearse, Gordon, Dunkerton, Valentine, Seaward, Wellwood and Gillan. A very successful party. The first lad comes about 7.20 pm and then we walk out on Gordon and Wellwood at 10 pm. Everyone said it was very original, and that Razmak had never seen the like before.

Yesterday I ran the bloody mile and got 11/20. Also a sore throat from coughing so much when I got back. Nick and I had drinks with Walter Purcell, and were then dined out. I reckon I consumed about 2 1/2 bottles of beer, two gins, two madeiras, a whisky and a sherry, and didn't turn a hair. Got to bed at 12.30

73

pm and up at 6 am with "dawn patrol". A good party last night. Col. Weld was there and I made his acquaintance officially. I hear a platoon of scouts met a hundred dushmen on Bare Patch the other day, and that the enemy told them to "bugger off, we don't fire at you" – and they did too!

2

September 1939 - October 1940

2nd Battalion
13th Frontier Force Rifles

Madras / Abbottabad

September 26th 1939

MADRAS

NOW IN MADRAS. Before leaving Razani, was given a farewell party in the Sergeants Mess – Miller made his same speech again, and when he sat down, CSM Blackwell said "I wish I had your command of English, sir." RSM then invited me to get up and beat it, which I believe I did with one or two cracks against the CSM of "D" company.

On Friday I was kept on the range until 2 pm, and that evening I had drinks with Colonel Weld in the District Mess. We had a pretty awful trip to Bannu, each with the front seat in an empty Bagai lorry, and stopped at the Narai to say goodbye to those present at Battalion HQ. Met a gunner, Tom Christopher (81 Field Artillery), and Donald Gordon at the rest camp, and had a swim, and saw the flick on the club lawn, very pleasant, as you sipped beer at the same time. It was there I saw the first woman for six months, since I saw a brace in Kohat.

Got to Mari Indus the next day safely, having said goodbye to Nick on the platform. We filled the Heatstroke Express (the train) with ice and were damn cool, it all dripping out of the door at the halts. Reached Rawalpindi early the next morning, and Christopher had us up to the gunner's mess for the day. I read all the "Times"s and bought a 10/- thermos canteen, which has been very useful since. In Bannu I found my cigarette case was missing, so I wrote to Micky Wardle to look for it, but I think I have seen the last of it. Gora Miller was left at Meerut, and I changed at Delhi. The restaurant Babu walked me round the fort, about five miles, and then I met Donald and a lad in 2/8 Gurkhas and we went to Maiden's Hotel. We drank beer and gin, and watched some beauties who were there, including a French girl. I then left that afternoon and reached Madras two days later at 1800hrs. In Itarsi was a train load of Germans, bound for an internment camp and guarded by armed policemen at every carriage door. The captain in

76

charge said he had one carriage of Nazis and one of Jews and they wouldn't look at each other, neither would the Jews drink Becks Beers.

Palmer met me in Madras, and we went out to the Mount in the regimental bus. I met Symonds there, and next morning Niven and C/O Smythe, Freeland being in the Fort at Madras, commanding the station. Drinks at Jimmy Smythe's and the Niven's houses. Madras is nine miles away, but John Palmer and I went in the other night for a drink at the Connemara to meet a girl of his, and then to the flicks afterwards. We met the girl – a Mrs Honor Ransome (hubby Royal Indian Navy) – in her room, and so did five other men, including one Freddie Holmes (Flt/Lt DFC), and a lad by the name of Mac. They all danced with Honor, and then Jo and I went to the cinema with Mac. After that we returned to his room in the Connemara, and drank beer and sandwiches and talked. I got to bed at 0130 and up again at 0530 on company training by Black Rocks.

John's girl Honor then came out here last night for booze with one May Green, wife of Lt Green RIN, as chaperone. John has a large notice 'Ladies' above the door of his ghugle khana *(dining room)*, and they use it, too! They are both now coming to dinner here tonight, in the "Ladies Room". So God help us – or me, as John won't need it.

LIST OF OFFICERS, 2ND BN, 13TH FRONTIER FORCE RIFLES

Lt Col Freeland R.A.B. MC Command Madras
Major Smyth J. Present C.O.
Major Goode R.L. GSO India Office, London
Major Gilbert C. on leave
Major Morris C.F. DSO on leave
Major Woods D.L.O. OBE S.W. Scouts
Capt Nash J.H.E. Jhansi Brigade H/Q
Capt Abbott B.E. Staff College

Capt Armstrong W.J. Staff College
Capt Keen P.J. Political
Capt Wainwright V.L.M. MC T.B.
Lt Niven R.W. Present Adjutant
Lt Elsmie R. T.B.
Lt Steward R. Commanding Trichinopoly
Lt France M.H.C. on leave
Lt Beale G.F.A. on leave
Lt Symonds R.H.B. present
R/Lt Palmer J.B. asst QM present

October 2nd 1939

Madras

THAT PARTY WITH THE HARRIDANS went off all right. They were only two hours late in arriving, and I had to look after the heavyweight May for many an hour, whilst John went about his business with Honor. Yesterday went out after snipe with Niven. Left here at 5.00 am with a shikhari[1], and no one spoke Tamil, so it was rather difficult.

Eventually we reached the place, and for three hours we waded through paddy fields. Some were so full of water that the snipe would need to swim to get anywhere but we saw three. Niven killed one and I missed one, after having opened up on a sandpiper by mistake (and missed him). Romany kite, Kingfisher, Paddybird, Bee eater and Blue Jay seen for the first time.

Yesterday afternoon went to Gordon Woodroffe's factory sports as some of Sikh Coy were competing. Met a lad by the name of Cole, who is one of the "Key-men of industry" here. He taught me the one word of Tamil essential to know, "Poida", meaning "Get the hell out of it". No mail from home since the war (started), and only one from Grindlays, forwarded from Razmak.

[1] Guide/hunter.

78

October 8th 1939

WORK, TENNIS, FOOTBALL AND BOOZE. Maitland, France, Gilbert and Morris returned from leave, having doubled half the Atlantic in a convoy and been attacked by submarines in the Mediterranean. A partridge drive is arranged for today, but the shikhari never turned up last night, so Ray cancelled it.

Did a Battalion scheme yesterday. I took two Indian officers out the day before, and showed them the ground, and gave them orders. Mahan Shand of course altered it a good bit, and as I not fluent in the language he gets away with it. I can't sell these damn carpets. The bloody furniture wallah won't come and won't cooperate. (Sent them to Hugh as a wedding present!)

October 14th 1939

MADRAS

ON THURSDAY WENT IN TO WATCH the Wiltshire's retreat, in the fort, had supper, and watched our Khatlak dance, which was laid on in the fort for the benefit of the troops. First one I ever saw, and it was good, though the ground was too hard for hurling themselves about, and in mixed company it was quite clean. After that we went to Connemara, John, Maitland France and self. I had one dance with Mrs Green, not being invited to the other party, but she had an awful, grim man in the navy department.

So I go up to Maitland who is sitting talking to a girl and I say "May I steal you away?" to the girl (not France), and Maitland introduces me and I keep her for the rest of the evening. One Celia Mockett, who's father is a judge here. One other gent asks her for a dance but apart from that, I do very well. A few catty remarks made on the way home.

I wonder if I shall see this war. The Koikhais think we shall go to Wana, and if so I reckon we shall be forgotten and left to rot – unless the Mashouds should decide to try their luck again. We never get any gossip here, as in Razmak, as apart from us and the Wilts (1st Battalion, The Wiltshire Regiment) in Madras, there are no other regulars. I read the Madras Mail in the mornings after breakfast, and the pictures of troops off to, and in, France that I see make me grumble over my lot for the rest of the morning. How long we stay here I don't know but John (QM), was asked yesterday by the powers above if we had accommodation for an imposing list of M.T. But then we are not equipped for war in Europe, and Congress are trying to blackmail London to give them Dominion status before India helps in the war.

Bought a 17/6d air gun – a Tell – for 38 rupees here, at Orr's – the bloody shark – for shooting tree rats. Good sport. 12 bore cartridges are 17/-, though last time I enquired before the war they were 12/- / 13/-, and they are surely the same stock, so it is only profiteering.

A guest night with the Wiltshires tonight, so I suppose I shall get no sleep, as I hope to go out shooting tomorrow at the crack o'dawn. No letters since the war, and I should like to see an English paper again. Must do something about these carpets.

I have the bloody job of learning Indian Officers' and keymen's jobs, being closely questioned every morning by Ray Niven in the orderly room.

October 18th 1939

Madras

The Wilts came to a guest night last Saturday. Met one Jos Redman, who seemed to get a bit pissed towards the end. After dinner the bloods played 'Crown and Anchor' (a dice game) which I got from Spencer's – seemed to go down very well. Next day, went out shooting with Niven. Not too good, as I got to bed after the guest night at 2am, and up again at 5. Missed a partridge right overhead, God knows why, except that the gun does not fit. We also saw, and walked up to, about eight of what the shikhari called prairie snipe (Golden plover) – got off two shots and missed them as well.

I get rather depressed sometimes over this war, after having read the papers, but I'm damned if I see how I am to get near it – let alone to France. God help me if we go to Wana, as we will be forgotten there, so God help us again.

October 21st 1939

Madras

THERE ARE ONE OR TWO FUNNY CHAPS in the Wilts detachment up here. There is a Major Bearen, with a damn pretty wife, who is the "compleat tennis rabbit". One Major Ludford, known as Babe, whose wife has a mind like a lavatory – their children's nurse is one Lulu, who is courted by the troops. 'Doc' Cunningham and Robbins, with little Audrey, and a madman called 'Dopey' Hamilton. The Ludfords had passed some remarks about Dopey at their table one day, and later on Ludford took one of his small daughters across to the PRI's store. He was there in conversation with a CQMS when Hamilton happened to go past. Daughter turns round and says "Look Daddy – there's that wet officer again."

Must get down to a bit of work for the Retention exam – all the organisation and interior workings of the Battalion.

October 27th 1939

Madras

BEALE RETURNED FROM LEAVE LATE, not having received his recall telegram. John, he and I spent last Saturday in the Connemara after dinner, in observation. A letter from Ma, announcing Hugh's

81

marriage to Peggy Farlow. Wrote to Hugh and Uncle Bill. I am informed I go to S.A.S. Sangor, January 25th - March 10th, and must pass the Retention exam before so doing – what fun.

Observed a very good sunset last Sunday from Elliot's beach, where I was bathing. We have done a bit of riding lately, towards the Adyar, though unfortunately over the golf course. British officers plus Indian officers vs Wilts Officers and sergeants of the detachment up here.

October 31st 1939

MADRAS

WERE BEATEN IN THE ABOVE MATCH 1-2. That night Jerry Beale, John and I went to the cinema, and then to the Connemara. We got in without paying Rs 2/- and had a few drinks and sat in observation. Doreen Hope, Lady, was there, she's known locally as the Red Streak. But very nice all the same despite her imbecile look.

On Sunday, went to Elliot's Beach for swimming, and extremely pleasant it was, and we went out on a catamaran and tried to shoot the surf coming back. But not very successful, as the man would not keep the catamaran straight. No sunset that day. The monsoon has now broken and there is plenty of rain.

The trouble here is bullock carts. They travel down the road at night in front of the bungalow, and their greaseless axles make a hideous noise, which wakes me up in the early morning. Then these Madrasis will shout when talking to a friend just six feet away.

Went out after snipe with Niven yesterday afternoon, on the Poonamallee road. I missed a couple, he missed a few and killed one. There were quite a few about though, and it rained during the shoot, and I felt that I might be in Aberdeenshire.

November 5th 1939

SOME MORE SHOOTING IN THE SAME SPOT – Ray and I and Nizam. Nizam killed and halaled a couple, rather like a good retriever. I fail to break my duck of course. I go down yachting with the Colonel. "Thistle" is Tomtit class, 18ft long, Bermuda rig and centreboard. I am instructed in putting about and in jibing, round and about the harbour. The famous 'Pansy' is there, looking rather like the minesweeper she was during the last war. Beer follows, and I apply to join the Club. Met one Dunn, of Wilts.

Went down yesterday and was more successful, though there was a bit of a wind blowing. In returning to our moorings, the Colonel brought her up, the paid hand pulling on the topping lift, and then I think I still had the main sheet, and he nearly went overboard. She listed right over, and the Colonel and I were just about to scramble onto the keel when she came up again. Went to an RAF hanger dance last night – not much good, as I didn't know anyone, so I left at 11.30 and returned to bed.

November 10th 1939

MADRAS

AN AWFUL RAINY DAY YESTERDAY. John and I went to the flicks at 6.00 pm and the Connemara afterwards, where I was introduced to a "Highball". A woman came in with another couple, whom we know as the 'S' bend, as that's how she looks when she's dancing. She observed our observation of her and eventually sent over Bannerji to ask if either of us would dance – John had one, I attempted one, in spite of the old man 'thumbing' me away. Eventually John goes over for another dance and the old man does some more 'thumbing' and tells him to go back to his kennel. After a bit of an argument the old man apologises, and asks John to go to dinner – I join them and get invited too. His name is Tingle of the Asbestos Cement company, and his wife thinks she is a bit of a vamp. She's a bit of a load to dance with, as she clings from the belly downwards, which I always find impedes forward movement.

November 13th 1939

Madras

I see in the "Statesman" that Razcol were in the Shaktu in October, and had two killed and eleven wounded – also an R.P. picquet was shot up on November 2nd and one killed with four wounded.

Yesterday went shooting with Ray, and got six snipe – he got seven. During one drive they were coming straight at me but I couldn't shoot them, as all the beaters were looking down the other end of my gun. I pretended to be a blade of grass and shot them overhead. Result was horrid, I only got one. I let off about twelve rounds rapidly, and couldn't load fast enough. Came back and the band was playing in the mess. I had invited the Spocket out (Celia Mockett), being the only girl I know in Madras, but I met one Mrs Hughes, an Australian.

Some days ago I went up to the Aerodrome and signed on for some flying. Tyndall-Briscoe, the instructor, gave me some ground instruction, and yesterday up I went for twenty mins dual, the first time in my life in the air, bar 5/- worth at Yeadon aerodrome some years ago. Went up to about 1000 feet and I took her over for a bit, and got a bit lost up there. Diving, climbing and steep turns seem rather to detach the pit of my stomach and I take it off too early, though I hope to god I will get out of that soon. I feel just like a chota peg[1] when I come down, but I managed with a cigarette instead.

I can't do any more dual until the medical form is filled in, and the damn man Hubbard won't do it until tomorrow. They also want a little bit in advance, the sharks.

I see that Gilbert R.A. got an MC for services in 1936-37, and Payne 2/7 and Doc Murray were mentioned for good work. Wrote to Mickey Wardle to see if there's a medal yet, but don't expect an answer. No vacancy for me at Sangar, and the Retention exam is suspended for the duration, so I have no 'homework' to do.

¹ Miniature jug used for individual servings of alcohol, Chota is the Hindi word for 'small measure'.

November 21st 1939

MADRAS

WENT UP FOR TWO TWENTY-MINUTE SHIFTS on Sunday – climbing and gliding turns, and then T.B. went up to 2000 feet and shook me about. I could take a climb and roll alright, but a spin rather caught me in the eardrums. Today did a bit of landing and taking off. There was a sufficient wind blowing to stall her at half throttle. There's plenty of water about on the ground, so if I ever get her up solo I'm going out to look at the sea.

Three BORs (British other ranks) killed and eleven wounded withdrawing from a picquet at Razmak on R.P., so says the Statesman.

This flying costs 30/- an hour dual, and I have now got in 1.5 hours – I feel happy in the air, only I can't land and take off yet, being unable to estimate height and gliding distance. A letter from Bill the other day. He is back in Palestine, and got his truck blown up by a mine not so long ago.

November 24th 1939

MADRAS

DINED WITH THE WILTS IN THE FORT the other night. Did us very well on pate de foie gras, asparagus and champagne. Played darts afterwards and I defeated Jack Newton, their QM and champ. Colonel Freeland observed doing a very smart hornpipe with himself. Last night dined out with Jimmy Smythe and Mrs, who is going to U.P. (Uttar Pradesh) as Military Secretary.

More hornpiping by the Col. ably supported by the others, and Rangru was made to conduct the band. I let off a brace of marriage bombs, which didn't go down too well.

Went up for half an hour on Thursday morning. Started off doing landings and take offs, but I mucked up my turns on the preliminary circuit, and spent the morning doing turns instead. Tyndall-Biscoe is a yogi I believe, and dines on orange juice and spring onions or some such combination. As long as he doesn't go into the 7th transportation at 2000 feet.

I look after the feeding and it's some job keeping my bearer up to the mark. He sabotaged last night's dinner, by making oyster patties out of oyster paste. Am getting a bit bored with this job. How I shall ever last twenty years of it I shudder to think. And what the hell will I be like at the end of it – heaven forbid that I ever become a 'typical army officer', especially an Indian army one. Waziristan was alright – and it didn't much matter where your puttees ended – but here, Christ! The Navy's the place for me – I always was interested in ships and it's a skilled job, whereas what I do now – its useful value is approximately nothing!

We go off to camp on Wednesday, so that might shake my ideas up a bit. We never got that dinner out of Tingle, the Cement King, as he rang up and said the Vamp was ill with fever – like hell. Jerry and I went and called on Westmoreland-Woods the other day – one daughter by the name of Elizabeth. With great difficulty obtained a whisky and soda and left.

December 1st 1939

IN CAMP AT UTTAPANAYSKANNA. Had a very pleasant fifteen mins flight before leaving the Mount. Did everything correct, including take-off and landing, and next time will be landing circuits, if T.B. remembers. Went out with Maitland to Barrington-Smith for a drink, and stayed to dinner. He and Maitland are a pair, and I reckon I am on sufferance only because of Harrow – they talk of English country houses and of English families and listen to me eagerly when I say what I know of the McLean hereditary litigation – but a damn fine dinner all the same, and it's the first time I have dined in someone's house in India, I think.

We leave the Mount on Wednesday 29th at 2.30 pm in two trains. I go in first with Golly, Niven and Beale. We dine at Villipuram, which is dinner for three provided by Spencer's man, and eaten by four hungry bodies. I meet Spencer's man there and have a talk with him. Arrive at Uttapanayskanna at 7am, and I get the bearer to work on breakfast, which he does fairly successfully. The second train arrives with Reggie Steward and D Coy, whose Indian officers come up and introduce themselves to me.

I then try to pack the Mess on the bullock cart transport which is waiting – QM has allotted one cart for the Mess and BOs baggage – but after much swearing and berating of drivers I eventually get it all off on seven carts. Am a bit worn out as it's very hot and then we have to march up here – about seven miles from the station. The road is a cart track, full of red dust, and I walk behind a mule. I find it impossible to keep time with the pipes and drums and their rifle regiment step, and march in step with the mule instead – long, slow and easy. The worst march I ever did, and the hardest worked day since I left Waziristan. The colour of Sahdu Singh's beard when we arrive is a good sight.

I have a 80lb tent – on hire – and have pinched a mess table. Also have boxes a la Razani, so am fairly comfortable. Hills all around here, so it looks like mountain warfare, and the place is being turned into a semi-perimeter camp. We have got (the CO arranged it) a mess car at four annas a mile, and twelve annas a day for the local driver, or give him bata. Also a frigidaire from detachment in Trichinopoly, which works by paraffin and will be a godsend in this heat. The war still goes on I believe.

December 5th 1939

UTTAPANAYSKANNA

"C" COMPANY DID A BIT OF MOUNTAIN WARFARE yesterday. I was horrified at it, but perhaps the methods I was taught are wrong after all. Anyway, no one will believe a word I say about it. Did a bit of field firing and ordered the local police to clear the range area by, say, 6.00 am. We then have to clear it ourselves, and start shooting around 7.30, having been just about to start once before and observed a man in dhoti up above one of the targets.

Two fat black policemen arrive at 9.30 and say sorry, had made mistake but now alright. One platoon has just finished firing and a local is then seen crossing the area, nearing the targets. I grab the arm of the fattest man and point a quivering finger at the apparition and threaten to get him sacked. He says 'excuse please' a few times and then sends his friend off to clear him out. The local is then seen doubling back out of the area like a frightened hare. We then ask fatty if we may start firing again. He says 'yes' so we ask him if he wants his friend to be killed – he had forgotten him, who is this moment coming back down the middle of the range.

Went into Madurai on Sunday to watch hockey against the police. Went in the back of a police lorry and nearly shaken to death. There had tea with Hamilton D.S.P. *(Deputy Superintendent of Police)* and drinks after the game. Whenever the D.S.P. happens to stand and talk to someone his Sergeant Major, a madrasi, falls in two men behind him. Hamilton looks around, they look a bit sheepish, so he asks the SM what the hell they are doing. SM answers 'to keep the sun off you, sar!'

Came back in the mess car which we have hired for four annas a mile and the driver's food, which is exceptionally good I think. After a hairraising drive in which we take the hair off a few old men and the driver strains her, by refusing to change down, we reach home, having got stuck in the sand whilst taking Golly back to his camp, where A and B Coys are. A letter from Ma, enclosing one she had from Peggy, who is by way of being the girl that Hugh married – Peggy, Pegs – I wonder!

December 11th 1939

Uttapanayskanna

WENT AND CLIMBED ONE OF THE LOCAL HILLS yesterday with Palmer and Awal Khan. We worked up a chimney but got foxed near the top and had to come down, making great use of Awal Khan's pagri *(turban)* as a rope. We then play football in the afternoon against the Madurai police in Usilampatti. They play in bare feet, and their goalkeeper gets his big toe badly cut by a boot. In fact the ball becomes bloody. After the game we wait from 5.30 to 7.30 in the police station for the home bus to arrive and pick us up – never again!

After having been instructed in bridge by Golly in St Thomas's Mount, I now find myself playing every night and am 58 annas up – Kent, the Doctor is 60 up and everyone else is minus.

Am getting a bit worn out here. Rise at 6.30 on parade from 7 to about 10, and get breakfast at 10.30, a barbarous hour – out again at 3.00 pm for about two hours, and then generally playing bridge up to about 11.00 pm – I can't take it.

There is very little scrub here, it is all cactus, of the bleeding sort, which drips milk and has an all round defence, so that you can't grasp it without being pricked. An answer to my letter to Bill

Webber, saying come when you like, but not especially enthusiastic.
I think.

December 16th 1939

UTTAPANAYSKANNA

WENT INTO MADURAI AND PLAYED FOOTBALL there, where
we defeated the local champions 5-4. After that, the secretary and
D.S.P., one whose name in Tamil means 'God Help Us', took John
and I to the station waiting room and got us pretty tight before
dispatching us back in the lorry with the team. That morning I had
gone out at 2.30 am on a night scheme, but got back in bed by 8.00
am until 12 midday, and didn't manage to football too badly after
that.

The battalion did a twenty one mile march the other day –
I wear boots for the first time in camp and collect a fine crop of
blisters. We do a flag march to Madurai on 21st, so God help me
if my feet aren't OK as it's all of thirty miles, and parade through
the town afterwards. Willie Armstrong arrived today from Staff
College. The Illustrated papers are out from home, and God how it
pulls to read about this war. Off to Madurai today.

December 20th 1939

UTTAPANAYSKANNA

WENT INTO MADURA WITH THE COLONEL and Golly – I was
due to stay with one Doakes, manager of the mill and drawing
6000/- a month. I arrive at his house, a palace set on the highest
hill around Madurai, and with a wonderful view, if it wasn't an
Indian one, and find no one there, he being still at his office. I have
the sort of 7th guest bedroom, but it has all modern conveniences
and a pair of good Persian carpets. I have tea, look longingly at the

swimming pool, and then drink the breeze from the highest point for a considerable time.

Eventually Doakes arrives, but doesn't expect me, as I should be with some others in the mills, the Essex's, who have arranged a party for me. I shift house and meet them at the Khatak dance we put on – then back to dinner at the Essex's. They have a Swiss girl – Hildegard – up from Tuticorin for my partner. During dinner Mrs Essex gets pretty tight, she is an Australian with a cockney accent. And we go on to the club dance at about 10.00 pm, everyone pretty tight, bar me and the Swiss miss, and calling me "Lootenant". Return from dance at 3.00 am having done pretty well keeping Swiss miss out of hands of proletariat – John and Reggie & co. We five are the only ones from the Regiment – and do pretty well in the Palais Glide, where Golly and John bend back so far they crash to the floor amidst loud applause.

Arrange to shoot with Doakes in the morning, but on waking up I can't take it, and don't go. Leave Essex's at 2.00 pm and home with the Colonel and Golly in the car. Out that night at 1.00 am until about 9 – sleep 10.30 am until about 4.00 pm and out again at 1.00 am, in bed midday until about 5.00 pm. Then last night in bed. I didn't mind going out at night in Razmak – there were bullets about, you knew that, and it made it more interesting. But climbing through cactus after 'Popeyekanoor' or 'Sodapaniswami' – I would rather stay in bed.

Last night Madurai came here to a drinks party, but some shite in the S.P.M.R., and the Mills I suppose, brought out the Swiss miss and kept her all the time. A pretty good party, and Mrs Essex in great form. They all reckon to come and laugh at us when we march into Madurai, thirty miles, on 22nd. General Norton arrived today to watch the company field firing scheme. He chooses C Coy, and as Pearson is manager, I have to do it. God knows what will happen – or I don't – and a night scheme tonight to catch one "Champagne". I shouldn't feel much like marching after that, to Madurai.

91

December 25th 1939

The night opp. goes off fairly successfully, and we start for Madurai at 4.00 am – arriving at 4.00 pm – 31.5 miles in all and with a stop for one hour. I find it pretty bloody on the feet, everything else being alright, but the Dogras look after me and feed me with fruit all the way. In Madurai we camp on the police football ground, and John and I nip off to the Essex's for a bath. I have two beers and one whisky there – then whisky in the club – and when I get to Brisley's the Collector's where we all dine, I feel bloody, but just manage to last the course, by consuming lots of lime juice during dinner. Next morning we march through Madurai, saluting the Collector on the way. All the locals (Essex's et al) are grouped solemnly on the saluting base, but I manage to keep a straight face, and pass grimly out of their lives (maybe).

Received Christmas card from Guy Hamlet, now on the staff in Quetta, also one from Biddy. Leicesters are in Agra now I hear. Arrived back here yesterday morning and went straight up to the aerodrome, where I did landing circuits, fairly successfully, though I was inclined to misjudge my glide, and had to use a bit of engine, or found myself overshooting. Had twenty minutes in the afternoon too, and find I am lighter on the stick, but a bit heavy with my feet.

December 28th 1939

A party of fourteen for Christmas in the Connemara (25th) – British officers and two wives (Abbots and Rays) – pretty awful party, although Freeland got a bit foxed. However, later on some drunks from the B.I. line ships officers (British India Steam Navigation Company), arrived and seemed to collect around Abbott. One said to him "Where do I get a good …". He pointed to his wife Rosemary and said "Over there". The chappie lurched over to Rosemary and said "Are ye on?". They all had fearful Glasgow accents, and Abbott's wife was furious, though he thought it rather funny. Willie and I, John and Pat Irwin went on to the Gymkhana Club afterwards.

Willie and I shouldn't have gone, as John wanted to get on and do some necking. Then two lads off the "Silver U" arrived, a 3rd mate and an electrician. They were 72 days out from New York across the Atlantic and Indian Ocean, and hadn't seen a woman all that time. I took the wind out of their sails by telling them of ten months in Waziristan and never saw one.

Got to bed at 5.00 am, and flying cleared my head at 9.30. Went sailing with Willie and Abbott, doing flying and sailing the same day, which I wanted to do. Yesterday John and I were invited to an early night do in the Connemara by May Green, one of the Horrors. Her husband, John's hairdresser friend, and Lt Hart (Royal Indian Navy) were present. Later (less husband) we went to the Gym Club, where I nearly got tight, having drunk whisky in the Connemara, as they started on champagne and then brandies came round. Had a very good 1.5 hours flying this morning, only it's a little bumpy.

December 31st 1939

MADRAS

FLYING AND SAILING, AND THE OTHER DAY Willie landed me on the 'Kallerati' ('Calamity' – her sister ship 'Deepuali' being the 'Depravity'). Had tea with one Sweet-Escott (Subaltern R.I.N.V.R.) He showed me over the works, and then Hart and the hairdresser Rene arrived, just as I went ashore.

Last night John and I went to the cinema and on from there to the Connemara. There John encountered Mr and Mrs Gordon (railways) and we spent the evening and night with them. Left Connemara at midnight and went to the Gymnkhana Club, where a fancy dress dance was in progress, with lots of drunks. Bed by 3.30 am – a few drinks in the Gymkhana, and then I did some useful elbow work and seized the Connemara cabaret star, much to the disgust and envy of those around and about. Forgot to ask her if she was married!

Gordon has done 150 hours solo, and took seventeen hours dual before it, so it doesn't look like I shall have much chance of going solo for many a month yet. Letters from Bill, Hugh and Peggy, and three handkerchiefs from Mrs Robinson. *(CDW's friend Bill's mother).*

January 3rd 1940

MADRAS

WENT TO DINNER WITH MAJOR MONEY – and then on to the Connemara and Adyar Club for the New Year. Connemara packed with a lot of lads, who looked as if they had only been there once, and that was last New Year's Eve. Saw the New Year in at the Adyar – it's like an old country house and is most beautifully decorated, the only drawback being the Governor's band, who perform none too well. Met Celia Mockett there and fixed up a flick for Tuesday – I collected her at Tippoo, and we saw 'Snow White'. After that, returned to Connemara and found I had made a balls up and it was Jack Bontemps' off day.

However, Celia suggested the Madras Club, so off we went there for drinks on her! On reckoning things out, it's the very first time I ever took a girl out, excluding Daphne of course, as she generally took me in her car. Funny that!

Am going off to camp for three weeks with the Wilts, as an umpire, though all the umpiring I ever did was that course of Jimmy's, and one day (or rather night) at Uttapamayakkannor. The weather nice and cool now, and there's a paper in from Waz District that we move on February 28th or so, arriving Wana via Manzai on 7th March. Saw in the intelligence summary that

Wanacol got heavily sniped one day recently, while out on column – that looks hopeful, but Golly doesn't seem to think much of the Wana Wazirs, at least not as fighting men.

What a difference in one's life good friends make. Here am I, having spent 21 years living behind a sort of mask of suspicion and social fright, and here I am sort of received with open arms and it's all gone. The Leicesters didn't do that, and with them I used to get pangs of annoyance, mistrust and even hatred sometimes, which I hadn't felt since dark days at Harrow. Certainly not at the R.M.C. *(Royal Military College, Sandhurst)*. All that is now gone, for ever I hope. I have even found my tongue – at times!

She is a nice girl, that Celia is.

January 7th 1940

IN CAMP NEAR PUTTUR

IN CAMP WITH THE WILTS, AS AN UMPIRE, near Puttur – until 27th, dammit. Went solo on 4th at 6.30 am – T-B took me for a couple or so (three) chukkers first – dual – and then I did a couple solo, ten minutes in all. Beyond a great inclination to sing, which I did, there was no difference in it at all. Have now done five hours ten minutes dual, which is reckoned as pretty good, the normal pre-solo dual being about eight hours.

Came down here on Friday, and the only good thing about it that I can see is that in the Mess they have the London Times, which I haven't seen since before the war. The camp is situated under trees, on which all sorts of birds sit and make a bloody noise at night. One end is bounded by the road, and the other by paddy fields. It would be alright for mountain warfare, provided each man left his rifle behind and took a machete instead, as the hills are covered in thorn scrub, much thicker than any of that cactus at Uttapanayakkannor. The B.O.s seem to do pretty well, one even brought a chest of drawers along, but they don't seem to take much trouble over washing as they have no bath tent and we use these bloody camp baths. However, I manage to borrow a tin bath from Lees-Smith, who brought his own.

I have a 160lb tent, and God knows what it will cost. At present Hamilton ('Dopey') is giving his bearer hell for not understanding that "1. pencil, 2. foolscap" written on a piece of paper does not mean one pencil and two sheets of paper. I reckon I shall hit him before long if I'm not careful, and fail to control my temper.

January 12th 1940

In camp near Puttur

STILL IN THIS BLOODY CAMP and about another fortnight to do. I have been safety officer on some field firing exercise, alongside a bit of umpiring, but I might just as well be in Madras for all the work I'm doing here. On Friday went out twelve miles, spent the night, and marched back yesterday – at least the Wilts did, but I went out in a lorry and back in the Doctor's (Keyes) car. Spent the night with Jos Redman, who was the 'enemy', near Nagari, I being the enemy's umpire. Had dinner at Battalion HQ and drove out to where the enemy were spending the night, round a good fire. He lent me a blanket, as I only had my cardigan, and it was about eight or nine feet long, so I was able to wrap up pretty well in it.

We drink whisky for a couple of hours before turning in, and we discuss marriage, he being engaged and due for splicing in a few months. A bloody cold night, and up at 4.30. Very few chaps slept, owing to the cold that night, but I did fairly well, and on the Battalion getting back at about 2 pm a lot of the young officers departed to bed, had supper there, and appeared again the next morning for breakfast. Attam Khan *(Colin's bearer)* asks what's wrong with them, having only spent the one night out, and what would happen if there was a war on (?!) and they didn't get any rations for a couple of days.

A lot of holy monkeys round here, who live in the trees, and are known to climb up the tent ropes and then slide down the canvas sides. Also flying foxes. At last got licenses for my shotgun and a .22 Colt, with five hundred free cartridges, though I hate to think what the price of them will be just now at P. Orr's. No hope of getting back to Madras early, as some of the regiment are coming here on the 26th as enemy, but I am the only one here who can speak the language. Captain Crocker, Inniskillins, known as 'Hobo', is the other umpire.

January 18th 1940

IN CAMP NEAR PUTTUR

ANOTHER NIGHT OUT WITH JOS as enemy umpire. Went out at 10.00 pm and back by 11.00 am. We sat near a village and then went up a hill amongst the cactus. Never slept a wink owing to the cold. Used up Jos's iron rations – whisky! A letter from Ray, telling me to behave myself in this camp and explaining things. I sent a letter to Abbo. *(Battalion HQ in Abbottabad)* saying I didn't consider I was really wanted here, and would be more use at the Mount. However, I think I've been a bit of a B.F. One good thing – I think I mentioned before – is that they have the 'Times' in the Mess here. A letter from Aunt Vivy enclosing 10/- shillings for Christmas – a cheque.

January 31st 1940

MADRAS

RETURNED BACK ON THE 28TH. The intelligence section of the 2nd Frontier Force Rifles came down on the 26th for a scheme on the night of the 27th. This was the General's test scheme of the Wilts. I umpired Mickey Thomas. Hobo, Adrian Cooke and Tim

Money also arrived. Next day the General finished his talk at 3 pm. I left at 3.05 and the General at 3.06. Met Cotterill on return, and then Downe arrived from Lahore to join – he reminds me of Hamilton somewhat.

Went flying on Sunday – not much good – also Monday and Tuesday before parade, but I have lost the feel and bog all my landings. I do one solo circuit and try to land about five feet above the ground – a hell of a bump.

Went into Madras today and bought five hundred .22 cartridges at 3/8 a hundred. Also three "life buoys" @ four annas each. So now hoping for big stuff to come. Am living in Wilts officers quarters as everything else is taken. Feeling bloody minded about this flying, as all a damn waste of time and money, when I could land so well before I went away. I think I leave it too long before 'flattening out'. Just got Biddy's photo – I don't like it at all.

February 4th 1940

Madras

Went to Adyar tea dance given by the Sprocketts. John and I went with Appleton in his car. A couple of new RAF boys, "Dickie" Bird and "Peggy" O'Neill, arrived. The Wilts band performed, and the drummer boy had a high seat and grinned at all the women. One girl I danced with, Eve Maynard, I had to manoeuvre so she could see him. Not being a member of the joint, with difficulty I obtained two chota pegs, and when it finished at 8.30 pm we went to the Connemara – the two RAF chaps, myself, Celia, Daphne, Eve and one Joan Swann. John had found some'at else. When all finished, we went on to the Gymkhana, returning to bed about 01.30.

Thursday played squash with Jim Robbins. A training aircraft crashed the other day whilst the pilot, an Indian, was 100 feet off the ground, at some provincial landing ground. He got windy of the enquiry and on his statement put that he could remember nothing until he woke up in hospital. The machine was written off. Did a couple of chukkers solo yesterday and getting better, I hope. Whilst getting into one of those Blenheims the other day, one of the pilots accidentally pressed a button and the guns started off, pointing towards Madras!

On Friday 2nd we give our farewell "cocktail dance". Flowers arrive and I spend the morning helping Mrs Springfield and Jane with them. The racecourse lend us 'Pots, plants containing' and their head gardener fits them up in a few minutes. We hire a shamiana *(Urdu: an outdoor marquee for entertaining)* for the bar, the Wilts band in the ballroom and ours in the garden. John's room is, suitably, used as the Ladies room, and they all admire his photo round the walls.

Before the guests arrive, Lt Beale observed the shamiana boy concocting a 'white lady', brooding about alchemists and their work and wondering why it turned pink? They all arrive, about 150 of them. We are drawn up on the verandah at 8 pm, B.O.s and wives. His Excellency de-busses to 'God Save the King', and then shakes hands all down the line. After that – let the play commence. I have a dance or two with Celia, Daphne and then catch Marjorie Buller. Having hidden a few Pink Ladies (Colin's strategy to avoid peaking too early was to 'park' drinks) I am in crashing form, beating old boys on the back and telling them they look thirsty and explaining to dames that we don't keep no soft drinks here. Marjorie in cracking form too and I walk her "out of the out gate and into the in" – but nothing doing.

There's a supper bar in the eating room, and in the Frippets room a first class dining saloon for the Governor and those selected as fit by his ADCs. Sidelights – William had a gap in his conscious mind from 11.30 pm until he woke up in the morning. I got to bed at one and then up again to go flying at 6am. Yesterday took Sprockett to the cinema and the Connemara afterwards, but as I was suffering from Boozers Gloom, not very satisfactory.

February 6th 1940

Madras

HAD A DAMN GOOD FLIGHT TODAY, before parade, at 6.30 hrs –
did two chukkers dual, as T-B didn't like my first landing, which I
nibbled at, as I saw a plane going the other day in the dusk. Then
did four chukkers, perfect, though maybe two landings were a bit
pancaky.

We all went to a cocktail party given by Maj-Gen Wilson
ICS, yesterday in Guindy – encountered Michael Hunter, going
to France on Sunday, and Mickey Thomas, met Pam Holdsworth,
looked at, in the way that dogs do (as not officially introduced)
Anne Maconachie, and Jean Gordon. Maitland's friend, Marjorie
Buller, arrived too, whom I looked after last Friday. Well, I sit
and talk to her the whole time, and produce excerpts from my
experiences in Waziristan. Come back slightly whistled and have a
drink off Cotterill after dinner, in company with Bill. Being slightly
afloat, as I say, I sit down after dinner and write Marjorie a letter,
she having said how she adores them. I start "Dear Sir – " and
explain I was writing to the bank but somehow I seem to be writing
to her – hadn't I better see a doctor about it? In the light of day, I go
to the post box to get it back, and find to my horror it has gone. No
harmful effects, I hope. Later she rings me up – delighted with it.

February 8th 1940

Madras

YESTERDAY I WAS ALLOWED TO TAKE OFF from the beginning,
solo. They put out the sheet and round I go. I don't like the look
of the first one, so round I go again. Just as I am turning in, I see
the leopard about to take off, so I do a small circle right. I am still
gliding, am not paying attention, and she begins to stall at 100-
200 feet! I give her her nose and some engine, then full engine,

round and land. Coope nearly had a fit as high tension wires were underneath!

This morning T-B has one chukker dual, then OK, and off I go – I now have 1.10hrs solo. This morning Dr Dyson took me off for thirty five minutes as observer whilst we attacked the minesweepers. We went out to sea, they were a mile or two off land, and came down from the sun and a cloud at 3500 feet. He did glides and stall turns, then we circled for a torpedo attack and back home – delightful. I spot Freeland on one with my field glasses.

Last night a dance at Government House. John, Jerry, Tony Cotterill, Downe and myself all go in Tippoo (dressed up), and arrive to be the only ones in a soft shirt (I originally had silk shirt and cummerbund, but had to change them again). Had a good time, a few cocktails, supper with Celia and some dancing with Marjorie Buller. I also walk her out twice around dark and dim bushes, but she won't kiss me – though I give her a peck for luck. I am reputed to be mad here, so these frippets think, but I explain how I have only three more weeks in civilisation. Sent Marjorie a cap badge, with my love of course.

February 12th 1940

MADRAS

THURSDAY NIGHT PADRE JOHN and I went to the Connemara after dinner for a quick one. Met old Ruffle, who invited us to his party – pretty bloody awful, as I didn't feel like drinking and was rather tired. So Ruffle, who was in a worse condition, and I, drank Rose's lime juice. Hart, R.I.N. (Royal Indian Navy), and three hairdressers there. I dance with one Renee, so small you can hardly see her. Friday we all go to the garden party at Government House. The Governor arrives down a lane of bodyguards with the "old guard", including the C.O., drawn up to receive him – sing God Save the King – and we get down to it. The tea is foul so I drink orange juice. All the Indian stuffing themselves with both hands as hard as they could go. We all walk round and chat about this and that, I and Marjorie and the rest. Then I go back with Padre and Downe, the rest of the boys going to the Connemara, for an early night with Major and Mrs Springfield. I drink beer with them and then to bed.

Saturday sailing with Willie in "Thistle". We have a hell of a race with Low and Gibbs in Lapwing. But local knowledge and the better sailing of Low wins the day, though we lead on the start and nearly catch him up again on the second time round from Cassinode to Seamark. "Thistle"'s mast isn't stepped right and Lapwing just sails faster than we do on the port tack. We keep the spinnaker up as extra jib during the last home stretch, but his lead is too great and he gets away.

Back at 6.45 pm and off to a cocktail party in the Fort, given by Steve and Mickey Thomas to some of their lads who are going off to France, including Michael Hunter. I sit and talk to Marjorie for a bit and then she goes home, I having fixed a date at the "Gym" with her for 10.30 pm. I have had three gin and limes with water and feel damn drunk. I then have dinner in the Wilts Mess (free I hope) and then go along to the Sergeants Mess where I meet Sgt Webber, an old friend from Camp. RSM Milsom not there disafortunamente. Have a lime pani *(lime juice)* and feel sober again. Major Lloyd RIASC passes out on the floor and then I go to the Gym in Gibb's car, my own Royal Taxi having disappeared. Here I meet John and the Hughes' in whose party Marjorie is. I refuse all offers to booze, manage to collect Marjorie for a couple of dances and then push off.

I manage to get Mr Spencer's, presumably THE Spencer's, driver to drive me home, give him 5/- and am in bed by 1.00 am.

Saturday morning I go flying twenty minutes solo. T-B shows me the figures of eight. I try at 600 feetand in fifteen minutes have reached 1200 feet. I glide down and try again. When landing I am a bit tired and heavy, and only just pull up in time as she hits the ground. She bounces, I put on some engine, and eventually she flops to a rest. I notice a twitch in my left knee as I climb out – why?

At 10.15 Marjorie picks me up in the car of one Leslie Cooper, and off we go for a picnic at The Seven Pagodas (Mahabalipuram), some 45 miles from here. We stop and repair the back brake on the way, but eventually arrive at the canal, which is crossed in a sort of houseboat after much garbar *(Urdu: negotiation),* the cars being left this side – Mr and Mrs Buller, Annette and husband, Steve and Jean Gordon, Eve Maynard and Leslie Cooper. We bathe and have a picnic lunch in the Collector's bungalow. Then we look at the Five Rathas, have tea and it's time to come home. Casuarinas, acacias and some other flowers make the whole place particularly beautiful. There's a nice place for bathing, with rocks reminiscent of Tiree. I see a pleasant picture of a small cove with a long beach one side, and in the foreground this side a huge rock just at the water's edge, with palm trees at the edge of the beach, and Marjorie and Eve washing the sand off their feet in the sea. They wave to me to come down, and I wonder when I shall see such a scene, and in such a setting, again. Shades of Tiree, but there I had no picture for my frame!

A very nice drive back with Marjorie in the back seat. She gives me a hand and we talk sweet nothings. Forty five miles, a fine sunset, a bit of a moon, but it has to end at St Thomas's Mount.

February 13th 1940

MADRAS

YESTERDAY WILLIE AND I WENT OUT to train for the Ladies Race in the regatta next Monday. I asked Pat Turner, she said she was away, but try Ann Maconachie. Ann said she was already booked, but try Bang-my-arse, who said she would be seasick, but try Elsie Wadsworth. I have never met her, but ring her up and explain all this. We eventually take her out, and she's not too bad,

Willie managing the mainsheet and I manipulating the jib and mast halyards. We have a drink at her house in Nungambankam on the way home, and meet Ma and Pa – also some beautiful Persian carpets. Letter from Pop Jacobs yesterday, enclosing £2.

February 16th 1940

MADRAS

WENT TO A COCKTAIL PARTY in the Connemara, given by Jimmy Jamieson, the other day. I invited myself on Celia's suggestion. Not a great success. Stayed on with Marjorie afterwards then took her home, and she gave me one of Pa's whiskies. Almost engaged to T.R. Molloy of Northampton in Jhansi, whose badge she wears.

Yesterday went out flying in the morning, doing figure of eight's over the ranges fairly successfully, even though I pulled the stick in a lot to swing her round, and might have stalled and spun when coming out of the turn. Entered Elsie for Ladies Race, so Willie and I took her down in the afternoon. Fifteen knot breeze, but we had a bad start and finished last of the Tomtits (a class of sailing boat). Saw a huge turtle in the harbour. Rushed back to Bearen's cocktail party. They had a most villainous cocktail – I tried half but it seemed to be pure alcohol. Later on, John invited me to come with Celia and Joan Swann to Connemara – I said yes, and immediately invited Marjorie too. This made things uneven so I collected Gerald Dunn and off we went in Celia's car. We had a spot of dinner. I danced with Marjorie more than with the other two put together, but it really was fun.

Adrian Cooke, 'Franco' because of his sideboards, was throwing a party to celebrate his departure for France. Very drunk and yelling 'Viva!'. I replied with 'Zieg Heil!' and eventually he embraced me on both cheeks in correct continental style. Elsie asked me to a 'Lido' party tonight at Adyar – dressing as one would there (where? Brighton?). OK, I say, then Springheel says there's night firing tonight. I then have to tell Elsie I cannot make it before

9.15, but when I ask Springheel he kindly says I can go. I hope it will be alright.

Went dive-bombing today with Appleton in a Blenheim. She dived at 260 mph but I wasn't awfully impressed, and why Jerry was nearly sick I don't know. About four bombs stuck in the rack, so he went out to sea to try and unload them. This the gunner did, by opening a hatch and knocking them off with his hand. I was hoping he wouldn't be able to do so and that I should be 'bailed out'.

February 17th 1940

MADRAS

Did thirty mins solo at 5.00 pm yesterday – did figure of eights at 600 feetfairly successfully I think, though whether I can land on the mark I don't know. I did a few landings, sort of settle down ones, as it was a bit bumpy. Shut off at 1200 feetand landed, and took a look at the Mess. It was the best flight I ever had. Then I went out to the range and had a puncture and had to walk back. It took forty minutes, but I made 8.30 OK.

Wore white shirt, trousers, rugger blazer and a scarf – most chaps in shirt and trousers. Dined with the Wadsworths, plus Elsie and the two Mocketts and of course Marjorie, along with Steve, Jimmy, another Willie and a chap I didn't know. Some good beer for dinner and I upset my coffee cup on the table like a bloody fool. I find myself seated next to Marjorie at dinner. I was told to send the driver away as soon as I arrive, and am next told to take Marjorie in Wadsworth's car – everyone going in pairs – so I reckon Celia Mockett must have fixed that.

Arrive at Adyar and find it's a programme dance. Get mine (his dance card) filled with a few horrors, but allow three for Marjorie. Sign S. Marmaduke on a drink or two, with his kind permission. There were chaps playing roulette, and there were lilos and mattresses everywhere. I take Marjorie for a walk or two and some more of her lipstick, though she isn't very helpful. I don't know why – I'm sure she likes it. Meet Willie Thyne (bart) who says I'm his rival. This goes on until 2.30 am when God Save the King is struck up. I'm pretty worn out, haven't seen Marjorie for a couple of dances, and pretty angry. Bill turns up, the Colonel having gone off for a weekend in Madurai with Doakes. He is with the Barrington-Smythes and Mrs Dyson. All five girls get in Wadsworth's car and take me home. No parades today thank god, so I get up at 8.30am.

February 20th 1940
MADRAS

FLYING AND SAILING – the flying not too good as I seem to misjudge my landings on the mark, even from 600 feet, as well as from 2000 feet. The eights aren't too bad, though they are not consistent at 600 feet. But today I try again, and land within 20 feet of the sheet every time but one, doing forty minutes altogether.

Yesterday took Elsie out in the regatta, both her and her sister and two Mocketts. Marjorie said she wanted to come too. We get beaten by Gibbs and Thyne. We have tea there, Willie, John and I (at 1/8 a head - christ!), and then Elsie drops me at the Maynards where I change before going on to the Connemara early night. The party consists of Mr and Mrs, another married couple, Leslie, Marjorie and Eve. Willie and John were there too, very drunk. Most enjoyable, and after 10 pm back to their house for sandwiches and beer. Chicken sandwiches, tongue and sausage rolls, and beer in tall thin cut glass tankards. Simply wonderful. Eve is a kind girl and sensible. Then Leslie takes me home, my suitcase is put on the front seat next to him, Marjorie gets in the back, and there's room for me too. A pleasant drive home, and I feel compelled to kiss her a few times properly. She seems more responsive than usual too. Back in bed by 11.45, after a damn good night.

Two new chaps in the Wilts come out from home – one Scarlett (Colonel!) is 30, was a civil servant before the war, is now a 2nd Lt. John and he and his pal and Dickie Bird gave a party on Elliott's beach the other night. I swam, it was rather pleasant, and the Colonel insisted in going in in his glasses and then wondered why he lost them in the surf. But Mrs Buller would not allow Marjorie to go. "No", she said to me, "I have to draw the line somewhere, and I draw it at moonlight picnics, until she's 21!" The poor sweet being now just 19. At about 12.30 pm a figure was seen lurching across the sand, and it turned out to be Bill in his pyjamas and dressing gown. He had gone to bed, and ordered a taxi surreptitiously and come on down to Elliott's beach.

February 22nd 1940

MADRAS

COMPLETED TESTS FOR MY 'A' LICENSE TODAY. Monday I was bloody awful, Tuesday I had all the tests taped, so I booked Wednesday 7.30 am with four hours solo. I did the eights but mucked up my landing, being too far from the sheet. The next two glides down from 2000 feetwere perfect, and I nearly stopped on the sheet itself. That afternoon did two eights and landed on the circle, and passed that test. My barograph was OK, as I kept at about 500 feet, but she looked a bit drunken during my figures of eight. Then a spinning test with T-B in, and this morning I go up to make thirty minutes and complete my five hours. I climb to 5000 feetand do right and left spins down to about 2300 feet, then back up to 4000 feetand one long spin, pulling out of the dive exactly on 2000 feet. I keep my eyes on the altimeter all through the spin, and feel no effects at all. The aerodrome officer then questions me on Indian Aircraft Rules, which lay down what sort of lights a captive balloon, broken away, being towed by a glider, must display, when looping the loop.

This afternoon rang up Marjorie to come out and have tea, as I have to go into Madras for my 'A' License photos. She said the Ludfords and Jane were lunching with her, she was bringing them home, and so would take me out. She comes out and we go off to the Yacht Club. We take a walk around the Mole and watch the turtles and the minesweepers and then have tea on the lawn. "Thistle" appears on the water with Willie, John and the Grinder. She gives me a letter, not to be opened until she is gone. She had intended to post it, as she didn't expect to see me again before the station. I open it in the taxi after having put her home, about 6 pm, and it's rather touching. I try to ring up, but can't express myself well enough, so write her a letter. She goes to Marmagoa, but back on Wednesday, so must see her that night I hope.

Padre, Arsitarsi, John and I go to Connemara in the evening. Meet the complete drunk – Capt P.G. Hennessey 4/10 Baluchis. Nodding head, slobbering at the mouth, swaying, shaking and pukka blurred speech. I get the Padre onto him and we get him to bed eventually, talking French, German, Urdu and Pashto. A bit of a clever chap.

February 26th 1940

MADRAS

GO SAILING ON SATURDAY. I skipper "Thistle" with Cotterill as crew, and we come last. He is sick at one period, the effect of bad whisky at an RAF dance last night, so tells me. At Rajpuram I put about too quickly, and have to jibe to avoid hitting the buoy. I nearly capsize her once or twice too, and when letting down the sail at the end it catches on one of the wire hallyards and makes a tear about four inches long.

Then dinner with Jos Redman in the Fort, and we go to the Connemara afterwards with Mike Kerro, Cotterill and Scarlett. I don't enjoy it, have three gin slices and we get away about 1am. Abbott has a cocktail party that night, to which I am not invited,

always be a very happy memory.
I hope it will for you too.
I hope you'll forgive me
for writing this, it would have
been so much easier 'to say
it all with you to fill in the gaps,
however I expect you think
I am quite "mad"! But I
can't help it Colin. Hoping to
hear something from you. I hope
you thoroughly enjoy your last
week in Madras & I wish
I wasn't going away for it! or
perhaps its just as well, I
don't know. Yours ever
Marjorie

The last page of the letter from Marjorie, 'not be be opened until she is gone.'

and then they all arrive at the Connemara at about 11 pm. The only people I want to dance with are in that party, which makes it a bit awkward, and I can do nothing about it.

109

Last night John and I called on the Mocketts – having given warning – they don't seem very keen to see us...

February 28th 1940

WENT UP TO THE AERO CLUB the other afternoon and found Patterson Morgan and one Kathline Wilson having tea with T-B. I joined the party, and then he said go and show us what you can do. I went up to 4300 feetand spun to 2000 feet, then did stall turns very nicely. Most enjoyable it was too. Yesterday went to the station from 7.00 am – 3.00 pm, baggage loading, pretty bloody too. Breakfasted in the restaurant. Went to the Wilts Retreat and drinks afterwards. H.E. there. I had two whiskies and felt bloody. Bathed in Jos's room then Tony Cotterill and I went to dine with the Maynards and go on with the ADC's party to Government House afterwards. His Ex. there in the same suit he wore for the Retreat, less coat, as it was a 'Cool Kit' party. I became ill and was sick in the lavatory, then departed for bed. "Knees up Mother Brown" done by Douglas ADC, then we all tried our hands at it.

Marjorie back today so I arrange for her to come up to the Connemara early night and then on to the cinema, with a party of about eight. It's very nice to hear her voice on the telephone again, and I do hope it will be a good party, in spite of my illness. A bit of sleep will soon put that right though.

March 11th, 1940

WANA

JOHN, TONY, KING OF SWING AND I went to the Connemara on the last night. Two Mocketts, Wadsworths and Black Bess (as they call Marjorie), so we pick up Langford James there to make up numbers. We dance, eat fish and chips up top and then go to the

New Elphinstone (Madras's poshest cinema). Marjorie takes me in her car and I hold her hand in the cinema, being seated on two-seater sofas. Then to Gym (Club), where John is the only member and has to pay for all the drinks. I dance with Marjorie and back in bed by 1.30. Marjorie rather excitable and seems to be in rather a state, but prettier than ever.

On 29th I go down to the station at about 7.00 am and load baggage. Have breakfast, and lunch there at 3.00 pm. The farewells begin. Eve and Bang-me-Arse, and most of the Wilts. I catch old Buller eyeing me a bit queerly and have a word with him. Garlands of roses provided by Northland Sports Works, who provided us with kit in the Mount and took a lot of money off me. I am almost reduced to tears, and can only shake hands and chew my pipe. I then give Marjorie a quick kiss as the train moves off and get in quick. She gave me a horrid looking photo of her last night, suitably inscribed.

The journey is pretty bloody. I have Downe and Cotterill, and the latter goes ashore at Delhi, gets tight, and is sick on his bed last night – a horrid smell. I do a lot of thinking, and my life seems bloody. Why did I join the army? Any bloody fool could do this job, and there is no satisfaction of the craftsman in his trade. I could forget the journey quite happily.

Played football at Bhopal against State Forces on real grass, a polo field. First time since coming out here. Saw fourteen dead tigers in one lad's house. At Agra rushed off the train to see the Taj Mahal, but not looking very beautiful and fleeced of rupees at every turn. In Delhi we went to Cecil's Hotel with Major J.L. Jones, who made us drunk (John, Tony and I) and gave us a bath and dinner. The neighbourhood of AHQ and 'Marble Arch' reminded me of Harrogate Stray.

Arrived Mari Indus on the 6th, and I duly cross the bridge with Bill on foot. We are given tea by old pensioners in the Rest Camp. Spend two nights there, and reach Manzai on the 8th. A shocking place, where we spend two nights with the 3/8. Then a convoy to

Wana, and relieve 2/8 Gurkha Rifles. I pray for a hold-up – but nothing, though two shots were fired at 2/8 going down the day before in the Shahur Tangi (A defile where a British convoy was ambushed with heavy casualties in 1937 - see March 10th 1939). A grim place, the Shahur Tangi, and Mehr Dil (rebels) supposed to be about.

Met Lakri Woods, S.W.D. at Jandola. First glimpse of snow from Shahur Tangi above Spli Toi scout post. Wana is very bare, and full of heaps of broken bricks, dust and rubble. John about to be married in April, Jerry hoping to get a job at J.O.S. Sangur and marry Pat Turner, Bill off to the I.A.O.R. in two months or so, Willie and Abbott presumably off to Staff jobs, Paddy Keen expected to go back to Political, Reggie wanting S.W.S. A new 7/13 to be formed and B.O.s required for it. So it will be pretty bloody soon. When I got my "A" License I applied for seconding to the RAF and Freeland said he wouldn't hear of it ever, the old shite. I go on a gas course to Pachmari next month.

March 17th 1940

WANA

I HEAR THAT NO INDIAN ARMY BRITISH OFFICERS are allowed into the RAF. Michael Oliver here in 1/18, a Captain, also Pepe Savignon, Lyall, Arthur Murray, Collins, Taggart and Shaw. I am living in Gunners quarters. A bloody wind just now, like the old 'sting of death'. Reconstruction everywhere here, piles of muck and rubble and it all looks pretty bloody. The Brigade goes in ten days to camp in Karab Kot on 3rd April, which I shall miss unfortunately, as there may be some fun there. Have called on Gunners and Garhwalis (The Garhwal Rifles) and there are plenty more to do.

I buy a camera in the bazaar for 34/-, but haven't had much opportunity to use it so far. British officers commanding companies can be made acting Captain (to fill Battalion establishment) and if held for 21 days get paid too – but no one in this battalion has anything. The Army instruction is rather vague. It must depend on Freeland. Reading up on gas warfare. Jolly is a great help over this, with his A.R.P. booklets.

March 21st 1940

WANA

COTTERILL AND I HAD DINNER with the Gunners last night and then played poker with them. I got away with some money in my pocket. You never get outside this bloody perimeter except exercising – no R.P. There's shooting in Razmak, but not a thing here, although one Pir Nullah and his boys are reputed to be lying in wait for the Wana Hunt, wanting to kill a B.O.

Why did I join the army?

March 26th 1940

WANA

I GET SUDDEN ORDERS ONE NIGHT to go with the convoy leaving next morning, so have to pack in hell of a hurry. This gives me six days spare on the way, so I wire the Franklins in Jhansi that I am coming to stay with them. We get down to Mangai OK, then manage to catch the convoy to D.I.K. (Dera Ismail Khan) after lunch. Davidson, a dentist and I share a staff car. A deadly dull journey, a long straight road, a regular speed of 24 mph with the milestones and furlong posts slowly slipping by. A flat desert on each side, like the Mari Indus-Lakki Marwat stretch, only flatter, with hills in the distance. I shut my eyes and think of Tiree, and every detail of the house comes back, rather extraordinary, as I had never thought of it before.

Met Colonel Weld in the Club in DIK, had a drink with him and went to look up Jackson, Chief Clerk. He is out, so return to the Club. At about 11.00 pm Davidson and I set out in an old car for Darya Khan. We cross innumerable arms of the Indus, by boat bridges, and catch the midnight train to Lalamusa. He goes on to Lahore, I change for Delhi, change again and arrive at Jhansi 4.10 pm on the 24th.

The Franklins are staying in the Club, and I see them about 7.00 pm, only to discover they are heading for Bombay, and home the next day. I have dinner in the Club with Fenella (Fenella Franklin) and two of her admirers, Harry Lee of 2/18 and one Tony of the Northamptons. I spoil their tete-a-tete-a-tete and after dinner they leave eventually, one after the other. Fenella and I sit in the moonlight under a tree, and I play my cards wrong like the bloody fool I am. Anyway, both the other two sneak back to say goodbye properly, and I creep off to bed disgruntled.

I see the Franklins leave at 6.30 am, and that day I have never been so bored in years. Joe Nash is away, Gus Holland is in Bombay, and I have read all the papers in the Club. I wire Chemsie Motor Service and am leaving today for Pachmarhi, though I don't have to be there until 31st. How I feed I don't know, but it can't be a worse place than this. I see that Harry Browell is with the Warwicks in Razani, and that a platoon sergeant won a DCM at Lower Tambre Obo! – my first Razani picquet.

March 31st 1940

Pachmarhi

I ARRIVE HERE ON 27TH, AND AS THE MESS is not open I stay at the Pachmarhi hotel, very pleasant. It's fairly cool here, and a sight for sore eyes after Wana. Rolling 'downs', trees and a church spire topping it off make a picture like England. A sweet smell from the trees too. I play alot of tennis in the Club, next door, and swim in the Club pool. A couple called Shipway are in the hotel – IAOC, late 4/8 of Razmak, and knew it well. Strallan's commandant of this school, with a glamourous daughter called Joan – engaged to Henson of KOSB *(Kings Own Scottish Borderers)*. She's just adopted make-up on the strength of her engagement, and none too skillful in its application. Pam Shallow is also here, her Pa being Lt Col of AEC School. Went to call on Ted and Pam Ritchie, he being adjutant of this school and an old pal of John's in the Suffolks.

I move over to my quarters today, the Mess being open and some chaps arrived, though the course doesn't start until 3rd April. A letter from Hugh and Peggy and one from Marjorie, being pretty affectionate. I spend a lot of the time swimming, which is good sport, being a natural pool, and no chlorine in it.

April 6th 1940

PACHMARHI

SATURDAYS ARE HOLIDAYS, instead of Thursdays. Interesting work it is, although unfortunately I don't know all the parrot stuff in Urdu; or English for that matter. In the afternoon I write my notes, and then go and play tennis in the Club. After that a drink, come back and change, then I seem to be back there again, on the booze.

A lot of temporary soldiers on this course, and they are good chaps, although some are as old as 34, married with a family, and all on a 2nd Lt's pay. I go to Government House the other day for tea and tennis, most enjoyable, though I enter by the Governor's private gate and drive, and the ADC O'Neill tells me off.

April 20th 1940

PACHMARHI

DOING PLENTY OF WORK HERE. Up at seven, at it from 8.30 until lunchtime. I then relax for an hour or so, have tea and go off to tennis. We have all fallen into our groups and cliques now. I am

115

in one with Roger Green, Dudley Withers RAF, "Lord" Page, R. Berko and mixed up Mulhollands, Ox & Bucks, Retherwick Skins etc. We call ourselves 'the snakes', though Basil Henson[1] is my idea of one.

I am getting browned off with the social side, and saw my club bill the other day, so am laying off for a bit. I am now the underwater expert at Beedam, and last time crossed and re-crossed in one. They call me "Dornford-Yates" – it was "Sulky" with the Wilts. The course is interesting but confusing in the facts accumulated. I sleep very well here, out on the verandah, though storms get up occasionally.. I wish I had a gun. Adams, 2/19, has got a panther and a sambhar. One Pughe, Kings Own, went up for his medical for the RAF and is now told to report to Hamble, near Southampton, on 13th May. God! A letter from Bill, just up from Cairo, and even in the Middle East they have the "Journey's End" atmosphere, and plenty of fun with the nursing sisters, or so he says. Mac Bradley and Gillam 2/7 on this course. I have a 1/500 H.S. burn[2] and some neat H.S. on the other arm. Neat H.S. removed with ointment. I win the plate-lifting at Beedam – money for jam!

[1] Basil Henson later became a well known stage and screen actor in the UK).
[2] A mustard gas -'Hun Stuff' - burn, a result of the chemical warfare training he was undergoing.

April 29th 1940

SRINAGAR

I ARRANGE TO COME UP ON TEN DAYS LEAVE with Dudley Withers to Kashmir, and so write to Marjorie to fix us up with a boat, and here we are in Srinagar. After the final exam we depart the 25th for Lahore, where his squadron was (now Peshawar) and where his car is. I send Attam Khan on leave and we go to Faletti's for a night. We go to the RAF Mess, purchase a few things in town and go to the cinema. We leave Lahore 28th at 7.30 am and arrive

"En route to Kashmir".

here twelve hours later, having done 320 miles – at least Dudley did – climbing turns from Jammu to Banni Hal, then gliding turns all the way down.

Beautiful scenery all the way, and at about 8700 feetwe had to help clear away a landslide. A few snow drifts remaining on the Banni Hal pass. Country very reminiscent of Scotland and, in parts, of the Razmak area.

We go straight to Nedou's for a beer and a clean up, and then take a shikhara to the Buller's houseboat on Dal Lake. I receive a surprisingly warm welcome from the hen and cock Buller, and they have arranged for us to have a boat next door at 5/8 a day each. They give us dinner the first night, and Marjorie has baked us a cake. All very nice and very kind of them. We had asked Marjorie to tea to eat her new cake and she said she would be along. Then at 16.23 comes a chit from Henry Buller saying "Thanks very much for inviting M. to tea but you will remember that in Madras she was never allowed into a chummery[1] and I cannot relax that rule here." Our houseboats are not touching but about three feet apart. Slightly staggered!

This morning I wake up feeling grand, and we go and look at Srinagar and the "Bund", which reminds me of the "seaside" at home, with touts everywhere. We then go and look at Nagin Bag, which is where we wanted our boat originally. The Club annexe is there, and swimming, and not a dirty backwater like our mooring here. Dudley meets some friends there and everything looks rosy, if only we can get away from here without giving offence to the Bullers. I use my catapult on the peddlers and hawkers. Ma sent me out two pipes and a cigarette case, silver with my crest on. Her great scheme of defeating the customs (marking them as repairs) failed, and I have to pay 11/- on the parcel. It was damn hot in Lahore. Our houseboat is called 'Lighthouse'.

[1] A bachelor pad.

'The Good Ship "Lighthouse".' The 'chummery' referred to by Marjorie's father, Henry Buller.

May 2nd 1940

SRINAGAR

WE MANAGE TO GET AWAY TO NAGIN BAGH, and whilst in the Club a girl comes in and we send her a chit from Joan Strallan, who we had brought up with us. We hear it being opened and find that we have struck lucky. She is Elaine Doran, up here with her Ma in houseboat "Butterfly", and is a really beautiful English girl; all her own beauty too, just out from home in January and completely unspoiled. We fix up a picnic with them but rain stops that. We take her to the flics the next day. Yesterday we go into town with the Adams's, Dudley's friends, and then on return play gramophones on "Butterfly" with tea and games with the Adams's. A dance last night at Nedou's and we go there with Elaine and Ma. I get left a bit longer than pleasant with Ma, but still. A wire from Wana extending my leave up to June 9th, or six weeks, so presumably I shan't get any more this year. Oh, Elaine! Met Valentine up here.

'Elaine'

May 7th 1940

WE BOTH FALL IN LOVE WITH ELAINE and take her out every day. We drive into Srinagar some mornings, go to a dance at Nedou's and the Club and the pictures – something every day. John Palmer

Elaine and Colin on a shikhara on Dal Lake

and wife up here, and we all go to call on them yesterday evening. I saw him in the Club. Met Matthew up here too. Nagin Bagh really is a beautiful place, whether it be wet or fine. It is a curious situation with Elaine. We both go out with her, and I suppose my eyes look to Dudley what his look to me, when looking at her. However I am the junior partner, and she prefers him I think. Mother is a colossal snob, despite her place of origin being Putney, and Pa, who is not here, is reputed to be like the Big Bad Wolf. They reckon to go up to Gulmarg in June for three months, and leave Kashmir in September or October.

I haven't seen Marjorie again – nor do I want to after Elaine. I fall off 'Butterfly' yesterday morning and lose my watch in about 5 feet of pani *(water)*. I go round the boat, diving, this morning but there is too much mud and I can't find it. I've made a catapult for the local bumboat man.

The thought of leaving Elaine is beginning to hurt somewhat but I think it would be better to go to Assam than to stop here, though if I had the clothing etc I might go for a trek. But then I would probably put my foot in it, like I usually do. I don't expect I will get the railway warrants in time anyway.

We have another 'sticky' tea in the Club at Srinagar, but it's not such a success as the first one.

May 14th 1940

Assam

OUR LAST DAY WE WENT UP TO GULMARG with food. I am a bit sore in calf, through falling off the footplate of 'Butterfly', and I have a spirited horse. I get him under control on the way down though. On return we have dinner on 'Butterfly' and go to a dance at Nedou's – coming back pretty grim, and there seems to be something between Elaine and Dudley, which rather worries me. However, such is life. In bed at 3 am and up at 5.30 and we drive off to Pindi, a bloody journey via Murree with two punctures, and we are both rather remorseful. I spend the night at Pindi station with some free beers in the Club where I get in a circle with Robinson 3/10 and some friends of his. Change at Lahore and reach Calcutta on 12th in the morning. I get blackmailed over my excess baggage by the Babu, helped by a YMCA chap, and it costs me 10/-. A helluva job to cash a cheque at the Great Eastern, but after much telephoning of Uncle Stanley's friends I get it backed. *(He is on his way to stay with his uncle, Stanley Wood, a tea planter in Assam).*

Dinner on the Assam Mail, breakfast crossing the Bramaputra on a ferry from Amingoan. Then up through some real African jungle with the cicadas in full throat to Titabar station. Some pleasant shooting out of the train in the morning with my Colt, at Paddy and wading birds, including a stork. Not far out either. Pass a beautiful train smash, with telescoped vans, torn rails and an engine with a really drunken list. The Uncle meets me at the station

'Panbarry.' The tea planter's house in Assam where Colin's Uncle Stanley (Stanley Wood) lived. Colin visited twice, in May and December 1940.

and here I am. Uncle Bill is dead, I am told, and left me £200. Hugh *(Colin's brother)* put up a good show and hoping for a DFC. I'm sure I'll never see this war!

May 18th 1940

ASSAM

THIS IS UNFORTUNATELY A CULTIVATED PART of Assam, the nearest jungle being 40-50 miles away. However, I go round with my revolver and a Greener .310 of Uncle Stanley's to see what I can get. I fail dismally with the .310 as I cannot zero it properly, not that there is anything worth shooting. Some duck-like wading birds, king crows, crow pheasants, crows and a bastard cuckoo which says 'Who are you?' the whole time. I spend half a day chasing some jungle fowl. I do a quick draw when I flush them, and one squats on a tree near the .310 but I miss him. However, I shall persevere.

There is a half-eyed pony which I ride a bit. An Australian whaler, and his good eye is damn bad, so that he stumbles and walks into obstacles.

An enervating place this. Breakfast at 9.30 and I don't feel like rising much before. The green is a good sight, and very unlike the India I know. We go over to the Jorhat Club for tennis and tea. I see the AVLH *(Assam Valley Light Horse)* doing their stuff, but was only introduced to one or two. I suppose I am better off than an assistant tea planter on Rs 250/-. This is a peaceful life, and a pity there isn't jungle nearby. An ever still, rising and falling cadence of bird calls. All varieties, the crow and 'Who're you?' predominating. And me out of the war! God!

May 25th 1940

Assam

Forty eight hours steady rain. Nothing to do. Yesterday managed to bag a cormorant, 'Who're you?' and parrot with the .22. It seems to shoot high according to the sights, so it's all a question of aiming lower by so much and holding her steady. Wrote to Elaine and Joan Strallan. Also to Mowbray Burnett.

The drill here is, rise at 8.30 and then stroll around outside before breakfast at 9.30, of all hours. After the 10.15 news I either go out with the Uncle walking round the tea, or by myself with the Colt. Back at about 12 to read the paper and have a drink. After lunch read, write or sleep until tea at 3.30. After that, shoot or muck about until beer and news at 7.00 pm – and so to bed.

What a life! Forever mucking about is how my life seems to have been spent. Letter from Jobber Benbow, wanting to transfer to 2/13.

May 30th 1940

ASSAM

WENT OVER TO THE MARIANI CLUB and watched the AVLH at drill. Worse than a school OTC. There I observed one Lance Corporal and wondered whether I had come out on the boat with him. Two days later, while dozing on my bed after lunch, I get to thinking about the old days, and eventually about Skegness. I suddenly remember that Thom Allen used to plant tea in Assam, so I nip out of bed and look in the Assam directory. I see an Allan, P living near here and remembering Peter, I enquire off the Uncle. He tells me that he has a brother called Tom who used to plant here, and also that he is the Lance Corporal I had spied. This is too much evidence, and it turns out to be Peter Allan, after fifteen years, and he had been eyeing me too, he said.

Went over to the Government Tea Research Department at Tocklai and there one Benton, bacteriologist, tells me that to purify water, insert two rupees a third of an inch apart, as poles, and then a current through them from a 4.5 volt battery will purify one pint of water in 15 seconds. Provided there is no clay in the pani (water), which combines with the silver and falls to the bottom. I get my hands on a car after three years since I last drove. It's a 1929 Chevrolet. Some good coot shooting, and have opened up on a jackal.

June 7th 1940

LAHORE

WE GO TO THE MARIANI CLUB on Saturday 1st and then I go off for a night with Peter Allan, and what a night. Tennis, a drink and change, then a game of pools, some bridge, and then boozing in the bar with a chap who knew John Macneil, and we leave at midnight. Finish dinner at 2 am, and so to bed. In the Club I had retired at about 10 pm, and after that got my second wind OK.

The next day, tennis with the Butters and back home. We discuss Allan family history since I left them, and this and that. I push off to Calcutta on 3rd, and spend the 4th in the Grand Hotel (12/8). I go out to Dum Dum aerodrome, and am allowed up dual, which I manage OK. The next morning I go out solo, but a damn Indian smashes his undercarriage the turn before me, so no more flying. That being so, I push off to Lahore where I am now, in Falletti's hotel (signed into the book as "Marmaduke, Undertaker").

4th June a memorable day, for that night I discover a secret of nearly nine years standing, though I admit I had overestimated it. Enough said!

A bloody journey on the Punjab Mail, though met one Gilroy (ex 53rd), now AIRO in RIASC. Arrive here at 7.00 am and breakfast and off up to the aerodrome. After twenty five minutes dual, am allowed solo, and just circle and land, though a bit bumpy. I'm fed up with doing landing circuits for ever. Still, it certainly is an expensive hobby, and I can't see what good is going to come out of it ever.

Met Appleton, joining the RAF in Calcutta. Up again this evening for forty minutes. Walters, the pilot instructor, unable to teach me aerobatics, so I go on a recce over Lahore, about ten miles away. Keep at 2000 feet and try to take a couple of photographs. A bit of a haze and much smoke, but most enjoyable, and finish with a perfect landing. The damn man won't let me spin her, me who has spun at 3000 feet in Madras – he says he doesn't like chaps of only six or seven hours flying throwing the planes about. What the hell's he think I am? Met a flying British officer there, and was telling him what Adams had told me about Haig going to the RAF, and found he WAS Haig, and that they had accepted him and then done nothing more about it.

June 16th 1940

I LEAVE LAHORE ON THE FRONTIER MAIL and meet Attam Khan in Lalamusa, where I have to spend quite some time. Arrive at Darya Khan at 4.15am, and then by car to DIK. This entails a trans-shipment across the Indus in a launch, which of course goes aground half way across. Met John in the rest house, and with the aid of a chap in the RIASC workshops, we obtain two cars and drive straight up to Mangai the next day. We spend a night here, and after much telephoning for permission, manage to get a seat in an armoured car coming up the next day. Very comfortable, and a good breeze through the open slit.

In Wana, and find that Freeland has gone to District HQ, Guy of 5/13 is the C.O., Willie and Abbo gone off on jobs, Keen at Political, Maitland Jerry on leave, Niven in Razmak with Patiala State Forces. Present are Guy, Golly, Reggie (adjutant), Bill, Arti and Cotterill. Bill departs on leave and gives me the job of Mess secretary, besides C company and Gas officer. I try to get a grip on the work, and wonder how to lecture on gas in Urdu. I have Uncle Stanley's Mauser .430, which he presented to me, though shells are 55/- a hundred. I work bloody hard the first week, but am now feeling rather depressed. Bill and Toby in the war now, and bits of the Indian Army, but how can I ever be? New battalions 7/13 and 8/13 (13 Frontier Force Rifles) being formed, so presumably some British officers will have to go. What a nice thought. Still further from the war would I go.

JUNE 23RD 1940

A STILL GREATER BLOW. Reggie says that I shall have to go to the TB *(Training battalion)* in Abbottabad shortly. This is being expanded, as well as 7/13 and 8/13. That settles the war for me then. Christ! A PAD *(Passive Air Defence)* scheme here. I get the job of AGO and PADO *(PAD Officer)* and it is the nearest to the war we have got. Sitting for one and a half hours one night in a stuffy blacked out Battalion office, played poker with Maxwell and lost, and last night he comes down here and Reggie, Cotterill and I sit down on him. We each have 6/- and Cotterill gets 15/- off him.

Of course in Abbottabad I shall remain a 2nd Lt, and here the boys will all be acting Captains if not Majors. But what to do? It's my own fault for ever coming out here. The Mess lawn is nice and green and I have swum a bit, but it's not too pleasant. This time last year I was enjoying running up Dun.

July 2nd 1940
WANA

NOTHING OF NOTE. I find I am not bad at six-a-side hockey, after my Razmak rink training. Some football, and have got Rangu trained to bring me a Murree beer when I shout to him "My usual!" On an Indian Officers course, which reminds me of Sandhurst, and it prevents me going out on a Brigade day, though they are nothing here. Springheel returned from leave and started boasting to me about Wana in '21.

Due for the T.B. I suppose, this time next week on the convoy, and for how long I wonder. It puts me still further from the War I reckon.

Had dinner in 1/18 Garwalis mess with Miles the other day. Him I met in Nowshara in December '38 when visiting 2/11. Paddy Nugent killed, and Jeffries, and I can't even get a smell of an Italian, let alone a Boche. I seem to be always frustrated. Frustrated to miss that column with Brain & 59th in November 1938, missed Razcol in August '39, then the RAF, and the other day on the Brigade Day, and those RPs where they all caught it but me. Perhaps I am doomed to become a Babu *(a Hindu wise man)*.

A bit of swimming which is pleasant, and from the Brigade garden comes apricots and just now some battered peaches. Grapes in the garden, but pygmies. Some enjoyable bridge the other night with Jolly, Springheel and Smith, 1/18 staff captain. A colossal dust storm, almost a sand storm, arises and for four days visibility is about 1000 feet. Suddenly it shuts down to 200 feet and dust sweeps across the camp, like the rain squalls in Razmak used to. I sleep out for the first time, and wake up under a brown mosquito net. But worth it.

July 11th 1940

WANA

JERRY RETURNED FROM LEAVE having spent it down in Madras, after Pat Turner. No celebration on the 9th *(Colin's 22nd birthday)*. I play in the young soldiers hockey team against the RA, and then Lock and I have a few beers and he comes over for dinner. Had Ken Mules 1/18 up for bridge last Saturday, and Springheel and I bid a small slam, which I play and win. A lot of drinks with one Dowson (Signals), of Western Electric.

Nothing of note ever happens here. Razmak is alive with dead bodies and lead, and Campbell the Resident was shot up and wounded in the arm in his car near Asad Khel. The Worcesters at Razani, and the Suffolks at Razmak, have casualties every day.

A letter from Mowbray Burnett who is in the Gordons in Singapore. I am due for the Training Battalion on the next convoy, in a day or so I expect. I have no guiding aim in life just now. It used to be Urdu, 2/13, the War, my flying license, the RAF – but now I am sunk as far as the RAF goes, and I couldn't be much further from the War in Abbottabad. For twenty years I have dreamt of a war, and now it comes and I cannot take part in it!!

July 14th 1940

Manzai

Now in Manzai. Came down on the convoy two days ago, with ten British officers. We have to sit in the back, as we are too good an aiming mark in the front seats; or so they say. Up to Sra Kanda Narai I stand in the back of my lorry, being the most comfortable position, and then nip into an ambulance which is following and get a good ride the rest of the way. What a place. I try to sleep outside, and am nearly suffocated. Arthur left on the DIK convoy this morning, and I take the 'Heatstroke Express' tomorrow at 6.00 am with Shaw (2/2), Maclean and Collins (1/18). The 3/8 keep a good John Collins here, made by Andy the Madras Khitnagar.

July 18th 1940

Abbottabad

Not a bad journey on the Heatstroke, as the sky was generally overcast, and so not too much sun. A bath at Mari Indus and tea with the Suffolk BORs *(British other ranks)* there. Change at Daud Khel, reached Campbellpore at 2.45 am until 8.00 am, then Taxila and rail head at Havelian. No transport for getting up here, so I have to get a couple of lorries off the RIASC, and had to pay 5/- for one.

This is rather like Kashmir, and there is plenty of rain just now. Dick Shirley (who I met on the 'City of Venice') (the ship Colin came out to India on) is in the next room, on the same job as me. Met Ray and Peggy Palmer in the Club yesterday. Today a session with the dentist, an extremely comfortable one too, and I send a wire to Ma. It's a good looking spot, though not for wartime, and Ray tells me I shall have no chance of using the Mauser around here. What a war!

*'The Heatstroke Express'. So-called because it carried
passengers in open cattle trucks.*

July 27th 1940

ABBOTTABAD

I NOW HAVE A CAR, A TRIUMPH 8HP of about '31 vintage. I
went down with Pat Kenny to look at second hand cars and found
this, which the experts think is OK. Got down from Rs 650 to
Rs 525, and even then the fellow had a hell of a profit. Kenny did
the bargaining, I signed the cheque, having stepped in after Kenny
had refused to go higher than Rs500, and Dick Shirley made me
pay another Rs20 for three months free service. But I reckon my
driving won't do her any good.

On parade at 6.50 to 9.00 am watching jungly chaps right-
turning by numbers, then 10.15 to 11.00 am in the office – bah! –
and one afternoon a week from 5-7 pm, the rest free (unofficially).
That is the sum total of my day's war work. Useful results therefrom
accruing = nil. The 1/8th from Razmak are here, with Walshe, Hall
and some others I used to know. I haven't yet joined the club, and
there's no need to yet. The pool is too dirty for swimming.

August 5th 1940

ABBOTTABAD

THE CAR NOT TOO GOOD IN PETROL. The snake tongued salesman said 30-40 miles per gallon. The first two gallons went 20 miles and the next three since have done about 23 miles each. The carburettor needle is wrong.

Henriques and young Fisher killed, and Halliday got an MC, in Egypt. Had drinks with Abbott last night, and he told me stories of the chaps who went home for mountain warfare in Norway. A letter from Bill in an Egyptian desert.

Had to pass a driving test this morning for my bus. Took an '8 anna' police sergeant round the town and back OK.

August 8th 1940

ABBOTTABAD

DICK WENT OFF TO HOSPITAL and died on the night of 6/8. He had been ill on and off for three weeks, and it appeared to be stomach trouble. The post mortem said it was an enlarged heart which had choked him. He always was a runner, and I suppose he strained it. It didn't help pushing my car up yon hill either, when I took him, Bill and John Stephenson up to Kelfani, below Tandiane.

Funeral last evening with Gurkha bands. I had the sword and had to place it on the coffin and remove it at appropriate times. It's a pity, as I should be in Peshawar with him by now, as we had tied up to go this weekend.

August 13th 1940

ABBOTTABAD

WENT AND HAD A DRINK WITH RAY the other night. Abbo and

Willie expecting to go home any time now. Freeland apparently commanding Razmak. That'll be nice for them. Not feeling too good these days. I seem to be getting fat, and unable to chase a foot or squash ball with as much vigour as formerly. A very sleepy place this, though I don't in the afternoons. A chap called K.A.R. Khan, attached to the Dogras, is apparently going off to Wana to join the boys. I have not joined the club here and seem to manage very well without doing so. Squash in gunners courts, football, a booze in the mess. My first earthquake the other evening. The mess suddenly shook, and the sound of cracking came from the roof, as though a score or so of bearers were chasing cats across it. Pat and I were outside like a cascara tablet *(a laxative)*, but nothing happened and so we returned to our beer in peace.

August 19th 1940

ABBOTTABAD

WENT OFF TO PESHAWAR ON THURSDAY for the weekend. Had some stomach trouble, and car conked out at Attock – this was mended (carburetter) by a lorry driver, and I reach Peshawar Club and hand it over to Ghulam Sarwar. Dudley Withers in Srinagar unfortunately, and I know what he is doing! A chap called Dibben (1/4 GR) turns up, whom I apparently played rugger against at Stowe. Friday the car was mended, and I fix up to go to Landikotal for breakfast on Saturday, and to look at the Khyber Pass. Also saw Major Loreto DDI, and got a man to show me the bazaar. Bathed and drank draught beer in the club. Saturday Dibben and I depart, and at milestone five the car breaks down again. There is a police post nearby and I ring up the garage. Out comes a man, looks at it, says he must go back for new platinum points, and will be just five minutes. I spend the ensuing hour until his return in smoking and throwing stones at frogs. A mad fakir gives us a brace of corn cobs, our only breakfast. Then start off again, but a temperamental piston frightens me and we return to Peshawar.

133

Reggie Malone comes down after lunch and we spend the evening swimming, and then beer on the lawn. Jobber is in Derha Dun with 6/14th. On Sunday we go round the bazaar. The guide is a Turk, of the royal family driven out by the Russians in 1910, and speaking seven or eight languages. We see the money changers, the streets of the leather, goldsmiths, silversmiths and brass workers, and painted birds in cages. We go to the pottery works, the Police Post roof, and the Afridi bazaar. Jews, beggars, locals with rifles strut about.

I set off at 11.30 and at one stop for an hour on the roadside. Here my car is looted of some Punjabi slippers I had bought in the bazaar. Reggie had told me that Peggy Hennessy, of the SS City of Venice, lived in Wah, her father being chief Punjab cement man there, so I stopped in order to arrive for tea there. This I did and found them all in Murree, but was given tea by the bearer, a very civil bloke. The house palatial. The car now gives trouble. I have been nursing it all the way, but it gets fits of not pulling in top gear, being OK in second. This they say is due to bad carburation. I don't know though.

C.A. Blackwell, C.D. Yarrow missing at Dunkirk. Also hear that Peter Petit had his girl, "the Minx", staying out in Mhow when he was there. No second pips until two and a quarter years service or eighteen months of war, whichever first. Three more months to do for me.

August 25th 1940

ABBOTTABAD

LETTER FROM UNCLE GEORGE DATED JULY 12TH sympathising with the loss of Hugh. *(His elder brother, flying Blenheims for 21 Squadron, went missing over France on 6th June).* First I knew of it, and he doesn't make it clear whether killed or missing. I wire Ma, but I suppose one can't expect an answer these days. I must have done it by what I said to Bill in my letter – tempting fortune though it was too late then. And me sitting here watching 'Ek do tin, nama, ek dot tin'! (A popular local dance, 'One, two, three, let's dance!') God!

Letter from Dudley Withers and as he states "after two days I got so browned off with her dumbness and her foolish mother that I have broken off relations". Fancy that now!

A helluva walk with John Stephenson last night, three and a half hours, and back at 8.15. Peggy says the boys expect to go out on column in Wana shortly. Russell T.S. and Morgan Wall killed the other day, the former at Tabbi and the latter in Razani. Wish I was there, and not here. Managed to get off a letter to Aunt Molly, for my sins. Am due for a trip to Nasirabad with a draft for 7/13.

September 5th 1940

ABBOTTABAD

SET OFF FOR NASIRABAD ON 30TH. Took over train, but my lilo was punctured of course, and with John Stephenson I set off. Parted company at Lahore, where he went on to Solon. Got onto the metre gauge railway at Bhatinda and nearly shook my guts out. Fed very well on a tin or two a day with bread, fruit from the stations and pinky pani (potassium permanganate water solution used to wash fruit and vegetables in). Passed through Ajmer, a big railway colony, and looking prosperous with a car practically at every door. Keith Dawson objected to the boys arriving with their feet out of the windows, and on arrival Pinsent Q/M gave me a sort of operation order for unloading, which I promptly forgot and do no more about.

Lunch with the Dawsons, a bit drunken, and me trying to get a word in here and there. Sleep, walk and booze with Hugh Easton and Pat Thompson 2/11, ex Razmak, with their new battalion there. Bridge with Bill, Springheel who is making a nuisance of himself here, and Felix Williams, and I come back on Sunday arriving here on Tuesday night after a bloody journey. Nasirabad was evacuated in May owing to a water shortage, but now they have returned as it rained a lot recently. Expect to go to Bannu shortly, and relieve 1/12 who are due for mechanisation. Akhbar of 6/13 there. He said we had been going to invade Persia with that force and seize the oilfields, but now not, so expect 59th have gone to Egypt.

Rumours of the boys moving from Wana to Jallundur or Ambala shortly – what the hell will they do there? Sikhs in C.I.H. *(Central India Horse regiment)* refused to embark at Bombay for overseas, so half a dozen of them were shot by court-martial sentence. One transported for fifteen years, but not dismissed the service, so presumably will return on completion.

Abbottabad as bloody as ever, and depression gets worse. Kitty Cole gets married to a Captain Desmond Verney.

September 12th 1940

Abbottabad

LETTER FROM MA SAYING HUGH MISSING on 11th June. "He went on a raid in his Blenheim, the most glorious hot day and though no fighter was after him, he was under fearful A.A. barrage and went up to 7000 feet and was seen no more – " Peggy *(his brother Hugh's new wife)* produces a daughter some few days ago too.

I work in Brigade now, two or three days, as the battalion out training, an interesting interlude, what with all the secret stuff and seeing how things work. It's getting cold here now and depression, mental and physical, is setting in. I don't seem very fit these days, I must say, and nothing ever happens, one day succeeding another. And Hugh.

September 26th 1940

NOTHING OF NOTE. Letter from Tony Cotterill, Wana getting sniped, and the other day six B.O.'s and three orderlies out exercising hounds were ambushed by thirty Dushmen at 200 feetrange. Two horses were hit and the remainder missed. However, Arthur Murray and an orderly fell off in the general confusion and their horses bolt for home, and Mike Oliver apparently rode back in the face of the advancing tribesmen and rescued Doc Murray. Or that's the story anyway. It was a trap to draw out Wanacol where a lashkar was waiting for it. However, the bait was not swallowed. Only some armoured cars went out in pursuit, and the R.A. opened up rapid fire from the camp. Why do I always miss the fun? Campbell apparently can't quite understand life there, and when the gunners opened rapid he was having one of his reports debated before the C.O. The guns started and Campbell interrupts the C.O. with "My God sir, artillery!"

These recruits here are a mixed lot. Some of the Sikhs that arrive speak pretty good English, some have been impressed, some are Nai Sikhs[1], and then some desert after they have been here some weeks. The Dogras are mostly pretty good, and give no trouble at all. Kumaonis we take now, and they are proud and conceited. (A people from northern India). Some have been told to ask for Ghurka hats like the Dogras, and some speak no Kumaon tongue. PMs are alright, some madder than others, but the real madness are the Pathans, especially the Orakzais (A tribe from the North West frontier), with whom no other brand of Pathan is able to converse. There are eight training groups, they spend fifteen working days in each, and then know how to fire a rifle and salute, a bit of V.B., and elementary collective training and mountain warfare.

---

[1] *A caste of Sikh working in the haircutting or beauty profession.*

October 17th 1940

HUGH STILL MISSING. Nothing of note for a month now. I just live and eat and sleep – or seem to. Saw David Cole get married the other day. There won't be many girls left when I get home, if I ever do. A bit of bridge with Rosemary Abbott, though she can't really play. Abbo' is now at home (Willie too) having gone on a course at Minley. Now cracking with the Pashto, and not finding it too easy. Three months I've been here now, and don't see how I am ever going to get out of it. I tried for 59th, wrote to Brain once or twice, but nothing could be done as they have now gone off to Egypt.

3

October 1940 - January 1941

RAF training

Karachi

October 28th 1940

In September I was talking to some of the boys from 6 Gurkha Rifles and they mentioned a request for applicants for the RAF. I pricked up my ears and being unable to find it in our office, I went down to the 6/GR office and took a copy of theirs. It read "Suitable BCOs and ICOs wanted for secondment to the RAF – under 28 and with at least 1.5 years service. Previous flying service is not necessary but will be taken into consideration." I sent off a wire to Wana asking permission and then the TB sent up my name. At last, on 26th September, just as I was going down the Mess steps, thinking of Tony Cotterill's letter about the ambush, and how I always miss everything, an orderly arrives with this telegram: "2nd Lt D-W provisionally selected for secondment RAF – will be required to commence initial training about end September. Should be warned accordingly. Further instructions will issue shortly."

I am overjoyed, start packing and get drunk. I then get more depressed as the days go on, and eventually a wire comes on 25th October saying report Air H/Q for medical on the 28th. If pass, then off to Karachi for training!

I come down with Bobbie Elsmie, off to Bombay to be married, and Logan Gates, whose wife and daughter died the other day (I attend funeral). I stay here in the Cecil and go round to drink with Brain, who is now a military secretary here.

This morning I roll up at Air H/Q and meet Haig (5/19), Pringle (2/10) and Gillespie (1/10), all pilots bar the latter. We hang about for hours for our medical and interview by Group Captain Bussell. Major A.S. Lewis (4/12) is Air Liaison Officer and does all the paperwork.

I mention my eyes and they all look grave. I am walking around the quad, looking at the pretty typists (it's the Nizam of Hyderabad's palace) when I see the M.O.'s room and Haig on his exam – I also see the eye test board, so I write it down, (it seems to be a gift – "never look a gift horse in the mouth" etc.), memorise it, and am passed as 6/6. How long it will last I don't know. I reckon I will be pushed out after a few weeks, or even days, but it will be good fun whilst it lasts.[1]

Our course is six weeks at Drigh Road, Karachi, then 4 Air Training School Iraq, and back to Army co-operation squadrons in India. Rank Pilot Officer, pay Army or RAF, whichever is the higher. After a year we go into RAF uniform. Off tonight on the Frontier Mail to Lahore and then on to Karachi – the great deceit – how long will it last – and will I be court-marshalled – Quien Sabe?

[1] Colin's eyesight was poor, and he expected to be found out eventually.

November 2nd 1940

KARACHI

DRIGH ROAD[1]. We stop at Lahore for the day on the way down. Pringle and Haig went to see the Flying Instructor there, Walters. Gillespie and I sit about Faletti's and go for a swim out in the Cautt. Then down on the Sind Express, plenty of dust and no restaurant car. We ride a bit in the engine compartment – rushing through the night down south – arrive Drigh Road at 8.00 pm – met by a three-ton lorry and taken to Mess – filled with beer by F/Lt J. Chapple, Adjutant. We live in tents here, of the marquee type with concrete floor, a water point, and an electric punkah overhead. I open up at night and such a breeze comes blowing through that I can sleep with a blanket on. As "Red Hot" Jones, the civil flying instructor, is away, we spend about five days hanging about the works and watching things happen.

The depot here repairs all crashes, assembles planes shipped from home, and now that not so much is coming out, it is a factory for all sorts of engine parts. It's in the desert seven miles from

Karachi – a nice Mess, but rather regimental in its rules and with notices everywhere saying "such and such is verboten" etc. We couldn't get dinner at 10.00 pm the other night!

Went to the boat club for a swim the other day, it's on a creek of the Chinna and a pleasant spot. Bond is here, but mad, and doesn't take much stock of me. Dudley Withers arrived here suddenly two days ago, as Armament Officer for six months, whatever that is. He flew a Wapiti *(Westland Wapiti)* down from Peshawar. Well, we both went into town for one, and sat in the Boat Club for a few hours, exchanging talk and reminiscences. It was just like the good old days on Nagim Bagh, with Karachi all blacked out, looking like the other side of Nagim. We then called in at the Gym Club and had another.

Dicky Lonsdale, Leicesters, awarded MC for Waziristan – Razmak I suppose. Johnny Benbow's engagement in the paper! Christ! is the only suitable comment. Well, I've been about four days in the RAF now – pretty good going eh?

[1] *The four Indian Army officers are accepted for secondment to the RAF. In total, 60 were transferred under this scheme. The Air Ministry gazetted them as Pilot Officers attached to 'General Duties Branch, RAF' in the London Gazette (30/10/41), service numbers 47299 (Haig), 47300 (Pringle), 47301 (Gillespy) and 47302 (Dunford Wood). They are posted together to the 4th Intermediate Flying Training School at RAF Habbaniya in Iraq.*

November 8th 1940

KARACHI

'RED HOT" JONES GOT BACK MONDAY, so we have done four days flying since then. Circuits and landings and ten minutes solo the last two days. I get in a bit of side slipping for the first time. Jones takes us in a DH60 but he doesn't wear earphones, and you can't always understand him. Ground work, theory of flight and we learn to 'buzz' up there. We have a go in the "Link" (trainer) too – a beautiful toy. At 1000 feet all you can see is desert, with the sea

Tiger Moths at the Karachi Flying Club.

eastwards, not at all a bad sight. Went out fishing on Sunday, with Jones, Bowden and Dudley in a sort of dhow. Out past Manora and I was sick – caught the only fish, but too ill even to haul it up. It's easy to sit here and say how nice the sea is, and how I would like to experience a real rough storm, but it's bloody hell when you get there.

We go up to the aerodrome at 7.30 every day, and back at about 1 pm. We live in a sort of Ipi hut, with canvas sides and a thatch roof to keep the sun off the canvas. At night I open her up to a decent breeze and sleep with a blanket on. Jock McGrath collects a DFC at home, and has his picture in the "Sketch"! The beer tastes nice here, the old Murree!

November 11th 1940

KARACHI

HAD THE FIRST GAME OF RUGBY SINCE "BLIGHTY" the other day – didn't manage too badly, except for having bars in my boots

LICENCE 3.
RENEWAL OF LICENCE.
LICENCE 4.

Medical Examinations.		Periods of validity of Licence.		
Date.	Result.	From	To	Signature (or stamp) of responsible officer.
16.11.39	Fit subject to wearing correction to vision.	18.3.40	15.11.40	
18.11.40	Fit	22-11-40	17-11-1941	

and so unable to move. It is played on the mud flats here, quite softish, though I cut my knees a bit. Went out with Gillespie in the desert yesterday evening and I shoot a hare and a partridge – there's some sand grouse about, though out of range. A hell of a wind today, and I do three bad landings, Gogte using the engine each time to save the undercarriage. Hope I'm better tomorrow.

November 13th 1940

KARACHI

GOT THE LANDINGS TAPED – I had been flattening out too late. Did two hours solo yesterday and today. This morning went out to a village on the creek due east and then climbed to 8000 feet – it was damn cold, so I came down, doing a bit of side slipping. This evening we go up and I had prepared a trip to Hawk's Bay. But I have a preliminary chukka and during the landing, I seem to be going too damn fast. Well, I bounce four times, get my tail up, damage the undercarriage slightly, and take three inches off the

144

airscrew. Jones is not too annoyed, and eventually takes me up in the Tiger and shows me when to use my engine. Though I really knew all along.

Yesterday went to the Boat Club after dinner. Saw P. Bond and talked of this and that. Met one Hayes, who succeeded me in ULIA attachment to Leicesters, and is now in the Baluchi Training Battalion here. Also MacDowall, who is an acting major in 7th GR. And as conceited as hell. I only talk to him for about ten minutes but I am nearly sick! Damn me for a B.F. this evening!

November 18th 1940

Karachi

NEARLY SCUPPERED. As my 'A' License expired on 15th inst. I had to have a medical exam for the renewal form. Crimes of Paris! As the saying goes.

Well, I go snooping around the hospital on the pretext of getting some boric ointment, but am unable to penetrate the medical officer's section and obtain access to the eye test card. So I nip down to the RAMC Hospital on Sunday morning. The C.O. there is a bit deaf and says 'come tomorrow at 9.00 am', I explain that I shall be flying, but he just repeats himself. I then see one Captain Hanbury on the list of doctors (he was at Pachmari) so I chase him around the wards, but unsuccessfully.

I then run into the C.O. again who is a bit rude, so I pack off home. I go straight up to the hospital here with my heart in my boots, but the M.O. is out. However, I penetrate his office and write down the eye test card, which is C-O-O etc in unfinished circles. I learn this off by heart, and this morning I go up for the inspection. He is in one of the wards, and as he fills in the questions he says "Come along with me and I'll test your eyes." He leads me out of the ward but PAST his office, and I hear the angels singing. We then come to a placard on the wall, and damn my whiskers if it isn't the same one as I learnt in Delhi at Air HQ!

Well, I learned RAF climbing turns etc, and can now do steep turns and side slips. There's a small camp some 3-4 miles from the aerodrome, presumably Kings Own, and I do all my stuff there at 4000' and then shoot them up in the remaining 3000' to 1000' after which I go home.

A dance in the Mess here last Saturday. McDowell rings up and invites himself, with a colossal fat chap in Phipson's called Connie. He wants to come as all the "Popsies" are here and he wants to get amongst 'em. Suits me. I have a few dances, nothing much to write home about, and eventually retire at 02.30.

November 21st 1940
KARACHI

FLYING MORNING AND NIGHT. Went off solo in the Tiger (Moth) for an hour yesterday, and was surprised how well I got on. Yesterday Jones taught us loops, and today I go up for an hour and did fifteen of them, a spin, and half a dozen stall turns; I did one, and only lost 400'.

After I had flown the Tiger yesterday, "Red Hot" forgot to see how much petrol was left, and did a forced landing 400' off the aerodrome, in spite of his 12,000 hours flying. He gets into his cockpit with a little black bag every morning which, we have now discovered, contains his breakfast. This he has in the air when he has given it "over to you". Someone crudely suggested that he didn't only have breakfast up there.

December 1st 1940
KARACHI

WELL, "RED HOT" HAS SHOWN US LOOPS, rolls and half rolls, but apart from loops, the others get worse every time I practise them. I'm flying the Tiger quite a lot, but even so, these bloody rolls are the bane of my life. The other day Jones produces his Rocket Loop, and bloody well blacks me out for half a second or so. Not my idea of fun at all.

I have now been to Hyderabad solo and dual cross country, and there's nothing much in it. Interesting the first time there, but that's all.

A letter from Air H/Q that we leave on January 7th. Well I have about three hours of my solo left to do, the others the same, so Jones has written off to try and get us some more flying. The buzzing is progressing *(radio comms),* though I send better than I receive it.

Went to visit Mac the other day. Edward Hill is Adjutant. I nearly starve at dinner, but his Indian can feed five hundred with a couple of loaves and a fish!

Am slowly getting the mastery of the "Link"[1] and we are now dabbling in Lorentz approaches – though what bloody good that will ever be to us, I don't know.

Two letters from Bill, who seems to be working pretty hard, but doesn't say whether he has been in action yet or not. Reading Compton Mackenzie's 'Four Winds of Love' which makes life seem sort of peaceful.

[1] *A series of flight simulators produced from the early '30s by Ed Link, based on technology he pioneered in 1929 in New York. They were a key pilot training aid.*

December 9th 1940

KARACHI

MY SLOW ROLLS GET WORSE AND WORSE – I stick on my back and even Jones can't see why. My knee gets jammed up against the petrol pump by the stick at times, when she is right over to the right, and I don't think that helps much. Have half an hour solo, about two hours dual and two hours 'Link' left to do. Extra flying not sanctioned, so we are recommended to apply for about fourteen days leave and come back a week before we sail. Where the hell shall I go.

Went out shooting to Kalri near Tatta where there are three or four large jhils. (Hindi: shallow lake). Went on Saturday with Ian Pringle, S/Ldr Bowditch and one Evans, and their wives. We stayed in the PWD (Public Works Department) rest house, and had food laid on by the Mess and cooked by my bearer. Popsie Crick laid on the banda but then got malaria, so he could not come. Hid in a hide for duck on Saturday night, and got two for twenty-three cartridges, and lost one of those. Shocking shooting, but magnificent opportunities.

Then shot all Sunday morning and I got a duck and five snipe, two of which were lost. Driven snipe – bloody hard. A lovely place I'd like to go back to, and smoke and listen to the birds.

Bought a .22 Winchester five-shot the other day for 120/-. Traded my colt for 80/-. I thought he might allow me about 30/- for it, but true to character I asked 100/- and he just mildly expressed that it was a little high. I was then so taken aback, when asked for another figure, I was foxed, but managed to get out 70/-. Suleiman Omer, the gunsmith, then jumped at this so I said I would give him 40/- for the rifle – and there the deal closed. Unfortunately its spring American peep sight is U/S *(unserviceable)* and is only sighted up to about fifty yards. Though I have not really zeroed it yet.

Pete Gillespie is in my tent now as accommodation is scarce. We got talking last Sunday. I mentioned aims in life, one thing turned to another, and I discover he tried to desert when war broke out, and get home and join up. Got to Bombay and the only ship he could find was American, and the captain offered to take him to the States. However, he thought he'd rather go the other way, but was unable to find a ship that would take him. His money then ran out, and just as he thought of going to Goa, he couldn't do it, so surrendered to the SSO. Was court marshalled as AWOL and sentenced to six months loss of seniority. A bloody good effort I call it. He also passes bouncing cheques, without malice aforethought he assures me. But that's another person who thinks of life the same way as I do. The Gurkha in Pachmari was the other.

Went out with Dudley for a few drinks in the Gym Club the other day after dinner. We then came back and talked for some time in his car, a nearly new Ford 10.

The Aerodrome Officer spotted my "A" License racket, and rang up the M.O. to ask how was it the original license said "Fit (subject to wearing correction of vision)", whilst his form said my eyes were OK. So I rang up the M.O. and explained, laying myself at his mercy, and thank god we came to the conclusion that the aerodrome officer was a bastard, didn't understand good Scots, but was only doing his duty anyhow. Eventually I got it endorsed 'fit' but I bet he's reported it to Delhi, and I suppose that will be my undoing.

I am now wearing two pips[1], being fed up with being asked what I did before the war. I qualified on 26th November, but god knows when it will be through.

[1] *He was promoted from 2nd Lieutenant to Lieutenant.*

December 20th 1940

Assam

PUT IN FOR TWENTY DAYS LEAVE until 6/1/41 so as I could get to Assam. Sanction never came, but I was allowed to catch the plane on the 18th, and so I may yet be recalled. With 44lb, a suitcase, blanket and the Winchester, we leave before dawn in a Waco (a biplane), AKI Manilal the pilot. After Jacobabad I take her over, and do about 1 1/2 hours to Lahore, where some other passengers get on and cramp our style. Karachi-Calcutta 373/- return. Meals on the Coy I.N.A. In Delhi stayed at the new Imperial (13/-) and in the evening I walk round to the "Circle" for want of a better name to describe it, looking at the shops and wondering if this really is India or not.

The next morning off in a Beechcraft a/c via Cawnpore and Allahabad. The other two passengers get off at Allahabad, and I take her over for three hours then, after Manilal got her through a rain squall. The roof leaks on me, but the pilot reads a book, and I carry on safely at 7000'. These canals are the devil for navigation, as you never know which is the one on your map out of the forty on the ground.

Staying at the Grand (15/-) and last night went to see "Turnabout" and laughed like a drain. Also consolidated my objective again and, knowing the ropes, I got off 15/- cheaper, but is it worth it? Definitely Not.

Hope to God I'm not recalled, but I suppose it's too much to expect. That chap Manilal used to fly Croydon-Paris, and was a curious bird. You can always tell the Indian who has been to England, apart from curry servers in Indian pubs, from the Dera Dun etc product.

December 24th 1940

ASSAM

HAD A PLEASANT TRIP UP, and breakfast on the Brahmaputra again. Panbarry much the same, only so hot and much damper. Absence of "Who are you?" birds.

The Winchester is going damn well, as by chance I arrived at a position in the screw peep sight which is dead accurate at about 60-70 yards, aim 6 o'clock inner for under that range, and similar adjustment for longer ranges. Hit a paddy bird at 150-200' and also shot a vulture through the neck and down he came. Was inveigled into playing golf with the Ashleys, and saw Peter Allan at the Mariani Club – he remembered about my eyes, the old devil. The doves make a pleasant noise and in fact I should like to live here – but then of course I wouldn't.

December 27th 1940

ASSAM

ON CHRISTMAS EVE HAD A FEW DRINKS with the Kenwoods down the road. Christmas they came here for supper. Uncle Stan opens a bottle of wine, and there is laughter and much ado about nothing.

I spend my time shooting vultures, or so it seems, and they always seem to roost in the same trees, so after learning where the trees are, it's too easy. Yesterday went down to the only patch of jungle round here, a few acres and too thick to penetrate, and shot a monkey, there being no other inhabitants. This morning went out on a vulture parade and observed two jackals eating a vulture's corpse, so shot them on the spot. On finishing them off, I thought their heads didn't quite resemble pukka jacks, and then some Assamese villagers turned out, and I gathered I had shot someone's chowkidars (guard dogs), they wanted 500/- compensation and would fetch a policeman from Jorhat. Though I can't understand Assamese, or the language which the coolies speak – akin to Urdu.

A magnificent sunset yesterday – blood red, orange – and reflected on the Naga hills, which had low-lying fleecy clouds on 'em, and golden ones above. But impossible to describe. Damn cold at night, but the sun is just warming, and no topee required. A pity there's no jungle and big game.

January 5th 1941

KARACHI

I HAD ARRANGED TO LEAVE ON THE 29TH and was just returning to tea on the 28th, after a last dekko at the monkeys (I get into the jungle and slay a couple up trees), when a wire comes from the Aircraft Depot: "Return immediately." I come back at the normal time, after going to Peter Allan for supper on the 28th, and arrive

Delhi on the 31st, having been unable to fly owing to one of INA's directors being on board *(Indian National Airways)*.

I stay at the Great Eastern, good food and a dirty cell for Rs 10/-, then stay at the Cecil, and spend New Year's Eve in my bed with a book. On the 1st, go to Hyderabad House and ask about ranks, pay and why I was recalled. Not known. Also when in Iraq (if reached) do we get RAF pay, British Army with colonial allowance, or Indian Army with overseas allowance? They know nowt of course, but will look into the matter (if they remember). Actually, they were all staggering into each other's offices and saying "Oh I say, Claude – it must have been too many gin and tonics last night – what! – I feel awful."

Next day arrive Karachi, having flown most of the way myself. Manilal again is the pilot – we go to 9000 feet and then fly through and above the clouds, my first experience of them. On asking about this leave, J. Chapple said that the day I left on fourteen days leave, a message comes saying we could only have ten, so they let me have my ten and then recalled me – so I had 15 days in all. Met Dickie Bird in the Mess, from Madras, and we talk about the good old times and "who married who – my god, really?!"

Next day Chapple casually mentions we need passports for Iraq, but "show 'em to me in two days time." We sort out the Iraq consulate from the Afghan and Turk ones, and find we require passports to be valid for Iraq, vaccination certs, an official order detailing us there, and two photographs. We ferret out the passport officer from a mass of City Magistrates and High Court Officers and their clerks' counter directions and find we want another order from the RAF, as all passports are invalid in time of war. Get photographed and return to lunch, exhausted.

That evening Gribbon of the King's Own telephones – "wasn't I at Beacon with him? – yes – then come shooting tomorrow, OK?" (Colin's prep school in Sevenoaks).

He takes me out to Kalri again, where Evans of the King's Own, his Mrs and aged Ma and Pa have been in occupation for ten days or so. I am stuck in the water in a hide at 3.30 and leave it at 7.15 with two ducks and minus twenty-two cartridges.

A very jolly supper, and Nigel Gribbon and I exchange reminiscences well into the night on our beds. Up at six and off to a damn big jhil *(lake)*. The old man, seventy with Boer War medals, and I – he well greatcoated and blanketed – are taken away in a boat one way, the others and the lunch departing north. I shoot a coot with the Winchester on the way for the boatmen to eat, it being duly hallaled first. We maroon Poppa, and I am taken to my hide. I am handed off the boat first and am nearly up to my waist, and so without having got wet himself, the Shikari is able to judge it too deep, and they make me another. Then I am also marooned, the fellow going off to "beat", and promising lunch later.

About 1.00 pm, three hours later, I see Poppa has evacuated his stall and is thawing himself on dry land, so we whistle up the boat and return, with great difficulty, against an icy wind. Great anxiety at the base, and not much lunch left. On swapping notes, we find the boatman did no beating but spent his time cooking my coot under Poppa's blanket. Return to Kalri for tea, with a "spot" in it, and dropped here by Gribbon at 6.00 pm. A great weekend.

January 10th 1941

KARACHI

NOW THE NEWS IS IN THAT WE EMBARK ON THE 13TH, having been struck off duty on the 17th December. An "Iti" submarine reported off the Indian coast along Persia way, so I hope I don't lose all my baggage.

Letter from Bill in Cyprus – none from Ma since October.

On Tuesday I dined with Nigel Gribbon and then went to the boat club. He then left and I joined a party of the boys including the Simpsons – Mary Simpson – and one Violet, the latter being Alan Haig's fiancée. I am supposed to look like Simon, and his wife

'Easy morals at Sandspit.'
Mary, Pete Gillespy and Joan, at Sandspit beach.

Joan spends the whole time pointing this out to people. H.R. Irwin of Mahrattis and one Humphries of 17th have arrived to take over from us, also one Fairweather of 4 Gurkha Rifles. Humphries is banging glasses at this party to see how hard it can be done without them breaking, when quite rightly a neighbour objects, comes over, and they square up and above one another like fighting cocks. Pete then turns on Humphries and gives him no end of a dressing down. They go out for a fight but Haig smooths it over. Bed at 4 am.

Next day off to Sandspit *(famous beach southwest of Karachi)* – Simpsons, Mary, Violet, Pete, Haig and I. I ignore Mary at first, and after some whispering, Joan asks me if I have met her, I say no, and she introduces us. Mary then proceeds to vamp me – successfully, I admit, but most amusing all the same. All day at Sandspit. Bathed but damn cold. Roll on the 13th. I am not taking much kit, as I don't expect to last out long in Habbaniya.

4

January - June 1941

4th Intermediate Flying Training School

RAF Habbaniya
Iraq

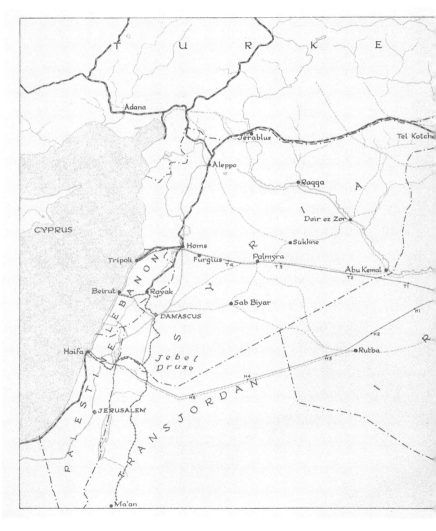

*A map of Iraq, Syria, Palestine, Lebanon and Transjordan in 1941,
showing Habbaniya just to the west of Baghdad, and the railway
running through northern Iraq to Syria.*

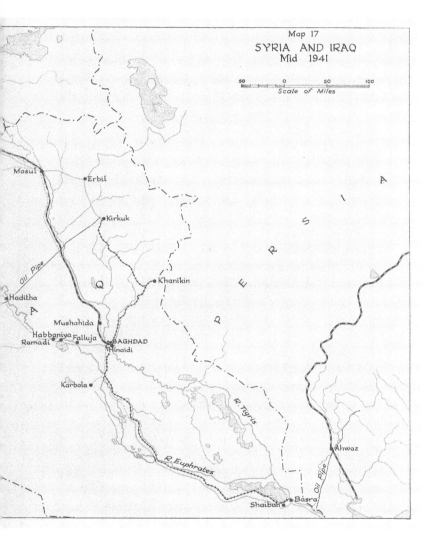

Map 17
SYRIA AND IRAQ
Mid 1941

Scale of Miles

Mosul

Erbil

Kirkuk

Oil Pipe

Haditha

Khanikin

Mushahida

Habbaniya
Ramadi

Falluja

BAGHDAD

Hinaidi

Karbala

R. Tigris

R. Euphrates

Ahwaz

Oil Pipe

Shaibah

Basra

*A line from Kirkuk shows the oil pipeline running to Haditha,
where it splits into the T branch, to supply the French in Tripo-
li, and the H branch, to supply the British in Haifa.*

January 14th 1941

BED BUGS AND BLACKOUTS...S.S. "BARPETA". A party on the 12th with Pete, Allan, self, Simon, Joan and Mary. A bit low. We go to the boat club and have supper and play the fool. Pete hurdles the chairs and tables and holds Mary upside down so that her knickers become exposed. Low talk by Simonson's concerning bananas. I get Mary on my knee and give her another of my "let me be your father" talks, which are quite good. In bed by 1 am. Irwin, brother of Pat in Madras, was at Delhi some time ago and saw in Hyderabad House (RAF HQ) a list of our eight names, with columns etc – age, regiment, qualifications. It read "A" License for most but by Pete's was "court marshalled for attempting to join the RAF".

We reach the harbour at 9.30 am yesterday after calling at 2 Bath Island Road on the way, and beating the girls under the bedclothes, and embark without fuss or formality. "Barpeta" is 3000' tons, with four other first-class passengers and a lot of deck passengers, and is a "slow" gulf boat. Calls at all the ports, Ormara at 4.00 am this morning, 150 miles from Karachi, and so on. Bed bugs and blackouts...

Out of India at last, but for how long? I suppose I shall be back in Abbottabad in a month or so, or even less, looking a damn fool. We are given thirty days advance pay before we leave. British rates less Indian income tax, so we lose about 200/- on the deal. At Pasmi half a dozen bunderboats descend on us like vultures and fight for places alongside. Bales of Japanese cotton are unloaded by Baluchis and some sort of black Africans. Small boats sell fish, some as long as four feet. Two old Sinbads with beards keep alongside for some hours selling fish, holding the tiller lines between their toes to keep their hands free for paddling. A barren coastline like the Red Sea. Pasmi is a great smuggling port as it's duty-free. The Jap cloth goes to Quetta, duty here being only 18%, whereas in Karachi it's 98%.

January 16th 1941

REPENT SINNERS, FOR THE LORD IS AT HAND. Yesterday called at Charbar in Persia. Mud buildings and forts. Last night big seas get up and I am twice soaked in my bunk before closing the port. A regular "repent sinners for the Lord is at hand" night. Muscat today, a small bay surrounded by Waziristan-like crags with picquets and sangars on them, all painted with the names of visiting ships from 1878 – 1941. Helluva swell on. Negroes come out and dive for coins. This must have been a den of pirates once. Round the corner another town, Muttra, looking through the glasses like an illustration in a book of someone's adventures in the last century. All the ships' boats are out in case we meet that submarine, which is supposed to have cut the Indian cable. A bloody cold wind in this Gulf of Oman. Chess with Pete but cannot beat him –

January 17th 1941

AT SEA

REACHED KUHAWEI THIS MORNING, a small island off Oman Peninsula leased as a naval depot. We land provisions for the R.I.N. sloop present in the bay. Saw some nasty-looking garfish. The Chief Engineer won't tell me a thing, as he says it's all top secret, but had it all from the first mate this afternoon. Now in Bandar Abbas and there's an Italian ship that's been taking refuge here since the war began. A low-lying coastline and a bit of a haze, but it seems a bigger town than any so far.

Two Italian submarines were caught by HMS Falmouth up here some six months or so ago. One was trapped, owing to its rendezvous being discovered in the papers of the captain of the one brought into Aden by a trawler some months ago.

SS Barpeta

January 18th 1941

LINGAH – AN OLD PERSIAN TOWN and apparently mostly uninhabited. After a long delay, boats come off to the shop and the confusion and noise of mooring and unloading is phenomenal, worse than anything encountered in India, everyone shouting at the top of his voice, and doing his bit of work irrespective of it dovetailing with his neighbours.

January 19th 1941

AT SEA

BAHRAIN ISLES – WE ALL FOUR GO ASHORE HERE and after purchasing a few things, call on Pringle's friend Dunn, manager of the local bank. We have a beer and then get into a taxi and say "Club". He takes us a twenty-mile drive across the island, through date palms, eventually petering out into desert, covered in mounds, apparently graves. We then reach the oil camp where there is a magnificent, up-to-date club (Bahrain Petroleum Co) with every possible, etc etc. We buy a book of tickets, walk in and meet Scottie Anderson, off the ship, who is going to Saudi Arabia. I have some beers and martinis and then we find it too late for lunch, as his launch leaves at 2.00 pm.

We escort him back and as our own launch goes at 3.00 pm we hang about till then. The shops are rather like Port Said and everywhere are luxurious American cars, not a single old crock being seen. Six yanks come back onto the ship with us, going on vacation to Persia. Quite a social joint apparently, but after the bombs dropped, all the American women were evacuated.

January 22nd 1941

At sea

Spent a day in Bushire in a gale and fog, waiting for the dhows to come off. Eventually cleared and they came out. The Americans gave a party last night and we all go into a cabin – twelve of us. Allan plays his accordion and we all sing, though only with difficulty do we find a song that both "sides" know. It's just like being at the films to listen to these boys.

Went ashore today at Kuwait – an exceedingly clean bazaar, streets swept, very few flies. Almost a free port, only 5% duty. All the inhabitants have queer puckered eyes, as though all afflicted. We see a plane, so hop in a taxi and say "Aeroplane". We find her landed in the desert, a 'Vincent' *(Vickers Vincent biplane)*, and I talk to the pilot, one Geary from Shaibah. We tell him we have been seconded from the army, and he says "Oh yes, airgunners." Airgunners!

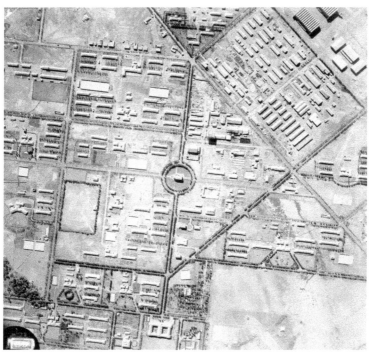

RAF Habbaniya from the air. Air House (the camp HQ) is the large building midway along the bottom edge, with the polo ground in the bottom right corner.

January 26th 1941

Habbaniya, Iraq

MORE DRINKS WITH THE AMERICANS (Joe Carroll) who get off at Al-Khamshah. We land at Basra, are met by an RAF Sergeant and then catch the evening train to Baghdad.[1]

The Customs pinch my .22 and shotgun. Basra is a pretty filthy joint with dim narrow streets, rendered so by the first floor jutting out over the ground-floor shops. I take in my watch for repairs and am told it will be 5/-. When I call later I put down 3/- and the chap says he wants 7/-more. I make it up to 4/- and he is quite satisfied.

We go to the Kit Kat Club and see the cabaret practising. A luxurious corridor train to Baghdad – soap and towels etc, and English-style coaches, but bloody cold in Baghdad. Here we spend two hours until the driver has finished his errands. The main street is like an English country town – thronged with chaps from all over the near and middle east.

The road out here (to Habbaniya) is sixty miles across flat open plain, and twenty miles of nothing, not even road, across Falluja Plain – a pukka sand desert. We are met on arrival and given drinks.

Much drinking last night, and met Garner, who was at Peterborough with Hugh. Dinner at 9.30 and a party at the next table, including Loyd (SWB and Levies), hurling whisky and sodas, plates of butter and pursuing each other over and under the table. Looks like we've come to a madhouse. Shops damn expensive – in Basra, Baghdad and here (25/- for a R10 pair of shoes).

[1] *Harry Hopkins, an advisor to Roosevelt who had recently visited the area, quipped: 'The Persian Gulf is the arsehole of the world and Basra is eighty miles up it.'*

February 2nd 1941

HABBANIYA

HABBANIYA IS A CAMP WELL LAID OUT, rather similar to Wana or Razmak, but vaster and better organised. Training here are a lot of Greeks and South Africans, and they had Norwegians and French before we arrived. We are the only four officers on this course, the rest being other ranks from Kenya and Malaya. We fly Harts, and I have already done four hours and not gone solo, and it looks as though I shall get myself chucked out – which would be the "irony of fate".

Up at 6, flying until 9, breakfast and lectures until 12.30. Then, next day, lectures until 10 and fly until 12.30 – and so on, alternately.

Went racing yesterday, first time since Blighty and on Pete's selection ended 100 fils to the good. A very nice boat club here on Lake Habbaniya, where the flying boats come down, where I went out on a whaler with Charles Braybrookes and some sergeants.

This is the middle of a desert and dust storms make life bloody. The Euphrates runs alongside, and last year the camp was evacuated to the plateau above the lake as there was a danger of the river bursting the bund. Flt Lt Cremin is my instructor and he is nagging and quite contemptuous of my efforts, which doesn't help at all. Saw a drinking game called "Cardinal Puff" yesterday, which is sheer murder by alcoholic poisoning, unless the victim watches his step.

My bearer is a bit of a wag, but not as good as Attam khan (I got him a job with Walker in the Pathans in Wana) – he has a ticket every year in the Irish sweep, and knows a little Urdu thank god. Will I be thrown out? Christ!

February 5th 1941

Habbaniya

My instructor is Cremin.[1]

First hour or so is spent in my U/S (unserviceable) telephones, with "Br....umph!" coming through them and me feverishly looking at all the bloody dials to see what I am doing wrong. Then I change them and go up with Sgt Baker – do very well, he says "well you know where the bloody ground is anyway!" and that I ought to go solo the next day. Then follows four hours with Cremin and I am bloody awful – he gets my back up with his tired, bored and pained voice: "Must you aim for the only plane on the bloody field?" when I am coming in, and thinking which side to go to avoid a plane on the ground. "Are you doing it on purpose?" when I get into

164

A Hawker Hart trainer

difficulties keeping straight on landing, and the plane continues turning.

Then I go up with Broughton and he shows me how the brakes work. Then Garner takes me up and I improve. Next day, Chief Flying Instructor Squadron Leader Ling gets in the back and I do a perfect circuit and landing, followed by three bad landings. More Garner, but still bad landings. Then Ling says "Well, you know the rules. I've told B flight to give you a couple of hours more" – and then out I go.

Today went up with Garner and did three landings, good enough, and am allowed solo, and do two not-so-bad ones. And that postpones the execution, but I still feel that the sentence has not yet been remitted. Played bridge with C.O. Ling and Broadhurst. Lost 230 fils.

---

[1] *Dan Cremin was killed in an air accident in March 1942 a few weeks after taking command of his first squadron, 66 squadron in the UK.*

February 12th 1941

THE OTHER DAY I WENT UP IN THE CLOUDS and was shown climbing and steep turns. Then up for 1.10h in an Audax to practice. Rain wet the aerodrome, and Harts can't even use the runaways *(runways were known as runaways in 1941)*, as water gets into the brakes and makes them U/S.

Got up today with Garner and I couldn't do climbing and steep turns, and then forgot to circle round before spinning. Why have I become such a B.F.? Did a bit of Duty Pilot, and drew 100 dinars today, advance of some pay or other. Have started learning Arabic, the colloquial variety, and will have a third lesson today I hope. I am introduced to Monopoly.

Nearly 3 1/2 months in RAF, by god. How much more? Whisky is 14 fils a peg.

February 22nd 1941

HABBANIYA

WENT TO HOSPITAL LAST WEEKEND with the crabs. Shave and put on some strong blue ointment. Now suffering from stubble trouble. Went out sailing in Braybooks's Moth the other day. My first three attempts to 'go about' failed through not letting go of the rudder, but soon mastered that, and had a damned good day.

Flying still going strong, and had CFI's test *(Chief Flying Instructor)* the other day. He said "See Y landing ground?", I said yes, so he switched off the engine and said, "Do a forced landing". Orders is orders, so down I went. I had two shots which he didn't like, and when we got home I explained I hadn't been taught them. Went up with the Group Captain (Savile) yesterday as passenger, and circled the lake and studied the trenches at Ramadi.

The Political Background in Iraq

What were these 'interesting things about Iraqi politics' that Colin referred to on February 22nd? To understand what was going on at the time it is useful to trace, briefly, the history of Britain's involvement in Iraq, which stretched back to the end of World War One.

After the break-up of the Ottoman Empire Britain was given a 'Mandate' to govern Iraq for twelve years at a gathering called the Conference of San Remo in 1920. Driving this was the necessity to ensure stability while the new gold – oil – was extracted by the Anglo-Iraq Petroleum Company, which had recently set up in the country, and to build and guard the pipelines constructed to ship it back to the shores of the Mediterranean. However, the Iraqis themselves were not fooled. In an era where empires were crumbling and 'self-determination' was the buzz phrase, they saw this arrangement as 'empire by other means', and the granting of the Mandate was almost immediately followed by a violent Iraqi revolt. Within a matter of months this had cost the lives of five hundred British and Indian troops, and the British exchequer £40m, and showed no sign of abating.

It was not the only uprising in British controlled dominions that year. There was another disturbance in Somaliland, led by someone dubbed the 'Mad Mullah'. Whitehall prepared to send an expedition to quell the revolt, but were told by the Chief of the Imperial Staff that it would require two divisions. Britain was extremely hard up in 1920, exhausted and bankrupt after World War One, and, mindful of the problems in Iraq, the Government was in no mood to get involved in a costly new conflict. However, the Air Chief Marshal, Lord Trenchard, suggested that he could do the job far more cheaply with two RAF squadrons – a new arm of the armed services that had only been in existence for a few years.

Instead of large and expensive ground forces, Trenchard argued that small contingents of the RAF with the new fighters and light bombers could be used to 'fly the flag' and, as a last resort, bomb the tribes into submission. He was allowed to test his theory, and so it proved, so the strategy was immediately extended to Iraq, where the six month revolt was brought to a swift conclusion by the controversial use of phosphorous bombs. A cost effective model for controlling large areas of territory had been born.

Soon after the Iraq revolt had been quelled in this way, Britain sponsored the 'election' of King Faisal to be ruler of Iraq following a rigged plebiscite in 1921. This allowed the Foreign Office to have a 'hands off' approach, with power in the hands of a friendly ruler. And instead of garrisoning ground forces to support him, Britain gave the RAF overall control of the region. This was 'softly softly' policing 1920s style, with the threat of terror bombing from the air. Since tribesmen had rarely seen an aeroplane in those days, it is not surprising that it was so successful.

Fast forward to 1930. The Mandate was about to expire, but Britain was not quite ready to give up its influence in Iraq, because more and more oil was flowing their way. The answer was the Anglo-Iraq Treaty. In return for smoothing the path to independence, and handing over the role on internal policing, the Iraqis would permit Britain to station troops and aircraft in Iraq at two bases, with a view to helping the Iraqis in a support role to keep the tribes under control. As part of this Treaty, a new base was to be constructed sixty miles to the west of Baghdad beside Lake Habbaniya, in a bend of the River Euphrates, to house the main base and command centre of the RAF.

The new airfield complex took five years to build. When it became operational in 1935 it was 'state of the art' for comfort and efficiency. There were miles of tarmaced road bordered with oleanda and eucalyptus; luxurious married officers quarters with all the mod-cons; manicured lawns, parks and a country club; and five hundred acres of well appointed accommodation for locally enlisted staff and militia, the 'Assyrian Levies', whose job it was to guard the base. These Assyrians were Iraqis, but a minority from the north of the country, and they were thought to be more loyal that ordinary Iraqis, with a relationship to the British Army akin to the Gurkhas – cost effective and locally based.

There was also a polo field and a golf course, and a comfortable Imperial Airways rest house on the banks of the lake where flying boats on their way to and from India and Egypt could land, refuel and overnight. Finally, there were fields for rugby and hockey, and a sailing club.

But two crucial factors made this base different from many others the military had constructed elsewhere in the empire. Being supposedly a friendly country, where a Treaty had just been signed, and for reasons of cost, it was considered unnecessary to duplicate essential facilities like the modern water filtration plant, its water tower, and the small power station for generating electricity. So there was just one of each, making the base extremely vulnerable.

Second, the airfield itself was left outside the main perimeter fence of the camp. It was laid out on the bare desert, with no bomb-proof shelters, no dispersal areas and no defensive arrangements of any kind. It could be seen for miles around, and was overlooked from the escarpment of the Falluja Plateau.

In the late 30s life had become so quiet in Iraq that there was barely any operational flying undertaken at RAF Habbaniya at all. It became the home of the 4th Intermediate Flying Training School (IFTS), a comfortable and sleepy backwater where trainee pilots could be taught in ideal surroundings. Since 1938 the base had been under the command of a semi-retired Air Force Officer, Acting Air Chief Marshal Reginald Smart. He was a stickler for rules and routine, the perfect AOC in charge of a flying school. His team of instructors were a mix of civilian flying club instructors in uniform, with no military training, and various ex-operational RAF pilots no longer required in the front line.

This was the happy and relaxed station, far from the front line, where my father and his fellow 'Musketeers' arrived in February 1941. How ideal, and how comfortable, they were soon to find out.

The four ex-Indian Army officers called themselves the Four Musketeers. Pilot Officers Allan Haig, Ian Pringle, Colin, and Peter Gillespy. Only Colin and Allan Haig would survive the coming battle.

Today an hour's Audax, and some "wheeler" power approach landings. A bit of rugger, and a bit of sunbathing in the afternoons. Was out walking on the bund the other night when I met a chap who said "come in and have one". He is W/C Jope-Slade[1], in intelligence in Baghdad, and he told me a lot of interesting things about Iraqi politics.

[1] *Both Charles Braybrooks and W/C Jope-Slade were to be killed in the battle to come in May.*

March 2nd 1941

Habbaniya

HAVE BEEN TRYING FORMATION FLYING, and am regarded as pretty dangerous at it, I think. I am also shown a forced landing, so have now got plenty to think about. The other night we went night flying. I get a bit depressed after doing three bloody awful bumps, but eventually satisfy Garner and am allowed up solo in the Audax, which is much easier. With all the lights on the camp looks like Brighton seafront at night. Life just "chills" on here, with nothing of interest to note. I flew over Ramadi with the official war map, and most of the old trenches can still be seen. (Ramadi was taken by British forces in November 1917 from the remains of the Ottoman forces).

I have got to volume III of the Official History, with one more to go after that.

March 8th 1941

HABBANIYA

HAD "LADIES NAVEL WITH CREAM" on the menu as a pudding the other day. *(A Turkish dish)*.

Did my height test, 15000 feet, successfully. Right in the clouds and could see the aerodrome occasionally. My fingertips froze and I spent the whole half hour diving and zooming, though not on purpose. I went on a cross country with Garner to Ctesiphon, Hindiya, and Falluja but I don't trust ETAs and make several blunders. We go at 6.30 am bang into the sun, and I don't see the arch until it's pointed out to me. Then solo, and I go Hit - Haditha and return in an Audax. A very pleasant trip up the Euphrates, and the villages are somewhat similar to Indian ones. Of course I tear off my navigating log and stuff it in my pocket before landing, so it won't blow away, and it blows out of my pocket whilst walking back to the flight office.

Today off in an Audax to El Aziziya, down the Tigris beyond Ctesiphon, which I find without much difficulty, though much of the ground is obscured by sandstorms. From there to Hindiya barrage and back to Falluja. The courses never work out, owing to the inaccuracies of the map, but one can usually see one's objective on the port or starboard quarter, say up to twelve miles, when the ETA is up.

Played in a sort of Cock House Match on Sunday last and won a Naafi bronze rugby medallion![1]

[1] *The Cock House Match was the final of the famous Harrow annual Football knockout competition, which some have claimed to be the precursor of the FA Cup.*

March 15th 1941

HABBANIYA

NEARLY CAUGHT OUT ON WEDNESDAY.

We were night flying, and before starting my instructor, Garner, says "be sure and use these plain flying goggles", handing me a pair – I think Christ, put them on my helmet and, when in the cockpit, I change them over for the pair with the lenses that I bought in Karachi. Then through the earphones comes:

"Are those dark bloody goggles you are wearing?'

I say yes, and I prefer them, but he makes me change them, stuffing my own pair in my pocket. So off we go, with me quivering and wondering how the hell I shall be able to see the signal light. But, actually, I can see it, and there is a full moon, so despite there being no Chance light[1]. I do four chukkas dual and then three solo in the Audax, and am fairly successful.

The CFI, Ling, gets his promotion to Wing Commander the other day and they all celebrate in style. At about 4 pm, all pickled, they make for the hangars, Levies and all, and away in the air. Luckily only one plane is crashed, landing on the polo field, but there are acrobatics near the ground, inverted circuits and God knows what. Cremin was the worst. Too pissed to convince anyone he could fly, he is taken in the back on an Audax with no parachute, and trying to bail out all the way. And coming back the same.

[1] *Mobile airfield flood lighting illuminating the landing area and the apron at night.*

172

March 17th 1941

I NOW OWN HALF A HORSE. Braybrooks and I were after one and asked Evans, the stable manager, if he could get one. He says "Oh yes, Finjan, £10, take over on Saturday". I arrange to ride on Thursday, but when I get there I find someone else out on him and Evans asking the fellow for £12.

I get most disgruntled, but in the meantime Braybrooks goes to the owner and offers him £10. The owner says Evans is selling it to someone else; Braybrooks thinks it's me, and says we are both in together. That gets us the horse, which Evans has in the meantime sold for £12 to the other chap. He settles it, however, by getting posted, so we get our horse, an arab chestnut and fairly tame. It's eight months since I last rode in Wana.

Yesterday met one Stoney, Armoured Cars, in the Mess, and stood him a few drinks, despite his protests, whilst his taxi was coming, and eventually he takes me off to dinner. There I meet Hilliard (also Armoured Cars) who knew Hugh, Cottingham (Gloucesters) an O.H. (Old Harrovian), and "Boozy" Bons in the R.V.R. I have a lot more whisky before dinner and shoot a line about India. Then halfway through dinner I realise suddenly that if I have another drink I can't be held responsible for the consequences. Not a comforting thought, but I preserve a calm and sober front, and manage to tell one of the bearers to get me a taxi, without anyone noticing. I stand firm against whisky, liqueurs and port and get the taxi when it arrives at 10 pm, my excuse being early flying at 5.30 am.

A messy "decontamination" when I return, and no head this morning. I go up and am unable to fly "straight and level" under the hood, performing two complete circles in fifteen minutes. Shocking!

March 25th 1941

Riding the horse and drinking a little. Dan Cremin went into Baghdad the other day and cashed a cheque for five dinars in one of the local bars. He then solemnly hands them round to the nearest five chaps at the bar! Went racing last Saturday but no luck. The flying is progressing, and am still riding the waves. A letter from Ma and Peggy, and Hugh now posted as killed apparently.

Ian Pringle goes to Baghdad on Sunday and gets hold of some Greek girl there. He has come back with a scented handkerchief which he keeps under his pillow. The A/Cs on this course got some extra drill as a minor punishment and we four are made to go and look on "to see any differences etc". An old thug of a warrant officer asks us the difference between 'move to the right in threes' and 'move to the right in column' – as if we should know.

Doing loops and stall turns.

March 30th 1941

Habbaniya

Last night I invite Stoney over, and with Pete (Gillespy) and Charles (Braybrooks) we go to the Club.

We have some of this eggnog and some food and eventually go and play billiards. Dan Cremin appears, still drunk from the night before, and I make some passes at him with my cue. This rather takes his fancy and the next hour I spend chasing him and others and doing points and withdrawals at all and sundry in a welter of flung water and pullings away of carpets from under one's feet. All in the form of raids from the billiard room. We get quite pally and then I go home in a taxi, reckoning I have had enough.

I find I've left my key in the Club so walk back for it. I stay for some more booze and get confidential with Dan C. For some reason or other 'socking' is mentioned and I stick out my jaw to him and invite one. I get it too, a right-hand swing, which staggers me and is about all I can take. I am sober enough to refrain from hitting him back, and Garner comes in to make the peace. Back at last at 2.00 am with Broughton, sentimentally drunk despite his bare 21 years.

Today I go out on Finjan to Medling Defile and back along the bund amongst gardens and date palms. Met Geary from Shaibah in the Club last night and one Hibbens of 3⁄4 Rajputs who's in Intelligence here.

Johnson and K.S. Smith, my drinking companions from Kenya, have gone – to the Middle East and Shaibah respectively. I have completed the small book on Arabic, though the words therein are committed to a very faulty memory, but have stuck at "Measures of the Verb", the Mesopotamian grammar. The interpreter who professes to instruct me says I am capable of passing the colloquial exam; which was worth ID15 (extra pay) before the war; but I don't believe him.

The Greeks all got drunk (not unusual) the other night when the news came that Yugoslavia had turned out their pro-German party. The result of this was some very excellent singing though I was endeavouring to sleep at the time and so didn't appreciate it. But I could just picture them with a bottle and/or girl in each hand.

April 4th 1941

HABBANIYA

COMPLETED MY 10 HOURS BLIND FLYING, and worn out a few instructors in the process I think. I have an hour to go to complete sixty-five hours of Intermediate Training, and next week we have our exams in ground work. Shades of Sandhurst again. Finjan turning out to be a polo pony, I have a couple of turns on him at the game, but am not very good at it; rather like my hockey, the ball goes under the bat too often. I go shooting with my Winchester for jackal, who live out on the plateau, but they see me first and disappear into small holes (caves almost).

Letter from Ma and Peggy and Hugh posted as killed. All my damned fault for tempting fortune by what I said to Bill in a letter. Uncle Bill said he "saw" he would get through all right, so trusting to Tiree second sight I never even bothered to scan the casualty reports.

Was shown slow rolls, rolls off the top and flick rolls, but have had no solo in which to practice them.

The incessant cooing of turtle doves here recalls Assam all the time, and there is also a variety of paddy birds, locally called storks, which is exactly the noise they make, like death rattling his dice. Then there's the sergeant/pilot bird which, at dawn and dusk, goes cookadoo, cookadoo-la.

Ian had a letter from Fairweather in Karachi and they are not coming here after all. The AOC happened to inspect Karachi Aero Club and happened to catch Jhadu or someone lecturing on ground subjects. So Bill Jones got his head chewed off and no wonder!! Mess bills about ID 10 *(Iraqi dinars)*.

INSTRUCTORS, "B" FLIGHT 4 IFTS

C.F.I. W/C "Larry" Ling
(gentleman but talks like Aunt Vivien)
F/Lt D.A. Cremin "Dan"
(never sober)
F/O D.A. Garner "Stooge"
(ex-policeman)
F/O H. Broadhurst
(ex-club instructor)
F/O J. Broughton
(21 and a gentleman)
Sgt "Joey" Baker
(definitely no gentleman)

April 8th 1941

ALARMS AND EXCURSIONS.

A few days ago the Regent was smuggled out of the country, the Prime Minister resigned, and the Army took over, one of the generals endeavouring to form a cabinet. Then occurs the most colossal flap. He is supposed to be anti-British, so the planes are bombed up, arms and ammunition dished out, everyone made to wear uniform and walk about armed, and no one allowed outside the camp. Yesterday an Iraqi aeroplane arrived, did three circuits and landed. The Gladiators were unable to get up to shoot him down, as they had been ordered to ring up the AOC before they took off, and his telephone was engaged. Chaps rush out to arrest the pilot, who says he has merely come for a meteorological exam, and he's right too.

Today a colossal formation is organised over Falluja and Ramadi, but there is so much low-lying cloud that it is postponed. The German news says we are prisoners of war and that Italian transports have arrived in Basra to take us away! And that the Iraqis have shot down some eighteen British planes![1]

[1] *A very interesting comment. According to the official history, the British were blissfully unaware at this stage that any real threat from the Iraqis existed, and that Rachid Ali's sudden attack three weeks later was entirely unexpected, but here is evidence that it was already being talked about, if only via German propaganda.*

April 11th 1941

HABBANIYA

IAN (PRINGLE) AND I PUT IN FOR WEEKEND LEAVE on the routine Valencia to Tel Aviv, and should have gone today if it hadn't been for the damn trouble.

The Situation in Iraq in April 1941

After the signing of the Ango-Iraq Treaty in 1930, although life had seemed deceptively quiet at Habbaniya, tensions had been rising across the country. There had always been a certain amount of inter-ethnic rivalry between Sunnis and Shias, as well as with the minority Christian Assyrian population, but in 1933 it had taken a turn for the worse, when the Iraqi army, under the prime minister-ship of Rachid Ali, had massacred 3000 Assyrian women and children at Simele, in an attempt to ethnically cleanse the northern provinces. This caused much anger amongst the Assyrian Levies, especially when their British masters refused to allow them home to help. Soon after the massacre the pro-British King Faisal died, leaving a much weaker heir, King Ghazi, on the throne. Rachid Ali resigned. However, the Germans saw an opportunity to weaken Britain's position, and they dispatched a T.E. Lawrence type character called Fritz Grobba to present his credentials to the the young and impressionable new King. Grobba's strategy was to gain influence with the Arab nationalists, and foment their growing opposition against the British and the French across the Middle East. Initially it was all about trade, but increasingly, Iraqi army officers began to be invited for training in Germany.

As the 30s wore on, the weak and ineffectual King Ghazi faced mounting tribal tensions until, in 1938, a group of Iraqi army officers known as the Golden Square seized power, bringing Rachid Ali back as prime minister. Groomed by Grobba, they were virulently anti-British, and they refused to declare war on Germany in 1939 as required under their treaty obligations, though Grobba was sent home. Suddenly Britain's toehold in Iraq began to look less secure.

So by 1940, despite the death of Ghazi in 1939 in a car accident (which many blamed on the British) and his replacement by a child king and pro-British Regent, relations with the military backed government were tense, with the British embassy in Baghdad reporting increasing activity between the Iraqis and the Axis powers.

To add further to British concerns, the Iraqi government allowed the Italian legation to remain open in Baghdad after Italy came into the war in June 1940, and secret plans were drawn up to divert Iraq's oil pipeline to Syria.

In early 1941, just a few days after Colin arrived, events took a further twist - Rachid Ali was ousted by a pro-British prime minister, Al Hashimi. During February and March the British worked on plans with Al Hashimi to remove the colonels of the Golden Square from their posts, but before they could act, a second coup took place on April 1st, and Rachid Ali was brought back. The original plot was to assassinate the Regent, but he managed to escape to the American Embassy dressed as a woman, before being driven down to Habbaniya in the boot of the American ambassador's car, from where he was flown out to Jordan on the 3rd April.

The British were now in a most vulnerable position. All military traffic between Baghdad and Habbaniya was stopped by the new Iraqi government, and the ambassador's radio equipment was confiscated, the embassy going into lockdown (Freya Stark was holed up there during this period). On 6th April Air Vice Marshal Smart cabled General Wavell in Cairo and the Air Ministry in London asking for reinforcements. However, his request came at a bad time - Rommel was advancing at lightning speed across North Africa and the British were on the retreat from Crete. April 1941 was probably the darkest month in the entire war from a British perspective. Wavell refused the request, recommending a diplomatic solution. Habbaniya were on their own.

So Smart organised that time honoured form of sabre-rattling, the 'demonstration flight', as recorded by Colin on April 11th. Another participant, Squadron Leader Tony Dudgeon, remembers it in his book 'Hidden Victory':

"48 pilots we managed to find, and so 48 aircraft flew. All instructors flew of course, plus a few of the more advanced pupils, and a couple of Greek pilots. Several different types

179

were chosen – 32 Harts and Audaxes, 13 twin engined Oxfords and the three Gladiator biplane-fighters. Those out of date fighters, of course, were not flown by fighter pilots. They were only based (at Habbaniya) because they had been superannuated from the Western Desert theatre as being beyond practical use in a fighting role. They were kept as a sort of flying sports-car for Headquarters officers to use for any local travelling. This great gaggle – it deserved no better word – took to the air. As may be imagined from the comparatively unpractised rag, tag and bobtail in the pilot's seats, the quality of the formation itself was terrible. There were five flights in all. One each of Oxfords and Harts, and two of Audaxes, all cruising at the same speed and, God willing, in the same direction. The three fighters, flying faster, had a roving commission and swooped around, above and below the main formation. Fortunately, no aircraft came into collision. The whole of this lot traipsed back and forth near two local villages called Ramadi and Falluja."

'The Demonstration flight'. The formation flight of April 10th over Falluja and Ramadi.

We do a formation flight the other day of four squadrons – Harts with Oxfords circling overhead, and the three Gladiators down below. I went in Dan Cremin's front seat and we went over Falluja and Ramadi. Ling showed me the air photographs of Falluja showing an anti-aircraft gun there. Heard last night that thirty Indian Battalions arrived the other day in Basra, being "Niblick" force. Alan Haig very drunk in the Club on neat whisky.

The 'Thirty Indian battalions' have now turned into a few Iraqi army troops.

April 14th 1941

HABBANIYA

THE 'ANTI-AIRCRAFT GUN' IS IDENTIFIED as a field kitchen.

Dined with young Stoney the other night and sampled some Mount Carmel wine. We discuss women – or rather they do. Letter from old Mike, in 2/West Yorks, with 2FFR and 6/13 GR down in the Sudan I believe. Today they decided to discontinue training and form two operational squadrons, ITS becoming Audaxes and ATS *(Advanced training school)* an Oxford squadron. I get detailed to the Oxfords as a bomb aimer of all things. When the hell will we get away – I hate to think.

Was graded an 'average' pilot, which isn't so bad as I fully expected "below average".

April 17th 1941

HABBANIYA

GOT MY 'WINGS' YESTERDAY. Went up and found W/V *(wind velocity)* by the three-course method in an Oxford and didn't do too badly.

Then a big flap yesterday and another formation flight ordered, this time presumably over Baghdad. I get a Hart to myself in S/Ldr Platsis's flight and we "stand to" from 8-11.30 when it is cancelled. Aircraft dispersed everywhere, and all over the polo ground too.

Piles of leaflets, printed in Jerusalem and Cairo, have arrived, so I hope I am allowed to drop some. Pete didn't get his 'wings', having failed in navigation. A year ago I had the mustard gas, and the mark is still on my forearm.

April 21st 1941

HABBANIYA

CAMERA OBSCURA AND WIND FINDING in Oxfords. Then the other night Ling says something about "Dunford Wood my ace operational pilot". I say "eh?" and then discover he didn't know I was in the Oxfords.

So today I go back to B flight and do message picking up, with White as my first passenger. My flying is shocking since it's a month since I last flew solo, and I can hardly see the message poles. I miss first time and second time break a pole; then it's time for breakfast. Irwin, Wall, Fairweather and Humphries (who went and married Mary Simpson in Karachi) arrive. They wear uniform all day in India now apparently.

Troops arrive from India at Basra. The King's Own came in Atlantas, B.T.s (with Dudley Withers) and Douglases. Also 2/8 GR with Mick Mackenzie and now, some say, 1/13 from Quetta.

April 27th 1941

HABBANIYA

I READ IN "AEROPLANE" about a new Waziristan medal for operations from December 16th 1937 to December 31st 1939, so Teddie Humphries, Reggie Wall and myself go out and buy one and post it up. After all these years, too. Douglases keep ferrying troops up here, and most of the King's Own are here. I met Nigel Gribbon and Byers in the Club last night. A most enjoyable party, majority army, from which I escaped at about midnight. Fairweather, Boozy Bons and myself get together over our black rifle buttons and get very confidential about it. The great thing to do is to exchange buttons. "Tiny" Irwin now has his own, free Greek, free French, RAF, RIASC and 16th Punjab, all on his tunic.

A.T.S. starts tomorrow, and I and Haig are in Stonehill's flight. 1/13 GR are not in Basra after all – it's the 2nd or 3rd battalion, 11th Sikhs.

I go to the Lake Hotel today with Wall and all the Malayan pupils. Also with us is Richardson, ex-navy and Imperial airways pilot, commissioned as a pilot officer for a fortnight to fly the Douglases from India, where he was holding a ground job in I.N.A. (India National Airways). Drinks and lunch and the conversation hops from Malaya to Bombay and down to Kenya, with interludes in Canada, and then back again to Singapore every time.

183

*'BOAC on Lake Habbaniya'. A BOAC Short Empire flying boat (G-AETX)
taking on passengers. The last flying boat flew out on
April 30th.*

Polo today but Finjan is a bit slow and wants some spurs. A pity that one can't have a few drinks and enjoy a party without having to have too many and stay up half the night. I reckon my system is the best, of parking drinks I don't want about the place, and if that is no good, of making myself sick when I come back of an evening.

April 30th 1941

HABBANIYA

YESTERDAY EVENING ALL BRITISH WOMEN and children were evacuated from Baghdad, and it is said that the Iraqis were about to resist a landing of further troops to add to the force already here. This morning the alarm goes at about 4.00 am and we go down to the flights and prepare planes for war. An Iraqi officer comes in by car to the AOC *(Air Vice Marshal Smart)* and out again, presumably with some sort of ultimatum. Then troops and armoured cars appear on the plateau, and at 8.00 am I go off with James Fairweather to reconnoitre them. I keep her at 1000 feet and we see three guns, nine or so AFVs and about one battalion of troops all lined up ready to fire at the camp. I then land her on the polo pitch and we report to AHQ. A shave and wash and some breakfast, and now what!?

Just done a two hour recce of the Plateau, Falluja and Falluja Plain in an Audax with Sgt Douglas, 13.30 to 15.30. What a time! Saw eighteen horse drawn 18-pounders the other side of Falluja Plain, and Bofors guns, howitzers and M/Gs on the Plateau. Simply grand at 500 feet and AOC very pleased with my report, and asks me to do a dawn patrol. I tell Ling and he says "Yes! Yes!" and details Haig for it according to his roster. Very tired, and with one of those chronic thirsts for iced water which I sometimes get.

May 1st 1941

Habbaniya

FLAP! FLAP!

Pete does a forced landing on Falluja Plain near the cement factory on his recce. I go up afterwards and much as usual, only they seem to have less troops on the plateau. I count twelve horse-drawn guns, but Allan makes it twenty-five. Ling gives us some maps made in 1918 and they're good, but roads etc have to be put in. We now have to stick to 2000 feet so will not be able to see anything. No more steep turns at 250 feet!

2130: C/O has told us we attack Iraqis at 0500 tomorrow. Under Ian as C/O our flight is ordered to stand by from 0500.

May 3rd 1941

WAR!

I went up at sunrise in the back of Broadhurst's Audax, without a parachute like a fool, and we drop 20lb bombs on the guns in conjunction with Oxfords and Wellingtons from Shaibah. I use the rear gun on an escaping lorry, but it's so damn hard when pulling out of a dive.

Next sortie I go up with Broughton, but we go too low and I feel something tug at my sleeve. Then liquid comes back over me, which to my horror I find to be blood. I can't see out of my goggles so stand up and find Jimmy B. in front is shot through the face and blood pouring out like a perforated petrol tank. I buckle on my parachute, but luckily he is fully conscious and we land on the polo pitch OK. I am a bit shaken, and we then get shelled on the polo ground and in the mess, without much effect. Ling, Garner and Broughton get shot, and Chico Walsh with two pupils Skelton and Robinson is shot down in flames in an Oxford.

Dan Cremin orders us four to do a continual patrol to Baghdad with R/T. I do one at about 11 am, and over Falluja Plain meet three Gladiators, but they pass me by and I take it they are ours. I see thirteen troop lorries on the plain and do a little front gunning, though not very successfully. We get shot up and bombed in the camp by Bredas, Savoia Marchettis, Northrops and "Peggy" Audaxes, but no damage round me.

These Iraqis have guts I must say. We are a bit windy about these Bredas, as we think of ours as a "suicide patrol" – we are sitting meat for them, we haven't been taught the slightest thing about air combat.

Pete (Gillespy) goes off at 3.00 pm and at 4.00 we get worried as he hasn't been heard of for an hour. At 4.30 Ian (Pringle) goes off on the patrol and finds his burnt-out plane in the desert near Falluja. He is himself attacked by a Breda with tracer but escapes. I

'C squadron (Audaxes) on the Polo ground'.
Alongside are the operations tents.

do a patrol to Najaf in the evening, windy as hell. I see a Gladiator and am off "through the gate" without waiting to see whose it was.

This morning at dawn there's a heavy shelling of the polo ground and, it seems, the room next to mine. Today I do a photography job, or try to (knowing nothing about it), over the Plateau and up to "Palm Grove". I keep at 6000 feet as their A/A stuff is known to fall down again at 5000 feet. Later we all do a bit of dive bombing. I am told how to let go the quadrant and a rough idea of it, and off I go. I thought I pulled out between 1500 and 2000 feet but anyway, my plane is U/S on return, and several bullets have just missed the water jacket. Funnily enough, after the pullout, I went sharp left, but all my holes were on the starboard side! All this is by Dhibban Village and do we give them hell! Dan Cremin and his boys! Phew!

Not much shelling after this morning's effort, and the Savoias don't do much damage. Dicky Cleaver in a Gladiator is seen to make a steep dive with smoke pouring out of it. We are lucky operating from the polo ground, and the operations tent is a sight to see. The

RAF Habbaniya Air Striking Force

Commanding Officer
Group Captain W.A.B. Saville

A Squadron
Wing Commander Selyn-Roberts
10 Hawker Audax (8 x 20lb bombs)

B Squadron
Squadron Leader Dudgeon
26 Airspeed Oxfords (8 x 20lb bombs)
(Previously the ATS's main training aircraft)
7 Fairey Gordons (2 x 250lb bombs)
(Previously used for target towing)
1 Blenheim Mk1

C Squadron
Wing Commander Ling
10 Hawker Audax (2 x 250lb bombs)

D Squadron
Wing Commander Hawtrey
12 Hawker Audax (2 x 250lb bombs)

Gladiator Fighter Flight
Flight Lt Cleaver
9 Gladiator fighters

Communications Flight
Flight Lt Skeet
2 Valentia (4 x 500lb bombs)
1 Valentia (8 x 250lb bombs)

The Battle Develops

In the weeks of rising tension that followed the coup in Baghdad, a number of instructors of the flying school had taken the initiative - without official sanction according to later reports - to ready their motley collection of superannuated biplanes for action. A key impetus had been the arrival in early April of Squadron Leader Dudgeon, who had been sent for some 'time out' and 'R+R' after completing fifty missions in the Western Desert, suffering from exhaustion. However, with his combat experience, he was ideally suited to team up with Wing Commander Ling in his unofficial project to convert their ancient Audaxes into bombers, designing bomb brackets and cobbling together ammunition. Both officers could see how the situation was developing, and that if they did nothing, their fledgling pupil pilots in their lightly armed trainers would be sitting ducks. Though Colin does not mention it in his diaries, one source of knowledge tapped by Dudgeon and Ling were the 'four musketeers', as these ex-Indian army officers, especially Colin, had first hand knowledge of how Hawker Audax biplanes had been used to bomb tribesmen on the North West Frontier.

They also recognised that the airfield they operated from was extremely vulnerable, being outside the perimeter of the camp and overlooked by the Plateau. After some quite considerable lobbying of the camp commandant, they managed to get hold of some bulldozers to flatten the polo ground and make it ready to take aircraft, beyond line of sight of the escarpment. It was from the polo ground that two of the reformed squadrons operated during the battle, and where many of the pilots slept in tents, yards from their planes.

Despite the refusal of aid from Wavell in early April, Smart was offered help from Auchinleck in India, who proposed diverting the 10th Indian Division (embarked at Karachi and ready to go to Malaya) to Basra. It turned out to be a lucky escape. The first elements, a brigade strong, sailed on 12th April, landing on the 18th, while four hundred troops of the Kings Own Royal Regiment flew direct to Habbaniya in transport planes in the world's first strategic airlift. As required under treaty, the British ambassador, Cornwallis, was obliged to notify the Iraqi Government of these troop movements, which he did at the last moment. Rachid Ali had no right to refuse permission, but he demanded they transit the country as quickly as possible, and it spurred him to accelerate his demands for help of his own from the Axis powers. When Cornwallis informed him on 23rd April that a second brigade would be landing, Ali flatly refused to allow it, declaring it an act of war. The disembarkation went ahead. It was then that Rachid Ali decided he had to make his move, as intercepted messages with the Germans revealed. He decided to march on Habbaniya.

It was at this point that Cornwallis, sensing a showdown was coming, asked Rachid Ali for permission to evacuate British women and children from Baghdad to Habbaniya. Their arrival is recorded by Colin in his diary entry of the 30th, and they reported sharing the road with advancing Iraqi troops, which Colin reconnoitred from the air the same day.

Faced with the Iraqi ultimatum to surrender, and reluctant to start a war without higher authority, Smart cabled London for orders. Eventually they came, direct from Churchill: 'Strike hard. Use all available force'.

In addition to the troops landing at Basra, Wellington bombers were sent from Egypt, and these 'Wimpeys' as referenced by Colin, took part in the initial strike. But the quickest route for relief to arrive was across 500 miles of desert from Egypt, so as soon as word of the outbreak of hostilities reached the Air Ministry, the Prime Minister and Chiefs of Staff cabled Wavell to put a relief force together. Wavell was again reluctant - first, he maintained it was India Command's responsibility to relieve Habbaniya and second, he had his hands full and feared a region-wide Arab revolt if a full scale war developed with Rachid Ali. He urged a diplomatic settlement. However, he was overruled by Churchill on 3rd May, and ordered to organise help. Reluctantly, Wavell acquiesced. Called Habforce, it was made up of mostly under-equipped and poorly trained peacekeeping forces from Palestine (all that Wavell could spare), many of whom were trained as cavalry but no longer had horses. In fact their lack of a means of transport was so severe that city buses and trucks had to be commandeered from the streets of Jerusalem to transport them across the desert. They were ready to march on 11th May. A rapid advance column called Kingcol, with members of the Arab legion under Pasha Glubb, spearheaded the force, racing ahead in the best available transport to capture the wells at Rutbah en route. Without those, Habforce would not have enough water to get to Habbaniya. They finally arrived on 17th May - some days after the siege had been broken by the pilots of 4 IFTS, as Colin recounts over the following days. This march across the desert, chronicled by Somerset de Chair in 'The Golden Carpet', has the air of a 'Boys Own' adventure, and was described by Glubb as "one of the most remarkable examples of military daring in history."

C.O. came up and said would we remove the empty bottles. None of my work, as I wait until we finish at dusk for mine.

Yesterday the Iraqis apparently listened in on their R/T and as soon as they heard the fighter patrols going home, in they came. But today the "Wimpys" *(Vickers Wellington Bombers, flying from Basra)* blow up Hinaidi *(Iraqi Air Force base outside Baghdad)* and nothing comes over after that.

Poor old Pete! I hope he was able to jump out. Water restrictions reduced, and we can now use the showers. The baths are kept filled with spare drinking water, but of course the Greeks have to go and jump in with their soap – if they use any.

May 4th 1941

HABBANIYA

SHELLING LAST NIGHT FROM 9.30 – 12.30 and then again at 4 am. I lie quaking in my bed, but they don't seem to do much damage. This morning we are all split into four-hour "watches" so I get a bit of time off in my bed and get a good shower. I go up in the back of Dan's plane on a bund bombing job, but 20-pounders are too small for the job. Then I fly a plane off the aerodrome onto the polo ground, and land dead across wind, with no ill effects.

A mechanised column took Rutbah and reached "H4" landing ground on the pipeline yesterday. Hope they get here before the Germans do.[1]

Blenheims and "Wimpeys" attack Hinaidi again today. Had a drink with Nigel Gribbon. Wish I had Attam Khan here (his bearer in Waziristan), as all the bearers are hiding under their beds in the civil cantonment and nothing is done. A plane is up continuously tonight so hope there will be no more shelling and I will get some sleep. Charles Braybrooks killed in a Vincent down Shaibah way. So poor old Sheila Nicholson in 'Pindi will be weeping. A few shells this evening before Dan Cremin took off.

I hear my photography job was pretty useless!

¹ *The relief column – Habforce – had not yet even been assembled in Egypt and Palestine, and would not leave until 11th, so this rumour is false. Evidently British propaganda was meant as much for spine-stiffening their own beleaguered garrison at Habbaniya as frightening the Iraqis. Second, it is interesting to note that the Germans are already being talked about as 'on their way'. Likewise, they were not to arrive for at least a week, and in fact their help had only been requested by the Iraqis some days previously.*

May 5th 1941

HABBANIYA

MORE SHELLING AT DAWN and at 9.00 am today, despite patrols in the air all night. Pat Weir and a platoon of King's Own do a successful raid Dhibban way last night, without any casualties. I am on at dawn, 4.15, then off 5-9, on 9-1, off 1-5 and on again to dusk. Mostly sitting around in our operations tent while "Doug" Baker presides with three telephones, fixes everything up, serves beer and washes up the glasses, besides having the tent cleaned out. With the help of W.O. Shawn Sheagh, R.E., we snaffle some ice to keep the beer cold in a zinc-lined parachute box which is the frigidaire.

I go up before lunch to bomb four cars in a copse and undershoot them. Then at dusk Dan, Gordon Arthur, Alan and myself go up to spot the guns at their dusk shelling. I am just coming home as the sun has disappeared when I see other planes in the air, so reckon I had better stay up a bit longer. I turn and notice a flash in a copse. I climb up and drop four bombs on the wrong copse, then four bombs on the right one (near "Camel Turn"), all of which overshoot. But I get in three good long bursts with my front gun at it, and Cpl Sanderson in the back does some good work with his Lewis gun. I report to P/O Shotter in the ops rooms, find the copse on a photographic map, and they are all pleased as it is a new one. I then find there was no shelling at the time I saw the flash, so it can't have been a gun!

'Iraqi M.T. at Canal Turn'. The remains of the Iraqi convoy.

May 6th 1941

HABBANIYA

I GO UP AT DAWN TO LOOK FOR MY GUN, with James Fairweather in the back, and find it's not there. How I take off I don't know, as it's almost pitch dark. Sit about doing nothing until 3.30 pm. The Kings Own attack and are held up at "Hell Fire Corner", the ridge above Dhibban. Dan Cremin and his boys (minus me) go and shoot it up, and they all come back riddled with holes. I get up eventually with "Tiny" Irwin in the back and machine gun the fleeing troops. They stop and shoot me up, but it seems slaughter all the same. Three Iraqi armoured cars come up, my bombs miss but Dan opens them up like a tin opener with a stick right down the road. Tony warns me they "bite" so I don't go too low.

Northrops come over while I am eating lunch in the tent at 3.30 and drop bombs right across the polo ground and get one of our "recco" Audaxes. The fire spreads to a Gladiator. Dicky Cleaver and Bob May wounded and some killed. Last night at

12.30 some 20lbers are dropped by Iraqi Audaxes and come very near my room. They also riddle our tent with bullet holes. Then a convoy approaches from Falluja and the boys go off, including Ian (Pringle), it being his turn. As he is buckling on his parachute I say to myself "He won't come back", and sure enough he doesn't. He does several trips and then Alan (Haig) and I go up. Both sections of the convoy are in flames, between "Canal Turn" and Falluja, and I put some bombs on the road and a good burst with my front gun. Two trips I do, and on the second I bend one bombing quadrant and am unable to even use the other, it being so stiff. So I use the front gun and return home, during another raid at about 6.00 pm. Some funny holes on the polo ground, like aerial torpedos, and they were obviously aiming for our line of tents. They must reckon 3 squadron the most dangerous one! Well, Stonhill sees a plane dive into the ground near the convoy at about 6.15, and it turns out to be Ian with Fairbrother in the back. But his bombs blew up, so he wouldn't have known much! What's the use? Hooray for the next man to die – Alan Haig or me.[1]

[1] *Of the four pupil pilot officers from the Indian Army – the 'Four Musketeers' – who had met at the medical in Delhi in October and who had started the course at Habbaniya together, two – Ian Pringle and Pete Gillespy – were now dead.*

May 8th 1941

HABBANIYA

I DON'T GO FLYING YESTERDAY. A bit of tip-and-run bombing from "Peggy" Audaxes, one of which is shot down by a Blenheim fighter. A Savoia and a Northrop spotted force landed in the desert, and are destroyed after a prodigious amount of bombs, S.A.A. (small arms ammunition) and Very lights have been used on them. Dan Cremin returning from the furthermost one meets a "Peggy" Audax going home, but as his front gun had jammed he does nothing. But the two planes on the ground are at 65 degrees

Fliegerfuehrer Irak

Just as the British were sending help from other theatres of war, so the Rachid Ali government was desperately seeking military aid from the Axis powers. And not just arms and money, but planes and personnel. Because he had been forced to act before he was ready, on account of the 10th Indian division's landing at Basra, the support he had been asking for since coming back to power in early April had not yet been signed off in Berlin, so in the days after his attack on the camp, a scramble was on to organise a taskforce. Not only the British were stretched - the Germans were too, with preparations for Operation Barbarossa well advanced and the invasion of Crete about to kick off. But Grobba (since 1939 in Berlin) persuaded Von Ribbontrop, and through him Hitler, that here was a golden opportunity to drive a wedge between Egypt and Britain's dominions in the east, and moreover to deprive Egypt and India of the oil that flowed from Iraq. There was also the tantalising prospect of diverting it to support Barbarossa instead.

So on 6th May Colonel Werner Junck of the Luftwaffe was tasked with taking a squadron of ME110 fighter bombers and a squadron of Heinkel 111 bombers via Syria to Mosul - the 'Fliegerfuehrer Irak' - which were diverted from Greece. Swift negotiations were concluded with Vichy France (the 'Paris Protocols'), allowing Italian and German forces to transit Syria, captured British arms to be released from there to the Iraqis, and a Luftwaffe base to be established in Aleppo. On 11th May Grobba returned to Baghdad to coordinate aid, and the first elements of the Luftwaffe arrived over the next couple of days, along with a Major Axel Von Blomberg, who was to act as liaison between the Axis and Iraqi air forces. Unfortunately he was killed by a freak bullet as his plane came in to land at Baghdad, fired by an Iraqi sentry who mistook the plane for the RAF.

However, the Luftwaffe was quickly in action, making an immediate impression by attacking Kingcol at Rutbah and Habbaniya on 15th - as recorded in Colin's diary. However, the next

IRAQ

YEAR 1941		AIRCRAFT		PILOT OR	2ND PILOT, PUPIL	DUTY
MONTH	DATE	Type	No.	1ST PILOT	OR PASSENGER	(INCLUDING RESULTS AND REMARKS)
						—— TOTALS BROUGHT FORWARD
April	21ST	Audax	7514	Self	Lac White	Message Picking up
"	22nd	Hart "T"	4916	Sgt Baker	Self	Front Gun Duval
"	23rd	Audax	K7514	Self	Solo	Forced Landings
"	24 Tlr	Hart	K4021	Self	Solo	Polo Ground to aerodrome
"	28th	HART T	4916	Sgt HORSHAM	SELF	I. F. SPINS
"	30th	"	4896	SELF	LT FAIRWEATHER	RECCO. OF PLATEAU IRAQ ARMY DISPOSITIONS
"	"	AUDAX	7530	SELF	SGT DOUGLAS	RECCO. PLATEAU — FALLUJA PLAIN IRAQ ARMY DISPOSITIONS
MAY	1ST	AUDAX	7518	SELF	Sgt DOUGLAS	Do Do IRAQ REPELLION
"	2nd	AUDAX	7543	SELF	SGT DOUGLAS	OPERATIONS — Do
"	"	"	7518	"	"	" RECE MAZARA CANAL
"	3RD	AUDAX	7530	SELF	CPL COPEROD	OPERATIONS — PHOTOGRAPHY (PLANE u/s) JEMO El DRIHAAN
"	"	"	3107	"	SOLO	OPERATIONS — Dive BOMBING - FRONT GUN
MAY	4th	AUDAX	3105	SELF	SOLO	AERODROME — POLO GROUND
MAY	5th	AUDAX	7504	SELF	LT IRWIN	OPERATIONS — SIRRIYA BOND
"	"	"	3714	SELF	SOLO	AERODROME — POLO GROUND
"	"	AUDAX	7514	SELF	CPL SANDERSON	OPERATIONS — GUN IN COPSE
"	6th	AUDAX	7503	SELF	P/O FAIRWEATHER	OPERATIONS — RECCE. GUN IN COARSE
"	"	"	3107	SELF	SOLO	AERODROME — POLO GROUND
"	"	"	3099	SELF	SOLO	OPERATIONS — CONVOY FALLUJA ROAD
"	"	"	3099	SELF	SOLO	OPERATIONS — CONVOY FALLUJA ROAD
"	8th	AUDAX	7521	SELF	SOLO	OPERATIONS — DAWN PATROL
"	"	"	7503	SELF	P/O IRWIN	OPERATIONS - PATROL FALLUJA-PLATEAU
"	"	"	7525	SELF	LAC. WILLIAMS	OPERATIONS — PATROL FALLUJA -MAZARA
MAY	9th	AUDAX	7530	SELF	SGT HAYLES	OPERATIONS - CONTACT PATROL MAZARA

GRAND TOTAL [Cols. (1) to (10)]
149 Hrs. 10 Mins.   TOTALS CARRIED FORWARD

Colin's pilot's flying log book entries covering the beginning of the battle. Not all sorties are entered here - in particular the first sort he made in the back of Broughton's Audax at dawn on the 5th.

day three Hurricanes arrived from Egypt to reinforce Habbaniya, as well as several more Gladiators and Blenheims, which took the fight to the Germans, attacking the Luftwaffe planes on the ground at Rachid air base on the 17th and again on the 18th.

After just two days, the Luftwaffe lost 30% of their strength. Although some Italian fighters started arriving in late May, by then the Germans were almost spent, and the Iraqi air force had been destroyed. It was too little, too late.

so when this is plotted on the map it leads to Baquba. Yesterday afternoon they bomb it, Stonhill, Broadhurst, Haig and Frewin, and only three come back. I am convinced it's Alan, but no, Stonhill was seen to force land near Baquba, so he must be a prisoner.

The C.O. wants to change our name to 4 Fighting Training School, which sounds OK. Night flying last night and they make me standby pilot, so I sleep out by our tent in a ditch on a camp bed. Today I do a recco of the Plateau and go down to fifty feet, and there's nothing to be seen between the camp and Palm Grove – Majara Road. I look at the convoy and see all the corpses. There is a platoon of Levies above Dhibban, and a section of our armoured cars above on the Plateau, manoeuvring and stalking Dan's burnt-out armoured cars at Canal Turn.

May 9th 1941

HABBANIYA

I DO TWO MORE RECCO PATROLS YESTERDAY and front gun a gun team (horses) on Falluja plain. Most of the time is spent low flying over the area and taking photographs with my camera. A sergeant pilot in an Oxford, at 2000 feet over Ramadi, has one shot fired at him and it goes through his heart. I go down to view all the booty in A.S.U. (ammunition storage unit) and get myself an 18lb shell case. There are all the guns and armoured cars and a wicked little Italian "whippet" tank. Some Valencias came up from Shaibah the other day and lost the way. One had to land at Hit, where the crew and passengers (15 Kings Own) surrendered after burning the plane. Galiani (Rachid Ali) has fled to Turkey, according to the BBC, after riots in Baghdad, so I suppose this little war is now over. The Blenheims raid Mosul yesterday, and one gets shot up and they have to bail out up there. Five hours flying yesterday and damned tired, with "parachute bottom". I get myself issued with an Iraqi .38 at the depot by saying I haven't got a gun, so it can't really be classified as "loot" or "booty".

Entry from the daily bulletin of 8th May, with the message to
AVM Smart from Churchill.

May 10th 1941

HABBANIYA

I DO A SORT OF CONTACT PATROL as our forces occupy Najara,
going out with them as a guardian angel. Very hazy today, and I sit
about in the tent all day, gradually getting deeper and deeper in
dust. As soon as my goggles break, I suppose I shall have to confess
to my sins, as I can't fit my spare pair of lenses. They need the edges
filing down a little first.[1]

Gruesome stories around of what the Levies did to any
prisoners they captured the other day. Most of them are Assyrians,
and have a lot to pay back. Pat Weir has been put in for an M.C.
– his platoon came under severe M/G fire, and he silenced one lot
with a V.B. fired from the shoulder. He then waved his platoon on
and got a bullet in the uplifted arm, severing a main artery. Some
Madras sappers and miners arrive by Douglas *(DC3 aircraft)* today.

---

[1] *Due to his poor eyesight, Colin relied on his specially made pair of google with*
lenses that he had specially made in India.

199

May 12th 1941

115 DEGREES YESTERDAY, and boy was it hot in our tent. I go out on a bombing raid to Musaib, where there is an arms factory, but fail to hit anything. Then this morning a two-hour patrol from 4.15 with Tiny (Irwin) to Falluja, El Musaib, Najara and round the back of the Lake to Ramadi. There I attempt to drop a stick of bombs on some barges, but am bloody useless at dive bombing.

Alan and I do Pete and Ian's things the other day, packing them up etc, and a more depressing job I never had. (Gillespy and Pringle, killed in the first days of the battle). We sort of give them each a dressing gown (no idea who's is who's) and share out the shoes evenly. I collect all Pete's bills and give them to the adjutant who will have some fun sorting them out.

Rashid Ali is still in Baghdad (not fled to Turkey as reported on the BBC), and a Heinkel was seen today at Hinaidi whilst they were bombing it. I should think my time will soon be up, unless I can keep up this deception. However, Quien Sabe! I forget all my Arabic by now. Nigel Gribbon in hospital with a nice bullet in his leg.

May 13th 1941

A FEW HEINKELS REPORTED by the British minister at Beirut, and the Turkish consul at Mosul. Russia has recognised Rachid Ali, so what to do – this isn't over yet.

Today, with W/O Frewin and Haig, went to bomb petrol tanks at Rachid, the old Hinaidi. For the first time I put a stick bang on what I aim for, but 20lbers don't seem much good. Yesterday Dan and his boys put eighteen holes through the factory at Musaib (the one I missed). One Brushwood, here, who was attached to the

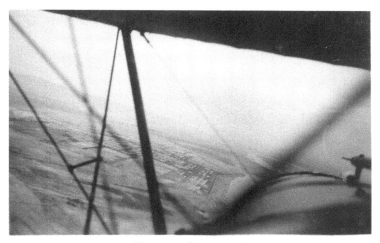

'Returning from a sortie'.
Habbaniya is below as Colin approaches to land.

Iraqi Air Force in some engineering capacity, knows exactly what is where in the target line. Much cooler today.

May 15th 1941

HABBANIYA

A RECCO PLANE VANISHES with Blackall and Ritz, pupils, on board. A Blenheim is attacked four times by an ME 110 at Mosul and six 109s are seen nearby in Northern Iraq. Five go off to drop leaflets on Falluja, which requires no small skill, and the prisoners' mail, addressed to the postmaster there. Yesterday I lead a formation to Rachid – Slack and Brown – but Slack cannot keep up and we go on alone. I miss my hangar but put four bombs through a house nearby, then overshoot with the next stick. Then last night I go up solo, from 2.15 to 4.30 am, half asleep all the time, and having nothing to do but think of MEs landing by moonlight and the first light of dawn.

A Bombay *(Bristol Bombay aircraft)* arrives from Egypt with a load of Marmite. We want guns here, not butter!

Today I do two half-hour patrols and shoot up some derelict cars on the desert road out of Ramadi. I spot seventeen lorries on the left bank of the Euphrates, opposite the ferry pier at Ramadi, and the boys go out to bomb them. Then I see a car on Falluja Plain. It sees me too, stops, and out get the passengers, being in too much of a hurry to shut the doors. I front gun the car, and notice the passengers are Arabs with rifles. I give one long burst, and I see one man lying in the sand and his body vanishes under the dust spurts, but he gets up afterward and runs off. I go down on another, but the Vickers jams, and whilst clearing it, I think this game is hardly cricket, so push off home and leave them.

May 16th 1941

Habbaniya

I have just taken off on a recco with Tiny and look back to see smoke over the camp, and three Heinkels high in the air. One is lagging behind, with a Gladiator on its tail. The Gladiator is then shot down, and we see the pilot bail out. The parachute fails to open properly and we go low over his body and the plane, which had exploded in mid-air. We return and report it and see one Heinkel with smoke coming out of one engine. It isn't seen anymore. Most of the bombs fall on the supply depot. Then off I go on recco and see some dust on the desert track north of Ramadi.

It's three lorries full of sacks which I machine gun and Tiny rear guns. I try some bombing and only get within fifteen yards – what the RAF call "in the target area", and blow up one of the drivers who is lying nearby. I return and report and Gordon Arthur goes and bombs them and sets them on fire, going so low that bits of 20lber hit his plane. He is the man who blew an Iraqi troop's topee off with his slipstream in the Battle of the Plateau. Then six

'A gladiator burning after a raid'. Habbaniya polo ground.

MEs get Reggie Wall, but the story is a bit confused and he is in hospital, not dead thank God. I didn't shoot at those drivers, Iraqi troops in uniform, but Tiny did. I don't like ring and head, would much rather an Aldis sight.

I am drinking too much - lime juice and water etc - and have had no exercise, bar two half-hour walks, since this little war began.

May 17th 1941

Habbaniya

SAW REGGIE WALL, who has a lot of superficial holes in him. He was testing a plane and doing a wide circuit when six ME110s caught him over Dhibban. He did a crash landing somewhere, got out and ran for shelter and they dropped a bomb near him. The ambulance, which had been collecting the body of young Hertage in that Gladiator, saw it and stopped for him, and was machine-gunned by the Hun.

Reggie had sent off a letter to Group Captain Bussell, telling him of our plight, as far as training was concerned, and that I had been saying that I ought to go back to the Frontier and the Army. Some lads, including Broadhurst, have now produced stories about the "Army officers having had it" and having applied to go back to the Army. Some people are damn swine.

Tiny and I had a drink with young Stoney this morning. Three Hurricanes arrived yesterday, to everyone's delight. Today two Gladiators shoot down two ME110s as they are taking off from Rachid aerodrome.

May 19th 1941

Habbaniya

ANOTHER ME110 DAMAGED AT RACHID. A new AOC arrives, Air Vice Marshal D'Albiac, who evacuated from Greece and so knows his stuff. Old Smart had a slight car crash and packed it in with shock.[1]

Yesterday a proper operation order came out, for the investment of Falluja by Levies and the King's Own on the Plain (going there at dawn in Valencias). The RAF are then to bomb the hell out of it, the bombing being interspersed with pamphlets, until the troops there surrender. I have two salvoes, miss the cemetery and brick kiln, and nearly get taken off the show, as they all land in the desert. Then I put four through the bazaar roof, and four bounce off its walls, so I get a bullseye. Dropping from 4000 feet to 2000' and then releasing at 1000 feet seemed to do the trick. But the town hasn't surrendered, and no one thought of what to do if they didn't, at least the army didn't, so the AOC has now ordered them to capture Falluja.

The "Phantom Column" has arrived, and is dispersed about the Rest House with its M.T.[2]

[1] *The original AOC, AVM Smart, had had a 'road accident' on 3rd May – some maintained a nervous breakdown – and had been evacuated out to India by air. For the last two weeks the battle had been fought without an AOC in charge.*
[2] *Called the "Phantom Column" as they had been so long promised and expected to relieve them from Palestine, but never materialised, until now. The story of this force is very well told in Somerset de Chair's "The Golden Carpet".*

May 20th 1941

Habbaniya

RACHID IS BLASTED AT DAWN THIS MORNING. Cremin arrives late and we take off in the dark and get lost. I never find the squadron, so go straight there myself, reckoning on being safe, as there are Gladiators about. Bombing not much good. A Heinkel, or Savoia, does a photography run this morning, and on the way back drops a bomb or two. I go for a walk this afternoon and three more come over and blast the hangers. These are followed shortly by four ME110s who come down front gunning. They had a crack at the Harts on the race course this morning, so they must hang about here all day.

One general, twenty officers and five hundred men are captured in Falluja yesterday. Iraqi air force strength on 2nd May:- 24 "Peggy" Audaxes, 15 Northrops, 7 Gladiators, 4 Bredas, 4 Vincents, 3 Savoias, 5 odds and sods. Total 62. Frewin went out yesterday with some civilian to find a convoy at H1-3, and saw some MEs ground strafing, so came right home.

May 22nd 1941

Habbaniya

NO FLYING YESTERDAY. Two ME110s come over and shoot up a Douglas on the ground belonging to Dudley Withers and Dickie Bird, who are here. I take them to the Club last night, and I find Dudley is engaged. This morning woken up at 5 am, as Falluja is being attacked, and Haig, Figgis and self go off. I put a stick amongst some lorries and miss two cars going flat out, with two bombs apiece. Front gun jams so I have to come home, quarter of an hour after the other two, to find the camp being bombed, and 110s just finished and they all think I have "gone for a Burton", as the expression is here.

Off we go again and we spot the Iraqi troops attacking Falluja. I find a lot in holes and a road cutting, with two lorries under desert-coloured hoods. I miss them with both sticks, but reckon I got some troops. I nearly fail to pull out of the second dive. Then down with the Vickers and two long, long bursts at the troops, who sit up and fire their rifles at me. Then number three stoppage1 so off home. The first sortie I got a number one every time after about fifteen seconds. A pity, as I had a runabout at my mercy, filled with troops with white hat bands crouching on the floor and hanging on the footboards. I always cut my knuckles on these damn bomb levers, and a bad one today.

[1] *The Lewis gun was notoriously prone to jamming, with three types of stoppages.*

May 23rd 1941

Habbaniya

I DO TWO MORE TRIPS OVER FALLUJA. One to bomb lorries at Khan Nukta police post, where I put a stick bang on the road, and the other to attack 100-200 troops who had come up to Falluja by the canal road south of the town. They had left their lorries and were sitting out in the open, so I spread out the bombs and cause a minor retreat of a few hundred yards. I believe they were all lying down on their faces with their rifles pointing in the air. Then the Sergeant Major would watch us come over and order "fire", and every man would pull his trigger with his thumb and a fusillade of shots would come into the air.

206

A aerial recce photo of Al Rashid air base, dated April 1941, used for raids in May.

At about 4.00 pm two bombs land in the Mess. One behind the C.O.'s quarters, some hundred feet from me, and the other one on the Mess lawn, five yards from our newest slit trench, which was full up at the time, though no one was injured. Also one through the roof of the depot NAAFI.

Reggie Wall is better, and now remembers doing a tight loop and a few aileron turns and getting one of the MEs in his sights. The King's Own have had three officer casualties yesterday, and the Iraqis had them forced back onto the bridge at one time. The local inhabitants also sniped them. Complaints that the Indian-made bayonets snapped off in the 8th body!

Germans dropped leaflets yesterday too, but from 11,000 feet or so. Two 110s over today, twice, but didn't fire, and reputed to have dropped a message on Air HQ.

May 25th 1941

HABBANIYA

TWO DOSES OF ME110S YESTERDAY, and the first finds us all in the tent and we all get hurt jumping into the same trench. Today a lackadaisical blitz on Ramadi, but I don't go up and haven't done so for two days now. Then some bombing by a lone Heinkel, and three 110s sweep by over the polo pitch and away. Cowley and I get the smoke candle and arrow working, but I doubt whether it will be of any use.[1]

Am fed up with this war. I get enough sleep, enough food and something cold to drink, but life is getting pretty monotonous and a lot of new chaps in the Mess whom I don't particularly want to talk with. But what to do.

[1] *A smoke candle was lit if the wind direction necessitated a runway change, to warn pilots coming in to land.*

May 27th 1941

HABBANIYA

I GO AND BOMB EMPTY PALM GROVES at Ramadi on the evening of the 25th, and then go off for a second trip. But the plane splutters during take off, so I throttle back, and long flames shoot out of the exhaust. I had opened the mixture control by mistake, according to Flt/Sgt Rhodes. Then up again to bomb the military school at Mushaid point, but bloody awful. Saw two flashes and two white puffs of smoke on the ground, so presume it was A/A fire, which Figgis (in the back) said he felt.

Heinkels at 0650 yesterday, but today's dose not yet delivered. Blenheims continually firing up Mosul. *(where the Luftwaffe contingent of ME110s and Heinkels were based.)* Met Masters[1] of 2/4 GR in the Club last night, shooting a line about battles round Basra. Went over with Dickie Cleaver and Allan after dinner, or "rations", to the cricket pitch to see Hugh Thomas and the boys and his Levy company there. Had a few whiskies, and we discuss hearsay tales of this war, and decide how it should be won. I must write to Ma again, but am too idle. A lot of funny fellows arrive in Blenheims here and recount their experiences in Greece innumerable times.

[1] *John Masters, who had served in Waziristan, and who later became a well-known novelist.*

May 29th 1941

Habbaniya

Yesterday "Kingcol" advanced on Baghdad. A canal had been dug across the road at Khan Nuqta, and the road flooded further down beyond that. We stand by all day to support them, but only one flight required, to attack some 1500-3000 tribesmen massing south of Falluja Plain. These turned out to be sheep.

Today Arthur, White and self go off to attack enemy "targets" in front of our advance guard, some 10-12 miles down the road from Khan Nuqta. We have as escort, one Gladiator flown by W/C Wrightman, and before we arrive he is attacked by three CR42s. We break formation and go down on the deck and see him shoot one down, the pilot sort of stepping out in his parachute, like going down in a lift. We fly low over him and his burnt-out plane and he looks a bit dago-ish in long trousers and a shirt, holding up his hands in surrender. We had previously seen what we thought were

Audaxes ground strafing, but which were really CR42s pulling out after diving on Wrightman.

I attack some lorries and miss each time, and White puts them on fire. I machine gun one, and then see our troops creeping forward and mortar smoke and explosions on the edge of a wood, so go down to look for a target in it. Am below 1000 feet when a burst comes up by my left elbow. It is deflected by a Lewis gun drum, but wounds my gunner, Williams, in the back. Only a deep graze I think, but I push off home, to find the whole squadron waiting anxiously on the polo ground as we are a long time away, and CR42s had been reported there during our absence. My bombing is getting bad again.

May 31st 1941

Habbaniya

The pilot was captured, an Italian who had flown from Rhodes only the day before. He said the Wops had relieved the Germans in this country, so that's why no Messersmiths (sic) had been about lately. Yesterday went and bombed Washash Camp, across the Iron Bridge and near the King's Palace at Baghdad. I put a stick between the ends of two long barracks, hitting both, then four 20lb bombs through the roof of another one. One Sanderson in a Gladiator force landed some days ago on Falluja Plain and walked in by night through Iraqi patrols. The Levies refused to admit him by the wire, so he had to spend the night in the graveyard, with all the new Iraqi unburied dead.

Rachid Ali departed for Persia, and the new Government gave back the Ambassador his wireless to send a message asking for peace terms. Letter from Bill. C.O. said we would go to an Operational Training Unit in Egypt, and the other boys to do their Intermediate training in Rhodesia!

June 2nd 1941

BAGHDAD TAKEN AND ARMISTICE GRANTED. Germans supposed to have arrived with fifty and to have left with twenty-two planes. An ME110 found on the ground today, and one Blenheim vanished on recco two days ago. Dan announced today the dissolution of the squadron and final dissolution of 4 FTS. The Audaxes are to be flown to Egypt, and instructors probably to form a fighter and bomber squadron here.

Nigen Gribbons turns up last night, his regiment being Brigade reserve out near the hotel by the lakeside. Bob May and I drive him back, slightly intoxicated, then stop for supper there, just like old Frontier days – eaten in a bare tent under a new moon. Stonhill back from captivity, having been taken up to Kirkuk and seen some Germans there. Thirty-seven prisoners returned, including John Addy.

June 6th 1941

HABBANIYA

31 SQUADRON ARRIVED HERE. Dougie Homes, Bird and O'Neil staying here, the rest in the AHQ Mess. They bring the 'onlooker' with them. Met one Walters, RIASC, at the swimming pool who left 56th in 1937. He said Willie Armstrong has a staff job in the Shatt-el-Arab hotel in Basrah. Nine Harts and nine Oxfords have gone to Egypt, but Allan (Haig) and I are still here. Germans, in French-type machines, raid Amman yesterday, so it won't be long before they are here.

Looked over an ME110 in a hanger today, built in 1940. Flew a Hart from the racecourse, to the main 'drome, and also gave it an air test. Nothing registered on the ASI (airspeed indicator) and it was a more frightening trip than any I did in this war. Landed with some engine and a good drop! – but she stayed down.

June 13th, 1941

YESTERDAY I GO UP IN A BLENHEIM with Stonhill down to Basrah. A drink at the airport, and then off to see Willie Armstrong at Force HQ, whilst Stony goes to the RAF station. Willie very busy, and only able to have a few words with him, but he says 56th still in Wana, Maitland France is with the 59th in Palestine, and Abbot's on a parachutist course at home. Then on to Shaibah, very hot and reminiscent of Manzai.

Lunch with Kenneth Smith in the Mess, and they have a skull on the mantelpiece with a plate on it "The winner of the high diving competition 19 – "

Return after lunch and I drive for a bit, but bloody awful and I can't keep on a straight course. Today they decide to send us to Egypt, and eventually Rhodesia for an ATS course, so Allan and I fix ourselves up with a Hart each. If we get there I expect I shall be discovered, *(that he had cheated on his eyesight test to join the RAF)*, but shall have seen a bit of the world beforehand. One can't take much in the back of a Hart, and I shall most likely be landed with a passenger at the last moment. More kit to lose!

5

June - August 1941

Advanced Flying Training School

RAF Ambala,
Punjab

June 15th 1941

Route:
Habbaniya-Rutbah: 190 miles
Rutbah-H4: 130 miles
H4-LG22: 81 miles
LG22-Asraq: 20 miles
Asraq-Ma'an: 137 miles
Ma'an-Akaba: 62 miles
Akaba-Ismailia: 180 miles

I leave in 6020 (a Hart)[1] at about 6.00 am with suitcase and kitbag in the back seat.

First stop Rutbah, despite my formation leader, a Hurricane sergeant, doing his best to lose the way, and doing a sudden steep turn across my bows. The Essex Yeomanry mob look on whilst we refuel, a lengthy process for 11 Harts, but we are able to get tea and bread and jam from the troops in the fort. Then on to H4, where an ME110 had been sighted the day before, and one of our machines' undercarts is written off. Then along the pipeline and away at LG22 to Azraq and Ma'an. On the way, Metcalfe, leading the formation, sees an unmarked landing ground and goes down to investigate, and of course all the other nine Harts land too. But we reach Ma'an, 3000 feet up, and decide to stay the night.

We three, and three more out of a Rapide[2] – Pollock, Dunlop-Mackenzie and an American from Beirut – are all put up by one Warren of TJFF *(Trans Jordan Frontier Force)*. An excellent dinner, booze and breakfast. Lovely sleeping out on his verandah, after my first dinner since bully beef and biscuits.

I take Col Pollock to look for Petra and on the second attempt, the map being wrong, we get the right place near Wadi Musa, but can't find Petra. A mass of great pink canyons, and the most wicked country I ever saw. On the 10th, flew down early to Akaba, thinking Lawrence all the way, then across the Sinai over low cloud to Geneifa. We land at the wrong place first, where Allan lets a South African take up his Hart dual and shows off, without telling him of the luggage stowed in the fuselage.

Geneifa's just a camp, newly built, and nothing is known of us. But we are told to clock in and stay. The Mess sergeant was a bit doubtful about quarters, so after one thing and another we dump our kit and go off in a lorry, with a suitcase each, with Metcalfe (84th Squadron) to Ismailia, where he is stationed, intending vaguely to take French leave and stay the night. Go through miles of tented camps in the desert, all sorts, including an Italian prison camp and a military detention camp, very grim, where could be seen the prisoners in rows on their knees picking up stones, which were then thrown down for them to do it again.

Tea in the Mess at Ismailia, where we saw two halves of a ship blown up in the canal by an 'acoustic' mine, then Allan says "How far to Cairo?" Someone says "I'm just going and have two seats", so he drags me off there much against my will, as I fear that damn adjutant in Geneifa. We go to the Carlton, then on to Tommy's Gezira Club. Some Egyptian girl, horrid, produced by a hotel bearer, and end up with Teddy Humphries watching cabaret at the Continental. He says we are due for India, Haig and I, so the next morning we go round to Air HQ, and find a signal from the Air Ministry ordering our return to India to "complete training". They decide to send us by air, and one Squadron Leader Jolley, Movement Officer, produces a staff car to take us down to Geneifa for our kit. We arrive back about 5.00 pm and are told we can't go next morning after all, but must wait till the next plane. Then at 6.00 pm, having tea in the Carlton, we are ordered to leave tomorrow and go round now for weights, and to get an identity photo. Christ! Allan Haig is sulking because he has to return to India and refuses to cooperate in my bandobast-making,[3] and is a wet blanket.

I go to the Continental, like the old 'Brass-arse', full of Brigadiers with hats over one eye, some with only one eye, and all a bit drunk. Then I take Tiny to Tommy's bar, Teddie joins us, and then off to bed. Up at 4 and are shepherded from Shepheards Hotel to the (flying) boat and off. Land at Akaba, circle Petra and down at Basra, where we meet Gordon Arthur. Then reach Bahrein at 6.30 pm. After dinner we get in a taxi and drive to the BAPCO club (British American Petroleum Company), asking for Scottie Anderson, Joe Cooper and the boys. They can't be found, but some old fossil looks after us, introduces us to the Club Secretary, and we have free drinks and dancing the rest of the night. Bacon and eggs in his house and get to bed on the rest house roof at 3.00 am, to be woken by dawn flies and hot sun at 5.

I bought a new watch in Cairo, foolishly, as with no duty here (Bahrein, at the time of writing) could have got a good one. We shall get to India before news of our arrival I hope. Very sticky here, and having my jacket and wings on last night made things a bit difficult.

[1] *The serial number of the Hart trainer biplane he was flying.*
[2] *The de Havilland DH.89 Dragon Rapide was a 1930s short-haul biplane airliner.*
[3] *A word relating to 'bandaid' – a Hindi word meaning 'tying together of things in an organised fashion'. Still used in India today. Presumably in this context 'packing up'.*

June 19th 1941

FLYING TRAINING SCHOOL, AMBALA

WE SPEND THE 13TH AT THE BAPCO CLUB, with one Wally Jones and his wife, swimming, golf and a cinema. On the 14th leave and reach Karachi, very sticky, at 5.30 pm. Difficulty with customs over my unregistered camera and my .38, but we get away eventually to Killarney Hotel. We go round to the Simonsons and they get a bit of a shock. Dinner there, and at midnight I go to the Gym Club and meet Dicky Bird, Small, the Evans, Phyllis

Macfarlane, and Celia Mockett and her husband John Mansel. I am congratulated on my return – "So glad you are alive old boy". And next evening we leave for Ambala as the embarkation people fixed up. They knew we were coming!

Stayed at Lahore, went and had dinner with the Walters at Model Town and tried to catch the 9.55 train. But I can't hurry a late dinner etc so we stay the night on the roof and leave next morning, reaching Ambala at 3.25 pm. They, of course, don't know we are coming, and are four weeks into the A.T.S. course[1], so we ask for leave to Naini Tal. Granted by the Chief Training Instructor, Harris, who says "keep your hat on". Then it's withdrawn until the CO returns from leave.

Today the CFI[2], S/Ldr Simpson, takes us up. Allan goes up, then I, and do some circuits and landings, though they are not liked, and I say "Yes sir, no sir, etc", and looking round like a giraffe. Then find it wasn't Simpson at all but one "Tiny" Howell. I am allowed up solo in an Audax[3] with strict instructions to do a few steep and medium turns, and be down in 20 minutes! Did I know how my parachute worked?!

[1] *Advanced training school.*
[2] *Chief Flying Instructor.*
[3] *The biplane that Colin flew in the Battle of Habbaniya, see Volume 1, May 1941.*

June 25th 1941

AMBALA

ALLAN GOES OFF TO NAINI TAL for the weekend to see his fiancée Violet, and I stay here. Go and see Peter Fisher, RA, ex-Abbottabad, and fix myself up with a horse. It comes round when I want it and I tip the orderly at the end of the month. Buy myself some bush shirts of my own design and a R12/- pair of jodhpurs to go with the horse, but the seat is so thin I have to send them back after two rides.

We are told to fit into the course and make up the leeway, best we can. Yesterday night we went flying with flares only. I have half an hour dual, during which I have no earthly idea where the ground is, and the instructor lands it each time. He sends me solo and I manage to get down twice, though damn bad ones. I also do an Oblique Pin Pointing flight, but so damn bumpy, expect it will be useless. These Indian P/O's (pilot officers) are like a lot of small boys in their behaviour. There are British P/O's from Burma and Mongolian looking fellows with them. India's white contingent are all Sergeants for some reason.

108 degrees yesterday and it's too hot to sleep outside under a net. The "Who're you?" bird is about everywhere. There's a swimming pool in the Mess, in which I wallow like a buffalo as it is too small for much serious swimming. The bazaar is very cheap, luckily, as I have to buy all my kit again.

June 29th 1941
Ambala

ANOTHER LONG WEEKEND, but I seem to be still here. I am introduced to air-to-air but seem to make rather a cock of it. My rifle arrives from Abbottabad, but there's going to be difficulty getting ammo as it all appears to have been taken over by the Government for 'parashots'. Do 16 miles on the horse yesterday, which rather shakes him. It doesn't seem at all as though I was once at the war. I feel I have been in India all the time.

Letter from John Palmer in a new battalion in Bareilly, but the 56th are still at Wana. I hire a table fan, R5/-, and sleep outside with it full on and no mosquito net, and am cool for once. Before leaving Habbaniya I sent my trunk, suitcase and spare bistar[1] to transport section to be sent to Abbottabad, but naturally nothing known of them. Annoying, as my .22 Winchester is with them.

[1] *Meaning unclear.*

July 6th 1941

OUT AT 3.30 AM IN A TONGA to the Nullah by the cantonment water supply. Off on foot to look for black buck in the woods north of Barana village. I do one stalk but find there are no spikes or buck so leave it, and am following some more through the scrub, when suddenly they turn and come bounding back. Have just time to step behind a bush which they all come past, giving a violent leap on sighting me. I watch the heads flash past and see a pair of horns, so swing with him and fire, bringing down a two year old (red) buck at about 10 yards, with a bullet from my .423 Mauser straight up his arse.

The shikari[1] produces a 10 inch knife, cleans it, and ties its legs for carriage back to the tonga. Then off we set, determined to get a proper "Black" black buck this time. I see a herd but nothing black and reach the tonga at 9.30 pm, carrying one shoe. I am wearing my new sambhar boots and they pinch so much I have to take one off.

Allan off for the third weekend running to Naini Tal. Am shown dive bombing and told mine is too steep – they do 5000 - 3000 feet here. Saw a lot of fox-like animals, locally called "longris". Give the shikari Rs13/- and the tonga walla Rs7/- for the day's outing. Wish I had my .22 which must still be in Habbaniya.

Have hired a small electric fan and sleep out with no net, and fan at half speed blowing straight from the foot of the bed, and get a very good sleep out of it. Have taken on a local bearer since the first day for Rs25/- and 3/- commission, instead of Attham Khan's[2] 32/- and 5/-. Wonder when I shall next get out of India, not this war time I expect. Does anyone ever get drunk in this Mess?

[1] *Hunter or guide.*
[2] *His former bearer.*

July 10th 1941

I BELIEVE I HAD A BIRTHDAY YESTERDAY[1] – rode the horse to my favourite wood and then filled myself with beer and Pimms, had dinner, and so to bed. I wish I had someone to talk with here over a mug of beer. Young Haig doesn't drink, but I could talk with him in Habbaniya, but somehow not now – we've drifted apart since returning to this country. It must have been those two days in Cairo! I should like to be sitting in Tommy's Bar, over a large cold shandy, with Bill Robinson and Mike Jacobs!

Peter Petit reported "missing believed prisoner". Munshi[2] Professor Khan Sahib Haidari calls on me yesterday. He shows me all his chits, a photo of himself, tells a few praiseworthy stories and just drips, oozes and humbles himself for ten minutes. All for the money he hopes to make out of me. I am nearly sick when he goes.

[1] *July 9th was his 23rd birthday .*
[2] *Hindi title meaning wise man.*

July 14th 1941

AMBALA

WENT UP TO MISSOURIE FOR THE WEEKEND with A. Haig. We get a lift in a car with Taylor and Scorer, two sergeant pilots on this course, and reach there about 7.30 pm. Tea in Dehra Dun and up through the mist to Missourie, 6500 feet. Very good shooting country, and round Dehra Dun too.

We go to stay with Captain A.J. Lys, Violet's uncle, where her people are staying. Of course Allan does not tell them he is coming and complete panic reigns as we catch them at dinner. Still, they put us up. A scotch mist and rain all day, spent in the "family circle", after a visit to Missourie in the morning. Reminiscent of Kashmir and Abbottobad. We return at last "gate" at 5.45 pm, arriving here at 11 pm, and damn hot. Still, a pleasant trip and some nice jungle, green and lush in the mist, and cold. Duggie Holmes arrives with General Wavell.

The instructors from 4 FTS formed into a fighter squadron and were operating over Palmyra from H4 and were ambushed by alot of Huns. John Craigie killed, Dan Cremin[1] shot down and got away. Peter Williams a prisoner, but presumably back with the armistice. Gordon Arthur took off one evening from Baghdad for Basrah and his burnt out plane was found the next morning. He had two American bankers on board I believe.

[1] *Colin's former instructor and flight commander in Habbaniya, see Volume 1, Jan-May 1941.*

July 20th 1941

Ambala

Two hits in the 50 yards ring yesterday, dive bombing. Haig went off to Naini Tal on Friday and one of the CGI's little chits came round on Saturday morning asking him to report. I say to bearer he is sick and later they ring up at lunchtime for him and I tell the boy "Nei hai..."[1]

I go out at 3.30 pm to the waterworks and we walk about in the evening unsuccessfully, though I shoot a hare with Reggie Wall's .22 BSA repeater, a shocking gun, over who's sights I haven't the mastery. I sleep in the open on a comfortable camp bed and pillow, after eating a cold meat salad meal, stuffed between two plates. I sleep to the bubbling of a hookah and the tonga wallah's pony's grunts. At dawn we go off and walk for four hours through the jungle. I get several good shots at a jackal, but owing to not knowing the sights I miss. Suddenly a big black buck leaps across a clearing, but by the time I have changed guns he is lost. Eventually find a herd sitting down bang in the middle of some fields on our way home. I am led up to some cover, disguised under a sheet as a villager, and the others go round. Eventually I get a shot from lying down behind a bush at about 150 feet and the rifle bounces on my shoulder and I miss. Drank a lot of water out of a well, and got home for a good bath at 12.30.

[1] *Meaning unclear.*

July 27th 1941

KARACHI

WAS PREPARING FOR A LONG WEEKEND in Missourie when Wigg suddenly comes into the pupils room to say that Dunford Wood and Haig will go down to Karachi tonight with Ft/Lt Gambert to collect three Audaxes. Johnny Benbow came down the other day from Karachi as Adjutant to the 7/15. Well, we left Ambala by Frontier Mail at 2.30 pm, actually 4.30 after we'd spent time waiting on the platform, and managed to get an air-conditioned coach from Rokri, after all the Staff College had got out.

Arrived here yesterday, and spent the morning checking the aircraft and trying to swing the compasses. I have a shot, correcting for coefficients ABC and the result is 342 degrees instead of 360 degrees. Eventually I try again and get it right.[1]

After lunch, Allan and I pick up Reggie Wall, and go to the Simonsons, and then I get thirty 10.75mm cartridges off Suleiman Omer. Then to the boat club for swimming and tea. That evening, after drinks with the Simonsons, and banter about twins and quins (as Joan's ETA is next week sometime) (having a baby), Reggie, Allan and I dine at a Chinese Restaurant off "Stillborn baby soup". Then on to the Gym Club and join up with Gambert ("Gosling"), Bishop and Nick Tremblett. A bottle of whisky is produced and kummels for Reggie and Allan, and down we get to it. Towards the end I get Horse Evans over, and the Gosling prepares to pull his leg, finally ending up by being damn rude to him – all over nothing.

Or rather over "us chaps who teach you young fighter boys to fly". Bishop in the meantime telling me about "2000lb overload and the soldier didn't know how to fire his anti-tank rifle". Saw Walsh, RA.

[1] *Aircraft compasses are affected by ferrous components, and have adjusting magnets which can be very finely positioned to counteract these effects ('taking out the coefficients'). What he is referring to is adjusting the magnets to take out as much inaccuracy as possible, with the residual inaccuracies being recorded on a 'compass card' kept beside the display in the aircraft, so that the pilot could mentally subtract/ add this figure to get an accurate compass heading.*

July 29th 1941

JODHPUR

ON SUNDAY I GO OUT WITH DICKIE BIRD to lunch at the Mansels. He is 1st Lieut in HMIS Rakardar, the RIN training school, and lives in Manora. There is a wonderful cool breeze all the year there, and they need blankets in June and July. After lunch, at 3, we go sailing, and then more drinks and back on the 10.20 pm boat. Monday at 11 am we leave for Jodhpur which we reach at about 4 pm. A bloody awful journey over Sind desert, the bumps are so strong I sometimes have to take both hands to the stick. We miss Jodhpur and we only find it by swooping low over the railway stations and reading their names. I am on gravity (reserve tank), with about eight minutes left when I land. The RAF have an EFTS[1] here, and it must be one of the best stations in India. They live in the State Hotel, polo and pig-sticking alternate days and good shooting nearby. Well, we are lodged in State Hotel and drink from 6 pm to 2 am. Hotel and then to Club and back to Sq/Ldr Bonnar's room for the last black Dutch beer in India. Pete Bond and his mistress there, and met the instructor at the flying club. Gossle in cracking form with his French Canadian accent and jokes (Napoleon etc). He was at sea and then in the Palestine police before joining the RAF.

I have a run of nimbus[2] about 11 pm which does me well and I remain sober, but A. Haig in a bad way, even smoking cigarettes! We go down again to Karachi for ATS and he is due to go tomorrow with advance party. However, I am changing over, as he wants to go to Naini to see Violet. So once more that damn train.

Gordon Arthur's crash killed four passengers from Baghdad. A bad show as he had been at a cocktail party, and none of them had signed "blood chits". Gozzle got a DFC for rescuing Leicesters on Green Dome, 21/8/39. Much concern that I didn't wear my wings and medal on my bush shirt. All the Army wear their medals on their shirts now and it looks damn silly to me. However, mine is a light one, but perhaps I might do something about it.

[1] *Elementary Flying Training School.*
[2] *Normally cloud, in this context unclear.*

August 3rd 1941

KARACHI

I TAKE A BATCH OF INDIAN AIR FORCE PILOTS down here by train, quite comfortably sharing an air-conditioned coach with Bhose and G.S. Singh. Here at Karachi I go into town to see Tylers for a car, but no luck, though I eventually manage to find a Rs 4/- per diem for hire. Then I go to the boat club and see George Holland's name on a list, so ring him up in the Baluchi Regiment. I have drinks and dinner with him, and hear all about Eritrea etc., in fact I can hardly open my mouth about Iraq at all, then to bed.

Saturday I drive in, and take out Reggie Wall shopping, and we have a drink with Joan Simonson, whose ETA is long overdue now. In the evening to the boat club to swim with Tom and Elizabeth Charters (40th Pathans) and no dinner. They drop us at the hospital at 7.30 pm, and Reggie too ill to go out further, and having a hospital curfew at 10 pm anyhow. So I change there and have a beer. Then I go out and look for a certain cinema, which I can't find, and I can't find the way to the Gym Club either, eventually ending up there at 10.30 where I meet Turner in the bar.

See George Holland later, but no dances and nothing exciting and bed by 3.00 am, after some pretty dangerous driving back to Drigh Road with most of the headlights blued out.

Today I spend the morning filling ammunition belts for tomorrow's shooting, and have a slight touch of the old malaise. (Boozer's gloom – though not caused through booze – just 'blues'.)

August 5th 1941

KARACHI

SUNDAY AFTERNOON I GO TO THE BOAT CLUB with a book, and in comes a stomach, surmounted by a moustache and eyeglass, which could only be Bernard Fergusson, a major, and so it was[1]. He invites me to dinner at the Bristol and introduces me to his travelling companion, Brigadier Bruce. Badly shaken, I beat it to Drigh Road and change into tunic and slacks and off to dinner. He came out with Wavell, on the Intelligence staff, and is off back to the Middle East on a flying boat the next day. He produces a bottle of wine and we discuss the lads on No 1 Company.

He was in Syria with Bruce and is very interested in my stories of Iraq. Coming back, the first time in my life driving a car whilst under the "affluence of incohol", I run out of petrol by Doc Ritchie's bungalow and have to walk the last half mile.

Next day I go front gunning, damn bad, but still get 11, the top score. Sergeant Baldwin got 16 but is disqualified for going too low. I get the afternoon off and go into town to swim at the Boat Club, and meet Horse Evans (Major Harry K. Evans, USAF). I arrange to pick him up at the Gym at 6.30 and go to the flicks. The car breaks down again by the B.M.H., petrol again, and I have to get the mechanic out of his hotel and go through the drill of filling the autovac once more. I arrive at 7.30 to find Evans playing bridge and just about to finish, but by nine he hadn't finished so I call on the Simonsons a get dinner, bringing Braithwaite home afterwards.

Today another very bad front gun exercise, clouds at 1000 feet and a No. 4 stoppage[2] which I fail to clear, after 74 rounds. I go into town after breakfast and buy a clock for Allan's wedding present (28/-). The climate is good here with that breeze I like so much, and reminiscent of Tiree[3]. Met Langford James here, who is an observer in a Blenheim squadron, and greets me like a long-lost friend.

[1] *Bernard Fergusson later commanded a column of Chindits during the Burma Campaign, part of Brigadier Orde Wingate's long-range penetration expeditions behind Japanese lines. See Operation Longcloth. After the war, he became Governor General of New Zealand.*
[2] *The WW1 vintage Lewis machine gun with its circular magazine was notorious for stoppages and jams.*
[3] *An island in Scotland where Colin was brought up by his grandparents, while his parents were living in Malaya. His father was a lawyer in Ipoh, and his grandfather, Hugh MacDiarmid, was the Factor to the Duke of Argyll on Tiree.*

August 8th 1941

KARACHI

WENT TO THE BOAT CLUB TUESDAY NIGHT and met one Crosbie, a sea captain, who staked 7/- on the fruit machine which I helped him lose. I get slightly inebriated, and join up with Boulton's party, and dance with Braithwaite's wife Mary. Next day I go to the zoo at the shrine of Mangho Pir and see 'holy' crocodiles, with Reggie Wall and W/C Selwyn Roberts, ex Habbaniya[1]. He says the instructors have all pushed off to Rhodesia.

Well, after 11, 10 and 7, today I score 50. This I do by giving up all idea of stall turns, but I just throttle down slightly, then turn onto target, letting the nose drop, and with her speed she does not swing so much and is easier to keep on target, or so it seems, and I was able to pull out once or twice above 400 feet.

My application to stay out to Sunday evening and shoot crocodiles is refused, and I have to return Sunday morning (by W/C Mead, damn him).

Met Firmstone-Williams in the Boat Club. Have been having my war dreams again. I remember seeing parachute troops falling and a German attack by tanks under cover of smoke (or fog!).

[1] *W/C Selwyn-Roberts had commanded one of the squadrons of the Habbaniya Air Striking Force during the Battle and Siege of Habbaniya in May 1941.*

August 12th 1941

AMBALA

I GO TO DRINKS AT THE COMMISSIONER'S HOUSE, am introduced to Mrs Clark. Dinner with the Commissioner, where Philip Lorraine is staying, then on to the pictures with George and Margaret, and then on to the Boat Club. Next day my shooting not too good, but I got in two good bursts and score 44. Some Indian gets 48 that day.

That afternoon I pay my bills, spend some time alone at the zoo, then drinks at Dirk's house where David Evans is staying and they take me to the pictures. I then go on to the Gym (Club) – party is Lorraine, Mrs Clark and Eileen Collins but depart early, 2.00 am, tired and bored. Next morning I drive the car to the station and hand it over to Allan Haig. See Sam Lewis on the train and he tells me to write about my pay to Baler at AH/Q. Off we go on a bloody journey to Ambala, no A/C, and my prickly heat spreading all the time. The rest of the gang are in a special coach which gets detached in the night and left behind.

Arrive back here at 7.00 pm, bearer out. However, a good bath and three Pimms improve things.

August 17th 1941

NOTHING TO DO HERE. This week I fly once and do three hours of lectures, the rest of the time being spent in sitting in lecture rooms as per programme, or watching other people fly. Our weekend is stopped as some I.T.S. blokes are caught AWOL.

Yesterday (Saturday) G.S. Singh suggests going to Delhi for a binge. I second it, and we get "Ginger" Baldwin and "Buster" Taylor. Leave at 4.00 pm in G.S.'s car, a Mercury, and reach Delhi – 120 miles – in just over two hours. We go to Maidens for drinks and dinner and then watch cabaret. I meet the Maynards and Manichal, and also Doc Cunningham, now in the Armoured Corps. Ginger and Buster (both Sergeants) get to work with a dance each, and then we go to the Gym Club at 1.00 am. Here I meet Richard Hungerford and his wife. The two Sergeants get a bit tight. Ginger does a lot of dancing – solo and dual – and looks the complete thug. I try to collect them all at about 2.30, but as I collect two I go in search of the third, and then the other two percolate back and start dancing again. We get away at 3.15 am, and end up with no petrol at a pump 25 miles short of Ambala at 7. They refuse to supply us without coupons, and Ginger nearly gets arrested for assaulting the pump. He gets the beaker filled up, but can't find the tap to let it out into the pump. A police Havildar looks on, but luckily does not take him in. Eventually someone comes back with some kerosene oil and we get back to Ambala at 8.00 am.

A double breakfast – then punishment "prep" 9-11 and then I sleep 11.30 - 5.00 pm. G.S. Singh is the brother of the Raja of Baratpur (near Agra). He has a few cars, a house in Ambala and Delhi, and a royal standard on his car. Spent 15 years in England, at Wellington (College), and as English as they make 'em. He doesn't go about with other Indians on the course, but with the British and one David Bhose, an Anglo-Indian in the I.C.S. at Madras (Indian Civil Service). He had his Jubilee and Coronation ribbons on last night and borrowed 300/- for his party! "Ginger" Baldwin – the 'compleat Thug'. 33 years old (how he is a pilot, God knows), ex-engineer on a Tea plantation in Assam, white hunter, also an ivory poacher and God knows what. Lost two fingers in fights, and wanted by the Assam police.

The rest of the course is Indian and Anglo-Indian pilot officers, the British being acting sergeants. Most of the Indians are a bit 'Babuish'[1] and not like Bikram[2] at all. A few – very few – make good pilots, but the average are pretty bloody. They read books and stick compasses up each other's bottoms in between, like a lot of small children. Now they are coming in as cadets, and about time too.

D. Braithwaite of the Burma Forestry Service heads a small group from Burma, including British, Burmans, Anglo-Burmans and a Chinaman. These Burmans stand out a mile from the Indians.

[1] *Meaning unclear.*
[2] *Hindi word meaning bravery, prowess, valour or power, a name given to the Hindu god Vishnu.*

August 20th 1941

AMBALA

DRINKS WITH GAMBERT LAST NIGHT and I consume three bottles of Muree beer at a sitting. I went out the other day down the Lahore Road to try and get a black buck, but the country was underwater. Walked for three hours in the afternoon sun, the heat reflecting off the mud – horrid. The shikari carried me over a few streams.

Some excellent formation flying the other day, the best flying that I have had here yet. Peeling off, low flying and Prince of Wales feathers[1], on a lovely day with no wind. Formatted with Wigg today above the clouds, and got the same impression of speed as in low flying formation.

A bit of football. My kit has reached Bombay but customs won't clear it. They required a certificate from my C.O. about my .460 service revolver, with which W/C Mead refused to have anything to do, the Shit. So I went to Harris, the C.G.I., and we compromised with a chit to the effect that he saw no reason to disbelieve my statement. Haig saw Dan Cremin and Frewin in Karachi on their way to Rhodesia.

[1] *A pattern of formation flying.*

August 27th 1941

AMBALA

WE HAVE A TACTICAL EXERCISE. Two flights at Jullandur, two in the A.T.S. hangar and two out in a field near the grass farm. I am out at the grass farm under "Logger" Powley. We have dispersed aircraft, tents and slit trenches and pupils as flight commanders, intelligence officers etc. It ought to be a good show if well organised. I do a day's work, first time since May, putting up tents and digging trenches. We are raided by Jullandur flight, who drop a plucked chicken, cleaned out, along with a note saying "Stuff it". We do counter raids etc. Yesterday was employed from 2.30 - 5.30 pm supervising "C.C." pupils digging, a thankless job. Haig in Jullandur. I have a drink with the C.G.I., Harris (Squadron Leader), and he is quite human out of office hours.

Nearly an incident today, when Mehra borrowed my helmet and goggles without my knowledge. Then, once in the plane, he throws mine out to Glover and changes them for some plain glass ones. But no one has commented on it so far![1]

[1] *Readers of the first volume of these diaries will remember Colin's poor eyesight, which he has so far kept hidden from his superiors, having cheated on his medical when he first joined the RAF. Secretly, he had some specially adapted goggles made with special lenses.*

230

August 28th 1941

NEARLY WENT MAD LAST NIGHT with toothache. Started around 8.30 pm, so I had no dinner and hopped into bed. Eventually Chandikar suggested going to get me some medicine, so I sent him off to B.M.H. and he returned with two aspirins. I took one, a drink of water to swallow it, and the ache left immediately.

This morning Taylor and I go off – we recco Dhuri railway junction, then do some flashbulb bombing from 6000 feet of Nakodar. Then he leads for a low level attack on Jullandur where I throw out Haig's letters. Taylor and I go in from different angles, in fact I cross under him at one point – I thought maybe I was a bit too low. We return via Nakodar where we do some practise dive bombing – on returning to Ambala I see the camp being 'attacked', so dive in and take three numbers[1]. I then land, and another flight of four comes in. I take off quick and pursue them, overhauling them about three miles beyond the city. I take their numbers, 'cock a snook' at Baldwin, who is leading them, and then home. Then I get my raspberry.

[1] *Taking an aircraft's serial number during an exercise counted as shooting them down.*

August 29th 1941

NIGHT FLYING LAST NIGHT IN FORMATION, led by F/Lt Tate to Jullandur and back. Over Jullandur, Tate goes down to shoot them up, leaving Thin and me in echelon going round in circles. I don't know what happens but I damn near crash into him, and we just manage to mutually bank out of the way. Thin tells his observer Poonen to fire a Very light to show up country to Tate – he refuses, saying it's not his job, and he won't "take the responsibility". Head back, and a good landing.

Today to Jullandur – low level at 500 feet as observer, and have never felt so ill for a long time. As we were formatting, the ship was never on an even keel and I got hell. Off to Jullandur tomorrow, where Taylor and I will no doubt pay the penalty for our 'beat up' yesterday. My kit from Iraq arrives, filling me with nostalgia.

6

September 1941 - Januray 1942

28 Squadron

Kohat
North-West Frontier

September 4th 1941

Haig and I suddenly get posted, he to 20 Squadron and me to 28. I am told on Saturday to pack up straight away, and leave on Monday at 15.45, reaching here on Tuesday at 17.30.

Alan's marriage fixed for 17th, and I agree to try and meet him at Faletti's[1] on 16th. I travel up with two Nepalese officers, who look a bit Scottish. I get a room and a bearer here, and meet the C.O. in the Mess and have a few drinks. The adjutant, F/Lt Johnson, is very anxious to strip me of my wings and medal, especially the latter, as it is not yet being worn by the RAF.

First day I take four naval ratings up for air experience, and then half an hour's engine test. Nothing to do today, but I fix myself up with an hour's morse[2], and spend the rest of the time in A.I.L.O.'s office[3] reading back publications of military interest, which I haven't seen in the last year.

Last night went along to the "Piffer Mess" (Frontier Force Rifles), but 7/13 out at Thal, though I saw Hugh Garton there, in the Club, and had a few beers with him. The Mess here is some way from the aerodrome, outside the Cantonment, and a lorry goes every morning at 8.00 am and back at 1.00 pm. Tuesday and Thursday they go 7 to 9.00 pm for some reason.

Peter Petit recaptured, and with his face in this month's "Onlooker".

Five Lysanders[4] on their way from Karachi, and then I will be foxed, as someone will remark on my wearing goggles, if they aren't noticed in the flight office beforehand, blast it.

---

[1] A well known Peshawar hotel.
[2] Morse code practise.
[3] Air Intelligence Liaison Officer.
[4] A type of aircraft used in an Army cooperation role, which Colin would become very familiar with.

September 5th 1941

KOHAT

I SIT ABOUT ALL DAY IN PENTON'S OFFICE and do an hour's bugger all. Raining today, and continual thunderstorms. The Lysanders were unable to land as it was too wet, so they went instead to Dehra Ghazi Khan. They now have to get the petrol shifted across the Indus to D.G.K.

I study A.P. 1176 "Army Cooperation". Suffering from a kind of foot rot and cut cuticle combined, and go about in one stocking and two chaplies.[1]

[1] *Indian slipper or sandal.*

September 10th 1941

KOHAT

THE LYSANDERS ARRIVE, and I have now done 1.15 hours in them, though I don't seem to have gotten them taped yet. Today I do a Tac/R (tactical reconnaissance) to Fort Lockhart at 6600 feet. Wonderful visibility. A 'V' on the hillside near Hangar and a '54' on someone's parade ground.[1]

My foot now much better and I get a game of tennis. Much bridge with Traill, Stilliard and Penton. In fact I am having a damn good time as well as behaving myself. The I.A.F. boys (Indian Air Force) prang the Lysanders the first day at Peshawar, by braking on landing and putting a wing in. 2 Squadron I.A.F. is now here, and we call them "The Brethren". They fly Wapitas.

28 (Army Cooperation) Squadron

Sq Ldr W. Coade AFC
F/Lt W. Traill DFC (now Sq Ldr)

235

F/Lt N.H. Elliot (my C flight C/O)
F/Lt A.S. Mann
F/Lt W.C. Duncan
F/Lt K.R. Butler
F/Lt A.S. Johnson (from Glasgow) Adjutant
P/O C.C. Dickson (Trained in Rhodesia and just arrived
in India)
F/Lt D. Stilliard – station adjutant
F/O Butcher – equipment officer
A.I.L.O.'s (Army liaison officers)
Capt Vir Singh – 14 Punjab Rifles
Acting Capt C.A. Penton – Border Rifles

In addition, F/Lt O.A. Hammerbeck and F/O E.O. Clark, war-torn horses from the Middle East, have arrived. I reckon they have had it! Hammerbeck took a Lysander to Risalpur today and shot it up. Sq Ldr Malling, C/O of 5 squadron, rang up and complained, and now our new station C/O, Wing Commander Thripp, has taken his flight away from him.

I meet Springheel on the golf links the other day, and see a 'Harlow'[2] over from 5 Squadron.

[1] Signals for incoming aircraft.
[2] The Harlow PJC-2 was a 1930s American four-seat cabin monoplane.

September 17th 1941

LAHORE

ALLAN'S WEDDING TODAY. I see Jerry Beale in hospital and also have Hugh Easton round for a drink one night. Then last Sunday Penton, Watson, self and Hammerbeck went to Peshawar in latter's car. We swim, drink gin and return after lunch. I see Basil Henson there. On the way back we run into a terrific rain storm on Kohat Pass and pick up some stranded travellers whose car had broken

One of the new Lysanders of 28 Squadron. They had a fixed undercarriage and a maximum speed of 212 mph, and were largely used in any Army Cooperation role, as they had the ability to land on very short airstrips. Most famously, they were used for landing Free French resistance agents and picking up downed airmen in occupied north-west Europe during the war.

down. As Clark has to have a medical in Lahore on 17th, I am allowed to do a cross country and fly him down.

We came down yesterday in an Audax – K4850 - left 09.30 arrived 11.28 – navigation was quite simple all the way down. We come to Falletti's where I see Allan, and after a rest we both repair to the Lettingtons for dinner. Here I see the Huggins, of 'City of Venice'1 fame – Eileen and Yolande are to be bridesmaids. I and elder Huggins finish off half a bottle of Irish whiskey and get pretty merry altogether. Then back to Falletti's where we waylay a chap and borrow his braces, as Allan hasn't got any. I wake up at 3.30 am bitten to hell and wet through as the fan has stopped, and take my mattress into Clark's room.

Off we go to church, in serge, Allan with his sword, when he decides his buttons aren't clean and off we troop back to the hotel. I go through the ceremony, a Roman Catholic one, as Best Man,

Allan Haig and his new bride, Violet Lettington.

and there seems to be a lot of bowing and scraping. Reception at "Stiffles" where I have coffee, champagne and a few meat rolls as breakfast.

Colin attempting to chat up a bridesmaid, looking nervous before his speech.

Then I have to make a speech to the bridesmaids and as far as I can remember I begin as follows:

"Ladies and gentlemen, before toasting the bridesmaids I believe I'm supposed to say a few words extolling their merits and virtues. In fact I had a letter from the Bride a few days ago with the curt instruction "Bring a prepared speech for the bridesmaids." Nothing about kissing them at all!

Well, I haven't brought one as I find it rather hard, not knowing them very well. I came out on the boat with them, but that was three years ago, and you know what shipboard life is like, so I think we might let bygones be bygones. Since then I have just heard tales of them, here and there, as they have flitted from place to place throughout India, but I'm taking them out tonight so tomorrow morning would be a different thing.

However, I think I'll take this opportunity of saying a few words about the bridegroom. I first met Allan Haig a year ago when we left the Army to seek our fortunes in the RAF, and we have had our ups and downs together from Ambala in the East to Cairo in the West. Now, in Karachi last autumn he was an ordinary, decent sort of chap – didn't smoke and didn't drink, keen on his flying, and studied hard at his navigation. He didn't go out much – though one day in January he went out one morning and we put his lunch and dinner out for him, but he didn't come back for four days! He must have been paying his bills!

We left India in January and I looked after him, helping him when he wanted help, advising him when he wanted advice – then I noticed a change – he suddenly seemed to come out in cigars and double brandies! He was quite honest about it – he didn't take any soda! So I watched him more carefully. When we came back to India in June we stopped in Lahore and he went and bought a ring. I didn't think it was anything to do with me, so I didn't comment on it. Then some three weeks later I saw him with a pipe in his mouth. I was rather annoyed, as I thought it was one of mine, but on going up to him I noticed it had some tobacco in it and he was striking matches. I asked him what he was doing, he said "Trying to light it" so I took it away from him, took the tobacco out, showed him how to fill it and light it. Then curiosity overcame me and I asked him what it was all about. He said "Well, it's always been my ambition to have a horse, a dog, a pipe and a wife". I hope you've got a horse by now. Then I began to put two and two together and thought "well, it may be a bit hard on some girl, but it's none of my business."

Later I was troubled by pangs of conscience so I wrote to Violet and told her that, as I thought she ought to know etc – a sort of unsolicited testimonial, and got an answer back, thanking me – she had noted the contents, would take the necessary action and ended up saying "well, I think I know him better than you do." So then I knew it was hopeless, and here you see the result

However, let us drink to the bridesmaids (Joan Lettington shouts out – "after all that") and if anyone likes to fix an appointment with me tomorrow morning I'll tell them all about them."

Sat down quick.

Saw Gage (5 Sqn) and Scowers (28 Sqn) at the hotel on the way back, and they said Harvey and Rao killed in low flying attack on Jullandur by a steep turn low down without banking over. Back to Stiffles for lunch, and am now in my room trying to recuperate.

[1] *The ship Colin came out to India on in 1938.*

September 19th 1941

KOHAT

WE TAKE YOLANDE AND EILEEN HUGGINS to dinner at Faletti's and to the cinema, after seeing the bridal train off. Next morning, while signing the movement book in the Adjutant's office, I see "JHS Broughton" down as orderly officer or something, and sure enough I find he and "Stooge" Garner working in the cypher office, being still off flying.[1]

Took off at 10.05 and got back in just over two hours to find that 2 Squadron had just had an accident. Muckerji and an airgunner, after low level bombing in an Audax, did a climbing turn, steep at 200-300 feet and slipped in, broke his undercarriage, turned over on his back, and both burnt to death on the bombing range. There's then a balls-up about the funeral, and I am the only British officer from 28 Squadron at the ceremony, though some of the others eventually make the burning party.

Today I have a shocking time in a Lysander, being unable to get it onto the ground. Twice I manage, but have to do ground loops to prevent going into the boundary fence, and third time takes about five circuits to get in. I must be using too much engine in assisted approach. I don't know.

[1] *Both flew with Colin in the Battle of Habbaniya in May 1941, and both were badly injured. Evidently they are still off flying. Colin was Jimmy Broughton's observer in an Audax when Broughton was shot through the jaw.*

241

September 25th 1941

I GET HELL'S OWN TOOTHACHE, so fly to Peshawar to have it done. One Major (S) Pank stops the tooth but not the ache so I go back there today, and he decides that it is the wisdom shifting the others, and so nothing to be done about it.

Yesterday Johnstone, Clark and I go to Jhelum in Audaxes. A very small landing ground and I muck up the first one and have to go round again; the first time since April before the war.[1] Then we have breakfast in 10/1 P.R. mess (Punjab rifles) and are due to take up some army officers afterwards. However, Johnny's and my planes refuse to start and we are late on the job, with the Brigadier fretting impatiently. I also take up the B.M. to look at some hills and he is apparently sick in the back, as I notice a funny smell on the way home, so we check in at Kohat and that's what it was.

After lunch we set off back, but my plane again bolshie and takes 30 minutes to get going. Last night I take Amrik Singh (4/12) to drinks with Jerry Beale. Neil Elliott goes off to command the Comms flight in Delhi and we give him a send off. Damn this tooth and jaw ache – the fifth day now!

[1] *He is likely referring to April 1941, before the Habbaniya war, when he was learning to fly an Audax, as he was not flying in April 1939.*

September 27th 1941

PETE JENNINGS ARRIVES AS C.O. and takes over from Coade. Many changes in the air, and it likely that we get down to some proper training. Today Hammerbeck, Dicky and I go and beat up Khushalgarh bridge and Jand station, having arranged with Pentonji (Capt Penton, Army liaison officer) that there are some

'Swimming and booze' - Kohat Mess, Colin on the right.

mythical troops there.

Much tennis these days, swimming and booze. "Happy days are here again" as they say.

Tooth quiet.

October 14th 1941

KOHAT

AM IN HOSPITAL WITH MALARIA FOR THE LAST FOUR DAYS. Aching all over one morning and with a slight head I went to see Doc Wilkinson and he says sand fly or dengue fever and I have a temperature of 103. But I have to hand over security files to Corporal Doughty and then return to the guardroom and wait for an ambulance and am sick there, so they decide on malaria, and so it is.

Last night terrific bangings, and very shaking on my nerves.

Pete Jennings got us down to plenty of training programmes etc, which seemed to work, funnily enough. I was sent on a 'dash sortie' to pinpoint and count a convoy which was on the Bannu road – 8th Cavalry moving out of Kohat – and "spotted" 54 out of a total of 53! Northern command exercises are on now and all I had was a practice blitz on Peshawar.

Well, first 'A' flight taxies out in no wind under Squadron Leader Jennings and puts up alot of dust, followed by 'B' flight, with me as number two, led by Mann. It's as much as I can do to keep his wing tip in sight, and suddenly 'A' flight thunder down the long dirt strip over the hangars. Mann then forms up at right angles to 'A' flight's take-off and off we thunder through this horrible dust. A third flight, of 1 squadron IAF, is just starting to taxi bang across the middle of the 'drome through the dust ('A' and 'B' had gone round the edge.) Mann misses the leader by inches but Scowen, no. 3, cuts half its tail off with his skid. Mann returns to survey the damage as Scowen lands again and I go on to Peshawar.

Garner has turned up as Intelligence officer for 'the duration'. I have been Security officer in the camp issuing passes to over 270 'Injuns', though I had the details filled in by the Munshi (in duplicate as required by AHQ.) We have also got some A.C.H.s as policemen, and have been on the lookout for fifth columnists who are in the exercise too. But now I'm hors de combat.

A carpet wallah rolled up one day; and always an admirer of Persian rugs I let him show me his stock, though having previously said I wasn't buying. I liked one rather nice 'pear pattern' Shiraz, so he insisted I should buy it. After much argument that I ought to buy something, to get rid of him I told him to leave it on the floor for a day and he says "OK, price 375/-". Next day I tell him to roll it up and take it away but he insists I make him an offer, so again to be rid of him I say 100/-. He of course mishears that as 150/- and spends half an hour asking how much more than 150/- (as he puts it) I will give him. Eventually he says OK and asks for 150/-. When

I explain I said 100/- he spends about an hour of sales talk which I take in, and am damn nearly mesmerised into giving him 150/- for it. When he coughs and asks for a cigarette I can see he thinks he's snared me, and nearly has too, so I pull myself together and say "take it away, I don't want it." That breaks him completely; he says "you're a hard man, Sahib," and as he mounts his bicycle he turns, and with tears in his eyes whispers "140/-" – then pedals furiously away.

After leaving hospital I shall be grounded one month, which means Cypher officer and then - horrible dictu[1] – a medical board! So it looks like "the end of a promising career" as they say! To say nothing of the questions as to how I passed the first one!! Back to the Army – Christ!!! Or will it be RAF stores – still worse! Still, I suppose I have had a pretty good year and can't grumble.

[1] A schoolboy expression, 'horribile dictu', a Latin phrase meaning 'horrible to relate'.

October 25th 1941

KOHAT

OUT OF HOSPITAL NOW FOR A WEEK. Put in for ten days leave to float down the Indus from Mari Indus to D.I. Khan. Granted I hope, and D.V.[1] I go off tomorrow night. Harman had arranged to go with me, but now he is being posted and can't go. I tried to get Scowen and then Dicky but both failed to get past the adjutant.

I bought some stores, lots of bully, and 200 cartridges, and hope for the best. But what a shot am I with a shotgun? My bearer, I hope, will cook? Amar Khan, the SSO's mali, is the best shikari, but he can't be spared, so they have got me another and boatmen for 140/- rupees, and I sent 50/- advance.

I receive 465/- in notes as my 'uniform' allowance according to regulations, but no sign of any pay for Jan-June 1941 in Iraq.

[1] D.V. – abbreviated latin, Deo volente for God willing.

October 26th 1941

FLOATING DOWN THE INDUS

I LEAVE LAST NIGHT ON 9.20 TRAIN, Moulding drives me in, arrive Jand 11.10, depart 2.00 am, arrive Mari Indus 05.50. I meet Jerry Springheel and Harman Singh at Kohat station and old Freeland himself [1] in Mari Indus waiting room. He commands Razmak Brigade and greeted me very affectionately.

Had breakfast in the waiting room and then found Amar Khan, SSO's mali, who is the shikari. He takes me round Kalabagh and we buy eggs and wood but nothing to buy in the salt factory. My boat is a small salt boat with a room rigged in the centre, of chattai (palm fronds) lined with cloth. For'ard in a sort of fo'castle live five boatmen, Amar Khan and two chokras [2]. Aft under a small poop in a sort of well, my bearer Ghulam Rasal does the cooking.

We are now a few miles down river and have stopped to gather clay and stones to build a fireplace. I sit in the sun on the 'bridge' and am regaled with the local gossip by Amar Khan. I shoot a turtle after lunch and Ghulam Rasal cuts his finger on the first tin of bully. We tie up for the night at Ganda and I shoot two black partridges with the help of two local villagers and an able pie dog retriever.

Hot at night and many mosquitos, but two blankets on before dawn.

[1] *Colin's former commanding officer in the Indian army before he joined the RAF, the one he referred to in Volume 1 as 'that old shite' for refusing his initial request to transfer,*
[2] *Chokra - a boy employed as a servant.*

October 27th 1941

FLOATING DOWN THE INDUS

TWO BLACK PARTRIDGE AND A QUAIL on the same ground. Then down to four grass huts called Kopriwala for the night. A

Colin's 'small salt boat' on the Indus River.

sortie after duck proves useless as they are too wary. The jungle at Kopriwala is thick grass, mostly seven feet high, so shooting not much good, though I did surprise six partridge in a small field, but they all got away.

Waited till 9.00 am the next morning for Kopriwala's two pet muggers[1] to appear but they didn't oblige, so we cast off. Spent the morning chasing duck and missed twice with the .22, and also a "Karmoor" which I stalked along the bank. Halted for tiffin as a mugger sighted in the water, but as he didn't come ashore after an hour, we set off again. Halted for the night at a place where there are plenty of white partridge, though I only shot one. A pet mugger kept, so after the morning shoot we all look for him.

[1] *The 'mugger' crocodile, a marsh crocodile common in India.*

October 28th 1941

FLOATING DOWN THE INDUS

I get four partridge and lose one, two being full deflection shots, so I am improving. The mugger appears but the sentry says it's grass, so Amar Khan and I go off in a small boat to reconnoitre. The 'grass' slips into the water, so we land just opposite in the jungle. Ten minutes later he pokes his nose up, has a look around, then lands on a mud flat about 100 fet away. Using Amar Khan as a sandbag, I draw a head with my Mauser on its neck and hit it too, following up with one in the back and a miss. Amar Khan wild with excitement, and we row across quickly and pump .22 bullets through its eyes. Ten feet, four and three quarter inches, and it's taken ashore and skinned, the corpse objecting to the whole procedure. I don't think I'll shoot any more, as must save the cartridges.

October 29th 1941

Floating down the Indus

Last night at Kaffir Kot, where I climbed up to see the fort and to shoot sisi round a homestead or two up there. No sisi and no chukar,1 not the next morning either. This morning crossed to Huran Wala and I got nine pigeon. Hundreds of them, in winter thousands, which hadn't been shot for two years, and I got four with my first shot. Long, thick grass through which one forces ones way under the trees in which the pigeons roost. Like African jungle, and almost romantic if it wasn't India, or was in Assam. I wear shorts and a topee, shoes and a shirt ashore, for the morning and evening shoots, but nothing else. A swim before lunch and tea, the water being icy and the current too strong for me in most places.

Later tied up for a partridge shoot, and got led into a swamp, but as Amar Khan said, my 'dil' (Hindi for heart) wasn't in it though I got one black one. From Hiran Wala a boatman was sent to Kundian Junction – five miles off – to get me half a dozen beers, as I'm fed up with whiskey and boiled Indus. He leaves at 1.00 pm and catches me up downstream in the small boat at 7.30 pm.

---

[1] Sisi is a type of partridge, and Chukar is the national bird of Pakistan.

248

The 'mugger' crocodile after it's been shot by Colin.

November 3rd 1941

FLOATING DOWN THE INDUS

MY LAST THREE PIGEONS HAVE GONE BAD, which has rather put my calculations out, as I had hoped to take some game back to Kohat. I shoot some more partridge and another quail. Also a "Kunj" (a crane) which the crew fancied for their dinner. I go out 9 - 10.00 pm in a village after bhik pig but though I see them in the fields they don't come near enough for a shot by moonlight. Reading Somerset Maugham's 'Altogether' again, and as usual it sets one thinking. No duck seen for two days now, and nothing bar that first mugger.

Then, all of a sudden, three partridge with six shots at Norang, where the Lambardar's son[1] took us round. Next morning two more, making 5 for 13 (cartridges). Certainly an improvement. The 15lbs of potatoes have run out, so now it's only game and chappatis. They all drink 'lassi' down here, sour milk churned up with ghee, but if you pour it straight down like medicine and don't worry about the taste, it's quite refreshing.

Chased duck yesterday at long range with the .22, and though I could place a shot amongst them, they never seemed to come to any harm.

I hope I haven't been recalled! Wonder how the war's going? They measure distance in "Kos" here, 1.5 miles, which I never heard before.[2]

[1] *Punjabi word meaning 'village head'.*
[2] *The kos is an ancient mathematical unit of distance that has been in use in the Indian subcontinent for over three thousand years. Colin was a bit out – it measures 2.25 miles.*

November 5th 1941
DERA ISMAIL KHAN

MORE PARTRIDGE SHOOTING, and offered lunch by a Lambardar but would take too long. Manage to get away with two brace for Kohat, but on the last day only get one with great difficulty for ten cartridges. I start with an average of one bird to 15 cartridges but eventually get down to one per two and a half.

It's moving by moonlight on the river, with the partridge calling on both banks and a glass of something in my hand.

Arrived D.I.K. at 9.30 am – sent Ghulam Rasul in for a tonga (2/8/- for some four miles) – and find my watch has gained one and a half hours. Now sitting in Darya Khan waiting room after a good bath. Would like to see a paper though!

November 13th 1941
KOHAT

'A' AND 'B' FLIGHTS GO TO QUETTA the other day. None of the R/T sets work but they get off. I hate to see them go, being grounded, and knowing that I may never fly again[1]. But I have put on RAF uniform now, so I have got so far. I ought to be a flying officer by now.

Went out with Stilliard and Glover, the new A.I.L.O., after birds, and saw quail and some sisi. These latter, hill partridge, are rock coloured and fly low over crests and up and down nullahs. Daniel killed near Razmak on a road recce. He flew into a mountain.

[1] *He is alluding to his imminent medical, where he fears he will be 'found out'.*

November 20th 1941
Kohat

I PASS THE MEDICAL! I had been practising holding my breath and due to bad training and a damn cold could only hold it about 50 seconds. Well, I hold the bit between my teeth, push 100 on the clock, and hold it there with distended cheeks, breathing normally through my nose meanwhile. Doc Wilkinson spots this, and fastens a clip on my nose, but I manage to get a little air past it and do 65 seconds. He then says "I reckon we can call your eyesight 6/6" and I have passed! Provided AHQ don't object to my high pulse due to 'cold in nose'.

Johnston, Nick Winter, Stilliard, Glover and self go out in a car in the morning, looking for shite hawks on the 'drome, with buckshot and .410 service rifles. Nine confirmed and a lot hit. I kill four myself.

Air Commodore J.L. Vachell M.C. comes over and opens his mouth in the Mess. A division is going to Iraq, the armoured division is for overseas, but we stay here, eventually going to Secunderabad. 20 Squadron going to Choklala. In six months we are to have two flights of 'Mustangs' and one flight of 'Vengeances' so if I can stay out of medical trouble I ought to have some fun.

Still overseas in 1943, and dead and buried by the end of the war perhaps.

251

November 27th 1941

THE BOYS ARRIVE, BACK FROM QUETTA, and this afternoon I hope to go flying. But Glover insists on going in the back, and remembering my last effort, I am wondering if I shall be able to do a landing in the half hour allotted to me.

There is much talk. A new squadron adjutant is arriving; there's a week's detachment of four a/c next month to Jallundar; one a/c to go to Calcutta at the end of this month, and I am detailed as one of two planes to carry the G.O.C. (General Hutton) from D.I.K. to Wana and back. But as I couldn't even land on this 'drome, and God knows if I shall manage it today, how the hell can I land on a postage stamp at D.I.K. and Wana? We have fitted wooden tail wheels, bound with metal, and if you do a heavy landing it breaks the stern post. This flying – Christ!

November 28th 1941

KOHAT

I MANAGE TO FLY OK, though with one ground loop. Next day I practise landing in small areas, and Bill Duncan is willing to take me despite the size of D.I.K. 'drome (he goes round twice himself eventually). However, the Wing Commander says there must be no mistake so Butler goes instead. There is no 230 anywhere (230 octane fuel) and they have to go to Miramshah to refuel.

Off to Peshawar in the 2nd X1 football team tomorrow – back on Sunday. Butler posted to F.T.S. Ambala (flying training school). The intrigue in the squadron is shocking. Johnston and Hammerbeck are known as "that chap" and "that other chap" and it all weaves around them. A bad spirit all round, all a/c on the ground u/s, no work ever done by officers, and no training for new pilots.

On the Mess lawn at the Peshawar Club - Colin centre.

November 30th 1941

KOHAT

I SPEND LAST WEEKEND IN PESHAWAR, going over for a football match. Go to the club at night with Dicky Cleaver, Glover, Knowles and Wagstaffe (AILOs), and meet Basil Henson who says he has fits and is being invalided home shortly. "Christmas" Nowel invites us over to his party, Air Commodore Russell's, and he gives me all the "gin". Dickie fixes himself up for a fighter squadron and he tells me we move to Karachi next year and then to Quetta. Suits me.

Lots of flying, puff shoots, dive bombing and front gunning, the latter not very successfully. I have an abscess where Pank stopped the tooth, so have to go over and have it removed. Drinks here and there, football or rugger most days. I go into Peshawar, to the Club, on a Sunday morning and sit on the lawn to listen to the band. All around are tunics and Sam Brownes. Some even have their caps on. And I am wearing my green roll-neck football jersey. Have I established a new record?

December 5th 1941

CALCUTTA

MANN LEFT SOME TIME AGO to take part in Calcutta War Weapons week with one Lysander. Having a girl in Calcutta, he arranges to go on leave there afterwards and to pay my fare down to collect his a/c. I leave Kohat on the 2nd and after two days in the train arrive in Howrah on 4th. I go to the Grand, and find Burt living there as there is no room in the Mess at Dum Dum.[1]

But now a new signal from Group to say that the a/c is to be allotted to 146 Squadron for W/C Wright's use, so it looks like I shall have to pay my rail fare back home again, as well as 10/- a day here. But we are waiting to hear from Pete Jennings first.

Yesterday Burt took me to the Saturday Club for lunch and at 2.00 pm I had a drink with him, Langford James and F/Lt Overton (Signals) in the Grand (chota peg 15 annas!)[2]. Then Overton and I go to the flicks and to the Casanova (club) for a drink where I see Corporal Hove and alot of dusky beauties, one of which (or whom) makes eyes at me until the joint closes down. Overton had just been up in Dinjan, in Upper Assam, where goes 146 squadron to protect the Digboi oil fields (in 4- gun Audaxes with a Lewis[3] in the back!). DC3s from Chongqing (in China, the base of Chiang Kai-Shek) connect up there in a through route apparently, all rather hush hush. Neil Elliot and Macmillan have arrived with Wavell and he says that Reggie Steward is with Abbot in the Paratroops.

---

[1] *The airport at Calcutta and formerly home of the British Armoury, where, in the early 1890s, Captain Bertie-Clay developed a bullet with the jacket cut away at the tip, to allow its soft lead core to expand on impact – the Dum-Dum.*
[2] *A half measure of whiskey.*
[3] *The Lewis machine gun.*

December 18th 1941

LOST IN MULTAN

NEIL ELLIOT AND MACMILLAN ARRIVE WITH WAVELL and we take out the three Sinnott sisters and Pamela Russell to the Saturday Club for dinner and dance and then to the 300, a low night club. All this on Burt Mann, as he is a member of both joints. I depart and am in bed by 2.30 am, my partner having been seen off home.

On Saturday, news from 28 Squadron that a/c is to be handed over and I have to return home, so I take Sunday morning's train. On Saturday Pam Russell comes to lunch but Neil and Mac are so gloomy that I have all the fun with her. They go to the cinema after lunch whilst I park and then we meet for tea at Firpo's. Then we see her home (11/2 Birdwan Road, Alipore 311) and meet Sir Guthrie and her scotch mama – 'Desie' – a scream. On the train back I am a bit gloomy and have lunch out of a tiffin carrier with an Indian gentleman. He gives me a cigar, whilst smoking a colossal hookah himself.

Japan declares war? *(Pearl Harbor, 7th December 1941)*

I meet Thripp and Teddy Tyson on the Lahore - 'Pindi train and Thripp and I go to the 'Pindi Club with drinks and dinner on Colonel Mike Gilpin. On arrival back at 06.30 I find I have to take Squadron Leader Scott to Karachi, and we manage to get away at 11.00 am after some doubtful telephoning about Multan aerodrome. Well, halfway there, visibility shuts down, and at 1000 feet I can just see the ground. I carry on and wait for the Chenab (river) to appear under me and when it does I turn down it and hope to find the railway bridge, as I daren't go straight on and hope to hit Multan. I am just getting panicky when it appears and I follow the railway to Multan. Visibility so bad, dust storms, that I can't find the aerodrome for some time, circling round and round the town.

Land, refuel, find Scott has been sick in the back and decide to stay the night, in case I fail to find the next stop, Padidan, in the dust. I picquet the aircraft with the help of two small boys in a dust storm, but God only knows if I shall be able to start it again tomorrow morning. Now after a bath in Multan's inspector's bungalow, am feeling better, though still dusty. My first time lost in an aircraft, and not pleasant. If I hadn't noticed the river under me when I did, I should have gone on I suppose?

December 19th 1941

KOHAT

I CANNOT START IN THE MORNING. Scott and I and a policeman and a greaser wind for one and a half hours. Then I ring up Kohat and am told to get the IAOC to look at the batteries. Ten out of twelve cells are dry, so they put in another to start it and I return to Kohat, Scott going on by train. Next day Bill Duncan, Clark and I go and do a V.B.L. (or B.B.B.) demonstration[1] and land at Akora. I can't hit anything with my bombs on it.

Today I go off early to Thal and take Colonel Gilpin to Islam Chanki, the Burma landing ground, and back to Kohat. He takes me up to the upper and lower Shinki bridges where he inspects the Tochi valley defence works which they have started building. We also have a shooting match with the contractor who wants a pass to take his Mauser into Bannu.

Beautiful flying and landings today.

I now have an RAF blue uniform for Rs144, having received Rs465 allowance for it, so it will put me about square on the pay question. Jerry Beale comes down for drinks and dinner last night and seems to be in good form. A letter from Pam Russell in Calcutta; not bad going.

---

[1] *Meaning unclear.*

December 20th 1941

Kohat

The Japs seem to be beating us. All RAF leave in India stopped and we are ordered to stand by to proceed to Burma at short notice. Complete panic and everyone flapping. Well, I don't feel so happy about this one as the last war I went to. (Iraq). Why? Haven't I always been a firebrand and hoped for war? As a soldier, yes. But I think this job I enjoy all the time, and go to bed thanking God for tomorrow and the flying I shall do, which I never did in the army, except the days before road protection in Razmak.

Some forced landing practise yesterday. I 'cut the gun' at 3000 feet and landed on the aerodrome without using engine which I had never done before in a Lysander. I have bought two tin boxes at 9/- and 12/- each. As good as the English uniform cases for £3-10-0.

A letter from Peggy[1] which seems fairly cheerful.

[1] *Widow of his brother Hugh, who was killed flying a Blenheim in June 1940 in the Battle of France.*

December 21st 1941

Kohat

We are moving to Burma next month apparently. 2 Squadron are to do our job in Karachi. Sgt Ridley takes off in coarse pitch and crashes over the 'drome boundary without hurting himself. I fly Penton to Chaklala with 20 degree drift, and yesterday fly Mike Gilpin Thal-Bannu-Peshawar. I try to land in Thal in weak mixture[1], but luckily the throttle won't come back and I see it in time.

A nasty aircraft skeleton at Peshawar where young Namgyal, heir apparent of Sikkim, undershot and went to his death in flames. It saves them burning his body I suppose.[2]

All teed up and nowhere to go! A party in the Sgts mess last night and I get together with Falconer and Sgt Sedgewick. Cpl Doughty teaches me to ride a motorcycle and yesterday I do the camp seven times, by day and by night, safely.

---

[1] *Pilots could change the fuel/air ratio with a lever near the throttle. Weak mixture gives economy but slow engine response to power changes. Usually pilots selected rich mixture when power changes were anticipated during take off and landing.*
[2] *The episode is told here.*

Christmas Day 1941

KOHAT

WELL, WE KNOW THE NAME OF THIS PLACE we are supposed to be going to but it seems to be spelled differently on the map. It's near Lashio and Mandalay, below the start of the Burma Road of ill fame. 60 squadron with Blenheims, operating from Burma, are supposed to have just four out of 13 left now. Still we go on peace establishment! Johnston has got himself posted to 20 Squadron... How nice for them.

I go down to Lahore with Sergeants Grey, Hilton and Deacon to collect four Lysanders. We go by car to Peshawar and cram into the Frontier Mail. We're all in first class, and four soldiers join us as the train is stuffed full. Henry of 1st Squadron IAF lends me his greatcoat and half his berth and I get quite a good sleep.

On the tarmac from 8 until 1.00 pm whilst they get the kites ready and take their time off for tea and buns etc.

Yesterday Mann and I go to the signal sergeants mess on the invitation of Sgt Falconer, "B" flight's boss. I do well and am back in bed at 12.30, having squashed a tomato on Sgt Sedgewick's head, which he deserved. On returning, see Dickie's light on and find him asleep in his clothes, having puked on the floor. I suppose I was young and silly once. Or was I?

December 26th 1941
KOHAT

YESTERDAY (CHRISTMAS DAY) with great trouble I raise an officers team to play the Sergeants Mess. They arrive drunk at 4.15 pm and start playing with bottles and cigarettes in their hands, which are removed. On being knocked over, most of them stay flat out until lifted up. We get eight before half time, but then the game breaks up as Sergeants Bower, Sedgewick and Philpots start fighting – the spectators meanwhile carry on with the football.

Dinner with the Scotts, he is chief equipment officer, and we play games with pencil and paper which I haven't done for years. Between 7.30 and 1.30 am I get three small glasses of beer, but knowing the ropes I went well fortified beforehand and was in cracking form.

Went down to the Signals Mess the other day and invented a new trick – "Do you play tomatoes?". Falconer and I happened to find some tomatoes in the kitchen so brought one out. Then I held it on a chap's head and we all put our hands on top "to lift him up" whilst Falconer clapped his down on top and squashed the lot. The Sergeants thought it rather a good trick.

December 28th 1941
KOHAT

WE GAVE A DANCE ON 26TH to which all Kohat comes. Hammerbeck brews a very good hot rum punch which is much approved. Jerry Beck very drunk. I have dinner with the Pentons first, which was really the best part of the evening as far as I was concerned. Teddy Humphries arrives last night after being 'lost' by

259

the Indian Government in Cairo for six weeks. "Tiny" Irwin swears he is a V.R.[1] to all and sundry, and is trying to push his way home. But now Teddy's been found, they'll like as not catch him too.

Our rail party has to be in Calcutta on the 10th, so don't suppose we shall leave (for Burma) before 28th January.

Peace establishment, British rates of pay, in rupees I believe.

[1] *Meaning unclear.*

December 30th 1941

Kohat

I GO OVER WITH JERRY to visit the Kohat Pass Arms Factory. A most "kachha" set-up (Hindi for raw or basic) and no sanitation visible. Small boys turn sort of bicycle wheels which work lathes for boring the barrels. Other men make the various parts and then you can have 'B.S.A.', 'Ishapore' [1] etc stamped on as you choose. One stamp was 'Ezfield' [2]. Arms are only made on demand, but you can choose your own barrel and bolt etc and have the lot put together in your presence with a walnut stock. Martinis sell for 40-50/- and Lee Enfields for 60-70. They also make shotguns, single bore.

Later went riding with Blackwell on the 'Piffer' horses and did some magnificent jumping, which I hadn't done for years.

A trip to Miramshah today to take a spare part over. 'Springheel' Jack is a Lt Colonel and off to Delhi to command 20/6 Rajputana Rifles, a garrison battalion. A farewell party in the Piffer Mess and I stay on late to dinner with Blackwell, discussing Burma and Army cooperation in general. A great party at the Pentons on the 28th – I am in cracking form owing to 'old Angus' and vodka. We play 'Murder' and 'Consequences' and some pretty rude ones turn up.

Air raids on Rangoon – the day Wavell was there!

[1] *The Birmingham Small Arms company, and the Indian rifle factory in Ishapore.*
[2] *Presumably a mis-spelling of Enfield.*

Relaxing in the Mess at Kohat, Colin on the right.

January 3rd 1942

KOHAT

I CELEBRATE NEW YEAR IN BED AS USUAL. Bill Duncan overshoots and writes off a Lysander at Miramshah. I have been there three days running, on various jobs – doing air to air which was damn bad, though I get one hole on the drogue.[1]

Today a signal is in requiring two Lysanders for shore patrol in the Andamans from Port Blair – only Nobby and Nelson volunteer, whilst I am still thinking it over. Sgt Ridley to go with Nelson and I get rid of my useless air gunner, Sgt Turner, with them too. I am put in charge of enrolling followers and it's a hell of a job. A Havildar[2] from 7/13th comes down to drill them daily. I am all

261

packed up ready to go. The rail party departs on the 6th, and will be in Calcutta on the 10th.

---

[1] *A drogue parachute – a funnel-shaped or cone-shaped device towed behind an aircraft as a target.*
[2] *An Indian army sergeant.*

January 11th 1942

KOHAT

THE TRAIN PARTY GOES OFF ON THE 3RD and ought to reach Calcutta today. It rains like hell, and we stand about in it as it takes them two hours too long to marshal the train. Then I have to find seats for the followers and the Indian other ranks of A.I.L. section in the dark. A complete shambles, with men jumping on anywhere, as the accommodation provided by the railway authorities was inadequate. At last they get away, most of the troops intoxicated, and we, the air party, start a deadly existence of waiting, waiting. Clay pigeon shooting one morning, and we go out on a long range another. But we can't go before they arrive, which will be 20th at least.

Bill Tait posted here in place of Duncan who retires to Movement Control at AHQ. We give him a party in the "Ladies Room" with 'Snippet' Coverton whom I used to know at Pachmari, Mary Humphries and one other. Hammerbeck brews Black Velvet and then we abandon the chairs for cushions round the fire. Potent stuff! I remember Bill Tait lying under a screen, myself sitting on a chair perched on top of him.

Bill Duncan can't manage and departs, ill, for home. His wife Alison and the rest sit down to dinner with "Tiger's Milk", another horrible cocktail of Hammerbeck's. Why spoil a good liqueur, though I never touch 'em myself. Devilish cold, and I wish I hadn't packed my flying boots.

In Burma my pay is 14/6d plus Rs72 allowance, less British income tax, payable in India. Less Indian income tax I'm sure! Teddy Humphries has written to AHQ about it – but what to do? "Pay to fly with the RAF."

January 16th 1942
KOHAT

MORE DOING NOTHING and a little baseball with the Sergeants. Yesterday drank with Joe Nelson and Teddy and Joe's girl Olga, who has come up from Bombay, and they hope to marry on Sunday. Alot of whisky, and dinner in the Park Hotel. Joe Nelson from New Zealand, and lately from Aden, and old Jack Moulding – 7 years in the Straits Police – are two people I can sit and listen to for hours. There's a sort of romance in these sort of people – only I can't quite place it. Sergeant Moyer, a young Canadian, and Sergeant Glass, a big brawny Australian, are two more. Nought to do but hang about, all packed up.

January 17th 1942
KOHAT

I GET JOE NELSON ROUND FOR A DRINK LAST NIGHT, with Olga, in the "Ladies Room." Pete Jennings objects to me ringing the bell so much and spoiling his news, so tears it down. Then he and Hammerbeck come and join us and then we go to the Pub for more whisky and back to the Ladies Room for dinner. I get rather tight, but in bed by midnight. Hammerbeck annoys me. He is always ready to talk about the Western Desert and the hours he has put in. He means well, poor chap, but does get our backs up.

Bill Bowden of 60 squadron recently heard over Tokyo radio!

What the brassiere said to the hat "you go ahead and I will give these two a lift."

I wrote to Baker at AHQ and told him my moans, but I expect he will be so fed up with us he will return us to the army, or post us to a squadron in India where we can't complain. I do want to see Burma – now!

January 21st 1942

KOHAT

TEDDY HUMPHRIES COMES BACK FROM LAHORE and prangs his Lysander – breaking the tyres and straining the undercarriage and wing. Joe married yesterday, but I'm not invited. I buy a bottle of whisky and we give Jack Moulding a farewell party in his room. Loftus of the 'Camels' there, and Pete Jennings in cracking form. Yesterday I go with Farr in the Valencia to Miranshah as second pilot. Rather like driving a ship in a heavy sea, but I manage OK. We inspect the "Scouts" Mess but no one in.

Today I go with Bill Tate to Peshawar as second pilot. Hammerbeck goes in a Lysander and attempts to shoot us up, but is outmanoeuvred by Bill who swings his Valencia into aileron turns and eventually puts her down to about 160 and chases him down to the ground. Then both landings are done by side-slipping turns.

I call at Grindlays (Bank) in Peshawar and fix up a few things; also I give Hammerbeck a piece of my mind when he starts being rude on the tarmac.

January 24th 1942

KOHAT

RAF VS AN OFFICERS TEAM RUGGER yesterday and I score a try. A cypher in last night that we move on 26th, so I will close this book as I must pack it. Here's hoping I shall live to open it again.

New Notebook

At this point Colin starts a new notebook, with the following inscription:

Being a continuation of my previous record 'Flying and Soldiering' which I closed, leaving many blank pages, on proceeding to Burma. This is the only book I was able to get in Kohat and somehow a different muse seems to live in it. That is to say, a scribbling, hurried muse, who records beauty, drama and tragedy like a mere official communique. Why? I know not. Perhaps he will change.

7

January - May 1942

28 Squadron

Burma / China

Background, January 1942

Colin arrived in Burma at a critical juncture. The Japanese army had first crossed into Burma from Thailand in late December, with orders to capture Moulmein and Rangoon and cut the overland supply route to China, splitting the Chinese nationalist forces under Chiang Kai-shek from their British allies. They also wanted to create a strategic bulwark to defend their gains in British Malaya and the Dutch East Indies.

The first Japanese bombing raids of Rangoon had begun over Christmas 1941, but by the time Colin arrived, the three main airstrips in the south of the country had been overrun, and the Japanese were able to provide many more aircraft to support their advance. It was becoming increasingly dangerous for RAF pilots in the skies over Burma.

January 25th 1942

KOHAT

OFF TOMORROW TO LASHIO. Route Lahore, Delhi, Cawnpore (night stop), Gaya, Calcutta (night stop), Chittagong, Akyab, Heho, Lashio. Sixteen aircraft and a DC2, and I believe 1 squadron IAF, are going down the same route.

Yesterday a party in the Club, and I get a bit whistled, waking up with a slight head, the first time ever, despite my famous 'Roman's trick'. Teddy and I get an advance of pay at Indian rates. It lays down we shall draw down pay at RAF Indian rates, but I didn't get that in Iraq and I don't see how I'm going to get it in Burma.

I take my head down to the hangars this morning and try to load up the Lysander, but it seems to have a hell of a lot of extra kit in it.

January 30th 1942

HEHO, BURMA

WE LEAVE AN HOUR LATE and I do a ground loop at Lahore and bust a wheel, and so am two hours behind. On reaching Delhi, I refuel and take off up to some gate or other as I can't get off the ground, and only manage to pull up with a few feet to spare. I run up on chocks and find the engine is OK, so take off again and set course. Then Flight Sergeant Fairbrother, my air gunner, says 'something's burning', it appears to be another fuse, so I come down again and stay the night whilst it is attended to. The accumulator overflows and rots a large hole in the fabric.

I put up at Comms flight mess, with Gunn who is in the Douglas, and then go to the Club with Mac, Dudley Withers and Neil Elliot. I meet Brain and Dickie Lonsdale and Pamela Russell from Calcutta. Also alot of paratroops, some with carpet slippers on and plaster on their faces, and despite telephoning all over Delhi, am unable to locate Reggie Seward or Abbott.

Next day, with Sergeant Glass, who stopped overnight with an oil leak, we set off and after refuelling at Cawnpore catch up the squadron at Gaya. As I fly over, they fire Very lights, so I watch which way their smoke blows and land accordingly, only to find they had been trying to draw my attention to a landing "Tee". But instead of a 'berry for my prang I am complimented on catching up the squadron! We reach Dum Dum that night and are put up at the Mess. No taxis available, but we eventually manage to get on some service MT and reach Calcutta at 8.15 pm. A drink in the Grand, then Joe Nelson, Teddy and I dine at Firpo's and return to bed by 11.00 pm. Burt Mann up all night with his girl and some of the others stay in town.

Next day we reach Chittagong and then set out for Heho. B Flight leading, and over some wicked mountains up to 8000 feet, thickly wooded. Near Meiktila Burt decides petrol is short so we land at a concealed landing ground at Pyawbwe. It's home to the Burma Frontier Force training battalion and we meet a BVAF chap (Isaacs) and his wife who give us tea whilst refuelling in progress. I have a long range tank and they don't fill me up, but I take a look and find an air lock in the tank. That's blown out, and we set off for Heho where the rest of the Squadron are, bar Teddy Humphries. He was last seen over the Irrawaddy and it later transpires he went back to Chittagong and the next day set out again and crash-landed at Mandalay. But a search A/C goes out to look for him.

At Heho we sleep in dormitories with bedding "on the house", the custom out here apparently. Over 3000 feet and damn cold; rolling downland with scrub; sharp stakes and tank traps everywhere. Off next day to Lashio and up to 9500'. Of course our heavy kit has not arrived, but we disperse to A/C "hides" and then up to the Mess some three miles away. We all go about with pistols and carry tin hats. This is the railhead for the Burma road, and lorries are everywhere. Mostly Chinese drivers, and one lorry is only supposed to last about four trips. We drive down to some hot springs where boiling water wells out of the ground. Everything hellish expensive as all the inhabitants have made fortunes out of "lorrying" up the Road.

A beautiful place this. A low depression with rolling hills on three sides, thickly jungled. The earth is red, but plenty of vegetation and flowers abound. The buildings are all wood and chattai, on stilts above the ground in Chinese fashion. Tomahawks of the American Volunteer Group arrive occasionally, but we never see the pilots. They get about 2000 rupees a month and 500$ in gold for each plane they shoot down, so they are pretty hot stuff.

A sudden signal for two aircraft to Rangoon for two months, and it is B Flight. Sgt Deakin and Nobby or I. We toss and he gets it and has gone. He hates moving and I like it, but I'm not ready, having just unpacked and not yet being "composed like". Now I am, I wish the hell I had gone after all, as there will be nothing to do here, until we are re-equipped with modern aircraft.

DC3's of China National Airways run Calcutta-Lashio-Kunming. If I had gone to Rangoon I would have seen some more war, as there are bombers every day there. Am I a fool or not?

February 3rd 1942

ZAYATKWIN

DEACON HAS TROUBLE AT HEHO and Nobby Clark returns for spares, so Burt Mann and I go down the next morning. We call at Toungoo where I meet Watson and then to Mingalodon. We are then sent to a satellite "Z" or Zayatkwin where we find a dump of tents, very little water and nothing to drink. Burt goes into Group and I play poker with S/Ldr Burberry (31 Squadron) and some others. Air raid alarms at night, and one Jap bomber comes over at 4000 feet with his lights on, does a dummy run, then turns round and drops a stick of A.P.[1] near the runway, damaging a Tomahalk only. We have no ground crew, no petrol or oil, and Group ringing up with different orders all the time. Some D/F calibrations in the afternoon, and we see Pat Jennings and Tate arrive in Mingalodon to find out what's what at Group. More alarms that night but no bombs, and next morning we go to look for Tate's aircraft at "Johnny Walker" (a landing ground) as tail wheel nearly gone on mine. We can't find it and return, then off to Mingalodon where I burst my wheel and hand the kite over to S/Ldr Majunder of 1st IAF, stationed at Toungoo. Burt and Bill Tate then return to Lashio with GOC Hutton and staff in the back[2], Majunder goes off and I am left with four airmen at Mingalodon and two sergeants at Zayatkwin and no orders, as the detachment appears to be finished, and we are going on bombing raids from Toungoo.

I telephone Group, who contact Pete Jennings and order me to "await further orders", so I fix myself up with a billet at the Rangoon Golf Club where I am now. Airmen and officers mixed, and plenty of beer and a dhobi of all things, so I am well off at last. Met some 113 Sqn boys who take me to town last night to the Savoy. Whisky 1/4 rupees and a damn good feed there. Met Stuart of 12 Frontier Force Rifles on the staff, who said they only had two 1/2 battalions at Moulmein and could have held it with one more, but Hutton refused it. Then we go and search for brothels, but though we get to several opium dives, no women seen, so we return to bed. Well, I reckon I shall miss this bombing trip, and how the hell I get back to the Squadron, I don't know.

[1] Small anti-personnel bombs.
[2] General Hutton was on his way to Chongqing to meet with the Chinese nationalist leader Chiang Kai-shek, Britain's ally against the Japanese.

February 4th 1942

ZAYATKWIN

BILL TATE FORCE LANDED SOMEWHERE, so they say[1]. "Z' and Toungoo bombed yesterday. Pete Jennings rings up and orders me to get his Lysander from Johnny Walker to Mingalodon and return to Toungoo after lunch. I phone Alec Johnston who fetches me, we visit the accountants and eat strawberries and cream at the Savoy. They (Army & RAF Staff) have a Mess in the teachers college where I have dinner, meeting Bill Adams (7/13) and Hugh Seely, now on the Staff.

Today some War Correspondents, including the famous Gallagher[2] of the Daily Express, drive me to Group where I try and raise a truck for the flight. I find out the detachment is to continue, but cannot find a truck. I then collect my ground staff from Mingalodon and here I am back in Zayatkwin, expecting two Lysanders any day. Saw Ronnie Alden, now in IAOC.

---

[1] *He crash landed with General Hutton in the back as passenger. While Hutton managed to escape the burning aircraft, Tate was badly injured and Hutton was unable to free him, with Tate dying from his wounds six days later.*
[2] *O.D. Gallagher.*

February 6th 1942

ZAYATKWIN

LAST NIGHT THEY COME OVERHEAD THREE TIMES, so we don't get much sleep. This morning we see a small Balbo[1] cross over to Mingalodon and fighters weaving trails in the sky.

The Japs break up, and we see a bit of a dog fight, the score being 11 for 0. The night before last some bombs dropped here, and my slit trench shakes. Yesterday I go to Pega in a car, 19 miles, with Dickenson, adjutant of 60 Sqn. A few shops still open, and we get the golf club opened and inspect it. Twelve anna Mandalay beer, a library, unopened weeklies and a ping pong table. On our way back we see seven Lysanders heading for Mingalodon, and I hear they did a successful raid the other day.

Well, here I am, nothing to do for the third day, out here under canvas. Not too bad, I wangle a bath tub, and have an excellent "lease and lend" campbed. The only trouble is air raids. The warning here goes as they cross the coast, telephoned from Command, and I get up and listen. If they don't seem to be coming, then back to bed and keep one ear open, but sleep's impossible, so what's the use. Into a trench when they come overhead, and back to bed when they have gone. Then I'm woken up by the "all clear".

Visited a company of Burma Rifles who live on roast duck and three veg whilst we sweat on rations. Two Burman officers, one who had been to a university in the USA, and the other lived in England 17 years; neither very sure of their own language. Burmans seem discourteous in shops compared to India. I went to Mingalodon stores and they gave me the only pair of flying boots, as walking about here there are clouds of dust, and mine are still in my tin box which hasn't arrived yet.

221 Group H/Q mostly India long-timers, with some ex-Singapore, so chronic! They all have cars which they smash, and Johnston thinks more about his car than his job. They discuss their cars endlessly. A very nice looking girl in the Air Staff office.

Out on the other Road (to Mandalay), there are rows of wooden car bodies in the rubber plantations, alongside chassis as they come off the ships for transportation to China. The AVG have "jeeps", and the war correspondents put a "flying 69" on theirs, as they had to have some sign![2]

[1] *Early WW2 RAF jargon, which often referred to large formations of enemy aircraft as a "Balbo". This was a hangover from 1933 when Mussolini's Minister of Air, Italo Balbo, put on a display of Italian air strength that impressed the world. It involved building twenty-five specially equipped twin-hulled Savoia-Marchetti SM.55X flying boats and then flying them in formation across Europe, across the Atlantic to the United States, on to the Chicago World's Fair and then back to Rome.*

[2] *The 1st American Volunteer Group (AVG) were nicknamed the Flying Tigers, and were initially formed to help oppose the Japanese invasion of China. After America entered the war, they became part of the 69th composite wing of the USAAF.*

The American Volunteer Group

The 1st American Volunteer Group was made up of around 300 pilots from the US Army and Naval air forces who had volunteered as mercenaries to go to the Far East to support the Chinese nationalists in their war against the Japanese. They were recruited by Claire Chennault, the American chief air advisor to Chiang Kai-shek, and signed up on the promise of a bounty from the Chinese government for every Japanese aircraft shot down, in addition to a generous salary.

Their recruitment and travel to the Far East was kept secret, the pilots posing as tourists or businessmen as they travelled to Singapore and Rangoon in the summer and autumn of 1941. They were formed into three squadrons under the leadership of Chennault, flying P40 Tomahawks, based out of RAF Mingalodon outside Rangoon and Toungoo further north. They were astonishingly successful, averaging around 10 Japanese aircraft shot down for every one of theirs.

After the Japanese crossed the Thai border into Burma on 22nd December, the role of the AVG was focussed on defending Burma, and control was transferred from the Nationalist Chinese Air Force to the RAF.

Along with the RAF, they began to operate from makeshift landing grounds, with names like Highland Queen, Johnny Walker, John Haig, Z, Park Lane, Sybil, Ritz and Lyons.

When Rangoon fell, they were withdrawn to Loiwing in China.

February 9th 1942

JOE NELSON ARRIVED and collected me from Z and he, I, and Dickie go to the golf club and get rather drunk with the war correspondents Gallagher, Webber and Stowe ('Snow White'). Next day I load up with two 250s *(bombs)* and get ready to raid the Moulmein area with Majunder and some 1 Sqn chaps. Raid cancelled at last moment and 1 Sqn returns to Lashio. Hammerbeck turns up with orders for all to return, so yesterday Nelson and I come up to Magwe, where the squadron has moved. CO and Teddy the only ones here, and 113 Sqn and some of 60 Sqn.[1]

Bill Tate dies as a result of his injuries. He force landed some 20 miles off Lashio near the railway, and General Hutton, despite a crack in the head, beat out the flames and pulled him out. Burt Mann ordered his passenger the ADC to bail out, which he did, and then crash-landed himself but is OK. They took off from Heho for Lashio by moonlight.

Sgt Hammet got hit by a bit of bomb at Toungoo, and various others were blown off aircraft or had miraculous escapes. Today orders received – send six aircraft, and six from 1 Squadron, to Namsang for a bombing raid on Chiengmai tomorrow. No fighter cover. We can only raise one, which is me, and off I go after lunch. It seems bloody dangerous, as no fighters this time. Last raids there were more fighter escorts than Lysanders!

[1] *These two Squadrons had been informally amalgamated as both had lost most of their aircraft and crews in the previous months.*

February 11th 1942

I GO OFF WITH F/SGT PERRY but get foxed by the satellite landing ground – Hilton and I, and four of 1 Squadron under Pritipal

Singh. Namsang is at 3,200 feet and pretty cold, though hot baths had been laid on for us by Sides, the Australian station master. Next morning, Pritipal and A flight go off and I lead the second with Hilton and an Indian. The latter is late, so by the time I get off, the first flight has vanished. We stooge over shocking country and the Salween river, and after 1.30 pm I come upon a town in Indo-China. I think it's Chiengmai, near the Mekong River, and having done 1.30 hrs don't feel like wasting time, so seeing nothing of military importance I set course for home and drop my bombs in a forest. The other two see them go, think I'm nuts, and return and bomb Chiengmai.

I reach home after 2.57 hrs in the air and Hilton's engine going for 3.15 hrs. It later turns out that my navigation was better than I thought and we were over Chiengmai all the time. Later we return to Magwe, I deduct 75 from 360 degrees and get my reciprocal as 285 degrees. It seems all wrong and after half an hour I check up again, find my mistake, and decide I'm lost. I turn a bit south with my heart in my mouth and eventually strike Thazi railway station on the two lakes. I then turn down the railway to Pyawbwe and set a course for home. Hilton doesn't fancy that and sets off by himself from Thazi.

Hammerbeck comes up. The Japs have broken through near Martaban and Lysander recces are required. I refuse to go down today, but will have to shortly, when the aircraft are fixed up.

February 14th 1942

Mingalodon (outside Rangoon)

PETE JENNINGS AND I HAVE DINNER with the DSP[1], one Benson, an excellent dinner after rations, though we don't sit down until about 10.30 pm. On Friday 13th the C.O. and I fly down from Magwe, as all serviceable 'Lizzies'[2] are required down at Rangoon. We all go out to a landing ground called "John Haig"[3] with 1 Sqn I.A.F. and spend two nights in the golf club. "Mush" Howells takes

Joe Nelson and self into town, and we meet Logan Gates, and then go to the Silver Grill for dinner.

Yesterday we stand by under a bit of chattai cover at John Haig all day, but nothing happens. We see Jack Moulding in the Silver Grill in the evening and Johnston with some "Chicklees" girl[4] he had picked up from somewhere. We tour the brothels again, but too smelly and horrible for words.

Today out to John Haig and off to bomb the ferry at Duyinzeik. We are taking off when it is postponed one hour. Off we go, and I attempt to drop mine on the village, but on the first dive, the bomb has a hold-up. I have another try and it goes off, though I stall the engine pulling out too steeply. Not much effect, and nothing much to bomb. Hammerbeck also has a hold-up so lands at Mingalodon. It drops off on his landing, a 250lb, and breaks in half, so he gives it full throttle and takes off again, having deposited his 'egg' on the runway.

They send us out to lunch at John Haig, stew, bread and tea, but no plates or eating irons! Today we are billeted in C.I.D. lines. We have an empty house as Mess, a bed or two, and we steal blankets and sheets from the golf club and bring them down here. All have gone to town for a meal, but I have to remain as duty officer, in case anybody telephones. There is a 24-hour dhobie service[5] at the golf club. I am happy anywhere if I can get a dhobie, a bath or cold shower, and hot water for shaving, but I doubt I shall get any hot water tomorrow morning.

We got three 'jeeps' the other day, for 1 Sqn and ourselves, but they are allotted to 135 Sqn today. The Japanese well across the Salween River and into Thaton, over where we went today; most of their air force appears to be attacking Singapore, but we shall buy it when it falls.[6]

The moon has started again, so more bombing shortly I expect!

[1] *Deputy Superintendent of Police.*
[2] *Westland Lysander aircraft, used in an army co-operation role, as it could land on very short, improvised airstrips.*
[3] *Improvised landing strips cut out of the jungle were given familiar names by the British.*
[4] *Meaning unknown.*
[5] *Dhobi or dhobie – an Indian washerman.*
[6] *Singapore fell the next day – 15th February 1942.*

February 18th 1942

MINGALODON

YESTERDAY I GO OFF AND BOMB Moulmein railway station. I follow Pete Jennings and drop mine between two engine sheds in what I hope is a slit trench. Then C.O. says "you and Dickie go and fly Hurricanes". We go off yesterday to Mingalodon and Dickie flies but I don't as the sun is setting a bit low. Today I fly, windy as hell, but manage three landings all right. Then I drive Bobby Clark home and Dickie and I toss up as to who will 'stand by' at Mingalodon and who will go to John Haig and perhaps go on a raid. I win the toss and elect to stay, as there is probably a reconnaissance to do in the afternoon. I ring up operations, and as there is nothing for me, I do another hour's Hurricane flying. I circle John Haig and see the boys taking off for a raid. The fourth kite to take off bursts into flames and turns over on its back. I am nearly sick in my cockpit and return to Mingalodon. Of course it is Dickie with Sgt Sedgewick in the back. Both killed. One of the aircraft taking off drop 40 lbers whilst taxi-ing, but Dickie is airborne so they explode underneath him and he and Sedgewick 'go for a burton'.

I have to do a Hurricane recce tomorrow and am "windy as hell". I always said that Dickie would be the first to be killed, and after Bill Tate, he went. Burt Mann arrives down here from Maymyo. I feel too intoxicated to write any more.

February 19th 1942

YESTERDAY I DO TWO RECCES in my Hurricane over the Bilin -Thaton area. The first time I see nothing, and then I drop two messages on a company of KOYLIs [1] who are cut off at Yimon. Later heard this was successful and the KOYLIs got away. Not very successful at the time, as I seem to be going too fast and I don't see anyone in the village.

Today I go out to John Haig as Nobby Clark is doing the recce. I start organising the squadron, and arrange to lead a flight in a raid, when the bombs arrive. Then I am ordered on a recce as Nobby falls sick. I go over to Duyingeck river, and see two rafts and a boatload of troops crossing the river. I dive down and surprise a platoon of Jap troops marching to the rafts. They are in threes, and I see them dash for cover, but for some reason I don't open fire on them.

Then near Thinzeik I see a few lorries and some motorcyclists or horses on the road. I then recce the Bilin river, and see a few logs, boats and an undamaged bridge. Got back, and had to take my kite to Johnny Walker where I waited an hour for transport, and got back here about 8.30 pm.

We give a drinks party last night, and a most beautiful girl comes at C.O.'s invitation called June, who works in the Group HQ as a typist. I talk to her for some hours, until Pete Jennings takes her home, not returning until about 5.00 am? Jack Moulding gets rather affectionate, and very confidential, before leaving, after shaking me warmly by the hand. He lost most of his worldly belongings in the fall of Singapore.[2] I find Dickie's keys and a few buttons amongst the wreckage of his Lysander.

1 *King's Own Yorkshire Light Infantry.*
2 *Four days earlier.*

February 22nd 1942

I HAVE TO GO AND RETRIEVE THE KITE from J. Walker. I do a recce whilst Burt Mann does his first one solo, then he does the afternoon one. I go to town, borrow Paddy O'Malley's motorbike, and go swimming at Kokine. A beautiful bathe with grass terraces alongside. Then back to find Johnston once more in the squadron. Pete Jennings arrives with orders for evacuation. A boat goes that night with Johnston on board, and most of the squadron. Hammerbeck leading the air party to Calcutta next day.

C.O., Teddy, Mann, self and Sgt Hilton remain, eventually to go to Magwe as one flight. Much looting in a warehouse on the docks, and I manage to get a bottle of John Jamieson. On the way back, Sgts Farebrother, Edgar, self and Corporal Johnston break into "Watsons", a big store, to try and get a watch for me. We stumble around with torches, but no watches. Then a shout of "come out or I fire", a bit of a commotion on the doorstep, shouts of "turn out the guard" as we are discovered. We come out into the street one by one, expecting a bullet any minute.

A man shouts "Looters! Bastards". I reply, then he says "Are you white men?" and we let in the clutch and away, but no shooting. Only a chankider *(nightwatchman)*, and old man Watson himself.

Yesterday we move into Inseim Mess, the Girl's Bible School, where all the drink is free. Masses of refugees on the roads out past John Haig, mostly Bengalis and Madrasis. We pick up a dead British military policeman. Teddy and I go to see the burning of some houses in town yesterday. Some looter drops a match, and many houses in the riverfront burn, as they are all wooden. Today I do a recce over Sittang River, and now Pete Jennings has gone as advisor or something to 17th Division, and told Burt and I to hop in our Lysanders when the fighters go, and make for Magwe. Teddy and Hilton left this morning. OK if our Lysanders aren't damaged in the meantime!

February 24th 1942

I GO TO BASSEIN AND BACK IN A LYSANDER. F/Sgt Falconer and his men drive off to Magwe, after I have gone down to the docks the night before and stolen what rations they want.

Yesterday we are all packed up to go, and Mann is sent on a recce to find out if the Japs have crossed the Sittang or not. If they have, we are to go off at once and evacuate the joint. Mann has a squirt at a Jap "Army 97" and sees it enter a fog bank at about 100 feet with smoke coming out of its wings. But not confirmed. I am trying to fuel up the Lysanders, and though I find some 230 (230 octane fuel), I can't get a bowser, and eventually put 100 octane fuel in.

Then I am sent on a recce. I go at 500 feet over the river and find no troops crossing, a look over our lines and then I make for the railway station across the bridge at about 1,000 feet. Suddenly, BANG by my right elbow, and the cockpit fills with hot smoke. I recognise it as glycol, my goggles mist over, but I head for our lines and try to climb, undoing my straps for a "bale out". At about 2,000 fteet the engine gets hoarse, oil pressure drops to 50 lb and the glycol stops pouring out. I look over the side, funk jumping, then see a small river with a stretch of sand by it. I lower the wheels, forget to do up my straps again, throttle back and make for it. I switch off and notice smoke coming from the engine, so she is about to seize up. I just can't make the sandbank, I "pull the nose up to lengthen the glide", and suddenly the light disappears and I am underwater. I have failed to reach sand, and stalled into two and a half feet of water just short of it. Only damage, one of the precious lenses broken in my goggles.

I wade ashore, meet some locals to whom I chat, when Pete Jennings and some soldiers arrive. They burn the aircraft, we walk back to 17 Indian Division HQ and find it was them that shot me down and were still firing when I was trying to land![1]

Walking back to 17 Indian Division HQ after being shot down during the Battle of Sittang Bridge.

Beer, lunch and I get back in Pete's car to Pegu, and get a lift to Mingalodon aerodrome from there.

Situation chaotic at the front. Most of the division is on the wrong side of the river, the bridge is blown and HQ not knowing who is where. They fire at all aircraft, having been shot up by Blenheims, Hurricanes and P40s.

Tea with some 12 ton American tanks. Met Kinnaird on 17 Division staff.

---

[1] *This episode became part of Dunford Wood family legend, Colin describing how he had been shot down into a 'crocodile pond'. Technically perhaps he may have been right, though there is no evidence of crocodiles in this diary entry.*

February 25th 1942

MINGALODON

YESTERDAY I DO A RECCE OF MOULMEIN aerodrome with fighter cover. Nearing it, I see a cloud of dust and expect something

The Battle of Sittang Bridge

The Battle of Sittang Bridge was fought between 19th - 23rd February 1942. It ended in a victory for the Japanese and heavy losses for the 17th Division of the British Indian Army, who were forced to retreat in disarray.

The Sittang Bridge was an iron railway bridge spanning several hundred yards across the River Sittang, and was a main crossing point on the road to Rangoon. The British commanding officer, Sir John Smyth, had wanted to pull his troops back across the river days earlier and prepare a defensive position against the Japanese on the West bank, but the GOC, General Hutton, had refused permission, so when the Japanese broke through and Smyth was finally given permission to withdraw on 19th February, his forces had to rapidly fall back to the bridge along 30 miles of tracks through the jungle, harried all the way by the enemy.

However, early in the morning of 22 February, it became clear that the bridge might fall at any moment. Smyth faced a hard choice - to destroy the bridge, stranding more than half of his troops who were still on the wrong side, or allow the Japanese a clear march to Rangoon. According to Smyth, "Hard though it is, there is very little doubt as to what is the correct course: I give the order that the bridge shall be blown immediately."

on the West bank, but the GOC, General Hutton, had refused permission, so when the Japanese broke through and Smyth was finally given permission to withdraw on 19th February, his forces had to rapidly fall back to the bridge along 30 miles of tracks through the jungle, harried all the way by the enemy.

However, early in the morning of 22 February, it became clear that the bridge might fall at any moment. Smyth faced a hard choice - to destroy the bridge, stranding more than half of his troops who were still on the wrong side, or allow the Japanese a clear march to Rangoon. According to Smyth, "Hard though it is, there is very little doubt as to what is the correct course: I give the order that the bridge *shall be blown immediately."*

Fortunately, once the bridge was blown, the Japanese disengaged in order to find another crossing point, reluctant to delay their march on Rangoon by mopping up the British units, and so in the afternoon, survivors of 17th Division swam and ferried themselves over the Sittang in broad daylight. However, they had to leave all their equipment and transport behind, and straggled back to India over the following weeks, having lost 60% of their strength. Rangoon fell on 9th March.

General Slim (later Field Marshal), who took command of British forces in Burma shortly after the battle ended, called Sittang Bridge "the decisive battle of the first campaign". Smyth was relieved of his command.

to be taking off, but no, and from 6,000 feet I see something like a DC2 and four fighters grouped round a hangar, and one fighter dispersed north. I come straight back, and some 2.5 hours later the fighter boys ground strafe them, catching several on the ground.

A recce today of where the Japs are supposed to have landed (the troops contacted them early this morning), but nothing seen. A lull in the war at present, but there's plenty of moon, so I expect parachute troops are being prepared.

Anyway, nothing to stop them.

February 27th 1942

John Haig landing ground

AM SITTING IN THE WATCH OFFICE and we see 12 Jap bombers come over. Then, like a bucket of gleaming fish, we see the bombs falling, then the whistle, and as they seem to be using the Watch office as their aiming mark, I think my last minute has come. C.O.'s Lysander and a Blenheim burnt. That night two more Blenheims go up. The Japs are now infiltrating round Pegu, and everyone is ready to make off, but apparently we are not going yet. What worries me is if a bomb damages my Lysander! I might get a seat on the convoy if I'm lucky, to Magwe, but I suspect the Japs will have cut the road.

Today a dawn recco, very frightened, and see nothing. Fired on by a Bofors, after taking off near Tankkyam. Reckon I have had enough war for the time being. What about a weekend in Calcutta or somewhere?

W/C Carey gets a second bar to his DFC. He also has a DFM. Watson and Underwood of 135 Squadron are missing, the latter after ground-strafing Moulmein landing ground. Burt Mann on a recco now. Reckon it's my turn again shortly, and not looking forward to it. Using John Haig today, and made a bum landing.

March 2nd 1942

MUCH CONFUSION – we expect to evacuate any minute during the last four days. The Army are withdrawing down Pegu road and North on the Poonie road. We, us and the fighters, move to Highland Queen[1] to support the withdrawal.

A few reccos, and yesterday in a Hurricane I see lorries and Japs crossing the Sittang river at Mokpalin. On returning, I land drifting to port and am so intent on looking at the ground that I fail to notice where I am going. After a few 'touch downs' I notice a Hudson and a bowser loom up (off the runaway) and too late I attempt to use the throttle and swerve away. The end of the main spa breaks on the bowser and I land on my nose. Luckily the wheels collapse and I leap out thinking "fire", being delayed by my telephones catching in something. S/Ldr Stone says he is taking me off Hurricanes. 'I need a rest' or something, so I wonder what the hell I do now.

[1] A landing ground at Hmawbi, a few miles north of Mingalodon.

March 4th 1942

AOC SAYS I NEED A REST BUT I'M NOT ALLOWED ONE, and have to do silly jobs in the Lysanders. I take one Mr Scott of the Forestry Department to Zigon, a damn small place, and back. I can't even land a Lysander now. Burt Mann gets shot down by a lot of Jap fighters whilst on a recco, and yesterday's recco fails to return also. He lands with wheels up and is then shot up on the ground, having to run about 400 feet with a piece of bullet in his foot. Some villagers rescue him and hide him under a bullock cart, eventually delivering him to the Burma Rifles and then to the

Royal Tank Corps. He is off back to India now, and never looked so happy before.

An Infantry Brigade arrived yesterday by convoy from India. 15 Jap fighters on Kya-ikto, but they got away before our fighters could get over them. Must be using it as an advanced landing ground for shooting down recco planes.

March 6th 1942
HIGHLAND QUEEN LANDING GROUND

I GO UP TO ZIGON AGAIN TO SEE S/LDR ANDREWS. The strip is now 1200 yds, and I have lunch and a rest. Very pleasant, lolling in the chattai shade and with a cooling breeze whistling through the side. Scott is there too, they are old campaigners and know how to look after themselves. After lunch we hear the familar drone which denotes Japanese bombs, and shortly afterwards seven silver aircraft go over, Jap bombers at about 1500 feet on a course for Magwe. Apparently they bomb Prome. I return feeling very refreshed and more like flying, to see G/C Singer in Group, and fix myself up to come to Magwe and collect 5000/- that Andrews wanted for payment of his labour.

I set off yesterday with G/C Seton-Broughal as passenger, after a Jap has been over Highland Queen on a recco. We head west for a bit and then sneak up the river. I find my tin box (Gunn having given me a map of how to find it) and then see SASO[1] A/Comm Parry-Keene[2]. He says I am to join the Communication Flight and then fly Hurricanes on reccos. I say I thought my squadron was transforming to Hurries, and he says yes, they are doing a conversion course at Risalpur. I then demand to go there too, but he says 'Oh no, you can fly them already'. Then we argue for a bit and he says he will see what can be done about it.

[1] *Senior Air Staff Officer.*
[2] *Later to become the first Commander-in-Chief of the Royal Pakistan Air Force, from 1947 to 1949.*

March 9th 1942

Parry-Keene says I am to stay here, and that he won't promote me if India won't. Some drinking with Lakri Wood, Neil Elliot and Dudley Withers who turns up here. Yesterday Lakri and I drive out to Yenangyaung, the BOC field where there is an American and a British Club. We have some drinks in both and a snack lunch. The British are most inhospitable, and unfortunately we meet no Americans.

Seton-Broughal takes up my case, and today tells me that SASO has been told to fix me up. He also says they want him to take a Wing to China!

Rangoon is supposed to have been blown up yesterday[1].

Just seen the AOC[2], he has promoted me[3], ordered me to be properly paid, and says I am to go to Akyab to do some Hurricane flying and then come back here attached to a fighter squadron as a/c recco pilot.

[1] *Rangoon fell on the day this diary entry was written. The Japanese found that the Indian, Anglo-Indian and Anglo-Burmese population of the city had fled.*
[2] *Air-Vice Marshal Stevenson.*
[3] *From Pilot officer to Flying officer.*

March 10th 1942

Neil Elliot takes me to Akyab as second pilot on his Lockheed 12a, rather like driving a car. I see 136 Squadron and do eighteen landings (yesterday afternoon and this morning and afternoon) on the Mark 1 Hurricane, eventually doing a couple perfectly. A place reminiscent of the Madras coast, and I have a bed in a house overlooking the sea. Good shops in the bazaar where most things, except beer, can be obtained at a reasonable price.

The Fall of Rangoon

The story of the fall of Rangoon is well told in O'Dowd Gallagher's book 'Retreat in the East' - he was the Daily Express foreign correspondent mentioned in these diaries. Rangoon, and Burma generally, was woefully unprepared for the Japanese advance. Civil administration in the city broke down after the bulk of the working population fled following the first Japanese air raids over Christmas 1941, and large amounts of military equipment bound for the Chinese nationalists and the small British military force in the jungles of the north had to be destroyed before Rangoon was finally evacuated on 9th March.

The only reason the Japanese took as long as they did to reach Rangoon was the heroic fighting retreat of the British, Indian and Gurkha troops in the north, and the astonishing successes of the three squadrons of the American Volunteer Group, supported by elements of the RAF and Royal Australian Air Force.

Farr here, driving a Valencia. I get awful drunk on my promotion, taking about four pegs of whisky with ice and fizzy orange squash. I then go off to relieve myself in the bushes near the Mess, and decide that one more drink will kill me. I have a quick dinner, walk to my bed, about 600 feet, keeping straight with some difficulty. I ease springs as usual, and have a hell of a time trying to climb up the stairs to my balcony where I sleep.

Harris, Sgt Hilton, and F/Lt Pierce of 28 Sqn arrive to fly Hurricanes in Burma (as per the order). Pierce is from England and was in 4 Sqn with Lysanders in France. We come on from Akyab, back to Magwe in the Lockheed 12a and find we are the Army Coop part of this "Burwing" under G/C Seton-Broughal, and that we are to eventually retreat to China! We are being given three Mk 1 Hurricanes from 17 Sqn at present and will practise on these until ours arrive, if they ever do. Drinks with Lakri and Neil in the Club last night, very pleasant.

March 16th 1942

MAGWE

WE GO TO YENANGYAUNG A COUPLE OF TIMES to swim, and yesterday hit a black partridge on the way home. Moule arrives from the front to be Paddy's stooge.

On Friday 13th, I take off in a Hurricane and wonder why the tail won't come up. I put the tail trimmer forward a bit and the stick and give it full throttle. The end of the runaway looms up, DC2s etc, and I just manage to get off like a Lysander. I then look at the revs and am horrified to see only 2000! I throttle back and they drop to 1600 and off the clock so I come in and land quickly, and find the constant speed[1] has not been properly connected.

A lot of Blenheims being lost on low-level reccos, so I expect we shall have some trouble, as Pierce seems to fancy this low-level stuff. A Blenheim got back the other day with the pilot shot dead, and the crew bale out over the 'drome.

We have a 'Lashio Bus Service' wagon as our flight office, and the PA's car which I obtained by a wangle. I still don't seem very keen on this flying, but I expect it's through having nothing to do. As we are non-operational just now, we have been made duty pilots, so I'm sitting in the office doing nothing. We mess in the Commissioner's house – very pleasant drinking beer on the lawn in the evening, though there aren't many glasses, watching the sunset on the Irrawaddy and listening to the Quoels *(Brainfever birds)*.

[1] *Piston engines and propellors are most efficient at a constant speed, so sometimes power changes are absorbed by altering the pitch of the blades to keep rotational speed constant, via a constant speed unit (CSU).*

March 20th 1942

MAGWE

I GO ON OPERATIONS AGAIN. Hilton and I fly to Park Lane, the Prome landing ground, and then try an R/T test with the army at Milestone 135 (north of Zigon); the R/T fails, so I go off and do my recco of Myogwin railway at 50 feet, with Hilton weaving behind me. He loses me once or twice but we manage OK. Hardly operational flying though, as it all seemed to be on our side of the "line". We have two Hurricane 1's, and Pierce and Harris go one day, and Hilton and self the other. That's the scheme anyway.

Another day at Yenangyaung, and Paddy and I buy a couple of bottles of wine, which we consume in glasses with ice, during a local beer drought which lasts for two days. Saw Penton at Park Lane (landing ground).

March 21st 1942

MAGWE

45 SQN BLENHEIMS AND 17 SQN HURRICANES as escort go off at dawn to bomb Mingalodon, now in Japanese hands. The PRU[1]

brought home some pictures showing aircraft all over the runways. They get attacked before their run-up and all the way back to Henzada. 45 Sqn shoot down a few, drop their bombs, and 17 Sqn get a few more.

I arrange to do an R/T test with 17th Division today and am trying to tune my radio with the ground station, on the satellite strip[2], when I suddenly see 18 strange aircraft in straggle formation. I head for the bushes, with the fear in my heart, as they appear to be coming down to ground strafe us. Then the sky fills with planes and a stick falls along the east-west strip of the satellite and also apparently in the town, where a petrol dump goes up.

We run further out into the bush and more and more formations appear. There is some high cloud, so they can be seen quite clearly against it. They knock hell out of the aerodrome, but don't appear to notice the satellite, and Navy 'O's swoop down in the smoke and machine gun it. Dog fights all over the sky and a Hurricane comes in low over our heads, quite slowly. Off they go, and we return to the dispersal. I then hear an ominous noise, so out we go again, to see 18 bombers heading south. More bombs fall, and then about 17 come in at 10,000 feet from the east with the ack-ack going through them, but bursting high. A DC2 looms through the smoke and goes away again, to come back afterwards and land on the satellite.

I return to my R/T and get it working by 4.30, so instead of beating the sun, I decide to do it tomorrow. Perhaps I will get a rocket, but I don't fancy flying after all that. But they may catch me tomorrow.

---

[1] *The Photographic Reconnaissance Unit*
[2] *A Satellite Landing Ground (SLG) is a temporary RAF base that typically consists of an airfield with one or two grass runways. These are designed to be hidden from aerial observation by blending into forests and other natural features, hiding the aircraft on the ground.*

March 27th 1942

I GO DOWN TO GET INTO MY A/C and see them all running for the bushes, so I run too, and over comes another raid. It is followed by a dozen '97's' turning and twisting like birds behind one another as they shoot up the 'drome, their red suns and undercarriages clearly discernable. Like toy Frog aeroplanes.

Then I go off on my R/T test with 17th Division near Zigon, but not very satisfactory. On my return, Pierce tells me we are off to Lashio, and another bombing raid starts. I count 27 bombers in formation.

Hilton in our Hurricane flies to Akyab, with the six that remain out of 19 Blenheims. I see Parnell land with his legs up, but not hurt. I load our van with rations, a case of beer, and a lot of maps for O'Malley. O'Malley in his jeep, Pierce in his car, Moule in his, the two new PRU pilots Van Rooyen and Thirwell in a Hillman, and self, form our own convoy. We leave Magwe at 8.30 pm and drive through the night until 2.00 am, camping by the roadside near some water, before Meiktila. Tea and tinned salmon for breakfast and then off again.

We get some fuel at Mandalay from a RIASC[1] pump near the gates of the old fort and then on up here to Maymyo. I am behind the Hillman and rather slow, with trouble from impurities in the petrol. Paddy is waiting at the top of the hill with some baskets of strawberries at 1.5 annas each! We park in the Club here, sleeping by our vehicles outside in case anything is stolen. We dine at Angelino's and watch the popsies, as nothing obtainable in the Club, and then to bed, to freeze under three blankets as it's 3000' here. Reminiscent of Dhara Dun.

[1] *Royal Indian Army Service Corps.*

March 28th 1942

WE DRIVE ON UP TO LASHIO. A beautiful drive and a good river near Hsipaw where I would like to camp for a bit. Lashio has changed a bit. More buildings, and it's full of the Chinese Army. Prices have soared a lot, and 50 Players cost at least 6/-. I get a watch for 55/- as the watchmaker at Magwe bolted with mine after the bombing raids.

Harris is here with the Tiger Moth, having flown around Toungoo at 500 feet looking for lost Chinese troops. A lot of B.O.'s on the Chinese military mission, and I see A.B. Millar's name in the book as having passed through and paid his messing. Also Major Theyre of Wilts on his way to command the DWs.[1]

The scheme is for 17 Squadron and us to go to Loiwing in China and reform and re-equip, and then come back down to the war, and for 45 Squadron to stay here and do the same. Strange birds call all night, and it's good sleeping under a couple of blankets.

Thearle and Van Rooyen are due to return to Egypt. Van Rooyen and I go round and find some Burmese nurses and talk to them through their windows, but apart from that, can't even get a chota peg under 2/-. Moule finds some of his kit here, but someone has stolen his gun from out of his case. Paddy puts his clock by his bedside, and when he wakes up it has vanished.

[1] *2nd Battalion, Duke of Wellington regiment. They trained as Chindits to operate behind Japanese lines.*

March 29th 1942

LOIWING, CHINA

CHINA! We leave Lashio (Pierce and self and one Merritt of 17 Sqn), and drive to Loiwing[1]. We camp on the road the first

A Chinese soldier at the China/Burma border.

night, light a fire and broach a case of beer. Bully, cheese and dry biscuits fried on the fire form an excellent meal. Next day on, and we reach here. Many hairpin bends on the road, and country very hilly in parts and like Assamese jungle in others. We arrive here near Pangkham village on the border and live in the PWD[2] bungalow, 17 Sqn and troops taking over the BFF[3] barracks. Excellent food out of tins etc, now living well on the country, and damn good sleeping at this height. We drive to China yesterday over a bridge where there's a sentry and a bamboo barrier.

China much the same as this, and at Loiwing is C.A.M.C.O.'s works[4]. The sentry has a Kachha-looking rifle with a bayonet and two stick bombs in his equipment. Also some sandpaper for cleaning his weapons, in a special pouch. A British tin hat.

I cross the river and walk for some hours in China yesterday up in the jungle forest, but see nothing interesting except red ant nests up in trees. No fuel at Loiwing (the satellite), and they have no permission for aircraft to land there. It's about 10 miles from here over the border. A Subedar of BFF fixes up all feeding and servants for us. Not too hot, and wooded hills all around.

Today Sunday, must go to a church parade, whilst I and Crossing, the QM, sit and talk to the Subedar and the locals about food etc. The Burma road is a good one, and full of Chinese lorry convoys, going both ways. Pierce pulls over in a narrow bit of road to avoid a US Army jeep and gets two wheels in a ditch. The jeep pulls him out, but too far, and he ditches on the other side of the road, throwing us all off into the paddy fields.

[1] *Now Ruili in China.*
[2] *Public Works Department.*
[3] *Burmese Frontier Force.*
[4] *The Central Aircraft Manufacturing Company (CAMCO), also known as the Loiwing Factory after they moved to Yunnan, was a Chinese aircraft manufacturer established by American entrepreneur William D. Pawley in the 1930s.*

March 31st 1942

LOIWING

I ORGANISE A SHOOTING PARTY, and about 50 chaps with rifles come, and naturally we see nought. The guide, a BFF Hawaldar, fires the bush to drive stuff out but I don't see it.

Yesterday we go and examine the landing ground, and I go for a walk up the river above the bridge, and sit on a rock and contemplate. The acme of peace up there.

A Jap recco plane is shot down over here by AVG who use Loiwing field. When I set off from Lashio I had all my kit, but my kit bag doesn't seem to have arrived and is lost. Contains all my footwear, but worst of all my helmet and goggles. All I have now is the third pair of goggles. I buy a pair of PT shoes, and with chaplies and flying boots, that's all I have. S/L Stone is very contemptuous of my organised shoot and brings back 15 doves last night saying they are wood pigeon!

Today the adjutant Crowther and I visit Pangkham market with the Havaldar, and many strange sights seen.

April 3rd 1942

LOIWING

WE HAVE A PARTY WITH A ROAST (or boiled) pig, and I collect a couple of American matrons too, Mrs Davidson and Mrs Porritt. We brew our rum punch and sing songs. Yesterday I go swimming at my "Somerset Maughan" pool and very nice, with Biles the cypher officer who has spent 20 years in the East in BAT and comes from Chiengram. Most interesting.

I go out one evening and walk for nearly an hour into the jungle, with a guide, after peafowl, but all I see is a badger-like creature with a long yellow bushy tail. Perhaps a civet cat.

Air raid alarms and excursions. Akyab, Namsang, Heho, Lashio bombed. Saw a signal "Burwing has now no aircraft", so expect we shall have to move soon.

April 7th 1942

LASHIO

I GET VERY DRUNK WITH BYLES on "Samsu" at 1/- a beer bottle full. Drunk for 8 annas and the G/C turns up. But I recover with a bath and am alright by dinner time. A troops concert where I render "Craven A" to no great success, but the AVG come and visit us afterwards with some bottles and they get very drunk. Tom Pierce and I decide to visit Lashio on the pretext of looking for my kitbag, and pack up and leave for here. We find it under the Mess verandah, and arrive to find most of the air staff had forgotten about us, but they are sending to 221 Group suggesting we return to 28 Sqn.

Penton up from the front said Kinnaird was killed at the Shwedang road block near Prome. We have drinks with Group Captain Seton-Broughal last night, gatecrashing him, and later with rum punch brewed in a thermos. He is getting a "bowler hat" *(going back to civilian life)* and G/C Singer has taken over. We sit around doing nothing and hoping to get away, drinking South African brandy and water.

Penton returned today, as all surplus AILO's are required back, but Paddy determined to stay and retreat to China.

Loiwing was good fun and a rest, but now I must go back to war. There was some talk of joining 17 Sqn, but I prefer my own mob to those shockers.

April 10th 1942

Lashio

NOT MUCH HOPE OF GETTING TO INDIA, it seems. Now as a sop to the army and the Chinese, we are to do reccos again.

Rikki and two others patrolling Loiwing above 10/10 cloud runs out of petrol, gets lost and they all prang. Yesterday Japanese Navy 'O's over Loiwing at 6.00 am and they ground strafe 28 a/c to their heart's content – i.e. until all their ammo gone. Result: 5 damaged.

At 15.30 yesterday nine Navy 'O's up there, six shot down by AVG, one by 17 Sqn, one of 17 Sqn bales out, another crashes into a mountain, where the engine rolls off and the pilot gets two black eyes.

I go out shooting with my .38 yesterday and wound a vulture. On returning, Pierce says we have a recco each to do. I am to fly to Heho for the night and recco the Chinese front by Bowlake. He will fly to Meiktila and next morning recco Allanmyo front. But after yesterday at Loiwing, there is only one Hurricane left, so he is using that today, and I shall do mine when he comes back. Then when 17 Sqn have their second Hurricane serviceable, we shall have it and do reccos.

Burma's total air effort!

Nothing to do here but read books and walk out occasionally in the woods. Some gin and some sherry in the mess. Air raid alerts twice a day, lasting for about two hours.

April 13th 1942
LASHIO

STILL ALIVE. The Hurricane arrives late. He tries yesterday but returns owing to bad weather. Today the pilot has taken her up to Loiwing to get some plastic wood for the airscrew.

Yesterday Doc Waterman and I go up to Namtu where the lead and silver mines are. We are invited into the Club for some beer before lunch but at lunchtime (2.00 pm) they all bolt and leave us. We get some at the rest house and start home, 44 miles, taking five hours as there is dirt in the petrol system, and the pump doesn't work (this is a Ford 'desert wagon'). We get towed in at 8.00 pm.

Thirwell over here for his kit and his PRU machine is now at B25 with a crew of seven in Calcutta. I don't think we shall ever get there, and the longer we stay here the more dangerous these reccos will become.

April 16th 1942
LASHIO

PIERCE DOES QUITE A SAFE RECCO and I go down yesterday evening to Meiktila. First time up for three weeks, but I manage OK and navigation is good. I have to taxi for half an hour under cover and over newly cut down bunds so that the engine nearly blows up by the time it's finished. At full throttle I can't get over some of the bunds and have to take a run!

Sides, the Australian, is there, and we spend the night in the PWD bungalow up the road. Meiktila has been reccoed and shot up daily, so they shift their quarters about, as there seems to be an

Colin drinking in the Mess

efficient espionage system there.

Some food by torch light, and I crawl under a mosquito net on a charpoy, though only get one hour's sleep for thinking of what the Japs do to their prisoners! Sides works from 9 to 11.00 pm getting the a/c out on the strip, and I take off at 06.10, but would have got off ten minutes earlier if the chap driving me there hadn't lost the way.

No task arranged with the army, so Chaplin decides on a recco. Sinbawngwe to Magwe along the east bank. Our own troops are at Magwe and some way forward. I set course in the dark, get up to 1100 feet and suddenly spot Satthwa, so turn off and dive down over Sinbawngwe. I then look back and see four aircraft following (I am about 2000 feet), but these dissolve into puffs of smoke, and that means ack-ack. I scoot round a hill and back east of the village to recco the road north, and see some flashes, and up it comes again. I scoot and wheel down low but am between the gunners and the rising orb of the sun, so plenty more comes up but I am soon away. The road is difficult to find, but I see some lorries, probably ours, some A/T, and eventually return to Meiktila, thoughtfully in case the Japs be waiting there. I land, refuel, see Chaplin the A.I.L.O., and am off in ten minutes. A straight course, but I hit the railway at a point south of Hsipaw, and I skim up the road home.

Three decent landings OK!

April 22nd 1942

Lashio

SHERKHAM OF 56TH IS HERE on his way to Maymyo and a staff job. He says 2/13th are in 17th Division and lost Lt Col Guy at Prome. I go down to Myittha for another recco as Meiktila is getting too hot. Best camouflaged strip I ever saw, and when you get there it's some time before you can see how to land on it and avoid the cactus. Taxiing into cover, the tailwheel prangs, so I take it off next morning and fly straight to Loiwing, do a wheeler and a bit of a ground loop, and pick up the other one from the satellite. Then return to Lashio.

Then down again, and yesterday morning I take off at 06.05 with one landing light on recco. Chauk and the Pinchaung north of Yenanyuang, but NMS *(no movement seen)* except bullock carts. I return home, circle three times, but no smoke and no corner strips, so I try a landing. Manage to get down, and then see Sides at the end waving me to stop; I can't run off the end, and after 20yds the wheels hit a hole, and up on her nose. I think she is going right over and on fire, but not enough momentum and she stops on her nose. I pull everything and leap out, having pranged my third Hurricane 11B and my fourth escape from death in one. Prop, wing tip, and wheels bent back but salvageable. Aircraft noises in the air, but we cover her in cactus, and Sides sends me home in his car.

Strawberries at Maymyo, two punctures and back at 7.45 pm, having left Myittha at 11.00 am. Saw half a dozen Sikh soldiers straggling up the road, but hadn't sufficient presence of mind to stop and question them. At Myittha we live in the PWD irrigation bungalow, with a four course dinner and all booze except beer. I sleep on a camp bed on the verandah and very hot, so I don't sleep much, especially thinking of what the Japs do to their prisoners - again!

I have now done 57 ops, but no respite, though I can't go on forever, alive!

April 25th 1942

THE JAPS ARE COMING, YO-HO-HO!

Pierce does a recce between Heho and Namsang on the road where they have broken through. He sees lorry loads who fire rifles and tommy guns at him. I am sent off in a Blenheim and we go down as far as Loilem without seeing much, though we get fired on by Bofors. Lorryloads of Chinese troops pour past the mess and down the road to stop the gap. Very bad weather prevents me going down last night, but Pierce goes off this morning and they are coming up the road near Kehsi Mansam on the road to Lashio.

Everybody packing up and making ready to go to Loiwing, but not much hope of getting to India again. I am due off this evening to see where the Japs have got to, so hope I shall be alright.

April 28th 1942

LAST MAN IN TO BAT

I GO DOWN THE ROAD THAT EVENING and see nothing much, except a few lorries at Konghai-ping crossroads. Further up, I squirt at two lorries, the first stops and men rush out and hide, I miss that, but the second I catch in a pass on a winding gradient corner; but the burst kicks up the dust just behind it. I then see two aircraft, but avert panic by recognising them as two Blenheims, they get frightened too, and swerve off. Chaps rush for cover here and there off the road, but whether Chinese or Japs I don't know.

The AVG, 17 of them, blast a convoy on that road up from Loilem, the Kittyhawks with 40lbers. Next morning the Japs have moved up their Bofors type ack-ack, and Pierce has a hell of a time at zero feet. He squirts some troops on the ground, but no more to add to my one bullet hole through the top cowling. S/Ldr Stone then says he has no pilots to ferry the Hurricane to Loiwing and

The last Hurricane out of Burma

back for a daily, so much against my inclination I am sent, with orders to be back by 1600 hrs to do a recco.

I go to Loiwing, with some luggage in the back, but the weather takes a hand and I can't get off. The Burwing evacuation convoy comes in that evening, but the food is still as good as ever. I get off after lunch yesterday and have a wonderful trip down. Round the monster 7600 feet peak, as he is in cloud, but down alongside the Burma Road under the low fleecy clouds, and through the rainstorms.

Flap in Lashio!

Two '97s shot up the 'drome that morning and damaged a Blenheim there. Then two "erks"[1] mending a car down the road were ordered back to Lashio "as quick as you can", in English, by a Chinese officer. The two evacuate, and Chinese troops and tanks come driving back.

G/S Singer and his staff don't know what to do, are all packed up, and are just waiting to blow the joint up, and burn the damaged aircraft. As last man in to bat, I am sent off down the road to see what's going on. I take all my kit (most of it), which is tempting fortune if ever, and go down to Namlan, about 60 miles per crow. Pierce says keep out of range, so I do it a la Mingalodon days. A steady trickle of transport is coming back, and about seven miles north of Namlan, 50-60 lorries are parked facing north. Chinese or Japanese, quien sabe! I land, report, refuel and straight back to Loiwing, the last Hurricane out of Burma. Now the W/T seems out of order, but I expect a signal to go down there again anytime today, damn it. 60 operational sorties and still alive! Phew!

¹ Lowest rank RAF groundcrew.

April 30th 1942

Loiwing

Lashio in Japanese hands now. All they have to do is to drive to Namtu and then march by jungle tracks for three days north and they are here.

After writing the last entry there is an alarm, and the usual noise heralding the approach of Japanese aircraft. Very high, 20,000 feet, I just see between 12 and 20 bombers. They bomb the field and return home. Hundreds of holes in the runaway, a DC3 damaged and repaired next day. The AVG were away from home, ground strafing south of Lashio, where they shoot down some 17 Navy 'O's. One large four engine job seen, and suspected to be a captured Fortress.

The Lashio rearguard turn up here, and reorganisation is in progress. W/C Spencer is coming to command a small skeleton wing with a half a dozen refuelling parties, and when the rains have ended, aircraft will come from India and operate from China. Pierce is off in the Hurricane to Shwebo to contact the army and see what the position is, and tell them ours. After that, quien sabe?

17 Sqn have departed, hopefully, in lorries to India, by guess or by God.

May 4th 1942

I AM ORDERED TO FLY THE HURRICANE to Myithyina and then Dum Dum with long range tanks. Weather very bad, and much rain, and everyone leaves Loiwing for Myithyina and India. (Like hell I go to Myithyina!! I set course direct for Calcutta!!). But the road from Bhamo is down (up) due to the heavy rain. Paine and I are left, he to demolish, and I to wait for the weather. The AVG leave and all the villages are burning.

I set off on the 2nd through a hole in the clouds and do a bit of cloud flying, but lose control and suddenly see the earth above me as I come screaming down in a corkscrew dive. (I flew off the satellite because the main field is still O/S and we had to burn a perfectly good Blenheim there.) Then I lose my map, but continue on my course until I see the sea to port. This is all wrong and I stooge about at 1000 feet, absolutely lost for about an hour, then happen to strike Goalanda on the Ganges. Petrol is short, so I set a course for Maheshganj which is marked on the map, but turns out to be a seaplane base. On reserve tank I try to make DumDum, arriving with 10 gallons left after 4.5 hours.

Off to the Grand where I see J. Benbow. We go out to the Saturday Club and I see Mann and Reggie Cox, now a Brigadier in Ranchi where 28 Sqn is. I call at 221 Group to find I am still a P/O, as India have referred the case to the Air Ministry, Stevenson not being qualified to promote me![1]

A bit of shopping, 20/- of "bhaint"[2], shocking, and I go by train to Ranchi tonight. That first beer tasted nice. Met Donald Gordon again, mad as ever.

Two Chinese mission chaps turned up on May 1st at Loiwing and brought a bottle of Scotch so Paine and I had a party.

The monsoon came early I think, and today I hear that the Japs have got up towards Bhamo and 17 Sqn and BURWING[3] are in danger of being caught.

Three Japanese seaplanes bombed shipping off the mouth of the Hoogly the other day, and also two ports on the Malabar coast. Mann says Carey was after Air/Coop Hurricane pilots for some job or other, so I suppose I shall have to go.

Officially promoted F/O from 30/10/41. Haig in 155 Squadron at Risalpur. Dozens of new A/SD chaps in the squadron.

[1] *See March 9th 1942.*
[2] *Meaning unclear - possibly service charge in Hindi.*
[3] *BURWING, under Group Captain S. Broughall, was made up of No. 45 (Bomber) Squadron, No. 17 (Fighter) Squadron, and the few surviving pilots of the AVG. Alexander, the Army Commander, controlled its use and it continued to do all it could to support the retreating army.*

8

May - December 1942

28 Squadron

Ranchi
West Bengal

May 12th 1942

AM I NUTS? NOT QUITE. I arrive on the train and see all the boys at the station, who have come to meet Hammer's fiance and the bridesmaid Marianne Evans. We drink beer, 10.00 am, and then back to the mess. It's the white house in Hinoo which we have taken over, and would be quite comfortable if there was a fridge of sorts. The servants are pretty bum but we manage, and are on rations too. Well, yesterday was the marriage, and Robin White and I were ushers at the Cathedral. A "Lizzie" flew over and dropped confetti. Then back to the mess, and the binge lasts from 12 to 8 when the last guest departs.

I go off at 2.30 am and lie down as I have to play football, and through my room to his goes Robin with Joyce Knowles to lie down, as she is a bit tight. Later on she starts fighting him and I go in to see what's going on, clad only in a towel. She is keen on biting and I have to calm them down a bit, both of them half naked.

I go off to my football and end up in the Club at a dance. Meet Basil Seaton and Penton there, and do some dancing with the Marianne and Betty, the 14-and-a-half year old prodigy. The rest of the week seems to have been spent drinking late at various places. I take General Symes of 70 Div to Jamshedpur and on a recce of his area, and am due off to Calcutta with him tomorrow. We are under 70 Division and beat up their camps occasionally, but that's about all.

30 officers and 300 men got out of Myitkyina, and the Japs are now in Loiwing and Yunnan Province.

I thought I was doing well with the bridesmaid but Teddy has now taken her over, and anyway she is going back to Murree, a nurse in B.M.H., tomorrow. I have no aim and ambition just now, unless it's to get married, but who to? – and I'm not ready yet. Hope nothing contracted in Calcutta. It's going to be hot here soon, despite 2000 feet odd altitude.

May 13th 1942

I GO OUT TO LUNCH WITH THE BALDWINS and have a domestic afternoon playing with the Babe. Monday, I go down to Cuttack with Maj Gen Symes, and we recco Golapore on the Indian Ocean. Very sticky at Cuttack, where there is a Hudson-less Hudson Sqn 62, and two large runaways with "tees" on both of them. Then find Tom Pierce has arrived, and we go to the Club, where Burt Mann gets intoxicated and, along with Paintal (7 Rajputs) AILO, we dine with George Cutler, a great gross beast who supplies labour hereabouts and runs the Club bar. We escape about 11.00 pm. A good club, and the RAF are allowed to sign there, but not the Army, who have to buy books of tickets plus 20%.

Yesterday tennis with Pierce, some drinks, and we then feed with Raj Paintal and Joyce and the Nelsons on the floor of his tent. 'Desi khana' again[1], but not a hot one.

Today I fly round for 3/4 hour over Ramgarh where there is a POW camp, and 'shoot up' some camps, but too many shite hawks about, and damn dangerous. We go up to work at 6.30 am and finish at lunch, but if nothing to do, it means just standing around, which is what the airmen do all day. A letter from ADC sending five invitations to an "at home" to be given to "selected officers of your mess".

[1] *Urdu for local, indigenous food, meaning curry.*

May 17th 1942

RANCHI

JOE AND OLGA DEPART FOR AMBALA where he is to be an instructor. Tennis, football and drinking, and Pierce and I dine with Penton last night. My "Further Notes on Floating down the

311

Indus" is accepted for publication in the U.S.I. Journal![1]

No fun flying these Lysanders after my Hurricane! I don't seem to have an ambition just now. I drift along, and flying rather bores me. I wouldn't mind going to Waziristan and being a Tochi Scout or something, but I don't fancy any more operational flying if I can avoid it.

[1] See October 26th 1941.

May 22nd 1942

RANCHI

JUST PLAYED A GAME OF CRICKET, first for four years, and made top score (31). A little flying, not much good. A young I.A.F. chap tries to land in coarse pitch with wheels right back, overshoots, opens up and turns, then stalls, into the ground. I get the clock, as it's my old kite 4808. Passenger killed, and we have a funeral.

Reggie Cox is a Brigadier here, 23 Brigade, with Marriott of 2nd Leicesters as staff captain. Barlow, Clarcoates, Barder and a lot of others killed. Also Langford-James in a Blenheim. A letter from Bill (Robinson), now in Ceylon. Some girls in uniform arrive in Ranchi, attached to Signals, and Tom and I get in on it with tennis and dancing and whatnot. One of them, one Patience Farraday, knew Malaya and the folk1 quite well. Much drinking in the Club, though I haven't been tight here yet. Robin White and Teddy have a session ending about 6.00 am in our mess truck, filled with dhotis and ghandi caps which they tear off people in rickshaws. Very hot here just now and I collapse on my bed after lunch, which I never did before.

We are exchanging untrained pilots for trained ones from 20 Sqn, so I suspect we shall have to go back to the war again.

[1] His parents, Joe and Meta Dunford Wood, who lived in Ipoh in Malaya in the 1930s.

May 31st 1942

DRINKING AND TENNIS and some occasional flying. Robin White and I beat up 56 (anti-tank) Regiment crossing Ratu Lake, and one gun sinks. A most enjoyable flip. Bill Symonds here, raising a Provost unit, and we have a party. Also guarding the airfield is one Jeffries of South Staffs, from my term at Sandhurst, and a friend of Bill's. We get a lot of beer up from Calcutta, and are still drinking it after a week.

Nothing of note. I take over as mess secretary, being one of the few people capable of pulling out his finger. 17 Div is on its way here, so this will be the front line soon. More talk of these Vengeances we are supposed to get, but not in the country yet.

June 6th 1942

CALCUTTA

I MANAGE TO GET MYSELF ON THE FIRST HILL PARTY to Shillong for three weeks. One BO and 13 British other ranks. A horrid train journey, six hours late, and I go to stay with Paddy, as he had invited me, but someone else is there, so I am at 1 Bishop Lefroy Street. A bedroom, half a sitting room and bathroom for 5/-. Good food too. Went to Octavia Steel's, and found Uncle Stanley[1] in a new garden further up. Also met Pitcairn, 20 Sqn, who is in charge of their party. One Kochar of 353 Sqn IAF in the next room, and we go to drink at the Grand last night, as it's dry here. Met Everard and Warburton of 17 Sqn, the latter, having got himself engaged to an undesirable girl in Darjeeling, is being shipped off to the Middle East.

Saw an E.C.O. in the regiment in the Grand last night and I said "Are you in the 56th?"

"No," he replied, "I'm in Frontier Force Rifles".

"Good God, which battalion?"

"The 8th".

Some dialogue – the army's going to the dogs[2].

Hurricanes roar over the rooftops all day long here, but no air raids so far.

[1] *His uncle Stanley Wood, who was a tea planter in Assam, and with whom he spent his leave in Volume 1.*

2 *His meaning here is that the officer did not realise that the 56th (Punjabi Rifles) was the former name for a battalion of the Frontier Force Rifles, which he should have known.*

June 8th 1942

SHILLONG

I GO TO DINNER AT 48 THEATRE ROAD with Paddy, and then to the flicks. We go on to the Saturday Club and meet Singer and Devitt with a couple of girls. Singer rather tight, and shouting "Rape! Rape!" periodically. Actually it's "Wape, wape!" the way he pronounces it. He is quite funny, and I dance with his girl.

Next day, off to Shillong by special train, leaving Sealdah 11.30 am and reaching Amingoan 4.00 pm the next day. I see the station superintendant and switch myself onto the Assam mail, doing the same journey between 12 and 6.00 am. We pass some trainloads of troops, ex-Burma, and they invade the restaurant car and buy up all the beer. Breakfast on the ferry as usual, very full of troops, and I see Brigadier Ekin going the other way, though he doesn't recognise me. Up 60 miles by car and find we have got 8th Gurkha Rifles mess and lines, the regiment having left for Quetta. Damn cold, and all I have is a bush shirt (5000 feet in June?).

Shillong much like Abbottabad and the streets like Missourie. Full of wounded from Burma, so no liking for the RAF. Met Paine at Ganhati who is on the staff here, and apparently no transport, so the boys will have to stay the night down there when they reach the river.

314

My quarter looks out across the mess, with the smoke torn straight off the chimneys by the wind to wooded hilltops. Everything luscious and green. In the ghusal-khana[1] is an electric water boiler which I never saw before. A sort of cistern plugged into the main, which you turn on and the water heats up. A tap at the bottom lets it all out.

A nice dull day, bags of wind, and some rain. The sort of gloomy day on which I thrive, becoming all sentimental and longing for the company of a nice girl and a pot of ale. Thunder, doors and windows rattling, trees sighing, damn dark and further outlook worse – such weather always makes me cheerful, but sad with thoughts of romance. Sad because of no damn luck, though only due to lack of opportunities I'm sure. Maybe one day?

[1] *Urdu for bathroom.*

June 16th 1942

Shillong

Much drinking in the club and in the mess. Peter Allan up here; also met Jack Moulding and Tony Ward, the latter just off. Some people called Jim and Jane Lindsay of Calcutta, and quite a few girls. We have a bit of bother at the club the first night, and have to see the secretary and pay 21/- before we can get a drink. The C.O. has a girlfriend, also called Morris, and I spend a night in her spare bedroom, unbeknownst to her, as Boy Morris drives the car into a ditch on the way home, so I have to walk the woman home, and then can't find the car again until it's damn late, and I don't feel like sleeping in it.

Sunday I go for a walk to Elephant Falls, some seven miles up the Cherrapunji road, getting a lift part of the way. Coming back, it starts to pour, so I shelter in a small chai-khana (urdu for tea stall or cafe) with half a dozen Burma Rifles, eventually getting a lift home. I go for a half pint at the Club and then get myself in on a picnic at 14 milestone on Cherrapunji Road. Six of us – Jane, Peggy and Daphne Myer and assorted boyfriends, and we swim in a horrid cold pool full of sharp rocks, and then have tea. Tennis and squash yesterday with the Lindsays and Daphne. About 25 officers here now, from 221 and 224 Groups, and the men do a little PT and drill in the mornings and then have the rest of the day off. No dhobi, and we have to take our stuff (laundry) into town.

The weather improving, with only about one good shower a day. We have a ladies night Tuesdays and Fridays and the last one was pretty terrific. I'm now trying to snare them all again for the next one.

At last I write a letter to Peggy[1].

[1] *His brother Hugh's widow.*

June 18th 1942
SHILLONG

BAGS OF RAIN.

Shillong society: Jim and Jane Lindsay, he a "boxwallah" of Calcutta and she most attractive and with a liking for dirty stories – we have a sort of Ladies night here on Tuesdays and Fridays and I try to organise them out here. Daphne Myer, on whom a 7 G.R. (7th Gurkha Rifles officer) spends all his money, but who seems to prefer my company. She always asks me what I am doing tomorrow, am I going here and there, presumably hoping I shall invite her. But I don't – she comes up and asks me to dance with her – aged 21, with a sister Peggy who won't come out here, however much I try to coerce her. In love with a chap in the 8 G.R. who has now left, so presumably that's the reason.

There's the Assam Industries, with a sideline serving coffee and run by the local ladies. Here I encounter one Sheila Clarke, aged 28, still beautiful, though the first chap to whom she was engaged appears to have shot himself. Working with her is the real prize, the queen of Shillong, Pat Anderson, Tony Ward's girlfriend, who wears the 10 G.R. badge always[1]. Young and natural, and I hope to have snared her out for our mess warming party tomorrow evening. Damn Ward, who has now left for the frontier - the Assam-Burma border, that means nowadays.

Peter Allan, of course, up here on leave after road building down by Manipur Road. If Daphne was only Pat, I would fall, though as things stand at present I have to maintain a fairly impassive front.

[1] *Traditionally young women who were engaged or had a serious boyfriend would wear their cap badges, called sweetheart brooches.*

June 23rd 1942

SHILLONG

WE HAVE A PRETTY GOOD HOUSEWARMING PARTY, but Pat is unable to come at the last moment. I have a long talk with Sheila on the verandah. Jane Lindsay spends her time necking with this Morley Owen chap, 7 G.R.

Saturday, we go to the races, though I don't bet, being too preoccupied watching young Pat, then we go to the Pinewood for a drink and Peter Allan invites me to supper at the Club. I do a quick change and return to the Pinewood for a drink and then on to the Club with Pat and the Barclays, 10 G.R.

Sunday I go on a picnic and swimming with Jane, Morley and Daphne, and as the former two spend their whole time locked in each other's arms I find it a bit embarrassing. Then I try to organise a party to the races with Grubb Bell, Sheila, Pat and GB's girlfriend, and find that Pat is already going with the Barclays, so that's that.

I return to Calcutta next Monday, but in the meantime, I don't know what to do. I'll have to give up asking girls to do this and that. Chaps here include Tidswell, a very nice Aussie of 45 Sqn with whom I share a room; Bellinger of Park Street fame; one F/ Lt Marsland of 136 Sqn, a bit of a "chaw" and a "line shooter" but a good scout at heart; "Stinker" Murray the adjutant, once in the Guides; Mackwood of 62 Sqn, a Ground Defence officer; and old Paine, my friend from Loiwing, known as "Cherrapunji", it being the wettest place on earth and a few miles from here.

A letter from Aunt Babs, dated December and posted in March.

June 29th 1942

SHILLONG

I GO TO THE RACES with Mark and Grubb-Bell, the new adjutant, and we run a syndicate which only backs one winner, so not too good. Then we return a woman to the Pinewood, and G-B gets out to try out Barclay's car which is for sale – I hop out too, and get myself invited to Pinewood first, Pat there and all! Then we drive back to the mess in it, and then to the club, where I have to join a party of his, which rather cramps my style.

Pat arrives very late in a large party, and I leave it too late, and don't get a dance with her. I ring up today and ask her to the pictures, but she's going out, so I'm going to have tea with her instead. Let's hope I acquit myself well and don't put up a black.

Off tomorrow, but a bridge is down, so have to go by Sylbet way.

July 4th 1942

RANCHI

THE TEA PARTY IS A SUCCESS and we sit on the club verandah talking from 4.30 to 6.45 pm. Dusk falls, it gets dim, very pleasant, but she has to go out at 6.45. I go home and change and return to the club where I meet Colin Jaques, Benje and Bill Barclay (10 G.R.). We do some drinking, and then repair to Pinewood for some more. I find myself pouring treble whiskies and sodas away under the bar in an endeavour to remain sober. Jaques then takes me home, crashing in the ditch outside G.H. I get a cut on the head and the shoulder but am OK. We turn out the guard, who lift out the car, but it won't work, so Barclay takes me back, his car turning up shortly afterwards.

Off next day after lunch in two buses full of RAF, and Jane Lindsay and her Bedlington Boxer. Train at Sylhet, and then by steamer over the part where I got lost returning in my Hurricane from China. Then a train, and we reach Sealdah at 10.30 pm. Jane puts me up in her flat at Alipore, and next day takes me shopping in the market. I leave on the night train, and meet Paintal and Cpl Allward, the latter returning from town loaded down with booze.

Ranchi much the same, though rain cuts out my exercise which is a shame. Orders are to stand by to move to the frontier soon – why? Also the impending arrival of our Vengeances seems certain in everybody's minds – except mine.

Rather bored – I am just a stooge pilot, capable of commanding a flight, and I reckon I could make a better show as CO than Hammerbeck. I also seem to have forgotten a lot – both what I learnt in the army, and also at F.T.S. (Flying Training School). But I reckon I am a better organiser than anyone in the damn squadron, being capable of "pulling my finger out".

July 10th 1942

RANCHI

MY BIRTHDAY YESTERDAY, though you wouldn't have known it.

I go to the flight office in the morning, and the monsoon pours down, and eventually water invades the tent, despite my drainage system. Then Robin White rescues me in his car and we return to the mess. The 'drome under water, and only fit for flying boats. Then Teddy and I go down in the evening and visit Hammers and wife, who return with us to the mess for dinner. I get in a couple of squash evenings at G.H. with Teddy and Robin.

This could be a good squadron, if we had better leadership. Burt Mann, Pierce and White are the flight commanders, and they could be a lot worse (and better too). Eric Adams the adjutant, most efficient and hard working, Williams the censor and cyphers, and old Gunn. We are supposed to fly up to Kohat on Sunday, and flight ground crews go up by train. I haven't flown for about six weeks! So shall probably prang somewhere. Route Gaga-Cawnpore-Delhi-Lahire-Kohat. It was originally Miramshah.

My kite is having an engine change, and work has been held up due to the torrents of water pouring out of the sky. No exercise possible. Visited the Club last Saturday, but after Shillong and my Jane, it's a complete anti-climax. I see all the girls with whom I used to dance – Gawd! What shockers!

July 18th 1942

Kohat

I GO UP FLYING AGAIN. Engine test, and manage to land OK on the strip. We have some shocking downpours of rain. On 17th we leave, six a/c for Kohat, via Gaga-Cawnpore-Delhi and Lahore (night stop). Eight hours flying the first day, uninteresting, and we have our first beer for some time at Lahore. Yesterday we sit about at Lahore waiting for the weather to clear, and then reach here at about 11.30. Nice to be back amongst the home comforts once more!

One Larsen has joined the squadron, a seconded gunner (TA), and he seems to be one month senior in the RAF to me. Teddy and I find our names in the Gazette in the "Aeroplane" dated Jan 6th, and with all the names, dead or alive, "Oct 1940"[1]. I used 43 gallons (104 miles) in 1.05 hours from Ranchi to Gaga, and all the way to Cawnpore am looking for somewhere to 'force land', as it's 305 miles.

At Delhi we are sitting having some refreshment when the Movement Control Officer asks for a list of pilots and passengers.

He takes it and looks at it and I think "Perhaps he knew Hugh, and will ask who this Dunford Wood is?" Sure enough "Dunford Wood?" He peers at me – "You're not the one I knew" etc.

Ghulam Raval is now a bearer in Signals Mess, and when I mention Bengal, he says he can't come now until his Sahib has gone, but he understands there is a better rate of pay in Bengal! I have got one now who used to be a tennis and squash marker, and he is going to consult his mother about leaving the north first.

W/C Corkery, ex-Burma Communication Flight, is Station Master.

[1] *The time when a large group of Indian Army officers transferred into the RAF. Most of them were dead by this time.*

July 23rd 1942

KOHAT

I GO UP THE TOCHI and have a look at the Datta Khal area, where the forthcoming operations are to take place[1]. The fort has a 'T' and disc out, but I don't know what it is, so drop a message on Miramshah about it.

Pierce does a photo trip, and on the way back his engine gives trouble so he lands at Mirali, damaging the tail wheel. Sgt Gray, who is catching us up, takes off at Delhi and the rudder falls off the top hinge. He manages to get down on the runaway but prangs and breaks the kite's back. Then the CO returns yesterday with engine trouble. What nice aeroplanes we have!

Spent this morning in the canteen with peaches and a bottle of Kiaora[2], and there seems to be nothing to do, and Hammerbeck doesn't tell us anything.

A letter from Jane, who says that Guy Marsland and Peter – of 136 Sqn – fell out over Daphne Meyer and that Guy fired two shots at him.

[1] *They have been tasked with bombing the rebels in Waziristan on the North West Frontier, a return to his old battleground of 1939 - see Volume 1.*
[2] *A brand of orange squash.*

July 28th 1942

KOHAT

LARSEN GOES TO RAZMAK for an artillery shoot but bursts a wheel on landing. He mends 22 punctures in the inner tube but the valve has gone as well. Sgt Ridley flies up with a spare, does a ground loop and writes off his aircraft. Larsen complains of being sniped whilst salvaging the aircraft.

Yesterday four a/c go to Miramshah and then to bomb Narakai. Also nine Blenheims of 34 Sqn from Peshawar and 3 and 4 IAF Sqns. Robin White's engine cuts out, and he force lands up the Kazha Algad, overturning his a/c. He is seen to get out and wave, but his airgunner is still in the wreckage. Sgt Grey comes back and reports at Miramshah and Sgt Hilton drops 2 x 250 lbs on the target. Larsen goes off with medical supplies and sees two naked bodies 100 feet from the aircraft, so he bombs and shoots up all nearby buildings.

Later in the day they do another raid on the same target. Hammerbeck flies to Peshawar to tell them that leaflets have been dropped first, and then later has a lot of bumph to deal with and so misses both raids. Larsen gets a bullet in his engine cowling. Khassadars (local militia) go out and bring the bodies into Miramshah. Robin White was shot and stabbed in the back. Sgt Ellis had a hole in his head, presumably from the crash, and was minus his balls[1].

We now have three out of the seven a/c with which we left Ranchi. 28 Sqn dying a slow death, but not a hope of sending some of the aircrews on leave. I haven't done any 'ops' yet, only a trip to look at the Datta Khal country and some local formation flying.

Alec Johnston turns up as what is called 'Army Cooperation Advisor' – a sort of air staff officer, who writes down all we do, like an A.I.L.O.

S/Ldr Mehr Singh, CO 3 Sqn, once force landed in Waziristan, but he set fire to his aircraft, after having taken out the compass, then hid all day and navigated into Datta Khal by day. Robin was going to marry Joyce Knowles on 15th or 26th August, when we had gotten back.

[1] *This was a common mutilation carried out by rebels who captured British soldiers or airmen on the North West Frontier. Hence the name given to the ransom notes pilots carried on the North-West Frontier - the 'Goolie chit' - which offered a reward to return the pilot - and his balls - to British lines in one piece.*

July 30th 1942

KOHAT

WE HAVE A FUNERAL THAT EVENING FOR ROBIN and I am a pallbearer. I get the middle, a bad position, and the sweat streams down all over my body despite the hour, 7.00 pm. Then standing to attention by the grave during the service is an ordeal. Little tricklets of sweat everywhere, and I'll swear the flies balance on them and slide down my face.

CO writes Robin's mother a letter, and none of us approve of it, but that's that.

Page 3 of an airgraph from Ma – the first communication since Iraq and RS 50/- from the U.S.I. Journal[1]. I seem to spend most of my time up here by the mess swimming pool with a book. All I seem to do in the morning is a little link trainer[2].

[1] *In payment for his article 'Floating Down the Indus', based on his hunting trip in October 1941.*
[2] *A flight simulator.*

323

August 8th 1942

HAMMERS, JACKY, PIERCE, LARSEN, BURKE AND SELF go to Peshawar in the truck and stay Saturday night at Dean's Hotel (11/-). We swim in the club and then do some drinking, having a rather hilarious dinner with champagne at about 10.00 pm. Very stuffy in the rooms, and I wake up wanting a drink and have to drink tap water.

Sunday morning I take the boys down to the bazaar, with my bearer as guide, and we buy Hammers a young parakeet for his birthday. Lunch at the club, but I am feeling a bit tired after last night's bad sleeping. I get stung by a hornet on the way home, but suck out most of the poison before it takes effect.

Intelligence at Miramshah reports that Robin shot two, and wounded three other tribesmen, before he was killed. He had one bullet wound and a knife thrust, both in the back.

Getting bored with life again. Time I did something once more.

August 10th 1942

RAZMAK

I AM SENT TO RAZMAK with Falconer and 16 B.O.R.s to salvage Ridley's prang. We have to stay two nights in Bannu rest camp, a dreadful joint, but I am able to get rid of the Club tickets I have hoarded for all these years[1]. I spend the days swimming there and getting prickly heat. Also make some money at Bridge in the club. Then to Razmak by convoy. We have three Crosleys, a float, and a crane, and the two former are stacked with young unarmed Dogras. We break down about four times and get left behind by the rest of the convoy, but manage OK.

I get the B.O.Rs out to take up positions, but it's a pitiful sight to see, rifles in one hand and equipment in the other.

Between Greenwood's Corner and Razmak Narai I hear shots, and they make the sort of noise I always reckon they do when they are being aimed at you. Sure enough, the leading lorry sees them bouncing on the road in front of them.

In Razmak we stay with K.O.S.B.[2] but they are out on the Column and Courtney-Hood is in charge of the depot. We feed at district HQ mess, and the best food I have had this year. I meet the old Munshi in Boretts Park. We get the kite loaded up and are now waiting for the next road open day.

I go down and do 1.5 hrs roller skating at full throttle, then go home for a bath and get out shivering all over. No sleep that night, and next day I am aching all over and when I shake my head a large stone rattles in it. Eventually I get to hospital, and they take a malaria blood slide, but no result yet. I sign on a new bearer, Ayub Khan, a Poonchwala who was bearer to Agar of KOSB, killed on the Column. I feel a bit better today, so perhaps it's not malaria. Three Indians in this ward, and one plays Indian music on his radio all day.

[1] Kept from since he was last in Bannu in 1939 - see Volume 1.
[2] King's Own Scottish Borderers.

August 15th 1942

RAZMAK

REPEATED BLOOD SLIDES eventually disclose BT malaria and I am very ill one evening, but temperature normal next day and so on. Am now moved to a ward upstairs which is full of BOs. My bill for 48 hrs (3 days) at the Staff mess is Rs 15 – a monster!

Falconer and his boys got off and now I just lie in bed all day hoping to get away. One Major Hennessy of the Baluchis turns up. He was the chap whom I, John Palmer and the Padre had to put to bed in the Connemara (in Madras), way back, but I haven't approached him about it yet. The orderlies here are nearly as dumb as the Kohat lot, but more willing.

August 23rd 1942

KOHAT

I LINGER ON IN HOSPITAL, with sorties to the club for my morning beer. Eventually on the 19th I depart in a lorry with my revolver and my rifle, and a lot of other BOs discharged from hospital. We meet the Column coming back, and Brigadier Freeland and Morris Latham 3/1 G.R. pass close by, but I don't get in a word. We run into a battle just above Razani and the bullets seem to be coming over near the lorries.

A night in Bannu rest camp, where I manage to get a good berth and meet Major Speight of 3 G.R., ex-RAF in Iraq. We talk a lot, and then go to the club and join up with Brigadier Quyell, who was in Jhelum when we went there, and one Obsdell/Ulsdell of the Somersets. On next day to Kohat in an R.A. convoy, riding in the RAF W/T tender that had been out on the column. He nearly puts us over a khud![1]

Hammerbeck temporarily gone to some job in Bangalore, we hope for good, and Mann is acting C.O. of the squadron. Tom Pierce in Karachi looking for spares, the Rail Party due to go shortly, and the Air Party (2 a/c) gone already[2]. I am left in charge of the repairs, to make two aircraft out of three crashes, which will take months to do. So I shouldn't get away until then.

A new A.I.L.O. arrives, Major Rose, a regular gunner, and O'Ferrall got rid of, so we ought to be OK. My bearer now decides he won't come to Ranchi after all, so I'm giving up the struggle.

I see myself in print "Floating Down the Indus"!

[1] *A deep ravine.*
[2] *The squadron is being relocated back to Ranchi after the end of operations on the NW Frontier.*

August 27th 1942

KOHAT

THE RAIL PARTY DEPARTS YESTERDAY. I find repairs will take a month, so wire Ranchi, suggesting I return there. Answer is yes if W/C okays it. After much telephoning, I contact him in Peshawar, and he gives his assent. So I'm off tonight D.V., (God willing) though whether I will ever get through or not I don't know, as there are floods and riots everywhere. Major Rose shot a few on his way up from Calcutta, and I believe they are stopping people from travelling singly so I may get held up somewhere.[1]

Much tennis recently with Larsen, and we also play a lot of bridge, and I bid and made a little slam which is a thing that always pleases me.

[1] *On 8 August 1942 at the All-India Congress Committee session in Bombay, Gandhi launched the 'Quit India' movement. The next day, Gandhi, Nehru and many other leaders of the Indian National Congress were arrested by the British. This led to mass demonstrations throughout India, and thousands were killed and injured. Strikes were called in many places. The British swiftly suppressed many of these demonstrations by mass detentions; more than 100,000 people were imprisoned.*

September 4th 1942

RANCHI

I GO OFF ON THE TRAIN and reach Ranchi four days later, having passed the rail party. They change onto my train at Gaga. I feed myself well on bread, cold meat and sardines, with a pot of vegemite. We pass through a lot of burnt-out stations (during the present Congress riots), and they are mostly guarded by British troops. I collected a bearer at Kohat, but he is a bit dim and was a woman's before. The trains don't run at night but we get to Ranchi Road only one day late.

I meet Johnson and Carvel of 17 Sqn on 'Pindi platform going on leave. Burt Mann told by the 'allocator of a/c' in Delhi that we should be reequipped at the end of this month. No news of Hammerbeck, so presumably not posted, but quite a new spirit about in his absence. Tom Pierce still in Karachi presumably. Carmichael of 17th Dogras has joined us. We are doing a daily mail run to Patna, the other a/c standing by during the 'troubles' and doing armed reccos for rioters and what not. Rose gives a lecture on RTR[1], and it's an illumination after what we had before.

We go to the club last night and have one or two, but most of the old "kouhais" seem to have changed[2]. I bet these 'Vengeances' are a failure, if we get them[3]. Old, never been used before, and with Allison motors which cut out on take off. If they are good, why send them to India, and not more important fronts?

Parachute troops being dropped in Burma apparently, and then walking home, and Jap transmitting sets being found in villages along the Ganges!!

A patrol – BO Sgt, Cpl and two men – scuppered by a mob[4]. Bihar is the worst district, mostly Patna side.

1 Possibly Remote Transmitter/Receiver.
2 Juniors in Japanese - presumably he means junior staff.
3 The new planes they are expecting to be equipped with.
4 During the Congress riots.

September 7th 1942

RANCHI

I TAKE TO THE AIR AGAIN, WITH AN AIR TEST. A strong crosswind across the strip, but I manage three landings OK. Low clouds at 1500 feet so I try some cloud flying. I manage a few spells for 15 minutes or so, but then everything goes haywire and I see the ground above me and a hell of a speed on the clock. I open the throttle and just manage to pull out with about 300 feet to spare.

Then I go to Patna with an ICS (Indian civil service) official and bring back the Governor of Bihar. Weather not too bad, I go round the rainstorms and eat sandwiches in the Bihar Flying Club until H.E. is ready. He is impressed by my Tommy gun! We refuel at Gaya and I set course for Ranchi. Awful weather looms up, but I am blown off my course and pick up Ramgarh before I run into it, so I follow the road home at 300 feet in blinding rain.

Bought a fishing rod yesterday, but don't know what I shall do with it. Also wrote to Jane (Lindsey), as I reckon I am due a rocket from her. Bill (Robinson) coming to India on a course at Ahmadnagar.

Excellent dummy Hurricanes on the aerodrome. I was flabbergasted.

September 16th 1942

RANCHI

I DO ANOTHER TRIP TO PATNA, but an X is out[1], so I come back to Gaya and pick up Major Tweedie, the M.S.

I see a Sikh sepoy there of the 56th who remembers me and says the boys[2] are at Digboi. Much cloud on the way back, and I come on down the Ramgarh road again. Henry goes to Delhi for a medical, so I am now running the flying.

Yesterday went to an army demonstration - artillery fire, tanks and anti-tank guns, most interesting. Today, Paintal and I go out for 36 hrs with an armoured regiment but it rains so hard the scheme is cancelled at 4.30 pm. I meet Howes, M.C., ex 3 Company from my term at Sandhurst, in S. Staffs and now GSLO 70 Division.[3]

One of the Kohat a/c turns up and we now have three. Much work to do now, and to try and get the Sgt pilots & air gunners doing it too, which is hard, as they cut half the parades, and I can't always be there to check up on them.

Not much exercise, but fairly fit.

[1] *To denote a closed runway, presumably because of riots.*
[2] *His old comrades from the '56th', the Frontier Force Rifles.*
[3] *General Staff Liaison Officer.*

September 20th 1942

BHOPAL

A WEEK OF ORGANISING FLYING, and chasing the sergeant aircrews and cyphers as duty officer every third evening. I go to Aransol to have a kite repaired, and have lunch with Paddy O'Malley. I put up a black by asking "P" Staff (S/L Miliken) to post Hammerbeck, which he doesn't take too well. Hope it doesn't get back to him.

Now in Bhopal. Signal came for four a/c to go down, but we can only manage two, and 20 Sqn is sending two. I go off yesterday with F/Sgt Perry to Allahabad, around some clouds and then 320 miles to Bhopal in 2 hrs 55. Jaubert is in charge here, and Fyson and Bhose present. It's I.A.T.U.[1] – we are to co-operate with somebody, 77 Brigade presumably, who are at Sangar about 100 miles off.

Excellent shooting around here if it could be got, but I expect I shall be busy. 28 Sqn is bucking up at last, with Mann as acting CO and Carmicheal acting Adjutant, as the latter makes the sparks fly. Time I put this down:

28 SQUADRON

Flying

S/L G.R.W. Hammerbeck
F/L A.S. Mann
F/L T.R. Pierce (ex-UK)
F/O H.G.F. Larsen (ex-UK ex RASR)

Joe Soap[2]
F/O E.R.K. Humphries (ex 17 Dogras)
P/O H. R. Carmichael
P/O Douglas (ex PAVO – sick, posted to Ambala)

Stooges[3]

F/L E.R. Adams – adjutant
F/L F.R.J. Gunn – signals
P/O G.W.O. Smith – cyphers
P/O B.R. Williams – cyphers
F/L M.R. Matheson – M.O.
P/O Price – equipment

No news of our Vengeances. They are in Karachi but we are way down on the list for them. We manage to keep three 'Lizzies' flying, but we must get rid of Hammerbeck. How?

'Bud' Rose, Major ALO, gone to Risalpur for three months, he could get things moving OK.

No ambitions at present. Would like to get home but that is too distant. In the interim, stay alive, get some flying and attain that unfulfilled dream of mine!!![4]

[1] *Indian army tactical unit.*
[2] *He means him.*
[3] *Irreverent word for non-flying officers.*
[4] *Meaning unclear - presumably to secure a girlfriend/wife.*

September 24th 1942

BHOPAL

MILLER OF 20 SQN COMES DOWN and takes command. Yesterday we fly General Wavell and ADC to Dana near Sangar, a nasty little landing ground about 500 feet long. We then do a sortie each. I go and beat up Damoh village, and sappers there fire stuff off at me. It bursts in the air nearby and my a/gunner feels it and sees occasional puffs of smoke. After landing, F/L Longmore and some man with New Guinea on his shoulders1 drive us to Sangar. We bathe in the rest house, feed at the infantry officers' mess, and then have a couple of drinks at the club. Return to sleep under a tent at Dana landing ground.

A dawn sortie at about 0645 then back to breakfast on the flying field. General Wavell then turns up again and returns to Bhopal in the back of my Lysander. From the Nawab's Palace have come two colossal marquees for his three pilots, as Wavell is lunching at the Palace.

We eat off the royal plate and have a royal cold luncheon too. Dudley Withers is down here piloting Wavell in a DC3. Sangar's a pleasant spot, and I wouldn't mind being stationed there or here for a bit. The best shooting in India, and at one's front door.

Ground strafing Damoh last evening, I feel that uncomfortable feeling that I used to get in Burma. The 'let's get out of here' sort of thing. My nerve must still be bad yet. We return to Ranchi tomorrow, but Miller's Lizzie seems to go so much faster than mine and I don't know if I can keep up to Allahabad – 320 miles – so perhaps I shall go to Jhansi instead.

¹ Meaning unclear - possibly slang for someone with ceremonial feathers of the shoulders of his uniform.

October 6th 1942

Calcutta

WE GET BACK OK VIA ALLAHABAD to find Hammerbeck back in the chair again. Then the cock-up begins. We get two more Lysanders from Madras and they are pretty dud. I am now in Calcutta staying with the Lindsays. I came down in the back of a Lysander with Sergeant Hilton who was to take back a General today. Now Sergeant Cameron has arrived for another one, and both of them are now going, and Bengal Command want one a/c to go to Dinjian with a General tomorrow, and it scarcely has the hours. And I can't get hold of Cameron or Hilton!

Yesterday I go swimming at the "Tolly" Club and then to the Saturday Club where I see Peter Bond, Devitt and Logan Gates. I have a drink with Gates at the Great Eastern this morning. I think I shall make a cock of this trip unless I am careful, but S/Ldr Gill at Bengal Command insisted that it was an order, so that's that.

The Lindsays have a very nice flat out here in Alipore with a back garden overlooking a canal, and Hurricanes roar past all day long. Pat Anderson is engaged to some chap in the papers, of which I don't quite approve. Daphne Meyer has also hooked someone up there in Shillong.

A lot of Chinese wandering round the town now, and Americans as well.

October 11th 1942

RANCHI

CAMERON'S A.S.I. (air speed indicator) goes u/s so he lands back and the General goes by DC3.

I manage to get four bottles of Highland Cream from the Spencers, do some shopping in the bazaar, and then drive out to DumDum with Watson, who is down collecting transport for our A.L.O. section. I then have a drink at the C.N.A.C. canteen where I see the A.V.G.'s doctor again, and then fly Hilton sedately back to Ranchi.

Hammerbeck goes to Group, and comes back saying "You'll be able to laugh at 20 Squadron within a fortnight" – perhaps we are getting new kites? Like hell.

I retire one evening with the shivers. Doc Matheson thinks it might be malaria, but next day I am OK, and the day after I get it again so off to hospital. Dirty, blood stained sheets, cobwebs all round my corner, and yesterday I feel awful and cannot keep my eyes open. I doze for short periods all day, and am sick a few times and eat two biscuits. I drink plenty of nimbu pani (lemon juice) and keep down two out of four quinines.

October 14th 1942
RANCHI

A LITTLE BETTER DESPITE THE COBWEBS. I find a water beetle in my drinking water – a playful little fellow. Luckily I haven't much appetite as there isn't much to eat. Tom Pierce is in with dysentery.

Scott of the Intelligence Corps is very confidential with talk of four armoured and ten infantry divisions piling up in Egypt for a new offensive. My bearer brings fresh cold water daily and refills my thermos.

October 17th 1942
RANCHI

JUST WAITING, and taking Atabrin anti-malarial. A cyclone is 100 miles east of Calcutta moving north, so a signal comes grounding all aircraft. A wing of three squadrons is coming here eventually – 28 Sqn and 1 F/R Sqn at Ranchi and another F/R squadron[1] at Chara, wherever that is.

Young Margaret Sharp comes to see us several times, and brings me a large slab of chocolate.

The weather here is affected by the cyclone, and there's a strong blow from the north for two days.

[1] Fleet Air Arm fighter reconnaissance.

October 19th 1942

I GET OUT OF HERE TOMORROW D.V. (God willing), but still have five days of "plasmaquin" to do.

Hammers and Jackie come in to see me yesterday. I get a bottle of beer of an evening, but it is usually Solan, which is horrid, though I did get Murree at first.

We have a flight of the RAF Regiment on the aerodrome under one Micky Coyne, a dour Scot from the Dundee jute trade. They are quick on the draw too! The other night an Indian got onto the aerodrome at night and didn't stop when challenged, so several opened up but missed owing to their bayonets being on the end of their rifles. He was suspected of tampering with a bowser which was foolishly left out on the strip all night.

A week ago at night a lorry with lights blazing shot across the strip taking the short cut to Hattia, and passed the sentry hoarsely shouting to it to stop. He then fired two shots over it but it didn't stop so he took a bang at it, then another, and it eventually stopped. He found the driver dead drunk and with a bullet through his arm and one through his leg. Also three or four endorsements on his driving license for driving when drunk. He proudly said "Me racing driver Sahib".

Three others cross the strip one day, and as routine, they are asked for their paybooks by the guard. One is without one, so is detained and eventually spins a yarn about being brought from Burma in a Jap three-engine plane a few months ago, and being landed two days march from Calcutta. He looks like a Burman, and as I'm in bed with malaria, I send Cpl Doughty down to 15 Corps with him. They are very pleased, he is a Burman deserter, but I later hear that they have let him go. Some would have taken him to some secluded point, dug a hole, and then shot him!

Scott of Field Security says a few hundred Indian troops – ex-prisoners of war – have been sent over the border by the Japs as spies, with wireless and whatnot. One of them was caught and turned "King's Evidence".

I do a bit of shooting with my .38, a long-barrelled Smith and Wesson. At Sandhurst in 1938 they issued me with a Webley & Scott .45. I fired it in Razmak and found I couldn't hit a thing. I got it exchanged plus some cash for a long barrel S & W .45 which I found very accurate. In Habbaniya, after the Battle of the Plateau, I spent a morning amongst the booty, ranging from field guns, "Iti" (Italian) tanks to dummy rounds. I tracked down a .38 Webley in the armoury, spun a yarn about no pistol, and got it issued to me. In Loiwing, one of 17 Squadron had left his .38 S & W behind in someone's care, so one day I exchanged my Iraqi .38 for his. It's a lovely weapon, and I decided to fire off all my ammo, except for 12 rounds, as they are very difficult to obtain. On a river (stream) below the mess I found I could aim and hit up to 40 feet!

Out tomorrow, but no flying for a month is the order, and a medical board at the end! How shall I fare this time?!

October 24th 1942

RANCHI

OUT, AND SICK IN QUARTERS.

Lieutenants 'Art' J. Welling and F.J. Theison A.V.G. are staying in the mess for a few days. They produce a Chinese banknote and make me a 'Burma Roadster'[1]. I get out my .22 and shoot a couple of pie dogs around the mess - dawn and dusk sorties. One takes four bullets to kill, I miss another at 15 feet with my .38!

When Burt Mann was running Jean around, he used to dine at the B.N.R. hotel frequently and tell the mess corporal (Allard) to ring up and get a table. Eventually, the Corporal used to say "The usual, sir?"

That Jap a/c might have been a JU88. There has been a stripped-down one over several times (Calcutta etc) and a Hurricane got near it once, but the Jap pulled the 'tit' and shot away.

Colin's 'Burma Roadster' 10 Yuan banknote, signed by AVG pilots.

We have a society in the mess called 'The Red Hand'. We sit and discuss ways of getting rid of S/Ldr Hammerbeck and we chalk up the unit or formation to whom we have 'spread the gospel' – i.e. 221, 224 Group, 15 Corps, 70 Division etc.

We read in the papers that 'showers of flowers will be dropped by an aircraft in Ranchi on the R.C. Festival on 25/10/42'[2]. That's tomorrow, but we have heard nothing official yet.

[1] *Given to pilots who have travelled the Burma Road to China.*
[2] *St Crispin's Day festival.*

October 26th 1942

RANCHI

TWO YEARS IN THE RAF but no promotion yet, as they have swindled me out of five days and dated me October 30th[1]. I go out with Maitland France, 70 Division's G3 Ops, to lunch with the 56th. Bobby Elmslie there, the same as usual and talks to me exactly twice. The adjutant, called Penty, seems efficient, and my old Subedar Mohan Chul, now a Captain. Tara Singh (Sergeant Major) and I meet Subedar Abdul Rahman. There are to be two companies of mounted infantry on well-fed Tonya ponies, and two companies in 'jeeps'.

337

Last night we have a sort of dance out here. We polish the verandah floor and dance to Brown's accordion – about a dozen guests including Maitland, and bacon and fried egg sandwiches later on. I am starting a cold, and still a bit tired.

Saturday night Burt Mann lets off a bazaar bomb outside the club and blows two windows in. We hear it up here, two miles away. There are five APMs[2] in the club at the time, and he is talking to one of them when it goes off, as the delay didn't work properly and the fuse dragged on and on. Scott of F.S. Police is also on the job, but they all think it was a 'Congress wallah' trying to blow the place up.

[1] He was officially transferred to the RAF on 25/10/40.
[2] Assistant Provost Marshals of the military police.

November 5th 1942

RANCHI

W/C NICHOLSON V.C.[1] arrives to take over this new 171 Wing, which at present consists of him and five other 'Penguins'. He shoots the most dreadful and uncalled-for line in the mess one evening, and I consider him very definitely a 'chap'.

Played cricket yesterday and scored 12. Sergeant Doughty brought back my .455 from Abbottobad, and also my attache case, which is useful. A.V.M. Williams, S.A.S.O. at Delhi, was here yesterday and publicly stated that 20 and 28 squadrons would be reequipped with Bofors Hurricane 2Ds. I frankly disbelieve it, as so many have said so much that was untrue about our reequipment in the last nine months that I can't believe a thing. Wafflebeak of course believes the earth is flat – if some senior officer tells him.

I get a block of shooting jungle from today until the 11th, but it's now too late and Michael is going away with the bearer, so I can't have him for cooking purposes.

[1] The only pilot to be awarded the VC during the Battle of Britain.

November 8th 1942

I take to the air again. Doc Matheson gives me a medical yesterday which is a complete farce, beyond a little mercury blowing. Then I go off and do two landings, and then beat up the 56th at Milestone 12 past Ratu Tanh. This morning I do a few circuits and glide approaches, but not very successful. A little tennis – last night the RAF put on a show in which eggs are splashed into the audience. I am warned, and take three bad ones which I return, scoring a direct hit on the compere and two misses.

The parrot fails to return one evening and we reckon the cat got it at last. Its empty cage still stands, waiting, on the mess balustrade, with the door open.

A signal from AHQ saying "Post F/L Mann from flight commander to C.O. of 28 squadron", obviously a mistake. A.O.C. Hunter 221 Group rings up Mann and apologises, makes it plain Hammerbeck is getting the sack, and asks him to sign on for another year in India. Dribblebeak and Nicholson then ring up "P" Staff A.H.Q. and say Mann's time has expired and he wants to go home, whilst D-Beak keen to stay on. AOC Hunter gets to hear of this and rings up Nicholson in a furious temper telling him to mind his own business.

A/M Baldwin, A/Comm Parry-Keane here a few days ago and D-Beak and Nicholson do their best to "burn their loads". However, Nicholson himself is due to go, as posted here by mistake. W/C Muckerji is coming instead.

November 15th 1942

Signal in: "S/L H (Hammerbeck) to report supernumerary to 221 Group". Nicholson and he do nothing about it. Eventually "P" staff ring up, but H in bed (hospital) with malaria so Mann made acting S/Ldr and C.O. 28 squadron. I and Henry take over A and B Flights respectively, but our promotion not yet through. I meet Elmslie's wife Elizabeth here, and discover that Gavin Douglas of P.A.V.O., who was posted here but went to Ambala, is the same one who stole Pat Turner from Jerry Beale in Madras! I have dinner with the Elsmies at B.N.R. Hotel the other day. Much tennis, and am improving somewhat, though there is not as much to drink afterwards as there used to be. An RAF show here, which was rather 'pink' I thought – mentioned that last time.

Rs560 deducted and NO pay this month, for allowances drawn, though I paid them back on return from Burma. It makes me see red at times.

Tom Pierce posted as A.L.O. 4 Corps, so he won't be seen again for a bit. I wrote to G/C John Hawtry and he says it takes three months before promotions come out so I have another 2 3/4 as a Flying Officer to do.

November 24th 1942

Calcutta

We have a party in the mess the other night with Greta, McBlain and his girlfriend. Hugh Moule and his wife, and Elizabeth Elsmlie - Jackie too, who gets a bit weary on her first John Collins, pink gins and her first glass of port. Hammerbottom posted to 225 Group Bangalore, in some S/L A/C (army cooperation) job they have invented for him.

A signal comes in requiring Flying Officers and some armament B.O.R.s to go on a TAC/armament course for these Hurricane 11ds in the Middle East. I get put down for it, and eventually Burt Mann, Henry and I go, with Joel and Thompson of 20 Squadron and some BORs.

We come up here on Sunday morning, by train unfortunately, as no a/c available, and report to air transit officer yesterday morning. "Great Eastern at 4.00 am 25th" says he, and seats on BOAC flying boat all the way to Cairo.

We are staying at the Great Eastern Hotel and go to the Saturday Club and the "300". I have lunch with the Lindsays, and they have oysters and a few drinks with me at "Slap" yesterday evening. Met Doc Fowler, of Razani days.

November 30th 1942

Cairo, Egypt

Trip postponed 48 hours and then reduced to 28 hours. I go to a party at 17 Sqn Mess and introduce my 'Burma Roadster' notes. Also get rather tight on their rum punch. Eventually we get off at 4.00 am on 26th, via Gwalior, and make Karachi that evening. We put up at the Carlton and have a few drinks at the Gymkhana club, and then off again at midnight. Jiwani, Sharjah for an early tea, Basrah, Habbaniya, Kallia and Cairo. The only places we are allowed ashore are Sharjah and Kallia. Early breakfast on Bahrein quayside. Very uncomfortable 21 hours, and a lot of low flying over the desert for some reason.

At Kallia on the Dead Sea we have lunch in some rather exotic hotel, the Dead Sea surrounded by hills, and we come in to land over a salt factory, with large 'fields' rather like a sewage works in England. Then to HQ Middle East and find they have booked rooms for us at Shepheard's Hotel. We are all three in one room, with two washstands but nothing else, and this awful 19th-century French furniture. 40 piastres for bed only, and extra for meals, seems a lot.

Last night very tired, so off to bed after a few drinks. This morning to HQ Middle East, to find where we have to go, and later I buy a Tavanna watch for P£9, and the shopkeeper gives me £1 for my Tudor, bought for Rs60 in Lashio before it fell. Clothing etc far more expensive than India. Nasty-looking 'desert boots' for £3-10-0, whereas my sanbhar leather ones cost Rs18/-. Watches, cameras, razor blades are cheap – a lot of South Africans about, and uniforms of every imaginable nation. Excellent American tinned beer, and Shepheard's bar is a sight for tired eyes after the bare, bottle-less boards of India.

Mann hears about the Hurricane 11ds in HQME, and apparently more people have been killed training on them than in operations, so it doesn't sound very healthy for us!

Memories of that trip – a Catalina silhouetted against the glow of dawn at Bahrein, and the romance in the air of that hotel in Kallia on the Dead Sea. I hardly saw a glimpse of Habbaniya, as we weren't allowed ashore there.

December 1st 1942

Shandur (Heliopolis)

I go to the 'Badia' after Tommy's Bar on Saturday night, but am not much impressed. The mantlepiece with my name on has been wiped away at Tommy's Bar. Met McDowell, a Major now, in the Continental.

On Sunday we leave Cairo on a truck and come down here to Shandur where 6 Squadron's training flight is stationed, and with whom we are to train. The same road I took from Geneifa last year. It is dark at 5.20 pm here nowadays and we arrive after dark to find plenty of drink in the bar. Accommodation in tents, and bloody awful ration food. They root out some beds and blankets, and I manage to scrounge two sheets off the sick quarters, but the M.O. says this morning that he wants them back next week, so I shall have to find something else.

160 Squadron Liberators here, and also 7 Squadron S.A.A.F., plus 'tank busters' with 6 Squadron. 6 Squadron bust about 80-90 tanks in the battle[1], and only lost one pilot, though several aircraft got shot down. The morning spent on Hurry cockpit drill.

[1] El Alamein, fought a few weeks before.

342

Inspecting a tank in the desert shot up by 6 Squadron's tank busters.

December 4th 1942

SHANDUR (HELIOPOLIS)

I DO HALF AN HOUR YESTERDAY in a Hurricane I. The landing's OK the second trip, as the first time I don't throttle back enough. Yesterday up to 15,000 feet and I have to close the hood as too damn cold. Down the Canal to have a look at Suez and Port Tewfik. Today we get onto the range and watch IIds shooting the targets. Burt Mann and I think one or two are a bit "split", lifting a wing over the "tank" after firing, but perhaps it's the way to win a war. 7 Squadron S.A.A.F. have an ME 109F here, which is flying around this afternoon – it goes like a rocket.

Our tent is now fairly well organised, with hot water for washing etc, when the bearer can be found to fetch it. Bathing is under a cold tap originally designed for anti-gas decontamination.

Joel and Thompson of 20 Squadron are here with us. You have to fly at 240 mph, about 25 feet up, and fire at 700-500 yards range. Two 40mm "8" guns, each firing one round at a time from 15-round magazines.

December 7th 1942

WE DRIVE UP TO CAIRO on Saturday afternoon to see a tank demonstration on the Sunday. We stay at Pension Stanley as all the hotels are full. A nice bed and a bloody breakfast for 55 piastres – expensive. A few drinks at the Continental, dinner somewhere, then Henry and I go about asking the dragomen about "a nice place". Everything closed by the police, but a woman sitting in the shadows on the Continental verandah will oblige for £3 – we decide nothing doing, and so to bed.

I see Cleaver and Murdoch – ex-Habbaniya. Sunday morning to Abbassia barracks and we clamber over Matilda, Valentine, General Grant, Sherman and "Honey" or General Stuart tanks. A doze in the afternoon, and drive back at 5.00 pm, with the usual stop at the "halfway house" for coffee, an establishment put up by Messrs Thomas Cook, halfway along the Cairo-Suez road.

Everyone in Cairo seems to have a girl, uniformed or not, and I get a bit depressed at the sight, as I know no one and have no opportunity of striking up acquaintances, being in Cairo for the odd day only. I fire off the '8' guns[1] over Sinai today.

[1] 8 x .303 inch bore Browning machine guns, 4 in each wing of the Hurricane 11d.

December 11th 1942

Much firing on the range, but I never hit the target – a cloth tank. They all seem to fall short, firing at 500 feet, though I do get an occasional bracket of no value. Perhaps I ought to open fire a bit nearer the target than 500 feet as laid down.

Yesterday Burt Mann and I go to Suez to see his girlfriend and take her and another "Wren", Young, out to supper at the

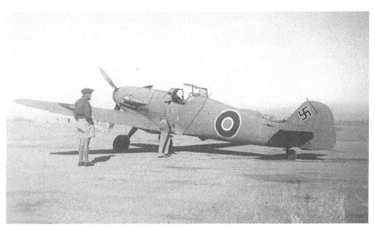

A captured ME 109 - 'it goes like a rocket'.

Suez Golf Club – at least he does, as he foots the supper bill. I go to the equipment officer and tell him about my valise that I left at Habbaniya labelled "Lt Dunford Wood, Geneiffa". He scouts around, and sure enough it has lain 18 months in a store at Kasfaret. I go over in a truck and get it. It has my best marching boots in it, amongst other things.

Plenty of beer here, and not bad, NZ and Canadian mostly, also some very excellent Palestinian beer. I did not bring my Arabic book, having sent it up with Sergeant Doughty to Abbottabad, and so can get nothing much out of these damn bearers. However, I can write my name, which impresses them no end.

A new moon yesterday, and I have a good wish. We do some interesting tank recognition here.

December 18th 1942

Shandur (Heliopolis)

We progress from 4+1 pr to 3+2 pr to 2+3 pr to 2+4 pr, and I get an odd 88% and 75% on 4+1 and 3+2 respectively.[1]

Tomorrow we leave for Cairo, and presumably go back on the next ship or flying boat. Not much on here: flying in the morning, a little reading in the afternoon, and drinking by night. The trouble is the early dinner – 7.00 pm to 8.30 – which means you have to go to bed around 8.00 pm or so, which is a bit of a bind. But by some judicious drinking I can usually get into bed in a fit state for sleep, so am OK. They posted us here from India, and so we lose our Indian rates of pay.

¹ *Meaning unclear. Possibly some kind of radio reception testing, or else gunnery scores.*

December 22nd 1942

Sharjah

We leave for Cairo and are told to wait at 22 P.T.C. Almaza, (a transit camp) near Heliopolis. In the meantime A.H.Q. fix us up with a trip to the Western Desert, but later cancel it and put us on a Hudson on the 21st. 22 P.T.C. – Christ, what a place! We get a palliasse "skin" and four blankets and are shown a hole in the sand, covered by a tent. I take out my "rezai"¹ and a sheet and manage to get really comfortable in the sand, but it shakes some of the others somewhat.

Next day we draw camp kit for our projected Western Desert trip, even though it's been cancelled, so are later comfortable with that. I see little of Cairo that trip, and off from Heliopolis on 21st – yesterday. We circle Gaza and visit Bethlehem before landing at Habbaniya, in a Hudson. We stay in the "Transit Mess", the old station H.Q. one, but it is peopled by ghosts for me. Everything dead, and a lack of booze and cigarettes. I notice half a dozen gravestones surrounded by a low wall in one of the wadis on the plateau, so presumably King's Own. All the trenches are still there, as well as the old Turk ones. Also round Jerusalem.

Next morning up early, and damn cold too, reminiscent of earlier days. Off we set for Sharjah. Cross over Basrah, also I see they have repaired the damage I did to Falluja[2]. There is a fort here, as when used by B.O.A.C., and we are living in the fort and feeding in the 244 Squadron mess. They have "Bisleys"[3] for G.R. work[4]. The mess is thick stone, with small "ports" heavily shuttered against the heat, though last night in Habbaniya was bitterly cold.

[1] *A quilt of silk wadded with shreds of cotton, commonly used to keep warm during winter in northern India.*
[2] *He is referring to the battle he fought here in May 1941.*
[3] *Blenheim aircraft.*
[4] *Ground reconnaissance.*

December 25th 1942

Karachi

We have a good party with 244 Squadron, who have a very well stocked bar, one of the best in the Gulf, and are very hospitable. Next morning about 0730 the only rainstorm this year arrives and pelts down through the chattai roofing of the mess. We can eventually stand it no longer and retreat to the kitchen which has a proper roof and make an al fresco breakfast there. Then on to Karachi, arriving on the 23rd. We find the only way on is by B.O.A.C. on 26th to Calcutta, the one Henry should be on, so we might just as well have waited in Cairo.

I ring up one Kathleen Lee (5567) to whom I have an introduction from Jane Lindsay, but she is going out all over Christmas so I can't see her. However, we all go to the dance at the Gym Club that evening and I organise a "Paul Jones"[1]. I ask all that I get if they know her, and the second one is her herself, so I go and gatecrash her party.

Here I must put on record that I was once put up for the D.F.C. (or so I believe). On returning from Burma in May, Tom Pierce said that with my 60 operational sorties (34 Iraq, 26 Burma) I was worth a gong, as they get them for far less in England now. Well, he and Hammerbeck organise it and H puts Tom up too, but changes his recommendation to "mentioned in dispatches". It doesn't leave the office as far as I can gather until late July, but since then I suppose it has been cut by somebody, though I should like to know by whom. W/C Majundeer got one, though for political reasons mostly I suppose, though he did a damn good job commanding 1 Squadron I.A.F. in Burma.

[1] *A routine where partners change during the dance.*

December 31st 1942

Ranchi

WE FLY TO CALCUTTA on B.O.A.C. "Cleopatra" and then by train to Ranchi.

Calcutta was recently bombed a few times – three to eight hostiles, a few on Kidderpore docks, all the coolies flee, and some also dropped near Dalhousie Square. We see a few broken trees and pock-marked buildings near the Great Eastern Hotel. Howrah station is defended by European police, who keep the mobs besieging every entrance in order. We get a seat, four in a coupe. Much change in Ranchi – 2 Squadron I.A.F. are here, and W/C David Yorke DSO has superseded "Nick old boy" (Nicholson). He says he doesn't like army officers, especially those that second to the RAF – he and Mike had had several 'set-to's'.

F/Lt Scott here, but Yorke says he is not fit to command a flight (as he is a boozy type) and so I have "A" flight and Henry "B". Scott runs training. There's a Harvard in the squadron, one F/O Gillies teaches on it, and four Hurricane IIb's, one fitted with cameras. Henry's promotion is waiting, and I find a letter from G/C Hawtrey addressed "Dear Colin" congratulating me on my flight lieutenancy. It is dated Delhi December 2nd, but nothing known here. But W/C Yorke having said "You seem to be on most intimate terms with the whatever-he-is" says it's good enough for him and I can put it up. So up it goes, and I only hope it is not a mistake.

Yesterday I fly the Harvard OK, though I don't like the brakes. Five new pilot officers in the squadron, all from fighter O.T.U.'s. This afternoon I shiver and have a bout of malaria. I consult "Watty"[1], and instead of calling the M.O., I have a hot brandy, two atabrins and a good sweat. Then a hot bath, clean sheets and two aspirins, and feel OK this morning. BUT will it come on again in the next few days??? This is the third time in six months and I must have malignant malaria. No use going to the hospital every three months for three weeks, then a month off flying, and not properly cured?? Or is it?

Amrik Singh is now a major, A.L.O. 2 Squadron I.A.F. S/Ldr Engineer gets a D.F.C. on the frontier, so I hear. Burke and Doc Mathieson posted away.

---

[1] *Possibly S/L Watts.*

9

January - April 1943

28 Squadron

The Arakan
Burma

January 6th 1943

I DULY GET MALARIA AGAIN, but we dose it away – Watty, Doc Fox and I – and I don't get it a third time. I lay off flying for a few days and fly Hurricanes again today – do some awful acrobatics. My loops all fail as she flicks round near the top, but they all say the same, so the kite I was flying must have bad rigging. Eventually manage some semblance of a slow roll.

I am to take a detachment of four a/c (Mike, Glass and Hilton) on operations to Chittagong, near the Burma border, but Burt Mann and Scotty are coming for a few days in Mike's and Glass's place until they have some more hours on Hurries.[1] Woe is me! I wish I was sitting at Risalpur on that job with Nobby Clarke. They posted me there in my absence to fill a F/L vacancy, but cancelled it as I was not available. But I have my Sandhurst marching boots with me, so here's hoping. Someone got back from south of Akyab the other day, so I hear.[2]

I expect we shall have to go well south to some satellite landing ground and live in a hole again.

I get a Christmas present of a chess set (pocket) from the Jacobs, and also shaving soap and one blade (all she could get) from Daph – now Mrs Blayney with a son. A colossal mail was waiting for me on my return from Egypt – about the best I ever had.

---

[1] This posting was to support the developing Arakan Campaign, launched into Burma against the Japanese on 17th December.

[2] Meaning a downed pilot managed to walk back from there to the British lines, hence his reference to having his marching boots with him. Akyab port and island was the objective of the Arakan campaign, to recapture it from Japanese hands.

The Arakan Campaign

The objective of the Arakan campaign was Akyab Island (today called Sittwe), an estuarial island on the west coast of Burma. If the British could re-take its port and airfield, it would give them a good foothold from which to launch a counter-offensive against the Japanese. Akyab was at the tip of the Arakan Peninsula, just across the water from Foul Point.

General Wavell's original plan was for the island to be taken by an amphibious assault while the 14th Indian Division launched a diversionary attack into the Arakan, down the centre of the peninsula. This was made up of a narrow, jungle-covered range of hills - the Mayu Range. However, the amphibious landing was dropped due to the unavailability of the necessary landing craft. Instead, the advance of 14th Division became the main effort, and once they had reached Foul Point at the extreme southern end of the peninsula, the plan was to launch across the narrow channel separating the peninsula from Akyab Island.

14th Division, commanded by Major General Lewis Lloyd, crossed into the Arakan from Cox's Bazaar on the India/Burma frontier on 17 December 1942. Initial progress was swift, as the Japanese screening forces along the border were ordered to pull back to join the main body Japanese forces near the tip of the peninsula.

However, the Japanese constructed a series of well-concealed bunkers at Donbaik to defend the approach to Akyab island, and on 7 and 9 January 1943, a determined attack by 55th Indian Infantry Brigade was repulsed. Lloyd asked for a troop of tanks to deal with the bunkers, and although the brigade commander protested that 50 or more tanks would be required, he was overruled.

Throughout the rest of the month, Lloyd's Brigade tried to shell the Japanese out of their foxholes and bunkers, as evidenced by Colin's diary entry of January 18th, to 'save the casualties of a full-scale attack,' but without success.

On 1 February, the Brigade, supported by only eight Valentine *tanks, once again attacked the Donbaik position. Again the attack failed, as the tanks became stuck in ditches or were knocked out by enemy fire, and the British were forced to withdraw.*

January 10th 1943

WE FLY DOWN TO CHITTAGONG via Dum Dum on the 7th. Lunch in C.N.A.C. canteen, and arrive Chittagong about 3.30 pm. Half an hour's taxiing to the dispersal, and then we have to wait from 4 to 6.15 pm in the duty pilots office until someone signs a 658,[1] and we can get to town.

We go to Group mess, where we meet Paddy O'Malley and More-O'Ferrell and G/C Hank Moore. We stay two nights. I find myself a bed in a small house, tended by some orderly who is so jungly[2] he puts his boots on the wrong feet. However, he brews hot shaving water, which is all I want. We go and see the effects of a Jap pilot who was shot down and captured. He had a map with some of the projected strips in Bengal, shown as pukka landing grounds, so the intelligence must be good. The usual F/L, and a lot of photos of a girl and of himself as a sort of cadet, leaning on the tailplane of his first aircraft. Also some Japanese rupees for use in Burma.

Well then, yesterday, I come down here, Maungdaw in Burma, to fix up this and that, as the detachment will be here eventually. Joel and two 'Lizzies' are here, and Major Vir Singh as A.L.O. It's a kaccha[3] strip, built by 'Scottie' (C.W.Scott, now a S/L), and we doss down in native huts. I go to lunch with W/C Ford, who is running 22 A.A.S.C. at 14 Indian Division HQ (Major General Floyd), and then try to fix myself a bed, as I have brought no camp kit in the Hurricane. I get a bamboo bed put up in about 40 minutes, borrow a valise, and stuff it with straw, and am OK. The jungle drips all night onto the tent, and in the morning everything is wet and steaming as the sun rises.

We are about 30 miles from the front here, and about 50-60 from Akyab, so should get hell soon. A moon is getting up now too!! Now I am standing by to do a contact recce, but have not the right way lights[4], so it won't be a great success.

There's an old Jap dugout near my tent, and all the villagers have Jap rupees, but those are all the traces left. They were driven out from hereabouts about three weeks ago.

All 165 Wing fighters are due down here soon, so the local peace and quiet will soon be shattered. We have to be self-supporting here, so Burt Mann has signalled for a cook and some utensils. I see I.N. Bayles (S/L) in Chittagong – I used to be at the Beacon[5] with him.

The birds and the scents are the same, and the atmosphere reminiscent of the last time I was in Burma.

[1] *An RAF form to request 'mechanical transport for duty'. i.e. to borrow a jeep.*
[2] *Urdu word meaning disorganised or uncouth.*
[3] *Hindi for raw or basic.*
[4] *For illuminating the runway for landing at night.*
[5] *Colin's prep school near Sevenoaks in Kent.*

January 13th 1943

MAUNGDAW

I DO MY RECCE – Donbaik/Laungchaung/Rattedaung – and get a bit confused, as I only have a one-inch map. I go in at about 50 feet but see nothing, except some bursts amongst the trees west of Laungchaung. I see Akyab from about 1000 feet only 20 miles or so away.

On the morning of 11th I see five fighters and recognise the red suns on them, whilst breakfasting with the RAF Regiment. Ten fighters come over with three bombers, who strafe the docks and a hospital ship at Maungdaw. Then a twin-engined job comes over on the way home at about 700 feet, having a good look at the strip. Bofors open up but they all fall short, the tracer being clearly visible.

We decide to move to the south strip, as we expect a 'Balbo' (a big formation) over soon to strafe us, and on landing there I taxi to the best dispersal. I am doing well, get over all the boggy ground, and have gathered speed to go up a rise, when the wheels fall through 2 feet or so of soft ground and the airscrew loses 4 feet off each blade. I gather some coolies, and by putting down bamboo rails we push her out and hide her under the trees. An Indian engineer then comes up and tells me there is a well there, which had been 'filled in'.

We also find a campsite near the other strip on a small stream. Three huts are being built, and C.O., Scott, Hilton and myself live in a 80lb tent. We do our own cooking, and three more recces are done, one by Hilton lasting 2.10 hrs! It is now my turn, but Major Vir Singh has nothing for me, so I am "standing by". I have my best Sandhurst boots (for walking home in)[1] and black half-puttees, which are most useful. As guards, we have some sort of "V" Force, an irregular body of pro-British Burmans armed with .476 Martini elephant guns, 1882 model. They stand guard day and night, and pour water over me when I am taking a bath above the stream in a camp bath. The coolies are putting up bamboo huts at 60/- rupees, so 'Scotty' tells me, each with six beds and three tables and benches.

'Scotty' went back to Ranchi yesterday to get another camera Hurricane, as the one I broke is our only one, also the only one with jettison tanks.

[1] Presumably he means in the event of being shot down.

January 14th 1943

MAUNGDAW

WE DRAW RATIONS FOR 25 MEN two days running, so the four of us have ample to eat. Also some rum, which we put in the tea, but which isn't too good. Vir Singh and Joel come and feed last night, and we cook and sit round the fire. This morning I do a recco – Launhchaung/Foul Point/Donbaik – but see nothing from '0' feet except some cattle, and a ship in the Kywede river opposite Magyichaung. I spend longer than I should have done redoing some bits, and looking for a missing Hurricane which I fail to find. I drop a message on 47 Brigade HQ, or at least where I think they are, and nearly 'spin in' whilst watching it being picked up; she does a flick, but I just manage to catch her with a burst of engine and am saved.

Burt Mann sees a Jap photo recco overhead, half an hour ago, but I miss it as I am exhorting the coolies to greater efforts in house building, having caught them sleeping on the beds they had just made. They all understand Urdu (so far) round here, so I am quite at home with everyone.

A stream runs through here, and we have managed to install a telephone, so it's fairly comfortable. So far, and touching wood, that is!

January 18th 1943

MAUNGDAW

THE GROUND PARTY ARRIVES and we get organised. Scotty also comes back from Ranchi, but without any booze, as he says they have none there! W/C Yorke broke up the joint one night, throwing soda water bottles and tomato sauce around the place. Yesterday I go down and get a rum ration for five B.O.s and seven Sergeants, which we consume with lime juice last night.

Yesterday morning I do a very successful contact recce, Changtow to Apankwa. "Soutcol" – 8/10 Baluchis and some Tripara irregulars – are attacking Ryauktaw, from the west and east banks of the Kaladan river respectively. I spend about 40 minutes overhead and see "Soutcol" and ground strips in the town on the river bank, so they are successful. I see an officer riding on a horse followed by porters with the mess crockery. On the other side, men in blue shirts with Gurkha hats put out an 'X', and then dive back into the surrounding forest. They are held up by the Japs, who all leave the other bank. I also count sampans between Kyanktaw and Apankwa – three Burmans leap overboard from one.

Then Mann, Scotty and Hilton are sent out to strafe the boats I saw, killing some Burmans, and Scotty gets a bull in a field. Later in the afternoon he and I are sent off to strafe a seaplane (seen by some Blenheim rear gunner) at Senbaik, but, fortunately, nothing there, and we carry on and I strafe a ship at Magyichaung, and some at Kalachaung, not very successfully. Also a tree with something under it south of the Pya Chaung. All a waste of ammo and flying times.

Japs raid Fenai and Chittagong yesterday, presumably from Magwe, as there are not supposed to be any aircraft on Akyab, though plenty of ack-ack is encountered there. Blenheims and their escorts pour over twice and sometimes three times daily, usually as close support I think. The Army Air Support Control (No 22) is functioning down here under W/C Ford and Major John Lewis of my old regiment.

I hear that Allan Haig was shot at Risalpur. He was standing by the range signals (as R.S.O.)[1] when some dimwit fired at the signals in a Hurricane, instead of at the target.

The guns are rolling all day, as we are trying to shell the Japs from their foxholes before Dombaik, and save the casualties of a full-scale attack. There is one company of them against our Brigade, and they are supposed to clear them off the Mayu peninsula today. The Inniskillens and 5/8 Punjabis are down there, and a whole regiment of 25lb guns, so they ought to do something.

[1] *Range Safety Officer.*

January 20th 1943

MAUNGDAW

LAST NIGHT ABOUT 8.30 PM three or four Japs come over and drop bombs on Maungdaw, returning home afterwards; all at about 15,000 feet or more from the direction of Magwe.

Yesterday Burt Mann and I go off down Foul Point way, with me weaving behind him. At about 1500 feet five Bisleys[1], coming back from a raid, pass under us at 0 feet along the coastline. I see Burt do a steep turn, so I follow round to see what he is up to, and during my turn I see an aircraft below me, leaping up like a salmon and with red balls and smoke coming out of his prop. I notice a bit of a Red Sun on his fin, so I pull the tit and away. I pull the two-speed blower first, but manage to keep my distance at about +8 boosts, nipping over the Mayu Hills in the meantime. He then appears to gain – I see two of them, keeping on top of the hills – and turns towards me, puffing out more smoke, so I pull the correct tit and away to Buthidaung, and then cautiously cross over again and land. The C.O. had seen him first – an Army 01 – intent on the Blenheims, and gave him a short burst, before he got on to me.

Later we go down, he to do a contact recce of the Donbaik battlefield, whilst I nip sharply round Foul Point, keeping a wary eye out for Zeros. I see a 15cwt truck half in water near Magyichaung, and a small tent by a dhow I used to strafe, then back home.

A good drop of rum and lime juice last night, following a walk back up into the foothills behind here. A padre – one O'Hea – is staying with us, and a regular Lawrence of Arabia, if his stories of counter-espionage and sabotage in Germany, Norway and France are to be believed.

The new airscrew arrives for the kite I pranged, and also some fitters to put it on.

[1] *Blenheim Mk Vs*

January 24th 1943

Maungdaw

OUR PARTY THE OTHER DAY was twenty Zeros jumping the five Blenheims over Akyab. Some said they were "01"s.

Hilton and Scott go out on 22nd to photograph Laungchaung at 9000 feet and are jumped. They run into some air effort of the Japs over the Mayu Peninsula. Scotty suddenly sees a yellow belly coming for him, but he remembers all about turning at him, and does so. Suddenly the reflector sight vanishes as a burst comes in from port. He gets away and lands at Bawli Bazaar eventually. On inspection, the a/c is riddled forward of the 'stick' including a cannon shell through the starboard tank and holes in the gravity tank. Hilton is not seen, but we hear his a/c and body have been found at Kyaukpandu. We go down there, arriving just after dark, but can do nothing, as his body is at an M.D.S.,[1] so we return.

Every evening we have to file across a "kaccha" bridge with one bamboo as cross supports, with another as a handrail. Twice at night, though once with moonlight.

Yesterday I go down with F/Sgt Clark and we bury Hilton's body in the hospital burial ground with the help of some Inniskillens. It is wrapped in a couple of blankets, drips a bit, and in my opinion smells. The hospital C.O. reads the burial service from F.S.P.B.[2] and we all then adjourn for tea. Then, with a guide, we make for the crash site through a mile or so of jungle and across a tidal stream up to our crotches. It is a mess, but no fire, all scattered in bits. No bullet holes, and half his head shot away, so they must have had a burst at him through the window. The photography was finished, but the films were scattered all around, so it will be hanging over our heads again. We get some coolies and gather up what we can, and set off home.

Scotty posted to Calcutta A.A.C.U.[3] (in command) and Burt flown off to Ranchi today to get some more a/c and pilots, leaving me in charge.

I do a recco today over the Myochaung/Kyauktaw area with one of 135 Squadron as bodyguard. Six pilots from 135 come down every morning and leave in the evening, so we hope they will lend us a hand. I didn't do me any good yesterday seeing the funeral, and hearing the stories about the Japs from the Inniskillens. However.

*'Joe Soap', Watty, Burt Mann and Mike at Maungdaw,
during the Arakan campaign.*

[1] *Main dressing station.*
[2] *Field Service Pocket Book.*
[3] *Anti-aircraft cooperation unit.*

January 28th 1943

MAUNGDAW

SIX FIGHTERS COME DOWN DAILY, and we get an escort of one section on our trips. I even get one to St Martins Island, where I go to drop a message. I try two, to make sure, but one sticks on the tail plane and the other falls, leaving half a streamer on. I see no one but two British officers with topees on.

Yesterday the fighters shoot up one of our M.L.'s,[1] which started the battle by clearing its guns in the direction of the island. They signal and say they are being shot up, so the party starts.

C.O. and Mike return, and I get awful drunk the first night on about four large pegs of "Old Angus". I even fall in the stream while crossing it, which is a poor show.

This afternoon I have to go around Foul Point again, which I don't fancy much. I would rather dabble in the Kyauktaw area.

The whole of 28 Squadron is supposed to be coming down here, when operational, and when equipped with some aircraft. I shall have to make out another scheme of objectives, as I don't seem to have any just now.

We have single aircraft crossing over here at night all the time, both ways, and it is a damn nuisance, as we go out and blow whistles and shout 'take cover!' etc. But God knows what they are, as they seem to go up and down and occasionally do a circuit over Maungdaw.

[1] *Minelayers.*

January 30th 1943

MAUNGDAW

I GO ROUND FOUL POINT AGAIN with an escort, F/L Mason of 79 Squadron. I don't see much, beyond a couple of camouflaged sampans, at which I have a squirt with mediocre results.

Yesterday two '99's, heavy bombers – with six 01's - came over, do a couple of circuits and then drop some bombs in the NAF. Some good shooting by the Bofors and one is reported shot down, further south on the beach. Some lad in a carrier on the quay fires at it and it gets annoyed and fires back, wounding seven men.

Pilot officers Brown, Dorman and Ardeline arrive last night, so we shouldn't have to do two or three sorties a day, though we are doing it with an escort most of the time.

Mike will insist on reading all night, which is a bind, as I like to go to bed at 8.30 or 9 round here, and start sleeping. Am getting good at being a dhobi now...[1]

[1] *i.e. washing his own clothes.*

February 7th 1943

WE START FLYING AGAIN after three days off. It rains in the night (30/31st) and both landing grounds become U/S for some three days, so we sit about reading books all the time. The Mess becomes organised – a 180lber (tent) dug down a few feet with two small tables and a few chairs. Here we do some evening drinking with what we have. One F/L Sinclair, signals officer of 165 Wing, stays over a few days, and drinks a lot of our scarce hooch, though I admit he pays for it.

I do a couple more trips, but of not much interest except one over Donbaik where I see a man in a yellow uniform, bending down with his back to me, scooping water out of a puddle. I'm sure he is a Jap! I watch the battle and see shells bursting etc. F/Sgt McTaggart comes back, following another TAC/R[1] machine, but misses the field and goes up to Bawli Bazaar. He takes off again to get here, loses the way again, and then returns and overturns on landing at Bawli Bazaar in the dark.

Burt goes away, back to Ranchi, and I am left in peace to organise the war. Two Jap prisoners are captured, who spill the beans.

A hell of an attack goes in with eight Valentines[2], but three get bogged down in enemy E.D.L.s[3] and are no good, because the infantry are late over the starting line. The Royal Berks are due to land behind the lines at Foul Point, but do not, as the tank attack is not sufficiently successful.

Before Burt leaves, we ask about whether we should carry on doing unescorted dawn sorties, and he says no until he has seen about it in Ranchi. He then hums and haws, and I eventually tell W/C Ford I can't do 'em, as C.O. says not. He sends a signal about it to 224 Group asking for an escort, and gets an answer "Concur with anything you have already done". But maybe the C.O. did not give a direct order? He never will say what he means.

I still can't think of any "objectives" to work for, beyond the three tasks which I am now giving to the new moons when I see them.[4]

I live in shorts, desert boots, and my famous glass-insulated hat.

[1] *Tactical reconnaissance.*
[2] *Tanks. See the note above about the Arakan campaign.*
[3] *Meaning unclear.*
[4] *I.e. making wishes when there's a new moon, presumably a superstition of his.*

February 10th 1943

MAUNGDAW

YESTERDAY W/Cs FORD AND SMYTHE tell me 224 Group's policy. That is that all low-level TAC/Rs are to be unescorted, and only medium-level or photography are to be escorted. OK. So off I go by myself to look for a 75mm gun near Laungchaung, but of course am unable to locate it. I do, however, see a sort of cave, or deep water hole in the hillside, but no one is impressed. I watch six Bisleys bomb Magiychaung and see incendiary portions burning around, but no apparent damage or destruction.

Tomorrow is the anniversary of the foundation of the Japanese Empire, so we are expecting a packet on this front. F/M Wavell was down, and has made a new plan, which is apparently to take Foul Point and hold it until the monsoon and then withdraw, presumably to India. Akyab to be left to the Japs!

No jobs today so far, but am expecting the peace to be shattered any minute now. My landings are getting very bad, and I expect to drop a wing tip in almost every time.

Ford wants us to do low-level recces of Akyab Island for the better education of 224 Group.

Impressions

- Coming home low over the hills and flying under cover of sheer steep sides;
- Sunset at 6.10 pm, a smoke and a drink then;
- Sitting in the 'dug down' mess consuming gin or rum, and rolling dice with Mike and Watty.

Smallwood and Major Wagstaffe come down as A.L.O., as Watty is sick. Freezing at night, but snug under three red hospital blankets. Ardeline gets a bullet through his fin on the Myshaung-Theyattabin road, of all places!

February 14th 1943

Maungdaw

WE GET THREE AVG MOHAWKS[1] down as escort for our photography. I am due to go up when the escort "scrambles" due to an air raid "red". Suddenly the Bofors open up at a kite I see over the strip. I dive down a trench, covered in overhanging foliage, and see nothing of the ensuing battle. Two "01's" race up the strip at nought feet and two Mohawks give battle, and a regular dogfight ensues. The noise is terrific, and I venture out once to see something attacked, roll onto its back, and dive towards the ground. The Hurricanes are up too, and the result is one confirmed kill (out of six '01's') and a few probables.

I then dash over to Rathedaung, where I catch a sampan on the ferry; one 'red lungi' leaps overboard, but I catch another one of the crew.

Yesterday Wagstaff and I and two pilots drive down to 55 Brigade. Our guns are firing all the time, and I am not used to it. We are taken up to Point 566, a gunner observation post, and observe Donbaik and the Jap front line forward of it through field glasses. The guns are shelling the front line, and we see a dump of some sort catch fire. A Jap mortar opens up, and we see the bursts in the hills on our left. A bit of 'tack-dunging' like in Waziristan.[2] As we are climbing the O.P.[3] three "97s" come over the hills through a perfect storm of Bofors and drop their bombs on Brigade HQ. Two land harmlessly, four on the beach and the remainder in the sea.

We have lunch at Brigade HQ in the jungle, very thick, with paths hacked from office 'hole' to office 'hole', and get back as the sun goes down. The 224 Group Welfare Officer has arrived with a bottle of beer for every man, and two bottles of "Old Angus" for the Mess. Add this to the rum ration drawn on Saturday, and we are ready to get as pissed as newts. However, I go to bed fairly early after not too much.

Today I do a photographic sortie around Laungchaung area and also the Jap front line with Peter Bond (S/L) and three other Mohawks as escort. On finishing, I give a good squirt to the Jap front line and come home. I very much doubt the photographs will be much good.

Day before yesterday, I and Wagstaff go and drink a bottle of gin that Hugh Moule has in A.S.C.,[4] and talk with John Lewis and one Major Brown, ex-Burma Forestry Service.

[1] *The American Curtiss P-36 Hawk fighter plane.*
[2] *Meaning unclear.*
[3] *Observation post.*
[4] *Army Service Corps.*

February 20th 1943

MAUNGDAW

SOME GOOD SHOOTING up on the Jap front line, and also by the pagodas on Foul Point, where I see a small concealed "hide". Garratt arrives, and Glass is promoted P/O. Much rain, but we manage to get off onto Ritz[1]. Then we try to make Hove, but it rains so hard whilst the pilots are getting down, they cannot get off, and we are bogged down for a day.

Today at dawn I go off up the Kaladan but it is too misty, so I turn down to Thayettabin, along the track to Myohaung. East of Myohaung I see some five sampans in the Lemro river at Panmyaung. I give one a burst, and it overturns with occupants, and see corpses in the water. I feel a bit sorry for what I have done, so shoot no more. But on the way home I realise that what I have seen is most important, being the Jap L of C (lines of communication) to Myohaung. At Myohaung I squirt the police lines where the Japs are reputed to be living, and return home.

Several days ago I went in a Tiger Moth with W/C Ford and fly to the Indin strip and then to Apankwa. Very nice, though he flies me too damn near Rathedaung to be pleasant. I watch the countryside and see several strange birds (Adj's probably)[2] at work.

Miller of 20 Squadron reputed to have a DFC for his "Lizzie" efforts down here. I photograph the wrong chaung instead of Laungchaung, and have a conference with Brigadier Cavendish of 6 Brigade[3] and a naval commander over his landing operations at Foul Point, for which he wants photographs.

[1] *Landing ground.*
[2] *Greater adjutant storks.*
[3] *Brigadier Cavendish was to captured and killed in April when 6 Brigade's headquarters was overrun.*

February 23rd 1943

MAUNGDAW

BERT AND "WINCO" YORKE come down in a Harvard and another Hurricane 11b. Winco sees General Lloyd[1], who says he has nothing but praise for our efforts, and apologizes for the rude signal he sent about us, which was instigated by W/C Ford, who has now been sacked and sent back to 221 Group. I go off on a trip to Kaladan where the Japs have cut our lines of communication, but my weaver tacks on to another Hurricane 11b, so I have to go

W/C Ford and the Tiger Moth on the Indin airstrip. This was to be overrun by the Japanese in April - see editor's note on Brigadier Cavendish.

alone and don't really do the job at all well. Brown gets a .5 bullet in his flaps over Myohaung, where there is apparently some force of Japs.

There's a commando raid on Myobin in Hunters Bay two nights ago, and they get six live Jap prisoners of the "Inland Water Regiment" or some'at.

We have a party in the Mess – Hugh Moule, W/C Smythe, and Major Cooper (G11 ops)[2], who was at Harrow, and commanded the trophy guns at Habbaniya.[3]

Four Jap 01s come over one morning from W to E at about 15,000 feet, and though I hear nothing, I see a parachute slowly descend. Two Hurricane 11cs had scrambled from here and attacked them, but were jumped by eight more up at 22,000 feet, and the second one, Boysen, a South African pilot who used to escort me, is never seen again. His Hurricane has now been found near Buthidaung, but no one can get near it.

Count Czernin spends the night, and, according to Mike, shot down his own brother in an M.E. and has another brother in Rommel's "panzers".

That night we go and drink with Hugh Moule, and find ration rum and hot water an excellent combination. Garratt doing photography now, and I am due for the next job over Laungchaung. Last time I did Gwedauk Chaung by mistake, being so used to seeing the country from 200 feet, that I didn't recognise it at 4000 feet.

A chap comes up from the front, and says "damn good show to the chap who squirted the Jap front line on so and so at 12h00". I look up and find it's me.

---

[1] *The commander of 55th Indian Infantry Brigade, who attacked but were repulsed at Donbaik.*
[2] *General staff officer Grade 2, operations.*
[3] *See 'The Big Little War' for the story of these trophy guns.*

February 25th 1943

MAUNGDAW

YESTERDAY I GO ON A VERY PLEASANT TRIP to Kamai and Batarai, with Brown 'weaving' behind me. I see four men run off a track into the bushes, and I give it a squirt on my way back, but am probably too late. Then last night, Smythe rings up, and says 6 Bde are going to raid Kyaukpyu and want us to photograph it – distance 135 miles as the crow flies over Akyab. But the crow would have to go out to sea on the way. We send for an escort and put the long range of tanks on, and I reckon it's me who has to go. About four runs over the town and jetty from 10,000 feet with an 8 ft lens.

However, Burt reckons it ought to be the next chap on the list, which is Garratt, so off he has just gone with two sections of 79 Squadron.

Burt Mann is a bit sour nowadays, and picks a lot of b-holes in everything, which I don't somehow think are warranted. I've just about "had him", as the saying goes.

March 1st 1943
MAUNGDAW

A MOST ENJOYABLE TRIP weaving on Mike up the Kaladon and down the Pi Chaung. I keep him in sight the whole way and the R/T works, or would have done if I had got the fine-tuning properly adjusted.

We have a game of football, RAF officers versus 14 Division staff, organised by W/C Smythe, the first exercise I take in about six weeks - a poor show, for me.

An air battle overhead just now, with lots of firing. We hear the Japs come over, too high to find with (field) glasses, and one parachute is seen to fall. Yesterday a couple of Hurricanes were lost I believe.

I am getting very idle just now I fear. I fly and do the bumph and read. However, as long as I don't put up too many blacks like painting "The black mamba of Maungdaw" on aircraft and sending them back to Ranchi, I may pull through yet.

A photo trailer has arrived[1], and I am trying to get it dug into the side of the hill, before it is blown up.

[1] *For processing images.*

March 7th 1943
MAUNGDAW

IN A BAD WAY TODAY. J. Benbow came in last night and I only have a couple of rums or so. But all complain of its strength this morning, so I cut my 'trip' and passed it on to someone else. A bad thing to do I feel. Yesterday Brown lands with his undercarriage and flaps up, and when we drop test them they are OK, so a clear case of finger trouble.

I sent Garratt back with a kite which wanted a new coolant pump, so now I only have two machines. Mike and I go over to Myohaung and recce around under clouds with 400 feet base, and I nearly pile in, the controls going 'soggy' in some downward current. I get fed up, and we come home over the clouds, an uncomfortable feeling silhouetted on a white background.

Yesterday whilst in the Controller's office we step outside and see a Jap Army "100" recce plane rush overhead at about 800 feet. It swoops around, dips a wing or two and then makes off for the nearest clouds.

March 10th 1943

MAUNGDAW

YESTERDAY AT "PRAYERS"[1] I see eight "01's" and two with undercarriages down, so they must be Army 98's. Teddy and Garratt arrive yesterday, and Teddy will take over from me. I take him to Divisional "Prayers" this morning in my famous hat, and introduce him to those whom he should know.

Today I do a last sortie looking for the 8/10 Baluchis who broke out of Apankwa and Kanzauk and made their way cross country to our lines. I see an 'X' at the bottom of a watercourse in the most shocking country. Previously doing a contact recce over Kanzauk I see a large "V" displayed, so I shoot up the place I think the enemy may be.

A bit of a party last night as we have a lot of beer, and have been saving up a small bottle of Scotch for a suitable occasion. AOC Bengal Command is down here and says "Burt for the boot shortly, and Tom Pierce to be the new C.O."

[1] Slang for senior staff meeting.

372

March 13th 1943

I DEPART ON 11TH after shooting up 14 Division HQ and giving a coloured display of Very lights from the Plessy gun. After refuelling at Chittagong, I strike a rainstorm whilst still over the sea, and have one or two anxious moments, eventually landing at Alipore in a crosswind, at the second shot, having nearly crashed going round again. A great long Chrysler is procured by the D.P. which deposits me at the Grand (hotel). I meet Gunn and Watty. A party with W/C Ford and Watty that night then Jane comes to my room at 9.30 and I throw her out at about midnight, having completed my plan[1].

Watty and I go out to see Charles Penton the next morning with a girlfriend of his – one Livia, ex-Malaya – and that evening I meet Jane at the Saturday Club. A rather drunken party joins, but I am feeling moody after a lot of gin, and eventually retire to the Grand for dinner and bed.

Today I come on to Ranchi to find Pierce as C.O. I get the impression "Oh, you're back are you?" – not at all the returned hero from the war that I was expecting. However, Quien Sabe!

[1] *Meaning unclear but can be guessed.*

March 20th 1943

I CONTACT BILL ROBINSON out at Piska, as we are having a party on Sunday at the Mess. I collect him from the Club and we do a bit of steady drinking in my room first. The party is quite successful, with about four women, and old Bill gets fairly tight. Next day I depart on 14 days leave to Assam to stay with Uncle Stanley, where I am now. Three nights on trains and all very full, so it's no joke.

Of course my express wire never gets to him, and I arrive unexpected, though the factory is only about ten minutes walk from Lakwa station.

Aunt Joyce is away in Darjeeling, but may be back. I wander around with a .22 but there is not as much life here (in Nahar Habi) as there was at Panbarry. I have some new I.C.I. .22 ammunition, which is pretty mediocre stuff. There are tigers about, but of course they won't kill whilst I am around, and though I took a bang at a green pigeon yesterday, it's about all I shall ever see.

Yesterday morning went to Nazira, where the Assam Tea Company has a very pleasant club overlooking a river, with jungle on the other side. We sit there drinking some beer we found, and I listen to tales of the Assam Road, and watch a fishing hawk at work in the river. Bar a few shots at adjutant birds and vultures, I have done nothing so far except wear myself out with the unaccustomed walking. A wire from Ranchi, that Ambala are still on my tail over mess bills, though I have paid them off. They want to know if deposited in a separate account.

What of the future? Ranchi for a bit, and then Maungdaw or Imphal I suppose, not a pleasant outlook somehow, as I see it.

94 sorties completed so far in this war. Isn't it enough?

March 23rd 1943

Assam

I GET A FEVER AGAIN, and spend yesterday in bed with 'Robinson Crusoe'. I expect another attack after tiffin today.

Rain and thunderstorms the last 36 hours. We get hold of a local shikari, who takes me out after jungle fowl one evening, but no luck. I stand in a clearing in the jungle for some time, but all I see is a damn great rat, and hear something pass by in the jungle. Then find the footprint of a small hog deer or something.

The papers are full of action down Arakan way, so I expect the boys will have suffered one or two minor 'shocks' by now.

A good Mugh cook here. There are tigers nearby in the jungle, but one hasn't made a kill for about a month, and Uncle Stan doesn't seem inclined to get anything done about it, so that's that – and I shall be out of luck. Actually, I shall be extremely lucky if I manage to shoot any damn thing up here.

March 26th 1943

ASSAM

NO MALARIA AGAIN SO FAR, and damn all to shoot either. The jungle chandikar takes me for four miles down to the bottom of the tea, and along the railway, and he and his friends beat the jungle for me. We see signs of deer, but nothing comes out of the beat, and we tramp wearily home. Joyce, the aunt, comes back from Darjeeling and cheers the place up a little, but still nowt to shoot. Papers full of the Arakan, and I'm sure we must have had some casualties down there, and expect I shall have to go back again shortly.

Pleasant rest up here, with home grown and cooked food more or less, and I feel no desire to fly an aircraft again just now. Greta Howard, Teddy's kept woman, wept on my shoulder in the Ranchi Club when I told her about Maungdaw. The selfish bitch! – expecting someone else to do the dirty whilst she kept Teddy warm in bed.

I have thought up another, in fact two or even three immediate objectives, but somehow I doubt if any of them will come off. If not, then I'm sunk.

Nothing yet published of what I told the Public Relations officer one day at Maungdaw, about army-co-operation, and especially about 'a pilot from the Indian Army' flying over his own former battalion (Mike) – he thought that was terrific. But kuchh nahin done.[1]

The 4th Battle of Donbaik appears to have failed, as I forecast!

[1] *Kuchh nahin - 'Nothing' in Hindi.*

Battle of Donbaik

The '4th Battle of Donbaik' which Colin refers to was the assault which took place on 18/19th March, when elements of the the 6th Infantry Brigade made a fourth and final attempt to overcome the Japanese bunkers at Donbaik [1], a village at the southern end of the Arakan peninsula that stood in way of reaching Foul Point and Akyab Island beyond. The attack was repulsed with heavy losses, with the Royal Welsh Fusiliers losing about 25% of their strength.

As Field Marshal Slim said after the war:

"It was a battle which should never have been fought, It is a hard thing to say but it is so …. The last and final assault…. Was led by the Royal Welch Fusiliers and on that day they showed valour which I think has rarely been surpassed. They stormed the position, they took it and were on top of those bunkers but they could not get inside them. They stood there until, I am afraid, most of them had been knocked out by the machine guns and artillery. As a place of sheer courage, I do not think it has ever been surpassed…"

[1] See the earlier attempt using Valentine tanks described in the Arakan Campaign.

March 31st 1943

I GO BACK ON THE ASSAM MAIL TONIGHT – 00.06 hrs, provided I catch it. Not quite so much rain now and I can get out more, but still nothing to shoot, bar shite hawks and vultures. However, it's very pleasant lying in a decent bed reading of a night. I study birds through field glasses, but require some book to identify them.

A pity I cannot get home[1] but the answer was "It is pointed out that – & – are seconded Indian Army officers and as such cannot be repatriated until the end of hostilities." That means another four years out here I suppose.

I have some of these 'Burma sweat rag' khaki shirts which I have been wearing for nearly a year now, and bought some more at Whiteway & Laidlaw in Calcutta. They are excellent in hot weather, though rather ugly. I wore my Sandhurst greased boots and puttees flying on ops, and most of the others took up boots too – for walking home. Also my famous sky blue overalls.

A hideous journey ahead, with three nights in trains to Ranchi, and changes in the middle of them.

What of my next objectives? I have four, but they are all more or less interconnected, and those that stand by themselves are impossible, on current form. So what to do?

[1] *Colin evidently applied to return to the UK after 4.5 years in India.*

April 5th 1943

ARAKAN, BURMA (MAUNGDAW AND VARIOUS LANDING STRIPS)

JOURNEY NOT TOO BAD, as I was quick off the ferry and got a lower berth. Pass two trains of Chinese going up. One had a lot of chargers in luggage vans. Got back, and find Teddy was killed in a crash a few days ago. He took off at Maungdaw and was heard on the R/T saying his engine was running rough, and he was landing again. He made an approach, north to south, overshot and opened up, raising his undercarriage. White smoke was seen coming from his exhaust, an internal glycol leak, and then he got slower and slower, until just over the hills she must have stalled, for she whipped a wing over and crashed and burst into flames. So I have to come down again. 24 hours after getting off the train I am on my way with Tom Pierce, and arrive here after lunch yesterday.

Bob Garratt running the show fairly successfully, but the Japs have cut the road near Indin, and 6 Brigade have withdrawn from Donbaik. A new general – Lomax – and a complete flap all round.

Damn hot and sticky down here now, and me on ops again, of which I am not too pleased. However, I had an awful nightmare my one night in Ranchi!

April 8th 1943

Arakan

I go on a trip to Indin and see the 6 Brigade battle in progress. More corpses than I have ever seen in previous battles, and a "T" out, though I feel the wrong end is facing the enemy. I go up to Rama and see Carruthers and W/C Forbes about our move up to 'Lyons'[1]. I fly back here, and am head over heels 'organising' things. Bud Rose comes down, and round last night for a drink. We get awful tight and confidential!

Tom Pierce returns to Ranchi. Damn hot and sticky down here. The Japs surround 6 Brigade, capture Brigadier Cavendish, and they have to fight their way out to Kyankpandu. Several burnt bodies visible.

An air raid on Maungdaw the other afternoon. I see ten (Army 99s?) through my field glasses and a lot drops on Maungdaw.

[1] Landing ground.

Brigadier Cavendish
& the 6th Infantry Brigade

On 5th April 1943, the 6th Infantry Brigade was positioned on the west coast of the Arakan peninsular, with its headquarters in the coastal village of Indin, when the Japanese attacked from the interior through the jungle of the Mayu Ridge - a route previously considered impassable by the British - and cut the coast road behind them.

About to be overrun, 6 Brigade's C.O., Brigadier Cavendish, ordered his staff to save themselves and evacuate north, leaving him behind, and to shell the area once overrun. He was captured, along with his adjutant and six staff officers, and the next morning, as they were being interrogated by their Japanese captors, the British artillery opened fire, as Cavendish had ordered, and he and several fellow officers and Japanese were killed.

April 13th 1943

WE MOVE UP TO RAMU - Lyons landing ground - leaving Watty and Matthews and a fitter on Ritz. We have quite a nice Mess, quite a lot of gin from Ranchi, squash, and a good supply of rum. The rum is now 8/- a bottle, so as we have drunk about 150 bottles we shall have to produce 1200 rupees at some point – horrid thought.

Carruthers is S/L admin, at Wing HQ, very useful and a great help.

Yesterday I go down to Maungdaw and do a couple of sorties, but not very interesting – by which I mean nothing of note. I don't like the look of the neighbouring bomb craters, but hope nothing will happen.

There are all these Assamese birds around here, but I cannot get hold of a bird book.

April 18th 1943

Arakan

DIVISION MOVES BACK TO MAUNGHNAMA, where there is a small landing ground some 900 feet long, on which I nearly prang. Watty, Matthews, the A.L.O. and eight men for refuelling are there. Also Cooper-Davies and Chris Glover, who, with David, are the three enemy aircraft detachment "investigators".

Cooper-Davies is a character. Fought in the last war, carries a pistol, a sporting rifle and a Sten gun, and has every imaginable bit of kit to solve any difficulty which he might encounter anywhere in the world. He and Glover have attached themselves to us as being a good place to hang around and wait for Jap aircraft to fall out of the sky (not to be confused with waiting for us to shoot them down!)

I go down for a couple of days and do a sortie down Alethangau – Indin way.

14th Division have now become 26th Indian Division, and all the staff changed, bar Higgins (G.R.1). Our serviceability is only one a/c at present, which does not give the army a very good impression, especially these new types. Rude letters and signals from Ranchi about the prangs, and my signals re. same.

There is a pleasant shower here, constructed by 79 Squadron next door, and we had some beer the other day from Maungdaw, so are fairly "khushi".[1]

[1] *A possible origin for the word 'cushy', as khushi means happy in Hindi. Most dictionaries prefer 'cushion' as a derivation, citing lack of evidence for the alternative derivation - though here it is.*

April 27th 1943

ARAKAN

I HAVE TO LAND BACK with an unserviceable A.S.I. at Ramu, a thing I haven't done before, but manage OK.

I go on a dawn sortie with Flynn, a new pilot weaving behind me, down Alethangyaw way, but see nothing. Land back at Sybil[1], and then go out weaving on Mackilligin, down towards Htizwe.

Since four days ago, I have been sitting about up here and it's damn boring, now everything is organised. Various signals from 224 Group that 2 Squadron I.A.F. are relieving us, and that we should move back to Ranchi by 28th, as the squadron is moving elsewhere. However, the last one says "take no further action re. move of 2 Sqn", and that's the last I hear. Not a word from Ranchi, but Bob Garrett set off from here yesterday by aircraft, and I hope to get some "gen" out of them – probably another rocket.

We put the tables and chairs outside the Mess of an evening, and still have some gin and a little rum, but squash is running low. Photo and visual recces report an increase of Jap fighter aircraft on their forward 'dromes, and numerous messages come in warning us to be on the "Que Vive".[2]

However, there is no air control at Sybil – or Somerset Maughan as I prefer to call it – and I suspect we shall buy it if anything happens.

I go on guard the other night – 8-10.30 pm – on the a/c, as there aren't enough "erks". Brigadier Cavendish of 6 Brigade confirmed died in Japanese hands after they raided his Brigade HQ at Indin. Two Hurricanes shot up Buthidaung yesterday, giving rise to the rumour that Japs are flying Hurricanes. They also shot up the Maungdaw - Buthidaung road some weeks ago. My God!

The last time I am at Sybil I see a storm brewing up north, so try and ring up Rami Ops. I cannot get through, so when I get fed up I go outside, and it is almost upon us. I, MacKilligan and Macmillan take off, downwind, and then I find it is so bumpy and gusty that I cannot control the aircraft safely. I shout "pancake!" into the V.H.F. (we changed frequency some 10 days ago), and turn downwind to feel the aircraft torn out of my hand and blown downwind at an alarming speed. On turning into the approach to land again, I am blown off and lose considerable height, but eventually manage to get down OK, followed by the other two. A black storm, soon over, and mostly wind, so later I return to Ramu after lunching with Watty on cheese and pickles.

[1] *Landing ground.*
[2] *On the lookout.*

April 28th 1943

Ranchi

Mike and Madill arrive, the former to take over from me, so after a day's handing over, Watty comes up from Sybil and we crack a bottle of 'Old Angus'. I return the next day with Mackilligan in another a/c to Ranchi. Mike and Flynn go down to A.L.G.,[1] and when I get back I hear that he (Mike) is shot down in flames into the Maya River by A/A fire from Magyichang. Well, 'Tiny' Irwin, if he is still alive, and I, are the only ones left now of the seconded Indian Army lot.[2]

We maybe move to Alipore soon, keeping the Arakan detachment and sending another one, me again, to Imphal when the monsoon comes. 2 Squadron I.A.F. give up their detachment there, which they took over from Henry – Henry left for Ramu this morning.

I have now got in 100 sorties and am not at all pleased with the prospect of more operations in Imphal. Tom is to be Wing Commander and Henry, Squadron Leader (flying) and me, Joe Soap, doing all the ops.

I go to the Club for tennis and meet David Cooper and all 14th Indian Division staff who are now in Ranchi, 70th Division having left. I have drinks with David and Tom Jones (14th Division), and they give me dinner at B.N.R. Hotel.

171st Wing is moving Madras way and "Waggers" left with the advance party. I have a drink with Mrs Roughton, and tell her of Mike's death. Not a pleasant job, as they were more than just friendly.

I am "windy" now, very. After 100 ops I can't go on forever. Also there seems to be this "hoodoo" on Indian Army types.[3]

[1] *Unclear which landing ground he is referring to.*
[2] *60 Indian Army officers were seconded to the RAF in 1940/41. Two years later Colin and Tiny Irwin are the only survivors.*
[3] *Meaning that the majority of RAF pilots seconded from the Indian Army have got themselves killed.*

10

May - September 1943

2 Squadron, IAF

Kerala
Southern India

May 4th 1943

On May 1st, a signal is received: "Post F/L Dunford Wood to 2 Sqn I.A.F. to command. F/L Dunford Wood to be posted Acting S/L from 1st May."

So I am to be O.C. 2 Sqn I.A.F.!!!

Bill Robinson, now a Major, comes in for a party and I see him off fairly well. I then move over to 2 Squadron Mess, and here I am. Things seem pretty chaotic from the administrative point of view, as the adjutant is a bit dim. Fortunately, there is a B.O.R. (British other ranks) corporal, most of the pilots are up in Imphal where there is a detachment, and only F/L Latif and nine aircraft are left down here. I spend the last few days on "bumph", great piles of it.

Two nights ago Tom Pierce and I go out to dinner with 14th Division – David Cooper and old 'GI Warren' in great form. Unfortunately I get a bad attack of diarrhoea, or something, and so do not enjoy it. I am also going deaf in one ear through a large accumulation of wax.

I wonder how long I shall keep this job? Presumably until I get the sack for putting up a black of some sort, or until an Indian C.O. is chosen and appointed. It won't be much fun going back to flight commander after having commanded a squadron for a day or two – (longer I hope – lekim quien sabe?).[1]

[1] *An interesting mix of Hindi and Latin - 'but who knows?'*

May 12th 1943

I go flying twice at Ranchi. Once to watch an artillery demonstration, and am stooging around about 2000 feet when up comes a mortar bomb above me, hovers a bit, and then drops. The second time I run into a lot of cattle at the end of the strip, but fortunately each one in his turn gets out of my way. I then come up to Imphal – leave Ranchi one morning for Red Road, but don't like the look of the approach, through a balloon barrage, so I land at Alipore instead. See Group (HQ), and spend the night with Reggie Cox, in their Mess, a beautiful house with electric fans, running water and iced beer.

We go to the Saturday Club and the flicks. Next day, despite the compass being some 10-15 degrees out, I land at Agartala and then Imphal. It looks just like Kashmir or Abbottabad, nestling in a plain surrounded by mountain ranges.

The two flight lieutenants, Nazir Allah and Latif, I find are in trouble – the one for beating up one of his pilots, and the other for refusing to fly at the latter's orders, as he considered himself the senior. Amrik Singh is here as A.L.O., and Group Captain Seton-Broughall is O.C. of the local Wing, and I see him and also A.V.M. Williams about some of my troubles. The Viceroy[1] comes up on a visit, heralded by a Lockheed Electra with his servants and personal baggage on board.

"Longcloth" – 77th Brigade under Brigadier Wingate – are returning from Burma. About 3000 of them advanced in several columns last December, crossed the Irrawaddy, and got nearly to Bhamu. Some have gone on into China, about 1400 have returned to India and others are on the way. We do contact recces to find them, and then aircraft drop supplies on them. They have been supplied by air the whole time, even boats being dropped to recross the Irrawaddy. Bernard Fergusson was one of the column commanders.

Nazir Allah and Latif go on a recce, but only Latif has returned, saying Nazir lost him – so that looks like a battle casualty, and the best man in the squadron too.

[1] *Lord Linlithgow.*

387

Operation Longcloth

Operation Longcloth had been launched on 7th February by 77 Brigade, consisting of 3000 specialist jungle-fighting troops under the command of Brigadier Orde Wingate. The main body of the force, the northern (No. 2) group, was made up of five 'columns' of c. 400 men each, and Colin's friend Major Bernard Fergusson led the 5th column. A southern diversionary group (No. 1 group), consisted of two additional columns. Named the 'Chindits' after the river Chindwin which was their first objective, the goal of the operation was to disrupt Japanese lines of communications in the jungles of northern Burma.

The concept was devised by Wingate - long range penetration (LRP) by mobile patrols on foot, supplied from the air, moving mostly by night, harassing the enemy in a jungle variant of the SAS long range desert groups of North Africa.

While the Chindits achieved little of immediate military value, other than blowing some bridges and disrupting Japanese supply lines, it gave a much needed morale boost to the defeated British, and invited the disastrous Imphal/Kohima offensive launched by the Japanese to counter the threat 12 months later, leading to their eventual defeat.

For an account of this expedition, see Bernard Fergusson's Beyond the Chindwin.

May 13th 1943

NAZIR GETS BACK ALRIGHT, and next day I set off. Two chaps go off on one sortie, but Amrik says Latif is ill and will go later if feeling better. I say "OK or get a couple of Mohawks to help", having laid on a tentative bandobust[1] with S/L Jefferies to that end. I am just about to take off, when Amrik gives me a message from W/C McMichael, the A.L.O. of 4 Corps, that he is 'very surprised' I didn't go myself that morning, so I expect he will try and put me in the dirt for it.

I take off, and reach Alipore via Silchar and Agartala, though without landing. Then on here to Ranchi, and nearly prang, swinging on landing. She has a small internal glycol leak, and I sniff the fumes for four hours on the way, and am violently sick when I get back.

Today a signal that Latif is missing on a sortie, but no details. Looks like Joe Soap will have to go up on Ops again as the fourth pilot!

Mike alive again.[2] Apparently he came up floating, swam ashore to Magyichaung, was offered a "V" cigarette by a Jap at the four Bren gun post that shot him down, and then kept in captivity for ten days. He had his leg treated and got constipated on a diet of rice. Then one night he walked out, round Foul Point, and then walked up the beach to Maungdaw with the help of some locals met with on the way, who got Rs150/- each for their pains. The march took him three days only.

I think I have slight jaundice following the cholera injection at Imphal, and that awful flight home. I shook hands with the Viceroy Lord Linlithgow when he inspected us and 15 Squadron at Imphal. He was wearing a two piece suit with three rows of medal ribbons! and a topee! Ah well, I should get my boots greased again I suppose!

Henry still at Ramu, and Sybil airstrip no longer being used. All my boys back now. One Jack Wales posted to 28 squadron in my place from a fighter squadron in Ceylon.

[1] *A word originating from Hindi meaning 'organization or an arrangement made to deal with something'.*
[2] *See entry for April 28th 1943.*

June 1st 1943

RANCHI

28 SQUADRON SEND UP FOUR PILOTS instead of my having to go, but Buckland is soon missing. Later it transpires he gets shot up and force lands at Chittagong. I get another whack of malaria and am in bed for two days, later getting the whole course of Atebrin etc from my squadron M.O.

I fly in formation for the Tunisian Victory celebrations[1], later going to the Governor's Ball from 7 - 9.00 pm. I get plenty to drink – Solar's No 1 whisky not too bad – and the A.D.C. is one Wood from 11 Sikhs who used to be in my platoon at Sandhurst. Later dinner at B.N.R. with Tom Pierce, his fiancé Jackie Marchant and some QAIMNS[2].

I go down to Calcutta a few days ago to see 221 Group. Stay at their Mess with Paddy O'Malley, and we go to see the film "Desert Victory". The next day, a/c is u/s, so I spend one more night, and then return here in a Dragonfly as a passenger.

Air Marshal Garrod[3] visits Ranchi and seems interested in my Indian pilots.

We are moving to Trichinopoly, and the advance party left yesterday. The route worries me, so I have signalled AHQ India and hope to get a reply, if they get the damn signal. Trichinopoly will be pretty hot and I suspect we shall have to live in tents.

Great winds and dust storms blowing here. Shall be glad to get away, Breakfast now consists of lychees and nimbu pani!![4]

390

[1] *On May 13th, 230,000 Axis troops had surrendered to Montgomery in North Africa.*
[2] *Nurses from Queen Alexandra's Imperial Military Nursing Service.*
[3] *Deputy Air Officer Commanding-in-Chief, India.*
[4] *Lemonade.*

June 2nd 1943

Ranchi

Wood gives a roulette party to which Tom Pierce and I go. Last night I go to a "dinner and dance" with Mrs Hoffman and Elizabeth – the former being the wife of the C.O. of the 56th[1]. One General and Mrs Moore of 39th Division are also there, and two U.S. Colonels from Ramgarh.

A goodly shower of rain yesterday. The Imphal detachment is not back yet, and the train party is due to go on the 3rd. I have asked for a route by air from Air HQ, but no reply so far. That's what is most worrying – whether we shall get there or not. Ranchi - Vizagapatam is 420 miles, Vizag - Madras about 450, and the monsoon is on the point of breaking, so we may run into some shocking awful weather. 6 squadron I.A.F. lost six a/c on one such long cross country, due to bad navigation.

Am feeling rather better now, having finished the malaria "cure".

[1] *56th Punjabi Rifles, now the 2nd Battalion of 13th Frontier Force Rifles, Colin's former regiment.*

June 8th 1943

Trichinopoly, Kerala, Southern India

I go to the Pierces' wedding on the 2nd. Then to a reception at the Sisters Mess. Not much fun, but I manage to keep off the booze and drink iced squash (this at 5.00 pm). Later

I go round to Elizabeth Elsmie and find Bobby in town, and have dinner with them. Mike back[1], but has fractured his spine, and will have to spend three or four months in plaster of paris.

Well, off we set at 07.45 on June 3rd. I lead the first flight and make Vizagapatam where there is a colossal runway. The last flight of F/L Nazir Ullah and three prunes[2] make a "cock up", and the three prunes go off by themselves, eventually getting down near Bezwada, where one of them dips his airscrew in soft ground. Then on to St Thomas Mount (Madras), which we make in record time, flying down the coast and "round the corner" from Vizag. On to Trichinopoly, and we are living in 173 Wing Mess until ours is ready.

Chapman has done plenty of work since he arrived with the advance party. We are living in 'bashers' with concrete floors, and well furnished by M.E.S. There is a strong west wind all day and night, which keeps me from sweating over much. There is also a small swimming pool in the officers mess. On Saturday we go to the Club, a quite nice one with the illustrated papers, where they lay on a helluva cold buffet supper for one rupee. Naturally all the best booze is reserved for permanent members only, and service members just get "Parry's gin".

This job of mine is quite interesting, I can fly when I want to, I have a nice car and get 200/- extra a month, but I do not seem to be as fit as I used to be. Perhaps the country is getting me down at last. It's just over a year since I spoke to a "nice girl" – in Shillong last May – but unless I can get away up to the hills occasionally, down here it won't do me any good either.

Wish to God I could get home!

[1] *See May 13th 1943.*
[2] *After Pilot Officer Percy Prune, a hapless character from a popular comic strip of the day - 'dutiful but dumb'.*

June 10th 1943

I escape into the air again – just sort of fly around – do a loop that fails, and then a nice glide approach and landing. If I could only shut business out of my mind out of working hours, I should be OK. But I keep myself awake of nights thinking of all the things I must do.

There's a detachment to Kolar for an exercise shortly. Chapman and I go to the Club Saturday evening, and have a few Parry's Gins. One S/L Vigors of Group comes down, and hears all my moans. I live in a house of plaited bamboos, with a stone floor and two feet thick walls too. I hope it won't rain much. No exercise for damn near six months, and I must do something about it.

I have an Indian adjutant – one Aslam Khan – a noted Lahore lawyer, who talks about "postal communications" for letters, and such like verbiage.

I wish I knew a proper "popsie" around here – I must go up to the hills – if I dare.

June 15th 1943

Kolar, Bengal

I fly up to Kolar, formatting on a Hudson at about 8000 feet. Very cool, and I have a blanket at night, but it blows a lot of red dust and I am always dirty.

Six a/c under Nazir Ullah and me are up here. We live in huts as at Trichinopoly, but there are no baths, and it is hard to get washing water if you have no bearer. We bring up a stone jar full of beer for the first two nights, but a contractor has now turned up and laid some on.

I fly around and look at Kolar gold fields, and today I examine Bangalore from about 500 feet as 10/10 cloud low down. Group

Captain Farquahar of Trichi is O.C. 171 Wing up here, as W/C Yorke is ill with malaria. We go and visit Kolar gold fields and have a bath, beer and billiards in the Club there. I pick up an article on the "Origins of Snooker" by C. Mackenzie – the inventor being Neville Chamberlain in Jubbulpore apparently.

Yesterday 258 Squadron from Ceylon arrive, and I have a bit of a party with two or three of them out of my bottle of "Canadian Club". I want to go into Group (HQ) at Bangalore and stay tonight, but G/C is too keen on his war (Exercise Roy), which starts tomorrow, and won't let me go.

Wagstaffe up here. I must return to Trichinopoly soon and see what sort of cock-up is being made of things.

June 22nd 1943

TRICHINOPOLY

I NIP OVER TO BANGALORE ONE MORNING and see a few "stooges" in 225 Group landing at the Hindustan aircraft factory landing ground. Then I hear a signal ordering me to report to Delhi for a medical board "to see if I am fit to continue service overseas due to recurrent malaria." So if they board me I suppose that I shall go back to the Indian Army as a Lieutenant – Christ!

An awful journey to Delhi before me by train. I came down to Trichi today in my Hurricane, a most enjoyable trip, and find a fair amount of cock going on in my absence.

June 26th 1943

DELHI

I fly over to Bangalore and spend the night in the West End Hotel. I see Jackie for tea, and have a helluva booze with W/C Yorke. Pleasant and cold at night, and the water tastes excellent.

Next morning to Delhi by Hudson with a stop at Nagpar – not very comfortable. No one to meet us at Delhi, but I find a Mess and meet Dudley Withers there, now a W/C with AFC[1]. I have to go in a room with no fan, and even on the balcony it is fearful, as no breeze. I lie in bed with a towel, and sleep for about an hour only. This morning to the Medical Board, and I am perfectly fit, even passing the eye test by squinting hard!!! Am told to return to unit, and that if I go to hospital every time I get malaria, maybe I shall be cured.

I ring up G/C Hawtrey and go and see him in the afternoon. Also A/C Baker (D.S.A.S.O.),[2] and one W/C Ashmore, about going home – but no luck. I also get a passage booked on a Hudson tomorrow, so if I get it and reach Bangalore, I suppose I shall have to go back by train.

Tonight I have to go and have drinks with John Hawtrey[3], provided I can get a taxi and find the way.

[1] *Air Force Cross.*
[2] *Deputy Senior Air Staff Officer.*
[3] *Wing Commander John Hawtry, former Inspector of the Iraqi Air Force, and one of the squadron commanders of the Habbaniya Air Striking Force that Colin was a part of in May 1941 in the Battle of Habbaniya - see Volume 1.*

June 29th 1943

Trichinopoly

I GET THERE FOR DRINKS, and we retell the Iraq campaign. I am produced to shake hands with A.O.C. in C. Sir Richard Peirse[1].

I get on the Hudson about 0630 and get to Bangalore in time for lunch at 2.00 pm in the West End Hotel. We fly at about 8000 feet and I get frozen and the shivers, departing to bed after lunch with several blankets. OK in the evening, and find my room companion to be one Tom Hudson (I was in the same room before leaving for Delhi), who was at Harrow with me, and in the police

395

with Hugh[2]. He is on rest from Catalinas in Ceylon, where is also Lawson-Smith. We sink a huge jug of shandy together, and then he introduces his 'popsie', one Mrs Coles, and we crack some whisky (mine), have dinner and go to the 'flicks'. I see June, now Mrs Brandt, whom I once met with Pete Jennings at a party at Insein mess in Rangoon.

This morning I fly down to Trichinopoly to find some prune using my car after I have given orders that it is not to be so used.

Letter from Aunt Babs that old 'Pop' Jacobs died suddenly in the lavatory on May 2nd.

[1] Air Chief Marshal Sir Richard Pierse was shortly to become Allied Air Commander in Chief, South-East Asia. However, his career was terminated early and he was flown back to Britain on account of his affair with Lady (Jessie) Auchinleck, the wife of his friend, Field Marshal Sir Claude Auchinleck, then Commander in Chief India. They subsequently married.
[2] Colin's brother, formerly in the Metropolitan police, killed flying Blenheims against German tanks in northern France in June 1940.

July 4th 1943
Yelahanka, near Bangalore

I GO UP TO KOLAR to find the boys have moved to Yelahanka just outside Bangalore. In the course of the exercise I fly on there and stay to the end, returning to Trichi on July 2nd. G/C Farquahar takes the boys into town and throws us a party at Chungking restaurant. I am given dual on chopsticks and manage very well. The food very good, and I manage to avoid eating too much, which is my usual failing on such occasions. Then on to the B.U.S. Club[1] where a dance is in progress. Later on we go to the Club again, and I meet Howes of 3 Coy, who says Bill (Robinson) will be down again here shortly.

We fly to Kolar for the conference – but have to leave at half time to get back to Yelahanka before dark. I have now come out in spots on my face, over half a dozen, a damn nuisance.

This job will drive me nuts soon – thank God for the car, the extra 200/-, and the fact that I can fly when I want to.

[1] *Bangalore United Services Club.*

July 9th 1943
Trichinopoly

I GO OVER TO BANGALORE with the Group Captain in a Hudson for a post-mortem conference on the exercise. Stay in the West End Hotel, and in the evening go out with W/C Beaman to "Funnels" for fish and chips, and then to the B.U.S. Club where I meet the Hammerbecks and Catherine Railton. Next day, lunch with Hammers, and I come back in the rear seat of an Audax which the G/C has gotten. Bad weather forecast prevents the Hudson coming back, but we manage to edge round the bad weather.

Cold last night, and I have to put a blanket on. F/L Nazir Ullah tells me a few things about the I.A.F. today[1], their principal moan being me as a British C.O. But the way they want to run their Air Force it ought to be disbanded. I don't know what the solution is – never had any C.O. a more difficult job.

[1] *Indian Air Force, whose 2 Squadron Colin commanded.*

July 17th 1943
Trichinopoly

THE INSPECTOR GENERAL OF THE INDIAN AIR FORCE, G/C Pround, with W/C Mazunder and Mukerjee, come round for a two day tour. Everything is gone into, and I find out a lot of things that I should have done something about are in a shocking condition, so I expect I shall lose my job, but I can't do everything myself.

We go to the Defence Services Exhibition last evening, and then on to the Club, where we have a damn merry dinner. I am getting a bit worn out, and had hoped to go away for the weekend, but cannot do so with all this going around. Chapman and I go up to Wing mess a couple of times for a decent dinner and some bridge.

I go out around a nearby lake with my .22, but nothing to shoot. I have as body servant one Nur Hussain, who answers to the name of 'Albert'. He is a lascar and son of the chaprasi[1] at station HQ Kohat, whom I used to know quite well.

[1] An office junior.

July 25th 1943

KODAIKANAL

RONALD CHAPMAN AND I come up to Kodaikanal for a weekend. We catch a train from Trichinopoly at 0645, and are up here by 14.30. Nearly 7000 feet, and damn cold at night and early morning. We stay in the Carlton Hotel which produces excellent food. It's years since I tasted a carrot like one of theirs.

We go to the Club on Friday night and I see Marjorie Maude (ex Buller)[1]. S/L Scott is up here too, and after some dancing we go to the bungalow of one Mrs Norris, who has half a dozen Sgt aircrew living with her. I take across, very foolishly, most of a bottle of "Canadian Club", which soon vanishes. Some French women from Pondicherry are there, and I leave first and take some woman home about 3.00 am. We row across the lake, and eventually I sleep on the spare bed in her spare room. She gives me breakfast the next morning, and I see she has a very nice daughter, about 16.

Yesterday I go for a bit of a walk, and then read the illustrated papers in the Club, and have hot rums with Scotty. A few retired people live up here, and it's pretty dead most of the time. But the climate is something.

A signal was in, asking for chaps for a special mission – "exceptional stamina and endurance" – another Wingate effort, and I have a feeling to go, but what's the use? All I want is to go home and find someone to bolster my morale.

A letter arrives from Bill[2], who's near Bangalore.

[1] *See Volume 1, when Colin was courting her in Kashmir.*
[2] *Bill Robinson, his best friend from Harrow days, who was in the King's Own Royal Regiment.*

August 2nd 1943

TRICHINOPOLY

LAST NIGHT AT KODAIKANAL, I go to dinner at some judge's wife's place with Marjorie, and down the hill the next day. I nip over to Banaglore on Thursday to see Group, and after doing my business, I try to get Bill on the line. But 70 Division telephone is down, so no success.

Drink some beer with W/C Banks in the evening, and then on to the pictures.

Flying home next morning I do three circuits of Yercand, the hill station above Salem in the Shevaroy Hills, but no'wt to look at bar a few schools.

Saturday to see "Desert Victory" again, and then to the Club, where I meet a Major Jones who I used to know in 1/11 Sikhs in Jubbalpore. We were both in the same car smash. I dance with a popsie called Joyce Cullan – Indian railways – whom we locally call 'the icicle', as she looks so grim when she dances.

6 squadron and 171 wing are moving here, but David Yorke is sick again I believe.

I get rather intoxicated last night at our B.O.R. Mess, on Canadian bottled beer, which is quite potent stuff. This squadron has five B.O.R.s now.

August 5th 1943

"1000 BOMBER BALDWIN"[1] comes round on a visit yesterday, but is not very impressed by me.

Today a signal is in, posting Tom Pierce W/C to 171 Group – David Yorke to AC Ops Delhi, and myself to S/L AC Ops 225 Group Bangalore – with Arjan Singh coming as C.O. to 2 Squadron.

I reckon I have got the sack after all.

[1] *Air Marshal Jack Baldwin, Deputy Air Officer Commanding-in-Chief, India. He was famous for having launched the first 1000 bomber raid on Germany when C-in-C Bomber Command in 1942.*

August 6th 1943

Trichinopoly

I TELEPHONE BANGALORE this morning to ask S.A.S.O. whether I ought to wait for my relief or move straight away. They put me on to the A.O.C., Mackintosh, who says "We don't want you here – await your relief." He (my relief) is from 1 squadron in Kohat, and God knows how long he will take getting down, and they may change the posting in the meantime.

I am sick of Trichinopoly. We work 7.30 am to 1.30 pm, and then I read a book or so to 6, and then either swim or do some "Strongfortism" exercises, with spring dumb bells on the floor, or lie on my bed if I feel too idle to do either. Then drink beer in the Mess, or go to 173 Wing Mess for a good dinner and perhaps some bridge, and the Club on Saturdays. They have an excellent cold buffet supper, all for 1/- rupees, and gin which runs out quite quickly – then rum and brandy (Indian) with ginger ale.

I do a low-level cross country to visit a jungle warfare school, and navigation is quite good at 200 feet.

I have taken on "Albert", a lascar, as my orderly, and very good he is too, despite his use of "tum"[1] to me. He was frontier constabulary, and stills wears his black hose tops.

25/13 MG Battalion is down these parts, with Victor Wainwright as 2nd in command. He and some of them come over to dinner and drinks, and we get through quite a good bit of hooch. Ronald Chapman (also 13th) and I meet them regularly every Saturday in the Club.

Hammerbeck, whose job I am taking over, said he spent most of his time travelling round the countryside on schemes and exercises etc, which will be pretty bloody, as I hate Indian railways, especially at this time of year.

[1] *The familiar form of 'you' in Hindi.*

August 11th 1943
Trichinopoly

I GO FLYING WITH A COLD – I go to 8000 feet and then dive down gently to earth, getting the most fearful pains across my forehead and blockages in my left ear. I rush off to the Doc on landing.

Today a signal from 1 Sqn that Arjan Singh won't arrive until 23rd, so I suppose I shall have to do this bloody exercise as well.

I fly over to Bangalore today to see 'P' staff *(personnel)*, and do some work for the G/C as the phone is not working. I have to lay on night flying next week, which I don't somehow fancy.

August 15th 1943
Trichinopoly

THE WORST HAS HAPPENED – Arjan Singh's posting is cancelled, and mine suspended. Presumably until they find someone to take over from me – and they won't easily, either. "1000 bomber

Baldwin" probably said something in Delhi, and I shall get a British adjutant, and be left here.

A little rain, and I spend practically the whole day on my back dozing. I tried some exercises yesterday, but didn't feel too good, so desisted. Met one Ferguson of 17 Sqn in Trichi Club, who came from Ipoh[1], and knew Ma. His brother is someone I trained with in Iraq.

I don't fancy night flying tomorrow.

[1] *Where Colin was born, in Malaya.*

August 25th 1943
Kolar

ON AN EXERCISE AT KOLAR AGAIN. One day in the Mess, Chapman and I get boiled vegetables only for lunch. We then find that Nazir Ullahas has said that they won't pay for British food for tiffin. I ask him about this, and he says "Yes, you can have English food, but you can pay extra for it." Was I angry!

I have had a cold in my nose for nearly three weeks now, but I fly up here successfully, and yesterday do a Tac/R at 5000 feet, seeing very little. 171 Wing, only, is playing on the scheme, with Hammerbeck the sole representative of Group. We manage to get some beer up here, and I have a bottle of Canadian Club, so am OK. I reckon I shall have to stay as C.O. and my Bangalore posting will be cancelled.

September 3rd 1943
Bangalore

I GO ACROSS TO THE SAPPERS AND MINERS MESS for a few drinks, stay to dinner, and then remain on, to compete with the jackals at singing.

The next day, drive over to Bangalore to see the Ear, Nose and Throat specialist, as I have had a cold for three weeks. He says it is sinusitis, and I must come into hospital. I go back and pack my kit, returning the next day with the remains of my beer ration as well. The road from Kolar is lined with trees, and troops of monkeys playing at the side.

Two accidents: Bhuller's aircraft gets a glycol leak whilst doing a slow roll at Trichi and the engine catches fire. He bales out at 5000 feet and lands softly in a paddy swamp with two fingers burnt. Then Sahibzada does a steep turn near the deck on a low-level recce, and manages to crash land somehow in a clear space – rather confused. His long range tanks catch fire and he is badly burnt.

So now I am in Bangalore, 38 B.G.H., *(Bangalore General Hospital)* sniffing a solution of boiling water and menthol every four hours, or when the staff remember. Every few days I go to the specialist, one Major Philip Scott, who dopes my nostrils with cocaine, and then shoves 5 inches or so of steel tube up my nostrils and through the bone, to siphon the muck out – a horrid business.

A lot of the orderlies are Italian prisoners of war. I lie on my bed and read books, and very pleasant it is too, in this climate. One of the patients, an observer, knew Hugh in RAF Watton. Food is excellent, much better than I get in 2 Sqn Mess, and I occasionally have a surreptitious swig from my 'Canadian Club' bottle. At the last issue I was given two bottles extra by the Mess secretary.

It's the old hospital routine of getting you awake at 0545, for tea of all things. I turn over and sleep until 0700, then up and shave.

September 6th 1943

BANGALORE

STILL GOING STRONG, and I get a touch of malaria yesterday. I do not disclose it, as that would mean another three weeks here, and I should lose my acting squadron leader position – so I just take ten grains of quinine.

Here let me record that, on returning from the Arakan, I made it pretty plain that I thought 100 sorties was pretty good, though only 160 operational hours with it, and I think Tom Pierce put me up for a D.F.C., but that was four months ago now, so I shan't get it. That's the second time of being put up.

There is an American pilot I meet here at meals occasionally, and he gives me the correct figures for their US pay:

- 2nd Lt – $150 basic pay plus $75 flying pay
- 1st Lt – $166 + $83
- Captain – $200 + $100
- Major – $250 + $125
- Lt Col – $275 + $135.50

Also 10% extra for serving overseas, and 5% extra for every three years service. $1 = Rs3, 4 annas.

September 14th 1943

BANGALORE

BILL ROBINSON COMES TO SEE ME in hospital and we have a few drinks. He is shortly moving out with his battalion to train for another 'Wingate' job of some sort.

Yesterday I am discharged from hospital, though still with a certain amount of catarrh. I go and book a room in the West End, and then ring up Hammerbeck, to find out if G/C Farquahar and Tom Pierce are in town. Hammers says "Congratulations" – a pause, and I ask what on – and he says "your D.F.C." And sure enough, a signal is in from 28 squadron to 225 Group dated 11/9 –

"Following received from A.O.C. Bengal Command. Warmest congratulations to F/L .... on award of D.F.C." (Distinguished Flying Cross)

Yesterday the A.O.C. throws a party for the two lodger squadrons in Yellahanka, despite the fact that S/L Proudfoot,

O.C. of one of them, spins in and gets killed that afternoon. I gatecrash successfully, and am congratulated by all and sundry. I meet one Mrs Pat Stephenson (nee Strangham) whose sister I met in Ranchi, and get on shockingly. She used to bring books round in the hospital. Buffet supper with her and the A.O.C., and he gives me one of his cigars. In bed by 10.30, though much noise and disturbances all through the night.

This morning I spend about two hours searching the town for a D.F.C. medal ribbon, unsuccessfully, until I go into a Gold and Silversmith, of all places. No accommodation until 17th on the Trichinolopoly train, so here I shall stew, I suppose. That 'gong' puts me one up on Jonah and Peter Petit I think, as I have the Indian General Service medal, 'Waziristan 1937-9' on the bar, as well.

September 17th 1943

BANGALORE

I SEEM TO GET SLIGHTLY PIXILATED on too much "Parry's" gin, and the next day, Bill and Dick Evans come in to see me. We sink 3/4 bottle of my best Canadian Club, and then have dinner. The regiment is off to do some intensive training for another 'Wingate' stunt[1], and I think Bernard Fergusson is the Colonel commanding them now. Meet Frank Fuller and Ormiston for lunch. The latter was G11 Ops[2], 26 Division, after I left.

I haven't felt at all well since I got this D.F.C., though I most certainly haven't drunk a lot. Last night I don't feel too well, but have a few gins, and am scarce able to eat my dinner. I go to bed early, and today I have some pains when I swing my eyes around.

I have been prospecting for accommodation here[3], but all the best rooms have two or three squadron leaders in them, and such a room is all I can get. Then I find a room down in some rabbit warren, in which I am now living, and with a bit more furniture it should be OK. I go back on the train to Trichi tonight.

[1] *See Operation Longcloth for the first 'Wingate stunt'.*
[2] *General staff officer Grade 2, operations.*
[3] *In preparation for his posting to Group HQ in Bangalore.*

September 28th 1943

TRICHINOLOPOLY

I RETURN TO TRICHINOPOLY in a shower of spots, which turn out to be dengue rash. Majithia[1] is there, and I get my handing over done before collapsing into bed. I then get moved up to a vacant room in Wing, where the food is better and the company more congenial.

After three days in bed in a perpetual sweat, I stagger out and take the next train back to Bangalore, having provisionally sent on 'Albert'[2], having arranged his posting to Group too, with my kit. I arrive, and find my room and kit all ready, so here I am in the West End Hotel. The food and cooking is excellent, but the bar prices are a bit steep for what you can get here.

I am still weary from the dengue and hoped for some sick leave, but A.O.C. A/C McWorth says this would be most inopportune, what with Hammerbeck going home on the next boat, and some Army jungle warfare scheme coming off soon.

I work out that I have had two months leave in five years, excluding ten days sick leave; largely through my own fault in not demanding any before.

[1] *The new 2 Squadron C.O., who is taking over from Colin.*
[2] *His bearer.*

11

October 1943 - March 1944

Air Staff, 225 Group

Bangalore

October 1st 1943

I HAVE DINNER WITH TOM JONES and his wife in the hotel, and go out for a drink with Catherine Railton, whom I also met. Tom Pierce comes over on a visit, and we have dinner together.

Then last night, I get mixed up with a most interesting chap – one Lt Col Cooper E. Yorks – who tells me all about Wingate's expeditions, and how they had 40 percent casualties.

I am heard on the radio this morning on American overseas broadcast from London, in the early morning. One of five DFCs awarded on the Burma front for "reconnaissance" and "supply dropping" – so I am told.

I work 8.30 - 1 pm, and 2 - 5.30 pm, each day, with one in seven days off – or two afternoons. Most mornings I go to the Southern Army 'prayer meeting' at 9.00 am, and get to the office around 10, so that cuts into the morning a bit. I hope to get out into the jungle on a local scheme out near Ootacamund[1], but S.A.S.O. doesn't seem to think I need to go.

[1] *A hill station known amongst the British in India as 'Snooty Ooty', on account of all the grandees who spent the summer months cooling off up there.*

October 8th 1943

I AM SITTING IN KUMARA PARK one afternoon and feel the fever coming on, so walk out and report to the M.O. that this is my ninth fever. They whip me into B.M.H., and after one evening's sweating, I am OK.

Food good, two nice nurses to sit and chat with, and a bottle of beer in the evening. The palm squirrels are pretty tame, and come down at mealtimes and leap onto the beds on the verandah, and are fed by hand.

I get two letters from Aunt Babs and Uncle George with D.F.C. marked on them – the first ever. Also a letter of congratulations from Grindlays Bank…!

Much rain, and I am quite happy in bed reading George Eliot's "Scenes from Clerical Life" and Dickens' "Old Curiosity Shop" – my taste in literature having suddenly swung back. I have "The Jungle Book" too.

Albert comes in every day with this and that, as I require them.

October 14th 1943

TRICHINOLOPOLY

I AM DUE FOR DISCHARGE TOMORROW. The treatment is now two days quinine, five days Atebrin, two days rest and five days Plasmaquin, or whatever the present substitutes. I get a bottle of Solan beer each evening, but am getting fed up with the chap who shares my room, an RIASC Lieutenant who insists on showing me how Indian sepoys salute and mark time. Me!

The S.M.O. W/C[1] says he will fix me another board in Delhi and have me sent to the UK. Like hell he will. If I am not careful, I shall get returned to the Army as a Lieutenant again, if not fit to fly out here.

Mike, I hear, is in Ooty, waiting for his boat home, but 'Tiny' Irwin appears to be back in this country, so God knows what the policy is. If I go home, I shall get bumped off in a Mustang, but it will be worth it.

We now get a lot of Canadian whisky and gin each month, per officer – a great improvement.

Madras bombed on the nights of the 12th/13th. One a/c dropped six bombs I believe.

[1] *The Senior medical officer, a wing commander.*

409

October 21st 1943

I HAVE THE JONES'S UP AGAIN, and also a party with Babneal and his wife. Meet a charming fellow called Broderick, a South African.

I manage to squeeze two weeks sick leave, and one casual, out of the A.O.C., and am off to Munnar in Travancore. There is an RAF hill depot there, and it's the centre of the planting community, but I have a horrid feeling that it will rain like hell, I shall be alone, and with nothing to do but read books all day.

I wrote to a chap in Ooty for some shooting, and he said he could fix me up in his bungalow in the shooting country, including food, transport and a tracker at Rs30/- a day, exclusive of baits and beaters. OK for the Prince of Wales on safari, but not for "Josope".[1]

[1] *Joe Soap, meaning himself.*

October 25th 1943

MUNNAR HILL STATION

I GET A BOARD,[1] and three weeks leave from A.O.C., and set off for the RAF Hill Depot at Munnar, Travancore, 4500 feet up. Of course, the train from Bangalore is late, and we (one Flo Withers and I) get to Jalapet at 1 pm, another train at 3 pm, and arrive Alwaya at midnight. We sleep in a comfortable tea company restroom, and leave by bus at 6.00 am. A few miles from Alwaya, the bus stops, the purser gets out, looks at us two and the bearer, examines the luggage on the roof, and gives me a bill for Rs25/-. Argument about the luggage is of no avail, and I have to stump up.

We arrive at the Club for lunch. It's well built, and furnished with sheets, towels and soap. The first night there is a cinema, "Coastal Command", and some of the locals come in and dance to the gramophone. One Marjorie Barnes is there, husband a POW in Korea, from Singapore. We decant half a bottle of Canadian whisky and are very popular. I get to bed at 2.30, and sleep well under three blankets.

Next day, I walk for about four miles, and come to a broken bridge and a barrier on the road. A car draws up behind, and I am asked what I am doing. I say walking, they get out and take me into Ma Barnes's bungalow for morning tea, then back to their own for lunch. A planter named Knight.

Later in the evening one F/O Raeder of the International Group gives a conjuring show, professional practically, and later I fox a few with my three card trick. The honorary manager, an Austrian whose husband is in Persia with the Gurkhas, gets into form with me, the conjuror, and one Girwin from Cochin, and with great difficulty I get away to bed at 1.30.

This morning I set off to climb a good looking hill, but after about an hour I find the leeches getting on my chaplies and through the outer socks faster than I can knock 'em off, so I return. One large brute gets a grip on my thigh, but I manage to flick him off before he gets a secure foothold.

A magnificent library here. I have brought up my artillery, but what with the leeches and the planters not being too keen on visitors shooting, I doubt I shall get anything.

In the bar are many heads, and the hats of those who have lived thirty years here and then gone.

[1] *Medical board or assessment.*

November 7th 1943

Munnar Hill Station

I GO OUT WALKING MOST MORNINGS, 9-12 am, and it rains after lunch and I go to bed with a book. I get up a good peak the other day, but am surrounded in cloud, so no view. Douglas takes me up to the Top Station, up and away another 3-4000 feet, and we call on some WAC(1)'s who have a secret job up there. I am nearly sick in the back of the station wagon going up, with hairpin bends and whatnot. We stop to see some black monkeys on the way down.

Wednesday night there's a dance for the RAF BORs, and most of the locals are in from a S.P.M.R. parade[1]. Much drinking afterwards, and the vultures close in on Withers and I when we open a half bottle of Canadian whisky. One old white hair doesn't believe it's really Canadian, and has to be pressed. But no one offers me any shooting. I get in a corner with one Dick Imray, divorced, and discuss life and marriage for about an hour. I get off to bed at 3.00 am, being not too well next day from the Travancore gin.

I march out seven miles to lunch with one Basil Matthews, arriving at 12.30 to find he and his visitor (one ex-Assistant Leckie of 7 Rajputs, on leave from the Middle East) are still in bed. They rise in their dressing gowns, we discuss the war, and they remember lunch at about 3 pm. No drinks though, but because they think it's still morning. I get away about 6 pm by car.

I read Gallagher's "Retreat in the East" – I knew him, Stone and Berrigan at the Mingalodon Golf Club[2] – some of his anecdotes are not quite true, notably Burt Mann's prang with General Hutton's ADC. He states that A.V.G.'s score in June '42 was 285 Japanese planes, for 15 A.V.G. pilots.

A letter from Ma, somewhat excited about my 'gong' in the 10th September Times.

[1] *Southern Province Mounted Rifles, a volunteer unit of the local planter community.*
[2] *Foreign correspondents in Burma.*

November 8th 1943

Munnar Hill Station

I GO OUT WALKING with bird book and field glasses. Weather fine now, with orange sunset over the 'cup of the saucer' in which the Club and grounds lie. Bitterly cold nights and mornings.

Saturday, I walk out to the Knights for lunch and tea, then play football for the RAF against the Town. The altitude gets to me, but I manage to put up a show. No one's around in the evening, and I get tired and go to bed at midnight to be kept awake until 2.00 am by locals dancing with WACs[1].

Withers and G.E. Corkin have gone down[2] and I'm a bit lonely, though the other residents and I stoke up a hot rum and lime before dinner. Shooting seems off, as Douglas is always playing bridge when the planters come into the bar, so he will never be able to fix anything.

A good life as a planter up here. Assistants get 250/- and managers up to 900/-, and nearly 50% extra as commission on a good garden. Beautiful country as any I ever saw, tea and jungle being practically one in parts, and excellent shikar[3].

[1] *Women's Army Corps.*
[2] *From the hill station.*
[3] *Hunting in Hindi.*

November 9th 1943

MUNNAR HILL STATION

I GO DOWN TO "STUFFY" STEVENS'S BUNGALOW for a day, and for tea he takes me out to a rock overlooking the low jungle country. Eventually we see a bison moving through the long elephant grass, with glasses. I return to the Club, and come back home with Ham Wilkes, with whom I am now. He has a beautiful bungalow, more like a country house than the usual, and breakfast and lunch on a sort of glass sun corner of the verandah. I go out by myself looking at birds, and see some black monkeys, and get lost on the coffee, having to get a guide back.

In the evening we go to shoot jungle fowl, though without success, though I see four scuttling away into bamboo clumps. In the evening we go for drinks to one Rowson, who has 19 rifles and

413

about a thousand heads and skins in his bungalow. A young stuffed black monkey holds a table lamp, and he also has a type of African nut that looks exactly like an anus.

I find the sun getting warm, and take to my Bright and MacIvor hat[1]. A lot of birds I see that are not in my book.

[1] *A fibreglass insulated jungle hat, made by Bright & McIvor in Calcutta.*

November 11th 1943
MUNNAR HILL STATION

BILL GIRVAN COMES OVER, and we three ride up to the grassland, having sent our kit on up by coolie to a boundary commission hut at Erivakdam. He has a rifle, and Ham Wilkes has a Jeffrey's .404, and off we go after Ibex. We sight a couple, and I get in two shots with the .404, unsuccessfully, and we then follow them up. I come across them twice on a convex slope at about 15 feet, but only see their heads before they are away.

Later, after lunch, I get in a standing shot at another two at about 60 feet and miss. We spend the night in the hut about 8000 feet up, and Wilkes's bearer lays on food and drink and a roaring log fire. My feet are a bit weary, as all I have is a pair of thin stockings and my rubber sole sambhar boots, which are almost in pieces, and no use for climbing up and down the slopes of hills sort of sideways.

Even a bath with hot and cold water from a tap is provided. The outlook is bleak, bare grassland rising up in thousand foot hills and spurs, with small clumps of jungle in the cracks between.

This morning, we set off home in the mist, damn cold, it later clears and I get a good shot at a sitting ibex (Nilgiri wild goat) from about 120 feet, with Ham Wilkes as a sand bag. And I have to go and miss it! I am officially not allowed to shoot, due to various decisions made by the High Range Game Association, as they object to the military coming up and flashing guns about and demanding a shot. I was damn lucky to get one at all.

Scrambling around at 8000 feet has done me good, but it's damn cold.

November 14th 1943

I ARRIVE BACK WITH WILKES to find Douglas has fixed for me to go and stay with the Gouldsburys at Yellaputti, and shoot. I come up on Monday and go back today – Wednesday.

The old man takes me out the first evening, but we only see a couple of wild pigs. Next morning I go out with a shikari after Nilgiri blue pigeon, and I miss two. I see three Malabar red squirrels, and take a long shot with the shotgun at it. Much coughing, and a barking deer, or jungle sheep, comes rushing down and past me. I get my first leech bites, despite an extra pair of socks, and spraying with some potent concoction of the old man's. I see another barking deer creep out of the jungle into the tea, but too far away.

On the last evening I go out with the shikari, but there is mist and rain, and visibility is only 30 feet at times. Just before dark, a sambhar leaps across our path and down through the tea, and we later see him nibbling the shade trees, at least the shikari does, and I can just make him out about 180 feet away in the dim light. I let off my Mauser, but it's downhill and I miss.

Last night the old man gets me a bit pickled on gin after dinner. He was with 5 G.R. in Mesopotamia and Ramadi[1], which I know so well.

This morning I look at his horses and go off for a walk with the daughter of the house, Phillipa – or rather Philippa - encouraged to do so by Mama I think.

Beautiful country, 6500 feet up.

[1] *In Iraq, where Colin learned to fly in 1941.*

November 17th 1943

I GET DOWN FAIRLY UNCOMFORTABLY by train, and find much mail waiting.

A telegram of congratulations from "Scotty, Nobby, Burt Mann". I also read in C.R.O.s that Mike got the MC for his escape from Foul Point.[1]

Hammerbeck gone, thank God, so I can get on with what work I have in peace.

My luggage from the Training Battalion in Abbotabad arrives, three years late. Meet one Sandy Webster DFC and bar, of 60 Squadron, a well-known character east of the Bramaputra, and we go to the Bus Club. Meet Catherine Railton, and go home to her bungalow for a drink. I leave at 2.30 am, and he is still there and not back when I go to work at 8.30.

The Medical Board will not let me fly, as the S.M.O. is taking my case up with Delhi, so I either go back to the Army, or get permanently grounded.

Well, I set off by "doodlebug", or Dodge recce car, to visit 171 Wing and 4 Squadron at Solar near Coimbatore. We go via Mysore and Ooty, and arrive about 9.00 pm. I should have spent the night at Ooty, as I miscalculated ETA and the slow descent from the hills. Ooty, Wellington and Coonoor not quite what I expect, and very close together. Tea and coffee on the way up, and vast grasslands, though they do not look open enough for ibex. The other side – to Coimbatore – with a dozen or so hairpin bends and dense forest all around. We run into rain, a bad road, and the market breaking up near Coimbatore, and find the lights will not work. Nobody knows of Solar there, but it seems to be on the Trichinopoly road, so we feel our way painfully down, the lights eventually functioning near Solar.

I have analysed what's wrong – I want to meet a 'nice gal' again.

Madras attacked again, but no bombs dropped, and a Beaufighter gets a shot in. Last month a four-engined Jap flying boat comes over, and drops half a dozen on the town. It strikes the coast to the south and is plotted flying up, but Control thinks it is a Catalina returning from patrol – why?

Indian trains - God! Dust and vibration despite all the windows, Venetian blinds, and wire mesh frames being closed, making it damn hot. The fans blow the dirt onto one's sweaty skin where it sticks. Nowadays it is hard to get a berth, and you have to reserve four days ahead, from Bangalore to Madras.

[1] *See entry for May 13th 1943.*

November 20th 1943

BANGALORE

WE GO TO A DANCE AT COIMBATORE and meet the Fleet Air Arm types from the RNAS station nearby. I am in great form with a WREN called Lila, or Lilo, or "Bubbles", and dance most of the evening with her. Fat, plump and 21.

Next day, Pat Lewer and I depart and reach Wellington by 12.50. We put up at the West Grove Hotel in Coonoor, and go to the Club in the evening. Meet Mary, and one Huggins, the brother of Yolande's father in Lahore. Damn cold up there. Lewer has a miniature dachshund which is trained to run up to women. They then say "what a sweet little thing", and he has his introduction.

We sit with a popsie from Bombay in the hotel after dinner, with a dreadful "chicks" voice, and she has this dog on her lap, which I stroke. Including her on the follow through – charming.

A long drive back to Bangalore, and this morning I find that 4 Sqn have pranged two a/c, and I have to go down for a Court of Enquiry tonight on the train. As Tom Pierce and 171 Wing are moving off, I have to stay and look after the joint – I suppose until

December 13th, and without any transport, which is going to be a bind.

I have a small "room" in the West End Hotel here – by the look of it where the bearer lived, and cleaned the boots. It's in a sort of warren, with four other rooms, nine beds, and a communal bathroom. But being on the outside I am OK, and no one can walk through me.

November 29th 1943
SOLAR

BACK AT SOLAR TO INVESTIGATE TWO CRASHES. On completion of that, 4 Squadron's C.O. returns, so I am pushing off on this evening's train. Basil Darlington, their A.L.O., and I, go and visit the Navy on Sunday night, having quite a party with the "No. 1", ending up in a search for a double hammock.

Last night we go into Coimbatore Club for a bath and dinner with the Wren – then on to the flicks. A very nice Club, and I see an excellent sunset over the Nilgiris from the roof whilst waiting my turn in the bath.

The 4 Squadron Mess is horrid; tin plates and tea soup out of thick glasses. Bearers wipe spoons with their thumbs, and dirt and neglect all round.

171 Wing under Tom Pierce is moving to Comilla, and this 4 Squadron is due in Ranchi after completion of the exercise.

Here are the squadrons I have known:

- *17 (fighters) under S/L Stone DFC, whose aircraft I flew and crashed from Highland Queen, and with whom I later went to China.*
- *135 and 136 (fighters), whose a/c I flew at Mingalodon and Akyab.*
- *45 and 113 (bombers), with whom I lived at the Mingalodon Golf Club and in Laschio Mess.*

418

- *20 (army co-operation), now on Hurricane 11ds under Pete Joel, with whom we went to Egypt.*
- *60 and 34 (bombers), whom I meet from time to time in Bengal, Arakan and down here.*

December 1st 1943

BANGALORE

I GET BACK TO BANGALORE, and continue doing nothing.

Tom Pierce is now up with Wingate's show. I take two afternoons off, and go and lie in the sun and bathe at the Bus Club. Then I get in a game of squash. I visit one S/L N.A.S. Allen, who used to be at Harrow with Hugh. I get a ride on one of his fire hoses, and we go into the Palace grounds. His wife is the daughter of one Colonel Willis, who commanded 2/13th way back in 1928 or so. I see the S.M.O., and hope to arrange a medical board in Calcutta, but I can't see any use coming of it.

I have to go out to Directing Staff camp in two days, for an exercise, "Malabar", taking place down in the jungle there. I have come to the conclusion that if I have to stay in India it is better to do something, rather than fester in 225 Group doing nothing.

Have now been turned out from the A.O.C.'s morning conference where I learned what little was being done in this Group. A letter from Aunt Vivy, as well as one from Bernard Fergusson the other day.

December 10th 1943

GUDALLUR CAMP, EXERCISE MALABAR

I GET MYSELF A JEEP AND A DRIVER, and come out with Albert to the Directing Staff camp for "Exercise Malabar".

The Camp is at Gudallur, at the bottom of the road to Ooty. 25 AASC[1] is here under Warren, and my job is as an RAF 'advisor' and

Air Director of the scheme. I live in the ASC Mess, and not very entertaining. I go out and visit both sides, and see some good jungle country. I also take the jeep down to Solar, and Basil Darlington and I go into town in the evening. We visit one Major Mollison, the officer commanding the evacuee camp at Coimbatore, and stop a beautiful Greek girl on the camp road and invite her out. Nothing doing.

Back to the Club for dinner, and meet "Bubbles" the Wren, who insists we go to a dreadful flick with her.

The drive up and over Ooty always makes me morose, as it is so nice and cold up there, and you can think of popsies all about, but it is a bit of an anti-climax when you reach the bottom. Below Coonoor is a great forest of palms, all planted within six feet of each other, and I always wonder about them when I pass. I meet one Major Ridley, who brought me out on the "City of Venice", and one Brigadier Hunt, who ran a young officers course I attended in Wana. Truly I have a remarkable memory for faces.

A boring place, this.

[1] *Army Air Support Control.*

December 12th 1943
Gudallur Camp, Exercise Malabar

This is all good shooting country. I go for a walk up a hill in sparse jungle, and fall into a bog. Tea and coffee are grown around here.

Today I take a party in my 'Jeep' to visit 14/10 Baluchis, who have constructed a position in the jungle. It's some position too – the foxholes and bunkers being unable to be seen except from about 20 feet. Fields of fire of about 30-40 feet, each covering the other, as by the book.

Very cool in the evening, and there is a boring conference 7 - 8 pm at which I sometimes talk about the 'Air'. MG battalion, 13

FF Rifles, has a company with them of 42 mortars, and I meet my friend whom I met before in Bangalore. Most mornings I go and visit one side or the other, and in the afternoon I manage to get a few hours on Warren's camp bed next to the office with 'David Copperfield'.

December 16th 1943

THE SCHEME FINISHES, and I meet Phillips (14/10 Baluchis), who used to be Staff Captain at Kohat, and he takes me back to lunch. This includes curry, and one Captain asks me kindly if I have ever eaten chapattis before?!

That evening I climb a hill and see a cheetah. Next day I'm off with Brigadier O'Carroll Scott to Mysore to meet S.A.S.O., and fix up some air cooperation for smashing Jap bunker positions. Then back to Sultan's Battery, where 25 Division are, and I stay in the Gunners Mess and enjoy a good few whiskies.

This morning we drive out into the Maharaja of Mysore's game reserve where the gunners are shooting, and where I have business to do. A great dark striped tiger leaps across the track ahead of our jeep, and the Brigadier stands up with his shotgun, which he had previously loaded with ball, and looks fierce, but nothing doing.

Much teak forest around here, and the jackals were noisier last night than I ever heard before.

Now sitting in my 180lb-er tent on my camp bed, which has again given way at the sides. I wear my blue battle dress of nights and it is damn cold.

I visit a jungle craft school today, where the troops are taught to make shelters etc, and the most fearful booby traps, with sharp fire-hardened bamboo dipped in poison meat. I love this country, and the High Range, better even than Assam.

A Christmas card airgraph arrives from Mhairi, and a letter from Tony Irwin, saying that Reggie Wall was missing at home.

December 21st 1943

I DINE IN 'A' MESS WITH ALL THE TITS, and then drive back in my jeep to Bangalore. Arriving about 4 pm, I find I have to get on the mail plane next morning for Vizagapatam, where I am president of a Court Martial.

I see SASO, and arrange to continue on to Calcutta, coming back on Christmas day. I go in and drink with Pam Allan, who keeps the horses, as Nigel is away shooting.

On arrival at Vizag, the Air Transit Officer sends me to the Filter Room mess, they being concerned with the Court Martial. Some WACIs are living there too, and I meet the station chief C.O., S/L Goldber, ex 240 Squadron, and some of 135 Squadron. We go to the Club in the evening, where I meet Ronnie Alden and his wife, and do myself pretty well in consequence. Some 'Pongo' Captain (15 Punjab Rifles) insists that I have a drink, it being "so nice to see some RAF with wings up." I collect Goldber and introduce him, with the same result.

This morning I go out to see one F/L Chapman, a member of the court and a lawyer by trade, as my last Court Martial was under instruction in Razmak days. On the way home we drive along the "front" and round the docks, but nothing exciting.

December 25th 1943

I FINISH THE COURT MARTIAL and deal out 98 days detention.

Then by air to Calcutta for another medical board, which has been arranged by W/C Stewart, SMO 225 Group, with the idea of getting me home. The aircraft does not turn up, and I am forced to get on the train, to my disgust. I get a coupe to myself, but with one Mr Row getting in later. Next door is the ladies coupe. I see an attractive woman in there, and she later gets out for a walk, so I determine to invite her to a drink later on, as she 'looks the type'. I take some Canadian whisky along at about 7 pm and she accepts the offer, and bids me enter. Her name is Joan Cory 28, wife of a M.S.M.[1] railway magnate 20 years older than she, and from whom she is in the process of getting a divorce. We get on well, and discover that Mrs Row, wife of my stable companion, is due in with her later on. So we agree to let them have my coupe together, and I move in with Joan. I then carry out a complete seduction, perfectly planned and operated, leaving at 8.30 the next morning and joining three gents in a four-berth compartment next door. God!!

I meet W/C Banks in Calcutta and we scrape into the Saturday Club as guests of W/C Dougal. I stay at the Grand Hotel, which has been cleaned up, and is now a hostel for allied officers and their wives. Also for nursing sisters.

90 Japs run in on a daylight raid some weeks ago, both navy and army aircraft, and the score is 10 all. They choose the one day when the Spitfires are away and their relieving Hurricanes have not arrived.

Calcutta is full of yanks and WAAFs, a division of whom are walking down the Kaladan.

I go for my medical, with the same result – "AIB Return to unit". I meet one Captain Richmond, Air Liaison Officer without any aircraft to liaise, with the WAAF, and we have a few drinks last night. I return today on a Hudson, not having had much sleep last night, with the noise of drunken Americans all over the hotel.

[1] *Madras and Southern Mahratta Railway.*

January 4th 1944

BANGALORE

NOT MUCH OF A PARTY ON CHRISTMAS DAY. I organise myself plenty of squash about three times a week. New Years Eve I go to our mess dance, and get rather intoxicated. I do a Highland fling with Fairweather, he in full Highland dress, and my own conception of a sword dance round an empty bottle of whisky. I do a "heavy line" with Mary Kinloch, one of the local blondes, and I think she gets rather frightened by my intentions.

Yesterday Ramsey and I go across to the Allans and play bridge. A letter from Mike Jacobs, now on the Burma border somewhere. I am trying to get my hands on a Fairchild (PT-19 trainer aircraft), as I have not flown for about four months now. No hope of going home. Tom Pierce is W/C a/c Delhi, and David Yorke a Group Captain. Farquahar is with Wingate, and I hear from Bernard Fergusson that it's no good me trying to cope with my malaria.

January 7th 1944

BANGALORE

I DISCOVER I HAVE A COUSIN OF SORTS OUT HERE – Donald Macnaughton, a cadet at the OTS, whose grandmother is my great aunt Susan. Much squash just now, and I am again as fit as I was up to the end of 1942. I try and borrow a bicycle, and have a shower and change at the Bus club afterwards. It's cheaper to drink down there too.

I go flying today in one of 4 Squadron's Hurricanes, and am pleased to see that I haven't lost the touch. I also get some dual in a Fairchild, 225 Group's communication aircraft, and do two damn awful landings and the third not so bad.

W/C Beaman is back from Staff College as Air Intelligence. I read in the papers that John Palmer gets an M.B.E. in the New Year's honours, and that "that chap" Johnston is mentioned in despatches for Waziristan "Oct 1941-42". Wish I was back on that train again![1] Another jungle exercise shortly. Here I sit, peering at birds with my field glasses through the door.

[1] See the diary entry for 25th December 1943.

January 11th 1944

RUMSEY AND I GO OUT TO DINNER with a battleship, one Mrs Wall, and drink King George IV scotch. Next day we take her to a "pagal" gymkhana *(sports day)*, which is pleasantly reminiscent of pre-war days, with a band and a musical ride by the Mysore Lancers.

I get in some squash, and 14 days leave is approved by AOC after this exercise, but expect I shall get malaria instead.

"Cheese" Gordon killed in Italy.

Here I sit in my office doing nothing. Smith (G3 Air[1], Southern Army) shares my telephone. Weather warmer now, but I don't sleep too well, despite my heavy squash, and much walking from the Club to the West End, some 2 miles.

[1] *G3-Air - Air Operations And Planning Officer.*

January 14th 1944

BANGALORE

Tomorrow I go out on another scheme called "Wynead".

Last night Jo Sellars gives a farewell party before going to Staff College, and we have a pretty good one. Gordon Grieve, who speaks gibberish at everyone, meets his match in me.

Today there is a dance at the Residency and Paratt, the Wren 'Babes' and Betty Jones are going. But Babes not yet here...

January 23rd 1944

GUDALUR

OUT IN D.D. CAMP AT GUDALUR, like the last time. I live in the main camp, and am fairly comfortable. Rumsey arranges for me to exchange my u/s camp bed. I have a jeep and so does Bill Beaman.

He goes out every day to both sides, and I sit in the AASC office with Ian Warren. At evening prayers[1], Beaman or I go over the day's air operations, being mostly imaginary aircraft. Then much gin drinking with the "pongos"[2] in the contractors mess. I meet Patterson (6 GR) who used to be at RMC[3] with me.

Not so cold as last time, and much more boring, though I walk out once or twice into the jungle with my field glasses to look at the birds.

[1] *Staff meeting.*
[2] *How the RAF referred to the army.*
[3] *Royal Military College, Sandhurst.*

January 27th 1944

GUDALUR

WE GET A DAY OFF, at least the Army has a truce for one day, and so Bill Beaman, Warren and I leap into SASO's car (he is here on a visit) and go up to the Savoy in Ooty for beer and lunch. Then we rush madly around shopping. This scheme finishes tomorrow, thank God.

Yesterday I go out for a walk and put up a small barking deer. I see a troop of monkeys, and also a malabar and squirrel. He goes up to one of the monkeys to see what it is eating, and it stretches out a hand and caresses the squirrel's whiskers. The squirrel has another sniff and then turns away. I am getting to know all these birds by sound, but damned if I can see them and name them.

February 1st 1944

BANGALORE

THE SCHEME COMES TO AN END, and Bill Beaman, self, driver and Bill's bearer leap into our jeep and climb the hill to Ooty, staying at Dunmore in Coonoor[1], which I had known of. We drink in the Club with the locals at the hostel, including a navy type who detonates mines for a living, and then return home to some liar dice.

That night, Bill snores so much that I make arrangements to sleep elsewhere the next night. Saturday morning, we go up to Ooty Club to lunch with a friend of his, one Marcelle Gauvain, who turns out to be the wife of a chap in the 5/15th who is missing in Singapore. Then to the Club in the evening for a dance, which I don't particularly enjoy, as I get a bit warm in my battle dress, which is all I have.

Next morning, down the hill back to Bangalore. I find nothing particular to do as usual in the office, and meet Purcell, and go and see the film "Spitfire". Tony Wagstaffe also appears today at lunchtime, and says I should be the ideal fellow to lecture at the Staff College in place of W/C Fox, who is a Catalina flying boat pilot.

Much hotter now down here. Am due for some malaria now, any time.

Before I forget:

225 Group Bangalore Air Staff

- Air Commodore P.H. Macworth CBE DFC - S.O.A.
(Senior Officer Air)
- Group Captain Howard DFC - SASO
(Senior Air Staff Officer)
- Group Captain J.E.W. Bowles DFC - Air 1
(Air Staff officer 1)
- Wing Commander W. Beaman - Fighter Ops
(Fighter Operations)
- Squadron Leader K.A. Perkin - Army Cooperation
(Army Co-Op Operations)
- Acting S/L Joe Soap DFC^2 - GR ops
(General Reconnaissance operations)

- Squadron Leader Babineau - Training
- Wing Commander T.A. Vigors DFC - Armament
- Wing Commander G. Knyvett - Intelligence
- Squadron Leader Green

& some others not really worth bothering about.

[1] *Today an Indian Navy holiday home.*
[2] *Himself.*

February 8th 1944

YELLAPATTY

I GET 14 DAYS LEAVE, and go up to stay with C.P. Gouldsbury, a tea planter in the High Range, at Yellapatty, some 18 miles from Munnar. I travel up in the train with one Daphne Acton, whom I met in a "conga" at Coonoor the other day. I spend the first night at the Club at Munnar, and Mrs G. collects me the next day.

We have quite a party the night before, with the two Boyd daughters and a couple of R.A. majors, breaking gramophone records on each other's heads.

Yesterday morning I walk out with a .22 in "Whipsnade", a prolific patch of jungle opposite the bungalow, and bag three malabar red squirrels, one of which I lose, as it falls onto the top of a dense thicket. I also miss an eagle of sorts, and see a couple of black monkeys, which are getting scarce about here.

Yesterday evening, out with Poosari, the shikari, looking for sambhar, but I only see a couple of hinds, and get back about 8.20 pm. It gets damn cold waiting from 5.30 to 7.30 for them to come out of the jungle, into the tea.

Today I go out with a .22 in the morning, unsuccessfully, and am now (4.55 pm) sitting on a mountain spur spying out the land – i.e. the jungle and the tea below. I am about 7000 feet, and below me is a saucer shaped valley of 6000 feet or so, with the factory lines, and much tea in it. Above me, towards the grassy heights where the ilex live, and away over the ridge lower down, I can see the plains forty miles away or so. I came up here on the back of a horse with two lads carrying my guns (.430 and a borrowed .303), sweaters and the tea. Poosari (the shikari) is now glued to the thin end of a telescope.

I could buy me a wife and live here, I think!

February 10th 1944

YELLAPATTY

I FAIL TO SCORE, as we do not see a single stag. Next day I collect five squirrels before lunch, and another four this morning.

Yesterday evening we go out and see a lot of barking deer, or jungle sheep - in fact they bark very nearby. We stalk a buck, but he has gone when we get up. Later I shoot a hind, as C.P.G.[1] is allowed to kill eight a year. It is downhill shooting, about 660', with the .303, and very good shots too. It's a bit small when we pick it up, but we see no stags that day.

Food here is grand. "Scotch" at night, and a good book in a good bed!

[1] C.P. Gouldsbury, Colin's host.

February 11th 1944

YELLAPATTY

YESTERDAY EVENING I go out with C.P. Gouldsbury after jungle sheep, but do not get a shot. We see a couple of red mongeese, with bluish grey heads and tail underparts – looks more like an otter.

This morning we ride up to about 7200' amongst the grassland switch blades, where there is a shooting camp. We have lunch, and then I am left with Poosari and a houseboy for the night. We go out at 5.30 am and sit on a hillside looking for sambhar, but only see a small stag about a mile away. The sun goes in, it gets rather cold, and we return to camp about 7.30.

Whilst discussing tomorrow's order of battle, I ask what time we go off, and the boy points to the moon. I think this is a bit odd, when he says 'big stag', and there behind us is a stag with its family on the skyline about 200-300 yards away. We stalk it, and I try a shot with the .303. The sambhar is below the crest, and it's so dark at 7.55 pm that I have difficulty in getting a bead[1]. I see the strike in front of his nose and he goes onto the skyline, where I get in another at his behind. I hear no dull smack, but he leaps in the air and vanishes – quien sabe?

I return to a bath and some whisky. The hut is wood and grass, daubed over with "matti", with bedroom, bathroom and saloon.

[1] *Bead sight - the little metal bump on the end of a gun barrel to aid aiming.*

February 13th 1944

YELLAPATTY

MY STAG IS HIT, and has gone to ground in the jungle somewhere. Yesterday I have breakfast at 6.30, and set out at dawn about 7.10, returning at 7.30. We sweat up and down the grassland slopes, up to 8724', but see no saddlebacks. Plenty of ibex, and one lot of five comes quite close. One decent stag, at which I fire twice downhill, nearly 200', and I miss and he gets away. I see a white hawk type with a black bar on his wings. Also a buck jungle sheep, but not worth shooting.

This morning, out at dawn, and plenty of sambhar, but the wrong sex. About 11.30, we beat some jungle and out comes a stag towards me. I miss first shot, and then stop him with a full deflection shot at about 50'. The boy serves up wonderful food, though he is not the cook, and he only has a grass hut to perform in. Many Nilgiri laughing thrushes around.

February 15th 1944

WE GO DOWN IN THE EVENING and see two huge stags come out. The Mudavan (guide) takes me to about 200', and though it's pretty dark at 7.30 pm, I manage to hit the best, a great black beast, on the third shot with the .303, then miss the other one, who had been watching in amazement. He crashes down, and falls about 20 yards, but when we get there he has gone.

Next day the Mudavan finds blood, shoulder high, for about 400' and then it stops, so he is lost. They found the one I got in the evening, however, though they only sent down the skull and not the skin. He is very small – well, too small to measure!

I go out yesterday with Gouldsbury, and miss quite a nice jungle sheep with two shots. I collect a couple more squirrels today, making 14 in all, though I lose two, and try and get a black monkey, but cannot get a shot. I wear overalls and greased boots on the hill.

February 17th 1944

YELLAPATTY

I GO OUT AGAIN AND GET THE JUNGLE SHEEP after an arduous search cum stalk. He is 4 feet long.

Yesterday we go down to Willie Laird's and beat for pig. No pig seen, but I knock off a hind, and later a doe jungle sheep. I should have had a buck too, but I rush after him too quickly.

February 20th 1944

BANGALORE

I GO DOWN TO THE CLUB for a night, and then to Alwaye by local bus. Arrive in Bangalore, and go to the office to discover that one Pinsen has been suggested by ACSEA as my relief, subject to

431

AOC's consent. Also an official letter saying I am 'tour expired', and will be repatriated to the UK – though when, it does not say. Most people hang around two months or so before they are called up, but no doubt I shall be an exception and take longer. Or they might even change their minds again and keep me in India!

I go and play some squash, but not much good. Also I get a shot of T.A.B. and cholera at the same time, and feel lousy for a couple of days.

Albert goes to Van Ingen in Mysore with my skins.[1]

[1] *From his shooting in Yellapatty. Van Ingen of Mysore (1900–1999) were famous Indian taxidermists.*

February 22nd 1944
Bangalore

I am reduced from acting S/Leader back to my normal rank of F/L with effect from 31st January, and S/Ldr R.M. Pinsen is posted here in my place, from Assault Wing. I am allowed to retain S/Ldr badges rank in accordance with some A.M.O.[1] So here I sit all day, and do nothing.

This Hotel West End is not too bad – 10/- a day, but the Government pay is 6/12, and gives me 1/1 ration money, so the balance is only a day. A lot of rain just now, a bit early for the mango showers[2].

I wrote to Abbottabad[3] about a month ago for the rest of my kit, but no answer. Now the Southern Army here has signalled to them to send it to Grindlays Bank Bombay, but still no answer. My pay is in a muddle again. Still being credited as F/L of 2 Squadron.

So we write to Delhi to promulgate again, also for 100/- per month extra for being with the Indian Air Force. Nothing will be done, and I shall probably get a bill at home (if I ever get there) for £300-400. Also, they deduct 100/- per month for the Defence Service Officers Provident Fund, but it is not paid into the fund.

I shall soon have to close this diary with some impressions of the East:[4]

• The sound of the birds – the Koel, the Coppersmith, the Green Barbet and the ook ook of the Crow Pheasant (Greater Coucal); the background being composed of various chatterings of the Myna birds.

• A cold iced beer after a hard game of football and a ghuzzle (bath) – especially in the silver engraved tankards of the battalion, with lids on.

• Sunset in Assam, over the Naga Hills, with a few loose cumulus about.

• Drinking "Mandalay" beer on the lawn of the D.C.'s house in Magwe (it was the RAF Mess) and listening to the Koels in the trees above the Irrawaddy.

• The zipping of bullets high above my head during operations on the Frontier.

• Riding home on my pony in the desert near Habbaniya, with the sun setting beyond the Euphrates.

• Walking on the Bund (at Habbaniya), around the same time, and wondering if I should ever pass the Flying Training School, especially the eyesight exam.

• Wandering in the forests of Yellapatty with a gun.

• A rainy afternoon in Shillong.

• The awful suspense waiting in Abbottabad to be called up for RAF interviews in Delhi.

433

• The night after Ian Pringle was killed – just me and Allan Haig left!

• Nerves in the siege of Habbaniya – going back to bed after the dawn stand-to.

• Walking home from the Ranchi Club to the mess after a game of tennis – in the good old days of Teddy, Burt, Robin White, Tom Pierce, Eric, Corporal Allward, and lashings of beer and hooch.

• A trip to Egypt in November '42 with Burt and Henry Larsen.

• Watching my boys landing and taking off from "Seaview" in Maungdaw.

• Mike, Waggers and co. in the dugout mess of a night over the rum.

• Driving my Chevrolet "Hsipaw - Lashio bus service" wagon from Maymyo to Loiwing.

• First days in Jubbulpore – getting dressed of an evening.

• Riding out into that small forest in Ambala – and a 'Pimms' afterwards – wishing I was in Tommy's Bar in Cairo.

• And last, but not least, all the thoughts and wishes that I might be in certain parts of the UK at certain times and which, if they ever materialise, will be stale and below par – an anticlimax in fact.

[1] *Air Ministry Order.*
[2] *Colloquial name for the pre-monsoon rains.*
[3] *His former home with the 13th Frontier Force Rifles, where he stored his Indian Army kit when he was transferred to the RAF three years previously.*
[4] *Since he was about to be repatriated to the UK, where he begins the last and final volume.*

February 24th 1944

BANGALORE

STILL HANGING ON.

With Bill Beaman and W/Cs Thunder and Gauntlet from Ceylon, I go to Winston's Chinese restaurant last night, and sample some fried noodles.

I am presenting a half tankard, and can't get a bigger one, to 28 Squadron. Yesterday they had done it wrong, and put "13th Frontier Rifles" on it, so I am hoping they will be able to correct it. On the reverse is "Round the bend – 1938-1944 – and back again."

I purchase Whistler's Book on Indian Birds, and "Birds of South India", which is rather technical and full of Latin.

February 27th 1944

BANGALORE

I LOSE MY IDENTITY PASS, and about 100 rupees and £1/10/-, at the Bus Club. I put it inside the cover of a book, as I have no pockets in my bathing costume, and later hand the book back to the librarian. He says it's not there, so it must have fallen out in the Club grounds, but I do not find it.

My relief, S/Ldr Pinsen, arrives, and appears to be as mad as a hatter, and has left a trail of adverse reports all around India and Ceylon.

The public relations officer catches me and writes up a short story about my gong. I tell him all about Mike's too, and suggest

435

he combines the two stories. However, the Indian Government will probably see it and say "Keep this fellow in India" – you never know.

I go to two parties – one is Jack Smith's (G111 Air) birthday in the Bus Club, and the other is Beaman, self and John Briggs, the RAF Regiment officer, at Group. Dinner and dance etc.

I break my English squash ball, and so I have 'had' squash for a bit.

February 29th 1944

Bangalore

Old Pinsen turns out to be saner than I expected, and we have a most interesting chat over my whisky last night.

A big flap on just now, as Jap fleet expected in the Bay of Bengal – Pinsen has to go down as station master at Tanjore. G/C George Howard suggested I go, missing my boat, and catch the next one! Bill Beaman stops it, and AOC tries again today saying "We can fly him back in three hours." Beaman wins again, but if the situation deteriorates perhaps I shall have to go, and miss my boat after all.

A letter from Mhairi out of the blue, and I go for a walk in the evening dreaming of a "rosy future". I write to Daphne, Babs, the Mad Aunt, Mhairi and Bill's father, who sent me 2oz of Gold Block, so I am more or less up to date.

That dance was some show, as Briggs and I spent all our time doing 'pincer movements' on pongos who kept coming up and trying to steal a dance from the girls, in particular Mary Kinloch, a blonde with protruding teeth and two eighteen inch guns. She can't dance, but waggles her bottom round the floor like a duck, and very comfortably; and Marcie House, in the mornings a F/ Sgt in our ops room. No light weights, those two. There seems to be something about me that makes these women – girls, rather – giggle and never stop. Must be my inane grin.

A fearful picture is developed of me for the Public Lavatories Officer[1]. Pinsen is a bird fancier like myself.

Four years today I left Madras with the regiment for the "frontiah"[2].

I have arranged for Albert to transfer his allegiance to F/L Peter Lewer, Group photo officer. I hand in my mauser and ammunition for transport by air to the Octavius Steel Company, Calcutta, and onward transmission to Uncle Stan in Assam – God knows if it will ever reach him.

I haven't got that boat yet, whatever they say.

Feeling rather turgid through lack of exercise, and concentrating on doing nothing for so long in the office, as AOC is back and I now cannot arrive half an hour late and depart two hours early: "Just going to the Admin buildings (Racecourse) old boy! If anyone wants me…"

---

[1] He means the PR Officer.
[2] The 13th Frontier Force Rifles left for Wana, in South Waziristan, on 28th February 1940 (see Volume 1).

March 3rd 1944

BANGALORE

STILL HERE DOING NOTHING HARD.

A signal from A.C. Sea today, asking for confirmation that I am available for embarkation, whatever that means. It never happened with anyone else before. I meet one W/C Phillips, just out from the UK, who gives me the lowdown – dry ships! There are far too many sinkings in the Gulf of Aden appearing on our Ops Room board for my liking. Just my luck to be sunk and, if rescued, then by a ship coming back to Bombay!

I purchase two small sandalwood elephants and a large rosewood one at Mysore "arts and crafts" department.

Bill Beaman, Phillips and one Swaley, a petrol king from Delhi, and self, stoke up on Cyprus brandy at the Bus Club last night, and then feed at Winston's Chinese restaurant. I have a great success with my paper darts made from menus.

AOC says to me "What? You still here?" So long as he doesn't ask me what I'm doing, I don't mind.

Indian Rates of Pay in Rupees (GD/ASD/Medical)[1]

- Air Commodore 1805/1725
- Group Captain 1680/1475/1930
- Wing Commander 1240-1470/1080/1510
  (also Lieutenant Colonel in Indian army)
- Squadron Leader 1010/915/1075
  (Major)
- Flight Lieutenant 710/640/755
  (Captain 690-710)
- Flying Officer 635/545/600
  (Lieutenant 535)
- Pilot Officer 500/455
  (2nd Lieutenant 480)
- Chaplain – 500 on appointment

[1] *General duties/Admin and Supplies Duties/Medical.*

March 6th 1944

BANGALORE

A DAMN GREAT CYCLONE OFF MADRAS, and a good drop of rain here. We lose a Catalina in it at sea. Another convoy sails from Bombay which I miss. S/L Ramsey lets me have his greatcoat for £8, in condition that I take a box home for his wife.

My pay is a complete muddle – back pay due from the difference between F/O and F/L from October to March in

Ambala. They offer me 190/10! P.O.R. re my Acting S/Ldr rank, and 100/- per month with Indian Air Force did not reach B.P.O. from 2 Squadron! My account debited 100/- per month for the D.S.O.P. Fund, but found not credited since Sept 1942?!

Apparently we get no 1939-43 Star for service in Burma, but as someone suggests, I should thank myself lucky to have what I have, without wanting more.

March 8th 1944

BANGALORE

THE AOC GIVES ME AN ADVERSE REPORT! Says I 'lack initiative' and made a poor show of 2 Squadron! Eventually he says he will wait until SASO returns and consult him – because Macworth (AOC) does not know me, and cannot even spell my name.

A signal in this morning that I have to report to Bombay on 21st March. I book a berth on the train for the 19th to arrive on 20th.

Not out of the woods yet!

March 20th 1944

BANGALORE

AOC SAYS HE WILL CONSULT SASO on my report when he comes in, so I put in a minute to SASO which he says is "bloody rude". However, he gets it changed, and tells me I shall not have to initial it. Half an hour later the AOC sends for me, gives me the report to read, and demands my initials. I discover he has altered the marks on the "scoreboard" on the front sheet, mostly to 4s, and consequently below average (5), and therefore adverse.

Am all tee-ed up for the boat, and hope that my kit will arrive and get safely on board with me.

439

25 Division has gone off to the Burma front, so I hear. They have collected about 40 prisoners on the show, and even had pictures of them in the "Statesman" – the first ever.

March 21st 1944
Bangalore

CONDITIONS FOR 1939/43 AND AFRICA STARS are out. As opposed to the Army, in the RAF you cannot get the Africa Star if you qualified for the 39/43 Star. The Army is the other way round. Aircrew get it after two months in an operational squadron, and one operation. Ground crew six months, aggregate, in an Army command:

Qualifying dates for 1939/43 Star (for operations in):

- France 3/9/39 – 19/6/40
- Norway 14/4/40 – 8/6/40
- Belgium 10/5/40 – 19/6/40
- Holland 12/5/40 – 13/5/40
- India (North West Frontier) 1/1/40 – 31/12/42
- Greece & Crete 7/11/40 – 31/5/41
- Iraq 10/4/41 – 31/5/41
- Syria 8/6/41 – 11/7/41
- Persia 25/8/41 – 28/8/41
- Hong Kong 8/12/41 – 25/12/41
- Malaya 8/12/41 – 15/2/42
- China 11/12/41 – 31/12/43
- Burma 11/12/41 – 31/12/43
- New Guinea 7/3/42 – 31/12/43
- Madagascar 5/5/42 – 5/11/42
- Sicily 10/7/43 – 17/8/43
- Italy 3/9/43 – 31/12/43
- Russian Wing 7/9/41 – 30/11/41

I send my blue tunic and battledress to have my 39/43 star put on, but expect I shall get told to take it down when I get home – if I get home!

March 22nd 1944

I LEAVE BANGALORE 8.30AM ON THE 19TH.

The night before, Saturday, is whisky night, and I have quite a party with Pete Lewer, Smith and some naval F.A.A. type from Ceylon. I am in good form, shouting "Fall out, all Brigadiers" at old Brigadier Ayles, who is propping up the bar as usual, and keeping a greedy eye on the few bottles of whisky they have allotted for the evening.

I travel most of the way with a Yank who has his ration lunch in a small cardboard box, all compressed and protected from the heat and the damp. I meet S/Ldr J. Hills and wife – he it was who introduced me to flying when he came over to our Mess at St Thomas Mount (in Madras) and told me how much it all cost.

Arrived Victoria station, Bombay, and met by Grindlays (Bank), who took over my heavy kit, and then out to Worli Transit Camp. I share a room with one W/C T.B. Morton, also on the boat, and we feed in a Mess arranged in a flat opposite. We spend last night drinking the worst possible Indian gin before dinner.

Today we go to town, I to Base accounts to see the Committee of Adjustment to try and buy a raincoat, but I get a shirt and two collars instead, off some corpse. Then to Grindlays Bank, but I find it's a bank holiday and only the shipping department is open. Meet Morton and G/C Seton-Broughall at the Taj Mahal Hotel for a rotten lunch, after a few sickly John Collins' in the "Harbour Bar" first.

A large convoy is in, and plenty of officers in shorts like drain pipes and carrying Wolsey helmets in bags. Some even are wearing blue uniform still. Bombay not too hot, but damn sticky walking around trying to get a taxi. Food is rationed and you only get three courses in the hotels at meals.

March 23rd 1944

MORTON AND I HAVE A "DEBAUCH" on Cyprus brandy with 1/2 a dozen wing commanders and squadron leaders straight out from the UK. Some retire sick, and all have fearful heads the next day, so perhaps the linings in our stomachs are hardened against this rot gut liquor. This is the worst Indian hooch I ever drank. I change a lot of money with them, and collect £10 travellers cheques from Grindlays, so that eventually I have to change £1 back to pay for my drinks.

Tomorrow we embark, and I have labelled all my luggage 'wanted on voyage' in the hope that I will be able to sort it all out on board. Maybe they will put it in the hold, if it ever gets on board, and I shall arrive in shirt and shorts.

There is a nice cool breeze at nights, and a strong smell of seaweed and excreta, as the draining is very modern, but they had not enough piping to finish off as far out to sea as was originally intended. I sleep damn well. I trade my spare valise, two sheets, a pillow case and a blanket for a blue raincoat, so I am now complete, except for a "fore and aft".[1]

I wonder how soon I shall be sent out again?[2]

[1] *Meaning unclear.*
[2] *In three years, as it turns out, just in time for Partition.*

12

April - May 1944

Repatriation to the UK

On leave
St Ives, Cornwall

April 2nd 1944

WE ARE ON THE SS ORONTES, and reach Aden yesterday despite plots of four submarines near the mouth of the Gulf, one German. We have "Dilwara", "Stratheden" and "Lancashire" in convoy, with five corvettes ahead. Aden is full of shipping but not much to see. We take on oil, fuel and water, and tomorrow will be "dhobie day" (washing day), as there has not been sufficient water so far.

The Italians cause trouble smoking on deck the first night at sea, and are then told that the guards will shoot at lights, so it soon stops. I find all my luggage in the "Wanted on Voyage" hold, and hope I shall not lose it all if we have to trans-ship in the Middle East, as is sometimes the case. I do some sunbathing, P.T. and deck hockey, and have had a drink most days too, though this is a "dry" ship. I think it has all run out now.

Quite a few women on board – some of them look a little better as the voyage progresses. Three generals also. Wingate has been killed in an air crash. His force has gone in – the Japs are attacking Kohima and are around Tiddim and Imphal. I meet one McKinley, Black Watch, at my table, who knows Bernard Fergusson very well, and has himself had a most interesting war so far. I have my army webbing all ready for abandoning ship, and am O.C. RAF boat stations. We hope to sit on rafts until help comes.

Much noise of children screaming all over the decks and the lounge.

April 9th 1944

WE REACH SUEZ AND EMBARK a few more passengers. It suddenly gets damn cold, the day before in the Red Sea, and I get my battledress out. P.T. every afternoon followed by deck hockey, a la Razmak, only no roller-skates, with the ships officers, and yesterday I get invited back for some beer – McEwans Red Label, which I haven't seen for some years. We pass Shandur this morning and are now going through the Bitter Lakes.

Sunset over that hill to the west of the refinery, and the ships silhouetted in the glow – the last one I shall see for a bit I expect. Italians singing to a guitar, heard whilst half asleep in the afternoon – always reminds me of Somerset Maugham.

April 12th 1944
The Mediterranean

We leave Port Said early on the 8th, and are now about level with Bizerta. I shout to Johnny Benbow on "Lancashire" in Port Said. We have a 16 ship convoy, but some leave for Italy, and another one has joined us this morning.

An air attack alarm yesterday morning, but nothing appears. We do one hour a day watch on the bridge for aircraft, very pleasant, though what the hell I am supposed to recognise I don't know.

P.T. and hockey in the evenings and I have a raging cold. Half an hour a day polishing all my buttons – hell.

April 19th 1944
Mid-Atlantic

We come through the Mediterranean OK, and are now in mid-Atlantic. The sea changes from blue to green and we heave and pitch a bit. Ritchie and I see an unidentified aircraft which acts in a most suspicious manner, but nothing comes of it yet! We pass a 75 ship convoy and see the snow on the Sierra Nevadas in Spain. Also about two million pink and black birds, long legs and necks,

445

so presumably flamingoes, going over to Spain in a long straggling line-ahead formation.

Ritchie and I get some gin off the Chief Officer after a morning session on watch, but that was a long time ago. Much hockey in the evening, before I get this cold which is raging in my head. The weather damn cold and damp too.

April 24th 1944
LIVERPOOL

WE TIE UP IN THE STREAM off Liverpool, but cannot get ashore for two days yet – having reached the bar yesterday morning. Visibility poor from Great Orme Head round to the "Tower" at Blackpool, and a glorious 'beat-up' by a Yankee Thunderbolt.

A great discharge of rockets as we come in, and all sorts of new aircraft tear across the sky. The first signs of life I see through my glasses are two jeeps and a crowd outside the Palace cinema – it would be! And a crowd on a sort of 'tour around the bay' steamer.

April 26th 1944
LIVERPOOL

WE DOCK ON THE 24TH and are met by a band. Off on the 25th at 5.15am on a train to London, Naafi giving us tea, buns and chocolates on Lime Street Station. Arriving at Addison Square, we are met and taken to the Air Ministry after some lunch and beer at the Endsleigh Hotel.

RAF P.D.C. A/M gives me a ration card, one month's leave, and "P" staff say I shall be a Flight Lieutenant again and go to an O.T.U. and some more Ops, but can stay in the Army Co-operation trade!! I then get a bed in the Nuffield Club in Halkin Street. A drink in the evening and a cinema and I meet Humphries, that

St Ives seafront

Australian photo type[1], in a pub for one drink. His companion borrows two cigarettes off me to "see him home". Today I collect clothing coupons and do some shopping, and tomorrow hope to catch the Cornish Riviera to St Ives and see Ma. As it's a restricted area and I have no identity card, this may be a little difficult.

[1] *Photo reconnaissance.*

April 30th 1944

ST IVES

I GO OUT AND SEE PEGGY'S FATHER[1] at Frewin Road and a friend of his, Bruce, an ARP Warden, comes in, and we consume beer.

Next day off down to St Ives where I am now, staying in the Trevessa Hotel. I set to work at once, and meet one Vivian Julian, who has a flat and an invalid mother, and one Denise Bennett, also

447

staying at the hotel. I take Vivian to a dance at the Tregunna Hotel and meet Denise and her American Major (Les Harness) there. It's terrific, and dancing with her puts my blood pressure way up, and the bell rings. However, the Yank is in, and is around all today, Sunday. I spend two awful nights 'sweating it out' as the Yanks say, and have a third in prospect.

(Too optimistic – the rest of my leave).

St Ives is full of cats, gossip and old Trout. One retired diplomatic service type gives me half an hour on the 'life of the salmon', after lunch. Ma takes me to tea at Corbis Bay with one Mrs Welch of Malayan days – first cousin of Vivian, and they hate each other like poison.

[1] *Peggy Farlow is the widow of Colin's brother Hugh.*

May 7th 1944

St Ives

BOTH OPERATION ORDERS 2 AND 3 FAIL[1] and I have to give up the struggle and see what God will provide.

Sunday we go to the American's tea (175 Regiment) where is fruit salad and ice cream and chocolate sauce, which apparently has never been seen in the UK since the war started. Then to Findlays for dinner where I nearly die of laughing, as everyone is deaf, and the noise of shouting is terrific. The old colonel even says "Wish I was twenty years younger!"

Monday I sit on the beach in the afternoon with Denise and discover that she doesn't mean half the things she says – so now I know where I stand. Also I go into "Sloop", which opens after having been shut about a week through lack of supplies. Meet one Barry Mitchell there, a Captain in the infantry.

[1] *He means his plans of seduction.*

May 9th 1944

This Denise dame invites me out on the sands, and we sunbathe and have tea. That is eat it, as there is no liquid. I proclaim that I am fireproof, and she sets to work, and we have quite a time. She says she cannot be unfaithful to her husband AND her lover (the Yank Major), but eventually tells me to come and make love to her properly in her room at night. OK, says I, and depart to the "Sloop" for some beer and then on to the flat for an omelette.

Having previously recce-ed all the stairs – which ones creak etc – I go in the door at 11pm to find her in bed and saying she didn't think I would come tonight, and I must go. I say 'why?', we argue, and eventually I am told that I'm a bit dim, so realise the score and leave.

Yesterday I sit in the garden in the sun after lunch and it's damn hot. Denise later departs with the Yank to Tregunna, and I call in there on the way home before the bar shuts, but he eyes me rather suspiciously, so I beat it.

May 11th 1944

St Ives

I reckon I am being played for a sucker, but I must learn somewhere.

Yesterday I go to a beer party at 9pm with the Sandons, but beer not too good. We play poker dice, and I clean up a lot of commandos and odd women.

Today feel ill in the stomach from beer. I invite Viv to Tregenna to dance, but she suddenly says she cannot, having to meet a train at 9pm or something. Actually her American boy friend is coming over for the weekend, so I get the old boot. However, why worry? Think where I was two months ago.

Am trying to get a keg of beer and throw a party. Ma and I go over to Lelant – me to be exhibited to her friends there, and drink much whisky – damn expensive too. On return I call in to the Sloop, have two pints of Bass, and bore Denise for half an hour. On to the flat for supper, and I get so tight I make for home and bed as fast as I can.

May 12th 1944
St Ives

WHO THOUGHT OF SUNBATHING IN ENGLAND!

I go and drink whisky with Jim and Sue Fraser (Commandos), stay to dinner, and we go up to Tregenna. Meet Colonel Warfield, and we get in a sort of party, but containing nothing worth looking at. Vivian looking a bit lovesick with her American. Get to bed 12.30 a bit depressed, and have to pull myself together this morning or I shall let it get me down – and what good will that do. Damn the Americans!

What I really require is a girlfriend after all the years living in goddamned places.

May 14th 1944
St Ives

A WEEK OF SUNBATHING. Denise tells me she is having fun at my expense, roughly, and departs to a house she has got.

Ma and I organise and put on a party last night with a firkin of Bass, which goes down very well, and a little gin and cider for the women. Viv condescends to come, but most of the women go with their Yanks to a Yank party at Tregenna. The Commandos come – led by Alan Greenhaugh, who organised 'bitter' for me.

I meet G/C Somerville and his adjutant in the Sloop (officer commanding Portreath) and he invites me over to meet Durrant, ex Maungdaw 'controller'.

My kit all appears to have arrived, and today I am contracted to take out a Wren I have never even seen – God! – to dinner and dance at Tregenna. She is sure to be a complete horror, and God knows how I shall carry it off.

No posting orders yet.

May 15th 1944

ST IVES

I TAKE THE WREN TO TREGENNA – C.P.O. Doreen Songthe. We later sit and drink Canadian Club in Gibson's back garden room amongst all my luggage.

Yesterday tea and supper with her, Ma and her aunt at various times, and end up smoking cigarettes in the dark in her aunt's flat, as we cannot find the blackout bandobast. But that's as far as I get, though I contract to go over and see her at Helston on Friday.

I write to Mhairi[1] again whilst full of Bass from the Sloop, a most peculiar letter, so I expect I shall dry her up altogether.

It's "Salute the Soldier" week here, and Yanks marching all over the town.

I play squash on Sunday morning with one Molly Allan, games mistress at Down's School, removed here, and sweat out a pint or two of gin.

---

[1] A childhood girlfriend.

451

May 17th 1944

No posting from the Air Ministry yet.

I go over to Portreath as a guest of Durrant – ex-Maungdaw controller – for drinks, dinner and a look at the Ops room, and one or two modern conveniences I have never even heard of before. Am driven back by a WAAF and we discuss Yanks, my usual bete-noire these days.

Yesterday I feel much depressed. I know what is wrong, but there is nothing I can do about it. The weather now turned squally and rather cold, and I appear to have starboard sinus trouble, as my right nostril is permanently slightly heavy and bunged up. Will keep me off flying again I suppose. I have removed all trace of my squadron leadership, and am now a common or garden junior officer again.

May 20th 1944

I meet Tom Slack (41 squadron)[1], ex-Iraq 4FTS, in the Sloop and we go drinking in the Queens and re-fight the battle, to the great amazement of one Wagg, a Yank in the same squadron.

Next day I do some drinking with them; they are staying in Tregenna, on the Nuffield (scheme) – one Jimmy Theale DSO, DFC is also there, and is found in the manager's wife's pyjamas and bed one afternoon about 4pm. All most uproarious.

I eat his dinner at Tregenna as he has passed out, then Tom, Wagg and I go down to the 'Sheaf of Wheat'. Wagg fearfully drunk, and throwing lobster shells about the place, and on the way down he picks up some women, gets sober on coffee at the 'Kettle', and joins us. This dame, Madge, spent many years in Burma and India, and Wagg takes her home, much to my annoyance, as we are doing quite well together.

Yesterday by train to Helston, where Doreen meets me, and we hitch down to Coverack where she lives. Lunch and tea in a farmhouse, Cornish cream, and we sit in the sun amongst a lot of thistles and nettles and I sunbathe. Progress is slow, but I get as far as combing her hair when it's time to go. Train is late for a connection, so I hitch a lorry and bus back to St Ives. Lovely country round Helston.

No word from the Air Ministry though I wrote a few days ago. Note from Mhairi, who seems a bit shocked by my description of the women of St Ives.

[1] *Tom Slack wrote about his wartime adventures in 'Happy is the Day'.*

13

May 1944 - January 1945

No 41 Operational Training Unit
Hawarden

No 5 (Pilot) Advanced Flying Unit
Ternhill

No 83 General Support Unit
Lasham

May 25th 1944
Hawarden (outside Chester)

Doreen comes over for two days, and we sit in the sun on top of a hill amongst the gorse bushes, and get down to things. Monday we have a farewell Bass in the Sloop, and then Doreen and I and Mama eat a lobster in the flat. Later we depart, and Doreen and I call in at the Gibson's shack where my luggage is kept. I come up against the armour of Roman Catholic principles, as on the preceding night, but it gets too hot for her, and I am eventually fobbed off with some typically Papist trick.

Day before yesterday up to London, and spent the night in Gig's flat. We drink masses of gin, feed at Manetta's, more gin at home, and bed at 2am, having discussed everything. almost, under the sun.

Yesterday I take my blue cloth to Flights in New Burlington Street and, foolishly perhaps, order it to be made up[1] – 10 guineas. Lunch on Gigs in a neighbouring pub, and then out to Stanmore RAF HQ. A muddle as to where I shall sleep, so I go along to 'P' Staff, one F.L Heyward, and am posted to 41 O.T.U. Hawarden as a supernumerary instructor-cum-pupil, which may be a bit difficult to cope with, before going on the dreaded Ops!

It is then 6pm, so I ring up Gigs and return for the night to her flat. We go to the Berkeley Buttery for a meal – rabbit called game, and some lager beer.

Now I am waiting for breakfast, and then off to Euston. My month's leave cost me about £30/- – half a guinea for b&b - so I must have drunk about 10/- a day on average. Cannot last out like that, or staying in London.

I arrive at Hawarden, and am put on the course, and stop me if Hammerbeck isn't the senior pupil! There is a dance the second night, and I get myself fairly well organised with a WAAF flight officer called Celia Spink, who is the boss here.

456

I take to the air again in a Harvard and Hurricane, but find on a dual and country I cannot steer a course properly, through not coping with the gyro correctly, and then we decide, F/L Brown and one F/O Trevor Mitchell, that an A.F.U. course would be good for me. So the C.F.I. is going to fix it, through 9 group.

We do our flying from Poulton out in the country near Chester, and live here.

Last night F/O Ashgrove RCAF, and Bishop and George Bainbridge (ex Army) and self go for drinks to Chester, and Bishop dates himself up with some telephone girl we encounter in a bar, and to bring a friend for me – tonight. But he has stomach trouble, so we may not go.

Tomorrow I go and see E.N.T. specialist[2] about my blockage in Cosford.

Very hot here, and I sweat like hell in my battledress, when I should be wearing shorts.

[1] Into a new uniform.
[2] Ear, nose and throat.

May 31st 1944

Hawarden

BISHOP AND I DO NOT GO IN TO TOWN, so I walk up with the Canadian to Hawarden for a beer in the local pub.

Two Sgt Pilots in an Oxford fail to find Cosford (for my E.N.T. appointment) and after circling Wolverhampton for half an hour we return, and now I can get no appointment until 6th June. What to do in the meantime?

An all ranks dance last night, and I get tacked on to this Celia dame and have to walk her home to Hawarden Castle in the middle of the night where the WAAF officers live. A sexless dame.

I beat the pants off the Group Captain, Alloway, at squash.

June 4th 1944

I AM SENT ON FOUR DAYS LEAVE, reporting to Cosford E.N.T. chap when it ends, so wire Sproats[1]. The weather is bad, so I have to go by train and arrive over in time for tea. Jarvis Blayney – F/L – also over at Fulford, and we do a lot of drinking together. Aunt Molly takes me round the house offering me bits and pieces when she is dead!

I spend a lot of time looking at Daph, and in wondering why I didn't make more use of myself in the old days. However, the day will dawn – maybe! Jarvis and I go up to Yeadon, and try and get me a seat to Cosford on Monday, but no luck so far. With great difficulty, manage to get the latest type mask and microphone – only through saying that I'm an instructor. I know what I need.

I leave my fountain pen at Hawarden so expect it's gone – hell! (The WAAF had it for me).

[1] His aunt Molly's family outside York.

June 7th 1944

HAWARDEN

I GO DOWN TO COSFORD after quite a party with Jarvis the night before, and put up in the Mess there. I meet one F/L "Dicky" Dee who has been having treatment for burns for 13 months now, and we go to see a show, and I am very taken with one of the stars, a WAAF officer, one Hazel Palit. Also I have my appointment with the E.N.T. specialist the next day and leave after lunch. He gives me an X-ray, and says there is nothing the matter except a change of climate, which I think is balls. A huge Mess at Cosford, and you telephone to the bar when you want a drink.

My posting not in yet, so I'm off to Poulton as C.G.I. tomorrow until it comes. Hope to get some flying, and one or two other things too.

June 9th 1944
POULTON

I MOVE OVER TO POULTON. "Ash" and I cycle into town and meet two dames of his staying at the Grosvenor. One Regina Grahame and Eve Porter, the former a Manchester typist with a shocking accent. We drink at the 'Pied Bull', then back to her room for some 'Canadian Club' which I have brought in with me. Eve comes in with two RAF types, but they go out again – very obviously – and I get busy.

This Regina dame is like a cold fish and I get her lined up on the bed and she moans she is a good girl and how she thought I was different to most men, so I get bored and leave at 11.30, and cycle home through the rain to bed.

'Ash' – Farrell Ashdown RCAF – is a helluva lad. Today I do a bit of office work, then spend an hour in a decompression chamber up to 25,000 feet – going up without oxygen and writing damn silly things on a bit of paper.

No squash court here – no exercise – no word out of Mhairi – no posting!

June 11th 1944
POULTON

MY POSTING THROUGH to SPAFU Ternhill[1], where they give you hell, so all the ex-pupils say! I go to town on Saturday night and go to 'Barlows', a pub upstairs in Chester, where one meets lots of women – I don't, but should do though. I meet my friend 'Bish',

459

and we go down to a dance at the Castle. We drink some whisky, then order and pay for half a dozen gins before they all run out. I dance with some dame, an 'excuse me', and three women cut in on me and nearly turn my head. One is an A.T.S. sergeant. I dance with her later on, and then for the rest of the night. If ever I saw love in a girl's eyes, which I never did before, there it is.

She is Jean Admunsen (or something) from Manchester, down in Chester on a baseball course of all things. I take her home to the 'Girls Friendly Society' where she is billeted, and we sit above the racecourse a little before midnight. I get busy, and find she is all of a dither, and stunned with pure love for me. She keeps asking what hit her, but beyond kissing her, I can do nothing, and take her home and wake up the 'friendly girls' at 12.15 am. God! I never met the like of her before – aged 20 – and her emotions bring out her Lancashire accent! I cycle home in the rain to not much sleep.

'Bish' well organised with one Betty Bevan, whose husband is a POW. I go flying in a Harvard after one hour's link (trainer), and find things easier. I also go and look at Haneck Oak, where I once stayed with 'Jonah' of Harrow and Sandhurst days.

[1] *He means No. 5 (Pilot) Advanced Flying Unit.*

June 12th 1944

TERNHILL

I GET FLOWN DOWN TO TERNHILL with my kit in an Oxford on Sunday. I go to the Mess, a vast building like a hotel, and meet the training wing adjutant, one Scott, who says he doesn't want to see me until the evening of the 13th. So I get my buttons cleaned, pack a bag, and leg it down the road for the Shrewsbury bus, which I just manage to catch.

In town I ask some RAF type which is the best place to stay, and he takes me to the George Hotel, where I get a room, though at first they deny such a possibility. I take a walk at 6pm, but it seems dead, so I return to the George at 7, beer time, and join two RAF types sitting by themselves. Various people join us, but my attention is on a girl on the opposite side of the room, with an RAF officer, and we exchange odd smiles. I meet him in the gents, and he has to go away to some other dame, so he introduces me, to take her off his hands.

My original party is off to the 'Post Office', some low pub, so we go too, but break away by ourselves to the Lion. She is one Sonia Price, private secretary to the boss of Swallow Raincoats in Birmingham. On closing time, we go down to the river and sit, and I set to work, but though very keen on kissing, nothing else doing. Seems odd to me, but then I know nothing yet!

We return to her hotel and sit in front of the fire for some ten minutes, and then she puts me out. I am to meet her this morning at 11am and go shopping, but then she may not be there! Quien sabe?

I can't get any damn matches in this town.

June 13th 1944

Shrewsbury

I ORGANISE MATCHES – and soap too. I collect Sonia at 11.00, and we go looking for fully fashioned stockings. Then beer and lunch at the "Lion". We then go down near the river, cross over by the penny toll, and sit on the grass from 2.30 to 7.35. I get busy, and so does she for that matter, but her principles are such that the result is another "Papist trick".

I get a bit tied up at various times with what Jeanie told me, and not Sonia, and what I said to one and not the other. We go back and have a meal of sorts at a cinema cafe, and then some more beer at the "Lion".

Good night Bass!

I hitch hike out to Ternhill this morning, as there are only three buses a day. I pass "Banky Bill" in the street last night, but can't stop with Sonia. I give her 10 coupons.

June 20th 1944

GROUND SCHOOL AGAIN, and I'm supposed to pass 8's in morse at the end of a fortnight. One Pete Mackenzie, a Canadian, and I go to town by bicycle and drink beer in the "Corbett Arms". Then on to some party in some woman's house where I talk to one Betty Fletcher, wife of a course pilot here, though now in hospital with measles. Same again last night, via much whisky (paid for by Betty) at the Stag's Head.

I go to the Parish Hall where there is a dance, and only get in with great difficulty at 10.30, as no one allowed in after 9.30. Pete not there, but I dance with his girlfriend, a WAAF driver from the M.U. in mufti. No joy in Market Drayton I fancy, so what to do!

A cook's tour in an Anson yesterday, and never saw so many flying fields before. Hugh's name in the visitors book (his brother), just before the war.

June 22nd 1944

PETE AND I AND TWO OTHERS go to town on Sunday. Then back to the Mess where there is a dance, just like India with some half dozen women. I set to with a Wren officer. On Saturday, I meet an a girl in the Corbett Arms who seems to falls in love with me and walks half the way home. She is a WAAF clerk in mufti and about 2 foot 6 inches high – God!

Yesterday we visit the "Stormy Petrel" and the "Castle" just nearby and I get to bed by 10.45pm. A letter from Mhairi, crossing one sarcastic one of mine in which I asked her if she was dead! It's taken about a week to be redirected from Hawarden.

I manage to get my hands on a bicycle by saying that I'm an instructor, but it will go soon I suppose.

June 23rd 1944
TERNHILL

I TAKE TO THE AIR AGAIN in a Master *(Miles M.9 Master trainer aircraft)* and go solo today, though I nearly bounce the a/c off doing a glide approach at 95, as they come down quite steep.

Hugh Roberts and I go to town and are admitted to the "Lamb" by Nancy Cork, the landlady, although it is shut. Two other women, two sailors and a Yank sergeant come in, and we all play darts and drink Scotch, being turned out about 11pm. Hugh and I are then asked to come back, when the others have left, as Nancy (a 12 stoner!) has her sister Elaine there with a sudden passion for Hughie. We go back and they are very drunk, but give us drinks and eventually bacon and eggs as well. Elaine wants to retire with Hugh but Nancy will not let her, and both being drunk, there is quite some argument. Eventually Elaine goes away and we are put out too, but Pete and I go down and drink with her last night instead of Roberts, who was supposed to meet her at 8pm in the Corbett Arms. We are going tonight and he is coming too, so I suppose I have had it again, as she is the nicest looking girl I have seen around here yet!

June 26th 1944
TERNHILL

I CUT ROBERTS OUT AND HE GETS ANNOYED and hasn't been in again since. Sunday I have lunch with them at the Lamb, and then go on to Mrs George Atkinson's, a friend of Sue Fraser's in St Ives, for tennis, which I am made to play until 20.30 – some gin and supper and return to bed.

Saturday I fly to Wrexham and Newport without getting lost, so am improving.

I go down to see Elaine, but she is serving behind the bar until 10pm, so I don't see much of her, though we go into the 'parlour' afterwards with some naval ratings and two Yanks who call each other "Slug" and "Teagarden" respectively. She gives me a demure sort of kiss when I leave.

Scott, the Wing Adjutant here, reckons I shall have to go onto twins with my eyesight, so I shall have to start all over again.

June 28th 1944

Ternhill

I go in on Monday and see Elaine, and we sit in the bar and drink mixed Guinness and Brown Ale until bacon and eggs arrives about 11.30pm. We have quite a session but no score again – though we have the joint to ourselves, Nancy being in bed suffering from "bad beer".

This (flying) programme is a bit of a bind, as it means up at 7am every day and we don't always finish until 17.45. The other day I sit in the flight office from 1-5pm waiting for a flight, and doing nothing. Yesterday I go to play tennis at the King-Hay's but am given a good supper, and so cannot play very well after it.

A cheque for £3 from Aunt Vivy.

July 3rd 1944

Ternhill

I am invited to stay the night at "The Lamb" on Friday, my day off being on Saturday, and go down there and do some beer drinking. Thursday I take Elaine to the Parish Hall dance and keep losing her in the general "excuse me's" when all sorts of women come and tap her off; she kisses me goodnight quite well, too.

At about 2.30am we go upstairs, and I am shown the spare bedroom, and eventually score a home base, though only just, as Nancy comes down from upstairs looking for Elaine and there is nearly trouble.

Next day, after breakfast at 12 and lunch at 4pm, we go for a walk and then I cycle home. Later to a dance at Buntingsdale, HQ 22 and 25 Groups, where I never saw so much whiskey before in England. I set to work on one "Penny" Penfold, a WAAF officer, and she comes over yesterday with Lady Chetwynd, who had invited me, to a hop here.

I don't seem to get much flying here, or much sleep for that matter, and Scott tells me the next course at Hawarden starts in three weeks time. A letter from Mrs Jacobs.

July 11th 1944

Ternhill

I GO IN TO SEE ELAINE occasionally, but no more home bases due to aircraft being U/S.[1]

I go down and look at the cottage at Bridgenorth, and not many chickens about. Also a few cross countries, fairly successful ones too.

Yesterday I go to a dance with Mrs King-Hay who puts up 10/- for my admittance. Free beer until it runs out, but not much else there, bar a lot of American officers. I get a bit disgruntled, and dance with some dame who I cannot see home, as I have to go back to the King-Hays for beer, and retrieve my bicycle.

Today I was going to see the Penfold dame at 8pm, but it was raining hard, and so that will be off too.

[1] *Military euphemisms abound.*

July 12th 1944

I COLLECT YOUNG "TUPPENCE" and we walk to the "Stormy Petrel" and drink beer until we are asked to leave. I walk her home, and put in a bit of fancy work in the garage, but nothing to cause any alarm.

Yesterday I go down to see Elaine in the "Corbett Arms" and we go back to the "Lamb" and I have to leave at 12.15 with Steve and Teagarden in their truck, as I can stand it no longer. I do some sodium flying[1] and am now in the night flying flight, and kick off this evening with "beacon bashing" dual at 3.15am, so what the hell I do until then I do not know.

[1] *Meaning unclear.*

July 14th 1944

TERNHILL

I GO NIGHT FLYING AGAIN, and do two solo circuits until 5am when it is getting light. Yesterday I go beacon bashing up to Hooton Park and I then drive straight into the ground.

I get a bad attack of Mhairi, for some reason, having had another letter recently, but from a careful appreciation there can be no joy, as the RAF say. I take Tuppence out for a walk in between supper and night flying, and it pours with rain and they cancel it.

I collect a clasp for North Africa to my 39-43 Star, for my services learning to be a tank-buster with 6 squadron, which seems a bit of a racket[1].

I would like to meet Mhairi in Edinburgh, but then I shall get no leave.

[1] *He is referring to the fact that he did not actually see any action in North Africa, just visited for training.*

July 17th 1944

I DO FIVE LANDINGS BY MYSELF, more or less satisfactorily, and then get the next night off. So I ring up Elaine but she sounds dubious, having a date with the Norwegian sergeant pilots, two of them, who have been around whilst I have been night flying.

I go to town with two pilots and drink beer in the "Corbett", where Elaine and Co appear, but all most unsatisfactory and we part later – or rather she departs with a flighty "Goodbye." We return to the Mess and I drink beer with a Czech, one F/L Donda, and we follow some women and their French boyfriends out, and we meet a dog, and I go to bed with a dead rabbit.

July 24th 1944

I POLISH OFF THE NIGHT FLYING and go to the gunnery flight. I also go to town to see Elaine, but she is a bit upstage, as a certain Norwegian sergeant pilot has undone all my good work whilst I have been night flying. His name in Biani, but I shall call him Piano. I sit around boozing, and later come back with Steve in his truck. She puts up her cheek to be kissed so I say "what's that for?" and depart.

Saturday, Pete and I and Charlie Ruck go in – Pete very drunk after eight or nine whiskies and grapefruit in the Mess, as he has just finished his night flying, and is on the loose again. We go to the Corbett and I see some dame eying us, so later, at the local dance, I seek her out and dance off with her. She is a WAAF in 22 Group, one Dorothy Lewis, and is in civvies and staying at the YWCA. She walks part way home with me, then I see her back to the YWCA and we do pretty well.

I date her for last night, and we drink beer in the Corbett until it closes, then she changes into uniform and we set off for home. I side track her halfway and we get down to something in a field, but nothing else, as she is on a "major", though if she were not, I have my own doubts too! I get her back in home by 23.59 and today arrange to meet her tomorrow. I expect that all I shall get for my pains is a trip to Sheffield – a double course too.

Thursday night I get a bit tight with "Tuppence" and two friends of mine in the "Corbett" and later I am foolish enough to spend 10/- on Pimms No 1 in the Mess ante-room.

July 25th 1944

Ternhill

I MAKE A RECCE FROM THE AIR, and then one on a bicycle. I organise some beer from the Mess, I brief myself and have everything on the top line, and all depends on how the enemy will fight – and what happens? – it starts raining. God! So the enemy won't even turn up I expect!

July 26th 1944

Ternhill

THE RAIN STOPS AND THE ENEMY TURNS UP and we sit in a wood and consume beer, amongst other things. Due to one or two technical hitches, the Papist plot functions again, not particularly satisfactorily either. We ride home in the dark, and I get her up to the WAAF quarters without getting arrested, and see her home.

July 29th 1944

I AM GIVEN SEVEN DAYS LEAVE, so wire Mhairi to meet me in Edinburgh. She says she can manage it at 12.30 on Thursday, then they cancel it and extend the course by a couple of weeks, and then give me leave again. I ring up Crail (Where Mhairi lived near Edinburgh) with some difficulty, and hear a distant voice on the other end.

Now I am going to Edinburgh on Tuesday and meeting Mhairi for lunch on Thursday, after which she returns to Crail. I have seven days, so what the hell I will do with myself I can't think. Aunt Babs ill in hospital. And what the hell will the lunch be like – a complete anti-climax no doubt.

A terrific dance last night, and I have "Tuppence" over, and she departs for Grantham today. Also the Atkinson dame, though I don't do much looking after her. This morning I have a cold – caught God only knows where.

July 31st 1944

ANOTHER WIRE THAT SHE CANNOT MAKE EDINBURGH before Friday, and I ring up Mhairi and contract to visit Crail tomorrow, if she can find me accommodation – so that will be that – and what do I do with my seven days leave?

I finish my flying and am on the list for Hawarden, but G. knows when I shall go.

August 3rd 1944

CRAIL

I MAKE EDINBURGH LATE, due to trains being delayed, and have to stay the night. I go to the Officer's Club, 2 Castle Street, and they fix me up with a bed in the Shelburne Hotel, and I drink beer there later. Next morning I go to Barnton to see the Virgin Aunt[1], who looks a bit ancient and lives in an attic with a view of a Jeyes Fluid advertisement.

On 1pm train to Crail, where I am met by Mhairi, and taken to the Marine Hotel, comfortable and good food. We walk around, talk, have a drink and she returns to her billet at 11pm. At work today and I see her for lunch and tea and again tonight, I hope, when she comes off duty at 11pm.

Now aged 27 and living in the past, or seems to be, with a memory like mine. We are a bit shy at first, but things improve, and tomorrow she has a day off, and then I return to Barnton and Aunt Babs's inquisition. I feel the old love of soul again, but am not sure of the body!

Crail full of smells and sounds reminiscent of Tiree, and Barracudas tear through the sky all day from the RNAS[2].

[1] *His unmarried Aunt Babs.*
[2] *Royal Naval Air Service.*

August 6th 1944

DUNBAR

MHAIRI GETS THE DAY OFF and we go to St Andrews and have lunch out of a bag on the cliffs in a damn mist. Then tea in someone's house who is out, and home for dinner and a drink, and a long sit by the football ground behind the graveyard. She was secretly engaged to one Beresford, who was killed some eight weeks ago.

I return to Edinburgh rather gloomily yesterday and stay in Barnton, meeting Toby in the Officers Club last night. We go the rounds and do some heavy drinking, and eventually collect three sisters in the "Aperitif", to whom I throw 'engaged' cards, as on the tables, and take them back to the Club. We dance and I manage to get rid of mine (they are all horrors) in a Paul Jones[1], and am a smashing success with my opening gambit of "which end of the bath do you sit?"

I have to walk home, as I have missed the last train through going to the wrong station, and am passed by many empty cars, but no lifts.

This morning I leave Barnton to stay with Toby, who is an instructor at 165 O.T.U. Dunbar, and here I am, returning Ternhill tomorrow. He is playing cricket and I have been watching, and eaten the Captain's lunch with them, as he went to his home for his. Mhairi still has the same fascination over me, which has lasted all these years, in fact I feel quite a pang at leaving, though I only see her one day and one evening, and two odd hours!

Aunt Babs ill, pretty awful, and most curious about my visit to Crail. She can remain so.

[1] *A ballroom dance in which the dancers change partners after circling in concentric rings of men and women.*

August 9th 1944

TERNHILL

TOBY TAKES ME TO AN EXCELLENT poker dice party and dinner in the Mess, and I return to Ternhill on Monday after an early start at 07.45 with no food. I stand, and sit on a table, most of the way to Crewe, and arrive back to find it a boiling hot day.

I go to the Bear in Hodnet for a drink with the ex-Pongoes (ex-Army) and then Collier and I go to the local hop, but all the women there seem pretty grim and I return home about 11.30 pm after an unsuccessful evening. I feel a bit odd about everything, and cannot decide what I want.

I fly over to Peterborough and come in against the circuit and two reds before I notice what I am about. No hope of a posting for a month or so, as Hawarden is full up and the war is finishing – or so they say. I shall be back East soon. The India Office say I cannot have the pay of Lieutenant of six years service – i.e. "Drumhead's Bob" – only 2nd Lieutenant, as I was when I was seconded.

Doing much flying, and gliding in every time satisfactorily. Elaine and the WAAF dame expect me to ring them up, but hell – I want to get away from here, and the tennis gang at the King-Hays.

August 11th 1944
Ternhill

I go to the Bear in Hodnet with Bill Conway and have a few beers with some aircrew from Peplow, including one who came home on SS 'Orontes' with me. Conway drinks so much beer, he crashes into the hedge two or three times on the way home, and I have to put the chain back on his bicycle and nearly die of laughing.

Yesterday we go to the Corbett Arms and on to the dance, but "no joy" as the RAF say[1], and I'm now approaching a gloomy weekend with Sunday off. I do a lot of flying and dogfighting with Thunderbolts over the Wrekin, but am getting damned bored.

[1] *Taken from fox-hunting jargon, "no joy" was used in radio comms by Battle of Britain pilots to mean "No enemy sighted".*

August 14th 1944
Ternhill

I do much battling with Thunderbolts over the Wrekin – but without much success.

"Sawn Off" and I go to the Bear on Saturday night and I end up with Charlie Rich at midnight with coffee and a pork pie with two dames in a house in Garden City. We are then turned out. Yesterday I play tennis all afternoon at the King-Hays, followed by some family bridge and return, exhausted, at about midnight.

No postings, as there is a bottleneck in F.T.C., and I go over to fly Hurricanes tomorrow from Chetwynd. I do an I.F. cross-country which is pretty erratic, and I don't seem to be much of a pilot at all, or to know much about this flying business.

But then I really know nothing much about anything, and should read to improve my education. My mind seems forever on one thing – and that I cannot have, or get rather – though I seem to spend many hours planning and thinking about it. What of the future? Nothing much to look forward to – I doubt they will keep me in the RAF, and I now know nothing about the Indian Army – I have even forgotten my Urdu.

Quien sabe? I'm getting fat, and even beaten at squash too.

August 16th 1944

TERNHILL

I GO TO HODNET and dance at the 'Bear' on Monday and meet a new dame. We dance around the dance floor, and I meet her in the Bear last night. Discover her name is Dorothy and she lives in Hodnet, aged 20, having been discharged from the ATS with a pension after a prang in a 15 cwt truck. However she speaks without the trace of an accent and seems to have some character, but that is about all her usefulness.

I go to Chetwynd yesterday and fly a Hurricane I, and find it a bit difficult to land after so many hours in the damn Masters[1]. Beautiful sun for a change.

---

[1] *The Miles M.9 Master was a British two-seat monoplane advanced trainer, which served as an excellent introduction to the high performance Spitfire.*

August 19th 1944

I GO BACK TO HODNET but the Bear is shut, and so we go for a walk and sit on a hill. I get a fearful thirst but can do nothing about it, and cycle gloomily home at about 10.30pm to three glasses of water.

Yesterday I go to town with Collier and eventually make the acquaintance of the "Hungry Vulture" and her sister, who are talking to my friend Donda, a Czech. She is another Dorothy, and Donda and I get invited back home when the pub shuts. But Ma and Pa are sitting in state and we have tea and biscuits. The H.V. is looking for a husband, so I leave hastily at 11pm and cycle home through the pouring rain. Tonight I am going to another of the awful Vardon dances, or parties rather, but do not intend to lose 8/6 at bridge this time.

August 26th 1944

TERNHILL

"HELL HATH NO FURY..."

I don't take much notice of the Dorothy dame at Hodnet's Monday dance, and she gets damned annoyed.

On 23rd we hear of the fall of France, and have a party in the Mess with the dozen or so French course pilots. I get up on a table and sing "A troopship leaving Bombay" with my own two verses, and then retire to bed. Later, I organise myself three days leave, plus a day off, and get a lift in an Oxford from Hinstock to Donibristle with one Lt MacDonald RNVR. We fly over Blackpool tower and Moffat, and see the Isle of Man to port. I get put up in the wardroom at Donibristle, and of course find that I have packed no lungi.[1]

This morning I bus to Crail and find Mhairi has organised a bed and breakfast, but nothing else. I have a beer and 20 Horlicks tablets for lunch, then Mhairi gets off 2.45 to 6.30 and we bus over to Elie and back for tea. Crail is crowded out for some reason. I am dissatisfied with this sort of life. I know what I want but cannot find it.

Some 3000 pewits on Chetwynd airfield.

[1] *Indian men's skirt, usually tied around the lower waist below the navel, often used for nightwear.*

August 27th 1944
CRAIL

I HAVE A SMALL BED AND BREAKFAST apartment with a gas bracket, and have high tea in the kitchen with the family. Angus Mitchell, a bus driver of some 24 seasons, buys me a few drinks in the local – the "Golf Hotel" – and then we hang around for some more when it has shut, and get some more.

Today Mhairi comes round 10 to 12, and we sit on the rocks and look at the sea, but her vibrations seem to be out of tune, and I reckon I made a mistake in coming up here. I should have gone down to see Peggy. However I must learn sometime, though what I do learn doesn't seem to be much good to me, as far as the results go. Mhairi has a half retriever, half spaniel called Mitch.

August 29th 1944
TERNHILL

WE SIT IN THE LOUNGE at the "Beach Hotel" in Elie, and have lunch and tea out of the rain. I ring up Donibristle but no aircraft, so after a walk around the beach I set course on the 4.21 train for Edinburgh, somewhat relieved, as I now know that I was in love with a shadow, and that its substance is a different shape. The Club fixes me up with B and B (3/6) in the annexe – the bed part turns out to be four blankets and a pillow on a sofa, but I manage OK when I get home at 1.30 am, despite no lungi.

Next morning I beat it hot foot to the Club after a bath and meet an RASC Lieutenant, a Canadian, and a naval Lieutenant, and we drink and sup together there. Then to the dance. I advance on some plain looking ringed dame, as a sort of stop gap, but she smells strongly of whisky and is quite gay. Name of Ray, from Manchester, as are they all. I see her home to the North British Hotel, skirmishing en route, and we sit in the lounge for a long time as her room is occupied by her sister and a Maori captain with an M.C. and a bottle of Scotch, which he brought all the way from Italy. I go on strike eventually, so we go out and I try to navigate my way home, remembering the position but not the name of the street I am staying in. I try to line Ray up on the way, but no good, though she comes to the door and spends a long time kissing me goodnight.

And today I return to Ternhill to find I'm on night flying again. A most odd letter from Nairn – Ma's landlord – in answer to one of mine.

August 30th 1944

Ternhill

A LITTLE STOCK TAKING after four months in England.

I don't seem to be a particularly good pilot, especially in instrument and night flying, not to speak of some pretty poor gunnery. Mentally I am stagnant, and cannot hold an intelligent conversation or argue on any subject – and seem to have no hold on anything.

I read the Times every day, but seem unable to absorb learning through the eye, despite having a memory like an elephant. I can organise damn well, but am on the level of a Canadian pilot officer at present, only my day flying is not as accurate as his. Then the presence of women in this country after the East has complicated things – warped my thoughts as it were, though principally because I don't seem to be able to score what other people do – or boast that they do!

Maybe the day will dawn, as I say to myself, but I may get posted East again before sunrise, as that is the present trend of postings.

I go around with Canadians – Pete Mackenzie, Charlie Ruck, "Sawn-off" Perkins, Hugh Roberts, the Englishman David Crook DFC (author of 'Spitfire Pilot')[1], A.J. Scott DFM, ex-Observer, who knew Hugh in 21 Squadron, Wilkinson DFM, ex A.G, and four seconded "pongoes" – Joe Hulme, Dennis Collier, Bob Martin, Tiny Price.

And to hear them talking, I realise how little I know of army life now. Someone once said "Jack of all trades, master of none" – but I'm not a particularly good Jack. Lazing in the flights or flying from 8 am to about 16.30, a game of squash, some beer and supper, then hot foot with one or more of the above in the Corbett Arms in Market Drayton, the Bear in Hodnet or the Castle nearby.

And then the local women with whom I am such a failure – Elaine Spender, who drinks more beer than I ever thought possible, took up with Biani the Norwegian sergeant pilot whilst I was night flying; WAAF Lewis of ill fame; the beautiful Vera and her girlfriend Irene; "Hell hath no fury" Dorothy of Hodnet – I walked out on her, bored; two others who live in Garden City, but no progress; Wilky's land army dame, but I can never find her; and the respectable hangers-on of the Vardon parties, who might yet be cracked, with skill.

Hell! I want a change of air! Or station rather.

[1] David Crook fought in the Battle of Britain with 609 Squadron, and afterwards wrote a book about his experiences, Spitfire Pilot. He was killed in a flying accident in Scotland in December 1944.

August 31st 1944

NO SOONER SAID, than I go down to the Corbett with one Reg Cooper for a drink and meet Elaine and Nancy Cork, proprietor of the Lamb Hotel.

We then proceed to the "Elephant" and the "Star" and back to the "Lamb". I make to go at about 12 after sitting in the bar with Elaine for some time, and she comes out to the wood shed, or byre, or whatever it's called in which bicycles and garden tools are kept, and I score a home run, as our Canadian friends say. And so to home.

Today I do some instrument flying and find it improving. There is a 8/6 dance in the Corbett Arms, and these two dames expect to see us there. Maybe, but I don't want to see them.

September 3rd 1944

TERNHILL

I GET POSTED TO HAWARDEN, together with A.J. Scott, Reg Cooper, David Crook, "Tiny" Price, Denis Collier and Bob Martin – also one Harris. Reg and I go down to the Corbett dance but it is a bit grim, though I get in without paying anything as the "heiress's guest" – Emlyn Williams.

Last night, Reg and I get to the "Lamb" and syphon petrol out of Steve's jeep and then go to the "Swan" in Newport, arriving home to bed at 2.30 – damn tired myself.

I am reading W. Churchill's Early Life and trying to enlarge my education.

Nine weeks at 41 O.T.U., one week's leave, one week at Larkhill, more leave and then to a G.H.U. in T.A.F.

It will be three months before I get to a squadron – and then the East again.

September 7th 1944

I GO AND SAY FAREWELL TO THE KING-HAYS, and next day drive to Hawarden with Reg Cooper. Celia Spink, thank God, is posted (away). We get ourselves all in a gang for huts and flights. Reg and I go to Chester the first night by car, under the tutelage of George Bainbridge, who is still here, having been suspended, and we go round all the pubs except Barlow's, which is shut. Then he leaves us at Quaintways about 10pm and we enter a dance there. I dance with some dame called Jill and later we part our ways, she with her sister home and I to rendezvous with Reg at the car.

Next day I bicycle in with Denys Collier to "Barlow's" where we meet Jill and her sister Sheila. We wander round the drinking dens and eventually we see them home, this Jill dame getting distinctly 'warm' at my side. I spend no little time kissing her goodnight and arrange a rendezvous at the Castle the next night, where I park my bicycle with the sentry. We go to the "Grosvenor" and consume 3 1/2 pints and then walk home, 'warmer' than ever. I cycle home and get to bed, having arranged to go down Saturday – though to what I know not.

Henry Larsen was here, home on attachment to get himself modernised, and is now over in France. He is claiming 22 months Ops, and says he is going to get Tom Pierce's job as W/C in Delhi. Just wait until I see him!! The beer is better up here than at Ternhill, and we are to fly Spits instead of Mustangs.

My lovely Jill – oh dear! I wonder...

September 10th 1944

I GET FLYING AGAIN AT POULTON. I do the pinpointing exercise in 15 and 20 minutes, much to everyone's amazement, but fail to find Welshpool on a dual cross-country in a Harvard, and will be allowed another try tomorrow. If I fail again, then off the course I go, damn it, and there's nothing left.

I go and meet Jill again last night and stop on the way home for a bit of kissing – she has even let her hair down in my honour – but find she is leading me up the garden path and then shutting the gate. She is 23 and married five years. I say I won't meet her again, but then arrange to 'close my account' tomorrow, foolish perhaps, as she may not turn up, and it's damn cold cycling home these nights. It seems to hurt more than I expected, as she really is a nice (no – charming may be the word) girl. So now I am no better off than when I arrived a week ago. However "better to have loved and lost than never to have loved at all."

I play some squash with David Crook and read his book "Spitfire Pilot".

September 17th 1944

HAWARDEN

I TAKE JILL TO THE GROSVENOR and "pay off ship"[1]. She is the wife of some Canadian W/C and refuses to tell me her surname. A pity. Next day I go into Barlow's with Denys Collier, but nothing doing.

Last night Reg, David, Collier and self go to Poulton in Reg's car to an all ranks dance there, but too many vested interests at work there and everyone organised. We drink much beer in the Mess, and I dance around with the odd Waaf, ending up in the back slums of the Mess consuming coffee with Denys and his friend "Loo". We have to wait around for Reg who is seeing some Waaf home, and the S.D.O. gets damned annoyed as he wants to close the joint up and go to bed. We creep out at last, and I lead the way down a lane of white stones, the others having bad night vision, saying "follow me chaps", and crash heavily over a bicycle as these 'stones' are concrete stands. I see it the next morning with its (wheel) rim bent and it turns out to be Scottie's.

I have nothing in my hand right now, and am damned annoyed to see everyone else around me organised.

[1] *A colloquial naval term meaning to close one's account.*

September 18th 1944
HAWARDEN

THIS IS AWFUL. We have today off, so I duly go in last night to do our worst. Bob Martin and I go to a dance at the Castle, but it is damn grim and costs me 4/-. I get home about 1 am, having seen some very grim women home on the way back here. Grim and as cold as icicles.

We do no flying the last two days due to bad weather, I have a cold in the nose, and am feeling damned depressed. This never bothered me in India, as there was nothing to bother about, but here it's pretty bad, especially with Chester having the reputation that it has. However, to quote Pelmanism, "The day will dawn."

September 20th 1944
HAWARDEN

WHILST IN THE "MONK'S RETREAT" last Thursday, drinking Guinness through necessity, not through choice, I see two Waaf NCOs with two Yanks. As I leave, I say to one of them "Whose country is this?" (her Yank is out powdering his nose), and we get talking and she gives me her phone number, and we arrange to meet on Monday outside "Blossoms". I ring up over the weekend, and meet her in town last night.

She is one Joan Hoffman, a Sergeant in the Waaf police in Chester. We sit in "Bollands" and then the "Pied Bull" – she looks into the office to see if the D.A.P.M. is out of the way, then we repair to a dark corner of the "Rows" for a cigarette and a natter. She gets playful, so I kiss her good and hearty, and return her to her patrol at about 10.45.

A wire from Ma that she is coming on Wednesday if I can get accommodation, so that will cramp my style.

I go to Elsie Dobbie that was – now Mrs McCoy – for supper tonight. An A.M.O. (Air Ministry Order) advising regular army officers to return to the army if they want to keep their commissions after the War, so it looks as though I may fall between two stools – no permanent commission in the RAF and not taken back into the Indian Army.

September 23rd 1944

HAWARDEN

I GO INTO TOWN AGAIN LAST NIGHT, and take Sergeant Joan out to a few pubs. We are thrown out somewhere at 10pm and she takes me to some dark corner of Chester under a tree and we sit on a raincoat and she kisses me – or I suppose I initiate it.

Then a policeman turns us out at 10.40pm or so, and we go and sit on some dark steps and carry on. This is too much for me, and I try baseball, but she won't play. Eventually, all my own work and no help from her, I score a home base, and cycle home getting to bed at 00.10. I was to take a friend and meet her friend tonight but no one would come, so I ring up and leave a message cancelling it.

Today we go and see tanks and guns at Rhyll, damn boring. No flying due to "clamp"[1] and if it keeps up it means no 48 *(hours leave)* this weekend – though what matter, as where the hell have I to go?

[1] *RAF slang for dank weather - wet with low clouds, sometimes fog.*

Barbara Paul

September 25th 1944

HAWARDEN

AT EL DOBBIE'S (Elsie Dobbie's) there is quite a nice looking girl, one Barbara Paul, and I ring up Andy later and find out where she lives and take her out to "Quaintways" dancing on Saturday night.

Despite a third of a bottle of Canadian Club I don't do very well, and the vibrations seem a bit out of tune. I spend the night on a camp bed at the McCoy's, and having the weekend of in between phases of the course, have lunch and tea at Paul's, which is just next door to the McCoy's. In between, Barbara and I walk to the zoo and back, and the air gets a little more clear.

I have a gloomy supper or two with Ma in her digs, and today I go and buy pyjamas and visit the Cathedral with her.

Henry Larsen is back here from France for a week before returning to India. He did an Op or two with Burt in 268 Squadron. I do a low level cross-country to Great Malvern and back, and some cloud flying, without upsetting myself – so am improving.

September 26th 1944

Hawarden

I go into town and take Barbara to "Quaintways". We get some beer in from the pub across the road, having had dinner first at her house. I spend the night there, and B. gets quite affectionate, curled up in a chair with me. In the morning, I take her to her office, and then meet Ma at the Grosvenor – she tries on a hat in a shop, and I get hysterics for some reason or other, to the amusement of the (shop) madams.

I get back to Hawarden for lunch and have now moved over to Poulton for phase two. It seems to me that I have fallen in love, for the first time to the best of my knowledge, and am due for an awful shock and much pain when I leave her with my proposals unrequited, or when something occurs that breaks up my whole house of cards.

"Better to have loved and lost than never to have loved at all."

In the near future I will be able to comment on the truth of this question – until then "roll on Friday", and I must remember to keep my mind on business when I am flying!

October 2nd 1944

I SEE QUITE A LOT OF B. and tell her my views on Saturday night after a dance at "Quaintways". I am told that I am only infatuated because I have not met many women, and on maturer thought maybe this is true. I spend Saturday night and return Sunday morning for a bath.

In the afternoon we go for a walk in the grounds of Eaton Hall. The brother Michael and his wife Patricia arrive to stay.

I do a lot of flying, and get annoyed at Bagley (an Old Harrovian), the G3 air liaison officer. Do some TAC/Rs and photography, and am lacking exercise.

October 6th 1944

I SEE MUCH MORE OF YOUNG BARBARA (24), and am glad to say I don't think I am in love, after all, and so hope I shall not make a fool of myself in any way before it's all over. At present I go in a few times a week, cinema or dancing or just to dinner, and get excellent food and beer in a most comfortable house, and a charming girl to play with (and that's about all.)

Harris and I go to the Isle of Man at zero feet and fail to find it, ending up over Holyhead on the homeward leg.

I have the afternoon off as well as tomorrow, but am Orderly Officer, of all things. I go for a walk in the fields behind, endeavouring to identify what birdlife there is, which is not much.

October 11th 1944

I HEAR FROM BILL (ROBINSON), back home again. Reg and I go and have a few drinks at the Trevor Arms, very nice, nearby. No flying for some days due to bad visibility and fog. I go in and take B. shopping yesterday afternoon, and then we go in the car into Wales and have tea at the Queen Hotel, whilst her father goes on for a consultation. Damn cold on the way home, and Mrs Paul produces whisky macs, and I swallow three and then take B. to dinner at the Grosvenor. We get a bit "warm", what with fun and games under the rug in the back of the car, and one thing and another, and I don't want to cycle home at all.

£1 less pay this month for some reason – must be more income tax.

October 12th 1944

HAWARDEN

I AM NOW MORE OR LESS ON THE SPOT. Having found that there is nothing doing with Barbara, I can't very well give up going there and start off from scratch again in Chester. It would be nice to organise something out here, but as we shall be leaving shortly, that seems improbable, so in the expressive words of the RAF, "I have had it".

October 13th 1944

HAWARDEN

I GO NIGHT FLYING IN A HURRY. The last two landings are OK after I have dived into the ground at 120 on the first. Thank God there is is a starlit sky, no cloud, searchlights and flares and Chester all lit up!

A fearful night of wind and rain, and Norman, David and I pile into Reg's car for a "night out". We go to "Barlow's" and do the rounds and back again, and eventually collect two A.T.S. dames, Jean and Milly, and return to camp where there is an all ranks dance. Someone has eaten our dinner and we get most annoyed. However, Reg and Norman take them home, so that's that. Barbara has had a wisdom tooth removed, and I haven't been in for four days.

October 19th 1944

HAWARDEN

DAVID CROOK AND I GO OUT DRINKING with Reg at the Trevor Arms and meet some half Italian ATS Sergeant whom Reg likes, plus her fat friend, and we all have to go to a shocking troops dance in a gymnasium with nothing to drink there. I telephone Bill Robinson, but he is off to Salisbury, and I cannot get over to see him.

Sunday I go to London, and spend the night with the Farlows, Peggy being at home. Next morning to the India Office where I see several Civil Servants of various ages, and eventually Colonel Erskine, Deputy Military Secretary. I am advised to return to Army duty – as "out of sight, out of mind" – and I may lose my commission after the war.

I then try on a new uniform at Flights, and return to Chester, spending the night at the Pauls, as the train was too late for the buses.

I see W/C Plumtree yesterday[1] and he reckons I shall not get a permanent commission in the RAF as my flying is bad, or rather, not 'above average'. I already hold a regular commission in the Indian Army, and my application was a bit too late, and no one would recommend it – only forward it on. Also, as David Crook says, the medical will be raised, and I shall be chucked out on my eyesight.

So what to do? Return to India on a fearful trooper as a lieutenant again??

[1] *Chief Flying Instructor, 41 OTU, later Air Vice Marshal.*

October 22nd 1944
HAWARDEN

I GO WITH THE PAULS AND ELSIE DOBBIE to "Quaintways" for dinner and dance at a doctor's thrash. I spend the night at the Pauls, as I have the next day off, and Barbara and I get together on the sofa before going to bed (1.45am) and I sort of get busy, the result being another "Papist trick".

Next day I buy her a pair of wings[1] (17/6) and we go for a walk in Eaton Park after lunch, and there comes about a bit of fiddle-de-de under a tree out of the rain.

That evening we go to a sherry party given by one Dr Wigley, but it turns out to be Pimms and caviar on toast. Everyone gets a bit tight, and I am dragged away by Barbara after the rest of her family have left. I just manage to recover in time for dinner.

I do a lot of washing today, which is drying now I hope before the fire, after a game of football against the other course.

[1] *A sweetheart badge.*

October 29th 1944
HAWARDEN

WE PROGRESS ON THE AIR FIRING with cine-cameras, but much hazy weather, with visibility two-thirds of the long runway preventing our doing much flying, and we have to stay an extra week.

Colin at home with the Paul family.

I go in on Friday and stay the night with the Pauls, a similar scene taking place on the sofa as before. The next day, Barbara and I go shopping in the pouring rain, and after lunch to visit the birds in the museum, though I don't see much of them, what with one thing and another.

Last night we go to Quaintways, but I am not in very good form, presumably being worn out from the previous evening. I sleep there, and return on the Vickers factory workers bus at 7.30.

No flying today and more football, but I strain a muscle and cannot cope. I visit Andy McCoy as a patient and find my sinuses are OK. He gives me some nose drops.

John Aitkin, ex-28 Squadron[1], turns up here on the next course.

---

[1] *Colin's squadron in India and Burma - see volume 2.*

November 5th 1944

A WEEK OF NOT MUCH FLYING, and then the last three days of intense activity in air to ground, and air to air firing. I distinguish myself with several complete "ducks".

I go to the Pauls Monday, Wednesday, Thursday, Friday, Saturday for one thing and another, including taking David, Norman, Reg and Tiny round one evening. David and I take Barbara to "Barlows" and "Monks Retreat" on Friday to give her a taste of low life.

Yesterday I rang up a bit tired, and am invited for the night. After a few gins with Mrs Paul, dinner and a whisky or two, Barbara and I are left alone in the drawing room, with the usual results of which I am not particularly proud.

We finish here on Friday evening. I then have to get down to St Ives, organise my kit, and go to Larkhill on Wednesday. I send most of it off in advance, expecting to go down in Reg's car, but he is now going to P.R.U. with David and Tiny, so I have to set off Saturday afternoon and it will be pretty grim.

My new uniform arrives from "Flights", a bit tight and nearly a good fit, though it seems I am a bit optimistic getting it. I shall be dead, or out of the RAF, before I have much time to wear it.

November 14th 1944

ST IVES

I GO AND SPEND THE NIGHT with the Pauls, with the usual results, and say goodbye all round the breakfast table, and get the bus home. Barbara sees me to the door. Then after clearance, down to town on the 2.30 train, after a drink in the Mess with the Group Captain and "Jumbo" Mazunder[1], who had suddenly appeared.

In the train to London are Mihalski, Plewcynzynski, Shirey and me, and one or two others, and we play pontoon, myself retiring before it got too tough. I spend the night at Nuffield House, and it's boiling hot at night, and I wake up to a couple of loud bangs about 1am.

Next day down to St Ives, and have bed and breakfast in Curnows, and other meals out or in the flat with Ma. I reorganise the baggage, and have a good kit bag of Daddy's. I am not too well, some common fever apparent in one's first winter in England, says Ma, so that's that.

Some beer in the "Sloop" and I see Vivian, but no more joy than before. After Larkhill I have to come back and wait for a posting, which will be pretty bloody, as I don't like this joint. I am fast getting a cold, despite much gargling.

[1] Wing commander Karun Krishna 'Jumbo' Majumdar, DFC, former c/o of 1 Squadron Indian Air Force - Colin commanded 2 Squadron - who he had known from Burma. See Volume 2. Majumdar was the most highly decorated Indian pilot of WW2.

November 22nd 1944

BOSSINGTON HOUSE

I HAVE A DRINK WITH VIV and her new girlfriend in the "Sloop" just before closing time, and then we make for the latter's home, but they become more interested in a stray dog found on the way than me, so I leave them for Curnows and bed.

After much packing I have a few, quite a few, drinks in the "Sloop" on Tuesday, all Ma's Lelant crowd come over, and then on with the Gibsons to the "Queens" for more gin. I get through Ma's supper and stagger home, losing the way in the dark.

Next day off to Andover and meet the other boys at the station. I have a slight sore throat. Thursday we go to Larkhill School of Artillery for lectures and lunch in a huge Mess there. I see George

Bainbridge as a gunner again, having been thrown out by the RAF. The coldest day ever, and my throat is so bad on return that I see the M.O. He finds I have a temperature, and packs me into the station sick quarters. I share a room with a Canadian gunner with quinsy or some such throat trouble, and fortunately I am not well enough to eat the food, which is airmen's, and at their times too.

After a couple of days I am passed on to Bossington House, near Roughton. A lovely country house taken over for the invasion, but short of patients, as the German air force did not turn up. Good food, attention also, but nothing much to read. My temperature is now down, throat almost gone, and I expect to get up after lunch today.

But – I have missed the artillery reconnaissance course, and next one is not for another two or three weeks. In the meantime presumably I go back to Hawarden, or to St Ives on sick leave, both of which will be horrid.

I have a huge kit bag of Daddy's but it tears in the ambulance and appears to be rotten, as well it may be after 20 years service. Also my useless camp bed.

November 29th 1944

Bossington House

This joint (Bossington House) belongs to Sir Richard Fairey[1] and the River Test flows past the bottom of the park. It also teems in pheasant.

I am due out today and have planned to go to town, and then to Deal to see Aunt Vivy, as I am not required until the next course on the 6th. I telephoned W/C Plumtree at Hawarden on this. But I spend 1/9 last night on telephone calls trying to get a bed at one of the London service clubs, without any success, nor could I contact Aunt Vivy, as they said she was not in the telephone book.

So it all looks a bit grim, as I want to go to town to take my uniform back to Flights, and also for other things which I shall most certainly not get, having no one as I do.

Typhoons scream overhead here, and pheasants and coots scream in the grounds, and I rampage in bed with my usual trouble[2]. I know what I should like in London, but it looks as though it may be difficult even to get there.

---

[1] Industrialist and famous aircraft manufacturer.
[2] He suffered from night sweats, possibly related to recurring malaria.

November 30th 1944

LONDON

I GET DELAYED IN ANDOVER whilst they run through me for a Board[1]. I pass the eyesight test OK, amazingly, and then dump some of my kit and get the first train to London. I try the Regent Palace, unsuccessfully, and eventually get a bed in the "Mandeville" – very dingy.

I go out in the evening to the "Windmill", which seems a pretty poor show[2], then for a drink (the first for ten days) at the Berkeley Buttery, and another at the Piccadilly Brasserie, where I meet two fairly pickled naval types, one Lt Ian Browne and Veronica McFadden, a Wren with a flat in the "Mount Royal" on Oxford Street. After some beer we go back to the "Mount Royal", as she has just been thrown out, and she manages to register again. Then we gatecrash the club underneath by getting odd yanks to sign us in, until it shuts at 10.30pm.

On to the "Coconut Grove", of which Ian is a member, and I ante up £2 towards a bottle of gin. Ian dances with Veronica, and I sit there gloomily with the gin, and then I have a turn. Then he retires to the gents and I go on dancing with Veronica, and he is seen no more, having taken his hat and left. This Wren cannot dance, being somewhat pixilated, and we repair to Lyons, off Shaftesbury Avenue, for some food at 3 am.

I walk her home by 4am and we go up to her flat, 729, on the 7th floor, where I set to work, but soon see that she has no idea what it is for, so I cut my losses and leave – getting to bed at 4.30am.

This morning I meet Bob Martin and some dame in the park, and arrange to have a drink in the Brasserie, and then I have lunch by myself in the Berkeley Buttery. I wire Aunt Viv and she says "delighted", and I hope she is, though little does she know that I have no ration cards! I cashed a cheque for £10 in Andover but not much left, though I have the remains of the bottle of gin to show for it.

It's 42 degrees and damn cold and my ear hurts, so I shall go out for a drink tonight and then retire to bed. Veronica rings up and leaves a message for me to ring her – but damned if I do!

[1] *Medical board.*
[2] *The semi-nude review show which was famous for having never closed throughout the Blitz and the war.*

December 3rd 1944
Deal

I GO OUT ON SUNDAY EVENING to a news theatre, and then look for a drink, but all the usual joints are shut. I eventually go to some pub off Regent Street where there are two RAF types, drink until 9pm, and retire to bed.

Monday I go to "Flights" and show him the uniform, then to Grindlays (Bank) and on down to Deal. A nice bed, and not too much food, and damn boring. I go out two nights in succession, looking for anything, having seen a few pilots in the streets of Deal in daylight, but despite visiting four pubs, not a soul do I see. There are some Wrens around and one was to be billeted here yesterday, but now she isn't coming, so I must resign myself to a week of "austerity".

The Aunt sees some fat girl she knows in Deal High Street and has invited her for a drink, but I think I prefer "austerity". Of course Hawarden may recall me before the 6th, in which case it will be OK. I feel better, though I can still feel my right ear and throat and do not sleep too well, having these damn sweats.

December 4th 1944

DEAL

I GET A WIRE FROM HAWARDEN to report on the 4th, so I ring up and find that I must go for a decompression test, however much I protest. So that's that, and I only hope I can fail it.

I go to tea with General Powell and two Waafs are produced. One goes home on duty, and I take the other to the "Cambridge Arms", and then back here for supper. One Josephine Dunningham, and she comes in again last night. We then repair to the "Drum" at about 10pm and meet all the Controllers, mostly from the local Ops room where Jo works.

I then see her home after a bit of necking in the road, and she seems excessively warm for her 20 years, but nothing else.

I go to the local reading room to read the Times yesterday and burn a huge hole in my uniform trousers on an electric fire. By the grace of God my new uniform had arrived by post half an hour earlier, so I am saved, but yesterday altogether a damned annoying day.

I see three 'Meteors' for the first time.[1]

[1] The Gloster Meteor was the first British jet fighter and the Allies' only jet aircraft to engage in combat operations during the Second World War.

December 7th 1944

I GO TO A DANCE AT THE LOCAL DRILL HALL which is pretty dead, though I dance with some dame, Jean Wallace, and her sister Renee. They then take me home for some food and cross examine me on India. They also turn out to be communists, and give me hell for half an hour.

Monday I come up to Hawarden and take the test on the Tuesday. Two hours at 37,000' and all I get is a slight pain in my right knee. Not enough to get out of it though. I go to dinner with the Pauls and am told I have lost weight – a good thing. Yesterday I walk to Chester in the morning, and meet Raynor and his girlfriend in Barlow's. I go in last night and drink beer from 7-10pm with a Canadian A.S.C. private – but no luck.

On looking back, I see my last home base was September 19th, damn near three months ago. As for Barbara, and her tricks, I have 'had' that, as it's no use. Everyone else seems to manage OK except me. I was a fool to drop Joan and pursue Barbara, but I had to follow my star I suppose – thinking that I was in love and all.

Damn cold up here, but I still cannot get what I want.

December 11th 1944

LONDON

I MANAGE TO FAIL MY DECOMPRESSION TEST, and so get five days leave before going to Andover on the 13th. I say farewell to the Pauls again, having tried unsuccessfully to get Barbara to come to town (London) with me.

I arrive on Friday and stay at Nuffield House. I join the 'Wings Club' and go round there for a drink, and meet an RCAF type, who promises to fix me up with a party on Saturday night with a

CWAC[1]. I then go to 'Shepheards' (Hotel), round the bars and to bed, after going with some tart up to her room and then managing to escape because I pretended not to be able to find the necessary £2.

Saturday I hang around "Wings" Club 6.15 to 7.30, but this RCAF aborts, so I go in a furious temper to the "Brass Arse"[2], where I meet one F/L Dudley Greenaway, and get talking to a couple of Wrens, but they have to go at 9 pm, and I seem to remember we all make a date for Monday night.

He then takes me to the "Rye and Dry" and then to the "Brevet Club". By this time I am a bit tight, and have some mistletoe in my breast pocket and give everyone the Croix de Guerre. I meet one Vera Barnes, disguised as a "Driver U.S.", and steal her away from her escort and take her home, to her flat in Bayswater Road. Another Canadian is there with her girl friend, and we all have some supper around 1 am. We then get busy, but with no success: she gets busy on me alright, but throws us out at 2.45 am before the worst has happened – thank God!

That morning I had lunch with R.B.T Morton, Major in 2 GR on leave from Italy in his club, the United Services. I recognise him in Nuffield House at breakfast. Sunday I go to the Overseas Club tea dance and collect one Agnes Hutchinson, quarter French, and in the French equivalent of the A.T.S. After it finishes I take her to "Shepheards", where we meet one Clarisse, a friend of hers, and the rest of the evening is carried on in English, Flemish and French. We then adjourn to the Archery pub off Lancaster Gate for sandwiches and beer after lunch.

I then take Agnes home across the park, but I might just as well lead a duck home. We all arrange to meet in the pub again today, and she gives me her phone number to ring her about taking her out this afternoon first. However, she seems a sexless dame, though God knows why, and only drinks spirits, so I am going to abort myself this time.

So I am now no nearer my goal than when I came here. Tonight I shall wander round the bars I suppose, and home to an early bed. I don't seem to have any luck at all since Joan. I shouldn't have concentrated so much on Barbara. I always say to myself that the day will dawn, but it never seems to do so!

¹ *Canadian Women's Army Corps.*
² *The Queen's Brasserie in Leicester Square.*

December 16th 1944

Larkhill

I wander out to Shepheard's on the Monday, and meet Greenaway again, and then to the Brevet Club and back to bed. I wake next morning with quite a hangover, which is dispelled when I have a few gins and a very excellent lunch with, and on, J.J. Saunders at the "Aperitif" in Jermyn Street.

That night I go to Shepherds for a drink, solo, and meet a marine, one Robin Graham, and some RAF penguins¹. I also grab one Marjorie Hicks, a V.A.D., and we all go on to the Brevet Club. I then take Marjorie home to the Strand Palace Hotel and set to work in her room, but am foiled as she declares she is cold, and I cut my losses at 12.30 and walk home to bed.

Wednesday I come down to Andover and meet Peter Mackenzie on Waterloo Station. We go over to Larkhill for a couple of days and see guns and do shoots from O.P.s. Today we start flying – but low cloud and rain and nothing until lunchtime.

Last night Loveless (RCAF) and I go to the local pub, and then to some village hall dance about four miles away, on our feet, but I don't get myself organised, though it seems to be there. Loveless gets a date and damn near a fight out of it.

¹ *Officers with no operational flying experience, from the fact that "Penguins don't have wings".*

December 19th 1944

I FLY AGAIN OVER STONEHENGE and do a few shoots on Larkhill ranges, quite successfully with 25lb-ers and 4.5 inch guns.

I go to the "Square Club" with a gang, and then to a local dance at the drill hall in Andover, where we discover a secret bar, run by and for the Home Guard. Later Pete, Gordon and I to to the "Bell" where I am taught to shoot craps, and we have a nasty journey back across the airfield in the mud and the dark. But nowhere do I get a date, though there seems to be possibilities if I was staying longer. My quest seems fruitless, and I shall have to amend my prayer to the new moon.

Exactly three months ago was Joan of Ross on Wye!

December 20th 1944

LARKHILL

BUD LOVELESS AND I TAKE TWO BATWOMEN, Betty and Pat respectively, out to Andover for beer, and then walk home to the Waaf dance, but no score on either side.

Scott, self, Raynor, Johnson, George and Robinson are posted to 83 G.S.U. at Lasham today, but their adjutant rings up and tells us to go on leave until the 29th, which doesn't suit me a bit, as I shall have to go down to St Ives, and would much rather get on with the job and cross over to Holland. After eight months in the UK I still haven't done what I wanted, and I am now about to leave again, though I am not going so very far away this time. On looking back, I suppose that I could have done better if I had been a bit bolder, and hadn't made that fatal change of policy in Chester. But that was a shot in the dark that damn near succeeded! There seems scope (slight) here in Andover if I was stationed here, but no one has had any luck in the week that we have been here.

However, as I say to myself, "the day will dawn" – I hope that I shall live to see it!

December 23rd 1944

St Ives

I ARRIVE IN ST IVES A BIT LATE OWING TO FOG, and share a room in Curnow's (Curnow's Café) with Allan, the gay commando.

Last night I am made to play bridge until 12.45 with the Sandons and am most annoyed. I make a scheme when I arrive, on the available information, but it has fallen through already.

Mrs Fraser over from Penzance for lunch, and afterwards I try and date up an American nurse I see in the "Kettle" but she has to go back to Plymouth tonight. So I seem to have "had it" before I have even begun.

Tonight, Saturday, I intend to drink some beer in the Sloop, then go to "Tregenna", spend 5/- on gin, and retire to bed in high dudgeon. Never will I come to St Ives again if I can help it, though it could be perfect if the cards fell right.

I get into my kit and get out a suit that I last wore at a garden party at Government House in Madras in 1939 or early 1940.

December 28th 1944

St Ives

ONE OR TWO PARTIES. Christmas dinner with the Langdale-Jones in the "High and Dry" Hotel, followed by a pontoon and whisky party in Bobby Brain's flat run by Vera Clayton. I cook the scores afterwards, and escape paying up about 6/- lost!

Then boxing night, Pat Rose takes Ma and me to dinner in Tregenna, and they discuss someone else's baby over my body for 20 minutes. Later Bill and Gertie and Felicity Findlay join us; and later still I get away and dance with whom I want to – a dark eyed

Spitfire XIV.

girl in a corner. She is one Gay Priestly from Ealing, down to stay with her brother-in-law and sister. We get on quite well, and I get her telephone number and go up yesterday evening for a drink at 6pm, before she goes back on the London train.

I go back tomorrow, but do not know whether to go to Basingstoke or Alton. Glorious weather, almost fit for sunbathing. I wish I met this Gay dame sooner – i.e. Sunday when she arrived.

January 3rd 1945

LASHAM

MY LAST DAY IN ST IVES I get a bit whistled before lunch in the Sloop, and meet Marnie Lowrey who's on a 48, a V.A.D. from Plymouth. Ma and I have dinner with the Lowrey's, and then Marnie and I go up to Tregenna and have a drink after hours on one of the residents. We walk back and down on the Portmeor beach and do much talking, and I believe we have much in common, but we part that night, having just become acquainted, presumably for

501

Ex-Indian Army Burt Mann, C.O. of 268 Squadron.

ever. A pity.

I reach Lasham – 83 G.S.U. – and am assigned a pitch in a Nissen hut. I manage to change my U/S camp bed. Much frost, all the pipes burst, and I have to wash in the Mess, rushing to be there before the others in the morning.

On New Year's eve Tom Raynor and I go to Basingstoke and drink beer in the Red Lion. We meet some dame, and then two more, and then one more and two Canadian pongos and a bottle of scotch and have a party in the pub, and later with food at a house shared by two of these dames. They are not much good, and Tom and I leave at 1am as we are not asked to stay, and get a taxi home. We still have one hour's walk, as we get lost, and I arrive back to find my camp bed broken, at 3am! It is mended for me the next day.

I then fly a Spit IX and in the afternoon (Jan 1st) take it to B79 airfield near Bergen-Op-Zoom, in Holland. F/L Ridley-Martin (Royal Corps of Signals) leads me over.

My first impression of the Continent, and Cape Gris-Nez, is the vast amount of holes, bomb and shell craters, in that area. Also the scattered farms with quiet work fields around, much smaller than in England, and many of them white – either through frost or chalky soil. We also pass Dunkirk, but no signs of battle visible. We land and leave our 'chutes and set off for Antwerp at high speed, and the town major gives us beds in the Century Hotel. I get a bath, as there are none at Lasham (the pipes being burst), and a good dinner with wine in the Excelsior, the officer's club next door. I see my first flying bomb, and we go out drinking later. We meet one Captain Webber, an A.L.O., whom I knew in Habbaniya as a F/L, and return to a most comfortable bed at 12, and a night hideous with the sounds of war.

Next day we collect our 'chutes from B79 and go to Antwerp airfield to try and get home. There is a clamp on (fog), so we organise beds again and go back to town, having heard a lot more flying bombs pass overhead in the fog. Then, last night out, we go again to the Latin Quarter, and there is a great flash – pause – then a ginormous explosion, and the odd bit of glass falls into the street as a V2 lands a mile away. We arrive at the "Robin Hood Inn" and are greeted by one Madeleine, who takes a few cognacs off us at 45 francs a time, whilst we drink 6 franc beers!

Back to bed, and today we go out to the airport and find a Lasham Anson about to return home. We embark, and make landfall over Deal of all places. Antwerp is dead, and damned expensive. The old German signs are still up on the flying fields,

503

and the whole set up reminds me of the Japs on Mingaladon (in Burma). No postings forecast for about one month, and I am allotted a week's leave on 14th January.

David Crook is killed in a prang at Dyce – some say his oxygen failed and he spun in.

Large notices in Antwerp saying P.A.C.[1] in the main streets, though not much to use them on. I went to Antwerp in my flying boots, my green sweater and a fleece jacket, and feel like the Yank pilots we used to see come in to the Grand Hotel in Calcutta, whilst one was immaculately drinking a chota peg. Roll on my posting. What to do with this leave? Go to London again?

[1] *Meaning unknown.*

January 17th 1945

Lasham

I GET IN ABOUT THREE HOURS in a Spit XIV and then set off to ferry one to 2 Squadron at B77[1]. I come down at B67 – Ursel near Ghent – due to bad visibility, and also because I am not sure which side of my track I am. It then starts snowing, there is more snow and fog, and I do not get off for some six days. I live with the local R+R party and am billeted on one Henrique Kaiser in a fairly modern Belgium farmhouse. He and his wife were 17 years in the States where he amassed enough dough to return home and retire. Under the Boche they had more food than under us. It was from Ursel that, on 11th December 1940, 54 C.R.42s[2] took off and only 9 came back from the Thames Estuary.

There is much snow and my flying boots leak. I sleep in pyjamas, a sweater and my socks, and manage to keep warm. I also pick up trench mouth and have to go to a field dental centre in Ghent for treatment. The lads take me to Knesselare near Ursel where there are supposed to be lashings of blondes, but no luck. I go to a few drinking dens in Ursel, but nothing doing.

Saturday 13th I manage to get off, and fly up to B77 where I stay the night, getting a camp bed in Burt Mann's room. He is C.O. 268 Squadron, and about to leave. There is a party in the Mess, and I get pretty full, and retire to bed, but get no sleep through my tooth. I see S/L Maitland, C.O. 2 Squadron, and try and fix myself a posting.

Next day back to Lasham in an Anson to find I am posted to 2 Squadron, and so miss the week's leave I was due, which is annoying, as I had ideas, including meeting Marnie Lowrey.

Today I get a whiff of gas and the doc, one F/L Fairfax, whips out my wisdom tooth – I then get myself cleared, and hope to go tomorrow.

[1] *Gilze-Rijen in the Netherlands.*
[2] *Italian bi-plane fighter aircraft.*

14

January - June 1945

2 Squadron

Holland / Germany

January 23rd 1945

I FLY OUT IN AN ANSON with Blain, Malcolmson, Raynor and George to 2 Squadron, and arrive to find Burt Mann still there. There is a continual clamp of snow and fog on, and I get as far as taxiing to the runway today but no further, to do an air test. On arrival we are greeted by a good view of a V1 at about 1500', and more all through that day. I also see a couple of V2 trails in the sky. We live in a Luftwaffe Mess which is fairly comfortable, and there are lashings of booze – too much in fact, and I seem to be up to my neck in it every evening with Burt.

I share a pigsty with F/L Chin and Selkirk of 2 Squadron, and there is a hot shower in the billets. My washing is well done by a Dutchman for a bar of soap and 20 cigarettes. There is much snow, and I go out and let off my revolver, but without much success. Burt and I go and visit 135 Wing Mess at the invitation of one S/L Patterson, O.C. of a New Zealand Spitfire squadron, and meet Group Captain Walker. I get rather intoxicated on champagne and stout, but feel better than Burt the next morning.

Today we are visited by Commander Brabner, Under-secretary of State for Air, but he does not seem particularly interested in us. There is nowhere to go when off-duty, and nothing much to read in the Mess. Some people even play chess.

January 24th 1945

I FLY AGAIN, A SORT OF TEST, with F/L Clifton-Mogg, but he goes round and round in circles and I cannot really cope. Then an air test, and today I go out with F/L Bob Mackelwain over Area 1 – Dordrecht, Rotterdam and the Hook of Holland area, and I seem to cope this time. Weather and clouds are a bit tricky, and I

The 2 Squadron Ops room at Gilze-Rijen - a requisitioned railway truck.

see some 20 and 40mm flak directed at Bob when he dives down from 6000 ft to 2000 ft to take some photographs.

No mail yet, and it's difficult to get hold of a decent paper, though three or four days late. V1s go over here day and night, if the icing conditions are not too bad, and Bob shot one down two days ago in enemy territory.

There is a very vicious bar here, and I am slightly flushed with wine writing this – *accounts for my handwriting!!

January 26th 1945

Gilze-Rijen

I DON'T GET UP AGAIN DUE TO THE WEATHER – fog and snow. V1s rush overhead all day today and yesterday, and we hear the guns opening up on them in the I.A. zone.

Yesterday afternoon, led by the Group Captain, we man the A/A Bren guns outside the Ops room and shoot at the blue Met balloons, with no small success. Today we hang around until lunchtime, and then it begins to snow. The 1st Canadian Army have a small battle on – "Operation Elephant" – to clear an island north of the Maas, and the guns can be heard all day, but we cannot help them. My camp bed breaks, though fortunately I bring a spare set of legs from Lasham. No papers, and all I can get hold of to read is Conrad.

February 8th 1945
GILZE-RIJEN

MORE SNOW. Yesterday I manage to get up as No. 2 to S/L Maitland, and see the gliders at Arnhem. Am pursued by some 88mm flak from Zutphen and arrive back with just five gallons, and try and land on the wrong runway. I eventually taxi back with 2.5 in the tanks.

V1s rush overhead day and night and one lands in the field the other morning, though without any damage. I hear from Marnie, and Bill, now at Staff College. There is English beer and stout in the bar, and Belgium beer which is rubbish. We get a ration of 20 tots of spirits a month, but every hour or so the barman produces a bottle "off ration". No eggs, but nine bars of chocolate and five oranges a week. I give my laundry and a bar of soap to a Dutchman and it costs 20 cigarettes.

Burt Mann retires to hospital with appendicitis and I cannot get a lift over to see him. My camp bed collapses and I spend one night on the floor, but now have it repaired again – though for how long?

February 10th 1945
GILZE-RIJEN

I GO OUT THREE MORE TIMES, one abortive due to weather, and another at Zutphen where I get another, more accurate, dose of 88mm flak. One bursts in front and above to the left.

Today as No. 2 to Selkirk who takes some obliques (photographs) – many aircraft in the sky and my goggles keep misting up, much to my discomfort. I burst a tyre taxi-ing out once, which delays our dawn sortie. Air Marshal Tedder comes round today, but seems more interested in the works than in the personnel.

I get Alec Johnston, S/L Ops 123 Wing, across last night, and he gets very full of whisky and talkative about himself and the Allied Control Commission. We later adjourn to his Mess, there being no more visitors' whisky in 35 Wing Mess, but I retire after a couple of gins. There is a Sabre test pilot with a George Cross there.

I go out egg hunting, getting two and then two and a half dozen in three days, much to the amazement of my colleagues. A continuous procession of flying bombs, but I have never seen one when I have been airborne.

February 11th 1945

GILZE-RIJEN

THE 1ST CANADIAN ARMY ADVANCES on the 8th into the Reichwald forest. We put up 30 sorties with 12 a/c and I do two myself. Continuous Arty/R (Artillery Reconnaissance) cover, which fails due to low cloud and a few Tac/R (Tactical Reconnaissance). I go out with Peter Crane, and he insists in flying round above the guns at 1000' above Nijmegen, irrespective of the air being full of shells. Later I do a Tac/R with him.

We lose Malcolmson, who came over with me, killed force landing on South Beveland, and Frank Normoyle, an Ops officer who just vanishes. I am damned tired, having missed lunch and tea, bar one and a half spam sandwiches, and am unable to stand up in the bar until after I have had about five large whiskies, when my strength flows again.

Yesterday I go on Tac/R as No.1 but have to return through R/T trouble, at which I am greatly pleased, as the weather stinks. Champagne in the Mess, but I can never grab a bottle. It's now raining, and I hope I shall be able to get in some reading.

February 13th 1945

Gilze-Rijen

I go up with Woodbridge and he works with a contact commander of 51st Division, "Longbow Mike". They ask him to look at various bridges on the Maas, and he dives down whilst I stay up at 8000' or so. I go too low once, and get mixed up in some light flak being shot at him.

The sky above this town, Gennap, becomes full of tracer, and then it bursts into grey puffs, not near me thank God. I go out again as No.1 yesterday, but low cloud at 1000' and so I investigate the flooding between the Waal and the Rhine, west of Nijmegen. Today more drizzle, and we are stood down.

I drink too much champagne last night, though without any evil effects. I see two flying bombs whilst on the circuit, there's just a glow if you are dead behind, but can do nothing about it.

I go to a party given by 123 Wing at the invitation of Alec Johnston, but am a bit bored, though I eat a few oysters, some grapes and an apple, and meet the famous W/C Alan Deere, and also one S/L Deakin-Elliott.

I have prepared five rules in case I am captured:

1. Answer all questions with "I'm sorry, sir, but I cannot answer that question."

2. Don't look the interrogator in the eye.

3. Try not to listen to what he is saying.

4. When put in solitary confinement, go in with something to think about – the future of civil aviation or something.

5. Beware of the first contact, probably a stool pigeon, and take stock twice a day on what subjects have been discussed the previous half day.

I have decided not to fly with a revolver, and will hope for the best without it, provided I reach the ground again alive.

Bob Macelwain shoots down a 109 (ME109), and Jeffries damages its No.2, on the deck in Area 111.

February 22nd 1945
Gilze-Rijen

Three days of fog, which lifts yesterday afternoon, whilst I am out with George Thornton getting some four dozen eggs. Steve got a bar to his DFC for a photo run down the Rhine by Emmerich the other day, and does the honours in champagne. I manage to do a No.1 successfully in area 4, but my engine oils up over Arnhem on the way home, and I am sweating all the way down to the soles of my feet, as it's damn rough and I see nowhere for a decent forced landing.

I also play rugger for 35 Wing against 123, and am pleased to be fitter than most on the field. Last night I go with a gang to Tilburg, where we drink some gin and beer in the officers club, and then go to a local dance, but not much good, and the scarcity of soap in Holland is very apparent.

February 24th 1945
Gilze-Rijen

I play rugger again yesterday during a 'clamp'. Today I go round area 2 as No.1 at 7.30am, a beautiful dawn, with V1s flaming across the sky as we go out to be briefed. I see not much, as there is a ground mist, through which stick the spires of Utrecht. Later I do a shoot with a 155mm gun onto a hostile artillery position, but when I dive down, I see no guns. One round lands on the Emmerich-Arnhem railway line.

A lot of flying, and as I mostly seem to be No.2. I look up the air force list and find I am a bit senior, but cannot break the trades union as far as I can see. Bob Mackeson takes me out one day and we get lost, looking for 202s near the Reichwald forest, and I get back with 10 gallons, very shaken, and touch down as the flare path is being lit.

Scotty and Johnson and Mumsford arrive from GSO to join 268 Squadron.

February 28th 1945

LONDON

I SET OFF WITH A BOTTLE OF CHAMPAGNE and six eggs on the Dakota on the 26th, and am now in town on seven days leave. I stay at the Wings Club, where I meet S/L Pallot, ex 268, on his way to India.

First night I try Gay Priestley, but nought doing, so I take Gigs out to the Berkeley Buttery and the Brevet Club[1], but she is not in very good form, and I leave her home at about 11pm and rush off in a sort of fit to spend £3 somewhere off Curzon Street. I don't even enjoy it much, but feel I have to, so that's that and pray God no consequences.

Yesterday I have a drink with Baffy Dugdale and then to Gig's for a party and on to Choy's Chinese restaurant in Soho. Met there is one Monica Peck, who might have stepped out of "Esquire", whom I see home to Chelsea, all the way on foot, and am enchanted – (divorced twice.) I arrange to give her lunch tomorrow, and get no sleep and all the usual over her.

Today I have to meet Gay Priestley in Piccadilly Underground at 1600hrs with a view to going to a tea dance. I try to get Monica

514

this morning, but she has a date, or I would have switched, and am now feeling a bit depressed over her, and have to go off and make hay with this Gay dame in about one hour.

I wire Marnie and Bill, but no replies as yet. I also get 20 clothing coupons, and see a good RAF dentist about my mouth and am a bit shaken about his treatment. Of course this Monica dame will be booked up all the week, or I shall have her and Marnie on my hands or something – and I get miserable.

[1] *It was at 11 Chesterfield Street in Mayfair.*

March 5th 1945

LONDON

THIS GAY DAME (Gaye Priestley) is pretty grim, and I have to cope with a tea dance in the Piccadilly hotel. Later, thank God, she suggests Shepheards, and then we go to the Brevet Club and I give her a couple of gins and have quite a good time myself talking to other people. I pack her off out of my life on the tube about 10.50pm, and she is annoyed I don't kiss her.

Next (plus one) night I go with Baffy Dugdale[1] to Lady Sinclair's flat after a drink at the Allies Club, and am very pleased to find myself talking to Mr Churchill's brother Jack. Bernard Fergusson is also there, and I had had a drink, quite a few gins in fact, with him the previous night in the Senior Service Club, after giving Monica lunch in the Brevet Club. I leave about 7.30pm, and rush off to meet Monica at the Wings Club.

We go to Mirabel in Curzon Street, but the floor is so crowded it is difficult to dance, and there is so much noise you cannot talk. Next day, Friday, I dash down to Harrow, and it seems much the same, though I feel like capping all the old beaks. J.W. Thompson tells me Peter Petit is home, so I go to call, meet his mother, and we go up to join him and his peculiar wife and June Petit at Scotts, later having lunch in the Berkeley.

I seem to have got my days muddled up. Saturday I meet Marnie and Bill who come up for the night – I collect Gigs, and we dine at the Brevet Club, and fool about upstairs, later going on to the "Nuthatch" Club in Regent Street, a low joint full of Yanks and French SAS. A French Canadian sailor sings most magnificently, and I get to bed at 3am.

Sunday I take Bill and Marnie to lunch at the Brevet, and then we walk around the park and feed the ducks. I lose my wallet somewhere, and identity card. I then take a bottle of champagne to Monica's flat in Chelsea, and she cooks up steak and eggs and gives me some brandy. We talk and drink and smoke and she sits on my lap and I almost make some proposal which would put an end to it for ever, but don't. She gives me a red silk scarf to fly in – or rather I ask for one and get it – I am pretty warm and so seems she, but I don't know how to go about it, as some others I know would. She is like a Varga girl from 'Esquire', and more lovely than anyone I can recall to mind that I know – with a VOICE – oh my God!

Gigs says she is her second cousin and older than her (Gigs 30+) and has just had her second divorce. I am going to see her tonight, but we have nothing to drink, and I shall undoubtedly make a fool of myself and get nowhere – how it will pain me tomorrow, going back to the War.

I get some sheets today for 22/- and no coupons, and my battledress smartened up a bit.

[1] *Blanche 'Baffy' Dugdale, a niece of Arthur Balfour and friend of Colin's mother. She worked for Naval Intelligence and was a well-known champion of Zionism.*

March 8th 1945

Gilze-Rijen

WHAT A NIGHT – We have supper and a drop of scotch in Monica's flat, and eventually I get talking and out it all comes! Surprise! The

Pilot humour.

most sympathetic and understanding woman I ever met, despite her claim to be 34. I leave at 1.30am after a passionate two hours or so, with ideas of returning on my next leave, if there ever will be one, and with Monica's wholehearted co-operation. I could write a screed on her, but as I hope she will take the opportunity of reading it, I won't.

I leave by Dakota the next day from Northolt, after a final telephone call, though doubts are expressed that I shall get on the aircraft due to the loss of my wallet plus identity card, 700 Belgium francs, some Guilden and 30/-. Not to speak of clothing coupons.

I find the Wing about to move further up, but no other change, except that Woodbridge had to bail out at 6000' above cloud, and only just came down inside our lines. Much mail and papers, and my bed is broken by these damn drunks.

Of course after this, something will happen to stop me going back on leave – it's bound to. And to a kiss like a.... I can't describe it.

March 9th 1945

MILL, HOLLAND

WE MOVE TO MILL – a pressed steel plate strip with a perpetual crosswind - and I take up residence with the A.L.O.s in the hope of sneaking a cup of their hot water to shave in the morning. Today I do a photo trip up by Leiden, and don't like it as I cannot get higher than 4000 ft. The engine is damn rough on the way home too.

There is a farm within 30 feet of where my washing is done, and I hope to get hot water there too. Tomorrow is my first effort at the dreaded Area 7 down by the Ruhr, and I am not looking forward to it. What with one thing and another, it seems too much to expect that I can get through to my next leave and go and see Monica again! God – what a thought. However, there is nothing I can do about it, and I hope I can keep my nerve.

Driving through the ruins of Goch.

March 13th 1945

MILL

I COPE WITH AREA 7 AS IT'S RAINING, and low cloud, and no one shoots at me. I see the Ruhr steaming in the distance. I then do a contact recce with the 11th Armoured Division, but do not see anything for them, except our tanks and S.P.s in action on the front, as it then is. The C.O. and two others are later attacked in the same area by 109s.

Today I go out Arnhem way but the haze is so bad I get lost several times and have great difficulty.

Reg Cooper arrives here to join 4 Squadron, and yesterday he, I, Reggie Hodge, Moss, Jimmy Chun and Jeff take a "cummer" after lunch and go out to loot Germany. We cross the Gennap bridge (over the Meuse) and go via Goch and Weeze to Kevalear.

Here we enter one or two houses and collect some chairs and crockery. I have a chair and some glasses, others have cut glass and an odd carpet or two. Goch in ruins, and most houses everywhere are holed. Mines abound on the roadside, a few dead tanks on both

519

sides, dead cattle, and two or three graves are passed. Any Germans left have to pin a piece of paper on their front door, with name, date of birth etc of the inmates.

I go to a local farmhouse and organise hot water for my camp bath, which I take in a clean (or was the last time) stall in a sort of pigsty-cum-manger, in company with some pigs and one horse. I give the women seven cigarettes, and one wants more. I sleep in the ALOs Nissen (hut) and take a cupful of hot water for shaving in the morning, and they always come to bed early and sober, so I am well in. They expect to expand, and want to kick me out.

March 18th 1945

MILL

YESTERDAY I DO A JOB OF WORK. The Army want forward facing obliques along the roads north of Emmerich for their next attack, and I take some. Chris Blundell-Hill[1] takes the first lot at 1000 feet, and I am briefed for two runs later on, the first over a 12 gun flak position.

I go out with Varley and dive down on the first stretch of road from 6000 ft. I level out at 420 mph and find I am at 500 ft, so just keep her there, follow the road round a forest, until I see a church spire, which comes at the end of my run, then pull up and jink through the gate and into cloud. I forget to turn the camera off and nearly ruin everything. I then look around for my second stretch, but the area is 9/10 cloud at 5000 ft and I stooge about for too long until I suddenly see it through a gap, and down I go. I skid around bends and then see Wehl, the end of my run, and pull up and around, but no friendly cloud. On a starboard bank I see two gun pits – flashes and rings of smoke – and tracer comes up past me from both sides. I twist and skid and turn and climb, and feel a little more comfortable at 4500', but still no cloud. Eventually I get clear and go home.

Looting in Kevalear.

2 Squadron, Colin seated to the right of the C.O., Dick Mitchell.

2 Squadron dispersed at Mill, 'a pressed steel plate strip with a perpetual crosswind.

Today I see the pictures – perfect and congratulations from all sides. There is one car, 16 HDT (heavy duty trucks), one flak gun, and an empty flak position. One nun getting off her bicycle, two men running away from the horse and cart they are leading, and many other pedestrians. Some cool and collected, others with guilty consciences.

Today Colin Maitland, the C.O., goes out for a further portion of the job and gets shot down. So it looks as if I shall have to do some more – and probably follow him too – as they are now well shaken up in that area and on the qui vive.

[1] He was to be shot down and killed two weeks later on April 1st.

March 24th 1945

MILL

THE FORWARD FACING JOBS are now postponed and cancelled, thank God.

One of 2 Squadron's Spitfires, clearly showing the pressed steel airstrip.

Hamish Selkirk finishes his tour, and there is the usual party, with 'B Flight' drunks very prominent. I get attacked, and have my tie chewed off twice, and bruise a rib on a chair during a fall. It puts me off flying for two days. During one melee I grab Johnny Young by the seat of his pants and he jumps around screaming like a cat on hot springs. Later he tells me that I have a grip on his piles!

I go down to Oysterwick and visit Griffiths, Ma's Canadian friend of Tregunna days, and he gives me a meal and quite some hooch. He is an Adjutant in the 4th Canadian Armoured Division. I get two letters from Monica, with some very nice bits in them! I am flight commander pro-tem, as Alan Clifton-Mogg is acting C.O., and I am enjoying myself with the first job of work for over 12 months! Today the Allies attack across the Rhine.[1]

Nick Bowen and I do an anti-flak patrol between Wesel and Bocholt to try and spot the gun flashes and get the "cab-rank" Typhoons on to them. There are masses of 88mm and 40mm about, but nary a flash do I see, and we reckon they are using flashless ammunition. We are expecting to see paratroops about, and at 10h I see them just as Mick calls up "Aldershot Tattoo", our agreed call.

Dakota's dropping the British 6th Airbourne Division as part of Operation Varsity, March 24th 1945.

Operation Varsity

Operation Varsity was an airborne drop behind German lines on the east bank of the Rhine that was launched on 24th March 1945 as part of Operation Plunder, an assault by 21st Army Group under Montgomery across the Rhine at Wesel on the night of 23rd March. Involving more than 16,000 paratroopers and several thousand aircraft, Varsity was the largest airborne operation ever undertaken.

The force was made up of two divisions - the US 17th Airborne Division and the British 6th Airborne Division. Learning from the mistakes of Operation Market Garden the previous autumn, when British paratroops had been dropped at Arnhem too far ahead of the advancing ground forces, Operation Varsity was only launched after the 21st Army Group had successfully secured bridgeheads on the east bank the night before.

The operation was largely successful, all the objectives being captured within a few hours, ensuring that the bridgeheads achieved by Operation Plunder could break out. By the afternoon of the 24th the ground and airborne forces were able to link up, forcing the Germans to retreat to the north. Within three days, the Allied forces had built twelve temporary bridges over the river, suitable for heavy armour, and 14 divisions had crossed the east bank, and within a week, they had taken 30,000 prisoners of war north of the Ruhr. The final defensive line of the German Reich had been breached.

However, it came at relatively high cost, with the 6th Airborne Divsion suffering 20% casualties.

We go and watch, and take some photographs, but due to the haze they are not up to much. The first drop seems unopposed, but the second comes through a hail of 40mm flak. The leading Dakota catches fire but continues his run, turns, and then the crew bail out. I see about six Dakotas burning, some crash, one puts out its fire in an engine, and one I see crash our side of the Rhine, with one of the crew about to come down in the river. I see a Typhoon smoking for a bit, and get caught up in the flak myself whilst trying to get photographs.

On the way home I pass a stream of tugs and gliders going out – the Dakotas of the previous drop passing underneath them on their way home. Later we do a TAC/R together, and I make a pass at a truck, unsuccessfully. My shooting is bad these days, and I have missed an m/c, a jeep, and today's truck.

Steve and Bob Mackelswain pick my wallet up at the Brevet Club and bring it back to me. The last four days have been hot, with not a cloud in the sky, reminiscent of India, and I do a little sunbathing – when time.

[1] *Operation Varsity.*

April 1st 1945

MILL

I GO UP AND TRY AND LOOT Wesel, but all I get is a bedside lamp. We pass 'Monty' himself on the way up. Down south of Welden the country is rich with German chickens etc, and many undamaged farms. The Rhine is fast moving, and we cross by an American built pontoon bridge.

I go out with Nick Bowen in Area 3 and we get a lot of flak which I don't see, though which he tells me about. Later I see flashes of light flak exploding, but a long way off. I had previously done a very successful shoot in the Stockhumer Bosch, north of

Emmerich, on two camouflaged gun pits, with many direct hits, and seeing smoke issuing from an unobserved position nearby.

Today a signal from Group to the effect that armed recces, and presumably us, is to be pressed on regardless of weather conditions and crosswinds. Consequently we have to waive our 'union rules' of 3000' and press on underneath.

The result has been one Spit (F/Lt Blundell-Hill), and two Mustangs hit by flak. I have to do Area 3, and as the cloud is down 10/10 to 1000', I send my No.2 home and press on. I get a bit lost at times, see nothing worthwhile, except one truck with its characteristic Bosch mottled camouflage, and near Wayringen I see a red golfball pass pretty close, so I leap into the cloud, cross the bomb line, and abandon the rest of my road.

But now? I have arranged to go on leave on the 5th, and had hoped to have seen Monica in Chelsea, but there are three days to go and I shall have indubitably have gone for a Burton by then...

April 7th 1945

LONDON

HAVING LOST 19 AIRCRAFT AND 14 PILOTS in the Group, the "press on regardless" attitude is abandoned. Dick Mitchell comes back as C.O., and says that David and I are to be his flight commanders. Fair enough says I – as Alan Clifton-Mogg is going home, as he will not serve under Dick, as he reckons he should have been C.O. himself.

I do one more sortie, abortive, with long range tanks, in the Zuyder Zee area, though after 15 minutes I open the engine, and it's so rough I come home. Just as well, as I am in 5/10 cloud and miles off track.

I get on leave and am now in the "Wings Club". We leave Gilze and reach Northolt around 6pm and I get up to town, but there is some mistake over beds and I have the 'emergency' one. I ring Monica, and she is waiting and says "come on down and I will cook something." My God! I go down to the King's Road with a bottle of "Cheval Noir 1937", and get home at 3am after another passionate session.

Yesterday I take my battledress for wings etc to Flights, and then collect her from her office at 6.30pm. We have a drink in Shepheards and the Brevet Club, followed by dinner there, and then get a bus home. It's raining, and makes her hair smell nice, and everything in the garden becomes lovely, so it's with the greatest difficulty that I am made to go away at 11.30, having started nothing, so that we both get a good night's sleep.

I had wired Bill at Camberley but find he is in town, and today meet him and arrange a party tonight. He is keen on night clubs, so I expect I will end up in one, very tired and against my will. The G/C, Anderson, got a bar to his D.S.O., and I start to think I shall get a bar to my DFC for those forward facing oblique photos. But it's too late now – and not even a mention. I should like an oak leaf!

April 12th 1945

London

I BOOK A ROOM AT THE SAVOY, a double with a bath, and Monica and I end up there after dinner with Bill at Quaglinos. On Sunday she gives me tea, and then I run dinner for Bill and his American dame and Burt Mann at the Brevet Club. I give them both German beer mugs.

Monday I meet Mama and send her off to Elstree with J.J., and Monica gives me supper, and sends me packing about 10.30pm. Tuesday I take her to 'Three's a family' and then we go home and 'Whoa!'

Yesterday Peggy and Mama and I go down to Farnham to see Frances *(his brother Hugh's 4 year old daughter)* but she won't speak. We miss the train back, and I just get to the Brevet Club in time to give Uncle George a drink, and then go down to Chelsea and eat Monica's tinned crab.

I get to bed early and feel fine today, though with a bit of a cold. I get a bicycle tyre (to sell on the black market) - the Customs will no doubt get it - but I cannot get Monica a wings brooch *(sweetheart brooch)* under 5 guineas anywhere.

Today I share a drink with Baffy in the evening, and later hope to visit Chelsea! We had a wonderful breakfast in bed in the Savoy on Sunday morning, and Monica manages to get her face cream on before I see her, so that I do not get the shock that she, not I, expected!!

April 17th 1945
MILL

MORE FUN AND GAMES, and I return to Mill on Saturday 14th. One chap goes through Customs with two bicycle tyres under his arm. Reg Hodge and I dispose of mine for 65 guilders, the market having dropped from 100.

I do a TAC/R west of Apeldoorn, where jet a/c have reported, and much M/T. I go right down to check up, but am only able to identify the odd one or two – the rest are shelters. I think I spot an armoured car, and get fired on, seeing the cigar rings come up. Next day we move north to Twente, a few miles from the German border. I have a small room to myself, thank God.

April 21st 1945
MILL

I FORGOT TO WRITE ABOUT A LUNCH PARTY at "Chandos" with Baffy on Friday 13th, whereat appeared Col. Walter Elliot M.P. and one Colin Coote, who I think is a leader writer for the Telegraph.

Most interesting.

Here is it delightfully green, and birds chirp around, though damn me if I can tell one from the other, they are all so drab. I sell my old battle dress to a Dutch boy who comes round our house, for 50 guilders, through the agency of Jock Trothill, our arch black-marketeer. Cigarettes, too, fetch 20 guilders per hundred!

Today there is oculus cloud and continuous drizzle and I am standing by in the Mess, briefed for Area 5 – near the dreaded Bremen and Wilhelmshaven. Thirtle of 268 was shot down yesterday whilst attacking a ship in the harbour in that area – but bailed out the wrong side of the bomb line.

I am reading Monica's "Droll Stories of Balzac" – and droll they are.

April 28th 1945

MILL

I DO A FEW TRIPS UP BY BREMEN and Emden, but all semi-abortive due to the weather or my tanks failing to come off.

I take one Peter Tredgett pair flying, and then slip off and photograph some gun positions near Leer by the Weser estuary. I find five 105mm flak guns, but the other positions have already been overrun by our own troops. Since then I have not flown, but hope to do so today.

Jock Toothill has been after cars, and through his agency, more or less, we now have three DKWs and an Opel in the Flight. I drove one back from Reine yesterday with Peter Tredgett, who claims to be a mechanic, and hope to get it serviceable. The local German province is green and beautiful and not much war scarred. All the women are wearing silk stockings, and look a bit sour about the non-fraternisation rule. We also see some German soldiers near a small hospital.

We are six in the Opel and after a quarter of an hour, whilst taking a corner too fast, she skids and falls on her side. We are so wedged in that no one is hurt, some airmen pick us up, and we drive off again.

I get a warning order to go to an investiture on 11th, and hope to get three days duty in town. No letter from Monica since I came back. Perhaps she has changed her affections.

May 2nd 1945

MILL

I GET A LETTER OK. I do a reputed "dicey" photo job over, or rather before, Oldenburg, at 2500 ft, but the flak gunners are all asleep.

We have a Wing dance on Sunday, and I steal the Group Captain's woman, a WAAF F/O called Brenda Scott. She comes down from Ghent periodically to keep him warm in bed, and I go up to him during a dance and tell him he is wanted on the telephone by Flying Control. I dance around in his place until he comes back and takes a lunge at me. Later I catch her coming out of the lavatory, and tell her that Andy has gone off to the Ops room for a few minutes and that I am to look after her, and keep her for about an hour this way. Later he tells me, rather rudely, to beat it, so I go.

Next morning he convinces everyone that I am posted back to Burma, and himself that I believe him. Harry Davison knocks out an ENSA girl, by mistake, having missed his swing at someone else.

The weather is bad, damn cold and practically snowing, and we do not do much flying. Two of my flight are overdue back from leave, and I am coming out in spots through lack of exercise. All I have had this year is two or three games of rugger in February.

May 4th 1945

MILL

I FLY AGAIN ON A WEATHER RECCE, plus Area 1 north of Emden. I get lost after about ten minutes, and have to get a homing back to base, and then start off again. Area 1 is not too easy due to the cloud formations, and at times I am not too sure where I am. Someone fires at me near Jever, two bursts of 20 or 40 mm, I think, but a bit inaccurate. I nearly prang on landing, and must be more careful in future.

Well, the war looks like ending out here, and God knows what the future holds forth, provided I am still OK. The Indian Army, I don't think, the RAF, who knows. I feel I should like to meet someone nice, marry her, and get a good job in her father's business – but what of the "call of the East", which I still occasionally hear?!

May 9th 1945

THE MORNING AFTER V.E. DAY, LONDON

I DO AN OP AFTER THE WAR is supposed to have ended, of the East Friesian Isles to Borkum, to see if they are trying to escape instead of surrender, but without seeing any movement. I also play some badminton with Mitch, Chokra and Peter Marsh. I dispose of the DKW for 275 guilders in the local black market, and have to drive it to a solitary farmhouse where it is hidden in a cowshed, the cart being taken out to make room for it.

I am now in London, and have to attend an Investiture on the 12th, but as the 84th Communication Squadron are having today off, I had to come over yesterday and was lucky to get a bed.

Monica I find is away, and as it is V.E. Day, I go out and see the sights. Two strange women insist on me kissing them in Piccadilly

535

Circus at 2.45pm, just before Churchill's speech, and I long for one of those red smoke candles which the Boche left behind in our house in Twente.

In the evening I go to the Brevet Club but it is sold out at 7.30, and Shepheards too at 8.30. I then wander back to the Wings Club where I meet one Van de Waale, ex Ternhill, and we have a drink or two whilst he discusses life and prospects in Belgium. He later (11.30) takes me to a party in a US warrant officer's flat in Atheneum Court, where about thirty people are jammed in a room which might hold 10 at a pinch. There is Bourbon to drink and a bad selection of dames, and I depart to bed unseen at 12.30am.

Today I go round to Wendy's and see Ma, and we have lunch in the Cumberland Hotel. I tell her I am engaged tonight, but as Monica is not back, God knows what I shall do. My kit weighs 62lbs and has to go on a different Anson to the one I travel on, and consequently I don't have to take it through Customs!

May 13th 1945

ROYAL INVESTITURE, LONDON

I GO DOWN TO THE KINGS ROAD and wait until Monica returns. The next day I take her to the Brevet Club for dinner, and then retire to her flat for one thing and another.

Mama and I have drinks at the Devonshire Club with one Dr Cullen, and another Andrew Maclaghlan whom I later meet in the Royal Empire Club Society, where he offers me a job in 'oil' in India, which I turn down. I organise two tickets for Ma and Baffy for the Palace, and get there myself about 10am, and remain for two solid hours in an ante-room with a hundred others or so, and nowhere to sit. At length I reach the King, who recognises my I.G.S.(India Star medal) and mentions my long service in India, and we then get out and go to Chandos for Baffy's Friday lunch. Of course there is a blonde there, Baffy's niece, who upsets me for the rest of the day. That evening we go to Kew for dinner with the Smyths, and consume Hock and champagne.

Yesterday I take Monica to "The Assassin", and though I have a room booked at the Savoy, I do not take it, as I do not somehow feel in the mood. Now I am off back to Croydon, and who knows what may not happen next. I wish these women didn't upset me so. Monica suggests a parting in peace, before we go in a row, but I say 'No, wait' and eventually we decide to maintain the 'status quo'.

May 20th 1945

MILL

I AM BACK HERE A WEEK NOW AND BORED STIFF. I sell my old sports coat for 40 guilders, and a bicycle wheel of Tom Raynor's for 100. We practise formation flying as a Wing, and though I miss the first two shows, there is one tomorrow over the Hague, where Queen Wilhelmina is holding a review.

We practise twice yesterday and there is to be the same today. Mitch is away and I am now C.O. and lead the squadron. We expect to move to Celle near Hanover any minute now, and it will be pretty grim with peacetime training, just like Hawarden again.

My view is that it is all a life without an end, without a glimmer, and what use is ambition at all. But then I am paid £480 p.a., and my board and lodging costs me practically nothing, and where would I get that in any job out of the Service? Somehow I am almost regretting that the war is over – it at least gave me a purpose in life. What is there for me now – not just 'soldier on', surely?

May 28th 1945

MILL

FREDDIE, GEORGE AND I GO UP TO MEPPEL to try and get a watch for him, and eventually end up in a Canadian officers club in Groningen. We go round some hospital grounds in a jeep with a slightly tight Canadian Captain, and all the women on their death beds wave back to us. We grab a couple of dames, and take them into the dance, but no good, and I make Freddie drive all the way back – three and a half hours, getting to bed at 1.30am.

The next day Jeff and I go up to Lubeck where we have heard of pistols for sale, and I buy two Lugers (one slightly u/s) for £7.10 and £2.10 off some airmen, as an investment – I hope. Lubeck is full of German aircraft, and on the way up we fly over Bremen and Hamburg.

That evening Bill Dodgson and I dash up to Groningen to try and get some gin but we cannot find the place, and as he thinks

Recently dug mass graves at Belsen.

538

A Visit to Belsen

At some point at the end of May or the beginning of June Colin visited the concentration camp at Bergen-Belsen, just 28 km north of the airfield at Celle where 2 Squadron moves on May 30th. The camp had been liberated by British forces in mid-April. 60,000 inmates were discovered, most of them sick and starving, as well as 13,000 unburied corpses. It was here that Anne Frank and her sister Margot died of typhoid, just 6-8 weeks before the British troops arrived.

The camp guards had been made to bury the corpses in May, so when Colin visited, he was able to witness dozens of mass graves. Soon afterwards, the camp was burnt to the ground by Churchill tank flamethrowers, in part to prevent the spread of disease.

It is surprising that he does not mention this visit in his diaries - the only clue being some photographs he took. However, there seems to be a page missing from the diaries at this point, so perhaps that was where he recorded the visit.

The remains of the incinerator at Belsen.

there won't be any chance of getting any dames due to the amount of Canadians about, we beat down to Meppel, where we had some success previously. But here too we are too late – 9.30pm – and the Canadians are already at work.

Saturday, we have the afternoon off, and Sunday off too, so Bill, George and I set off to Amsterdam. We have some trouble finding the town major, but do so, and get a bed in the "Red Lion" hotel. I only have 80 cigarettes, for which I collect 80 guilders and some bars of chocolate at 4 G each. Men approach you in the street with cameras, watches and even cufflinks for cigarettes.

We then set off for the Lido Club, Bill with some dame he picks up in the hotel lounge. She turns out to have a German accent, but, however, she satisfies him OK. I grab another called Helen and dance around, and George gets her friend, an old "Gladstone bag" by the name of Anne. We have some wine and beer that we brought over, and also a bottle of champagne, but later on my dame goes home. Anne is desolated, and she takes George off and they bring back one Tina, who is a lot more ugly, but quite perky and a bit warm.

Bill and his fraulein vanish, and we four go off in his car to Anna's flat, plus a box of our food, and Anna's gramophone. No electric light, but candles, and we eat bread and tinned sausage and dance. I get browned off and pinch out the wick, much to the dames annoyance, as they seem to want to dance all night. George and Anne retire, and I get busy on a sofa, but there is no joy and it ends in a sort of compromise, though not the usual 'Papist plot'. As George is in for the night and I don't know the way home, I have to stay too, and eventually we creep in and join the other two in bed – or rather we stay on top in our clothes rather like on a railway train – it's a large bed and takes four abreast easily.

Next morning we beat it as fast as possible back to the hotel and breakfast, though much to the disgust of the two dames. We then wander around, taking Bill's woman out to Haarlem, and end up for tea in a rather smart officers club in Utrecht, and back home

540

in time for dinner. We see a woman get 12 players (cigarettes) from a waiter for 20 guilders in an Amsterdam cafe.

Children come up and demand autographs. We see columns of Germans with their HDT cookers (heavy duty truck cookhouses), all driving quite happily, and pranged vehicles on the Appeldoorn-Amersfort road. In Utrecht a food convoy is going through, and one small boy gets onto a lorry and lets the back fall, flooding the roadway with potatoes. In a moment the crowd gather round, and there is much argument.

Now we hear of a flying control job of sorts in Copenhagen, and I must go and see the G/C about it.

June 1st 1945

CELLE, GERMANY

I GET MYSELF PUT UP FOR THIS CONTROL JOB – air traffic officer at Copenhagen, and another at the Hague. SPSO Group tells me to go and see T of Rear[1] about it in Brussels. I fly down on Wednesday.

Meanwhile the rest of the squadron moves to Celle, north of Hanover, where I now am, and all set for the Occupation. I get a bit lost on the way and have to get a homing to Brussels. The G/C I must see is away until the next day, so I get my kit off the aircraft and get put up in a shockingly awful transport command hostel.

That night I wander around the bars but do not meet any women I fancy, and retire to bed rather bored at 10pm. The next day I go shopping – perfume and 'silk' stockings for the boys, and eat a bag of cherries. The G/C – one Salmon – appears a bit vague on the subject, and I discover they have given the Copenhagen job away to a chap in 2 Group and that the W/C has promised the Hague job to a friend of his in his office. As the W/C is away and won't come back until Saturday, I return to Celle and hope to go down and see them both tomorrow. Meanwhile I am due for leave

541

on the 31st, and as all aircrew leave is to stop on the 4th, unless I get away quickly I will have had it.

Brussels is full of uniforms, and the shop windows are crowded, though at a price. I feel a bit tired due to an overdose of cognac and beer (I wrote notes to an Ensa girl at dinner in the Palace hotel on the strength of it) and have a lodging here with David Greville-Heygate. Outside, German girls are doing the washing, very nice ones too, and I for one will find this non-fraternisation order a very hard one.

[1] *Meaning unclear.*

June 7th 1945
Celle

I go down to Brussels again, well and truly navigated as of India days, and see W/C Andrews, Air Movements, who turns out to be an old acquaintance of the 1st Burma campaign. After a lot of negotiations I am given the job, as there is some stooge in the office who has to be satisfied first, but on returning to Celle I find no posting signal in, and I had planned to leave tomorrow. So perhaps I will be foiled at the post again.

Of my several nights in Brussels, I live in boredom in the Palace hotel and wander round at nights spending francs. In one joint – the 'Cosy Club' – some hostess sets to work on me and I buy a couple of rounds, cognac and fruit "cup" for her, costing 175 francs, and then get her away. We go to some cafe of her friends, where she warms up a bit, and eventually tells me to go home, but that she will keep with me all the next night, and we arrange a date for 2pm the next day. I wait until 3.05 but of course she does not turn up. I also do a bit of drinking in the RAF Club.

Andrews and I set off one day by car to the Hague. We arrive and go to SHAEF Mission Air Component, and also visit the air movements people in Valkenburg, the Hague airfield, and I get my office and bed provisionally promised in the Terminus Hotel, used by the Boche and now taken over for RAF transit officers, but actually inhabited by some ancient permanent residents and the town major's staff.

We have lunch at Mission, and dinner at the airfield Mess, and then go drinking gin at some local Dutchman's house in the Wassenaar residential area. We booze Bols from 9-10.30pm, and I meet there some 28 year old dame called Kieks Henny. She is brought in by some other RAF type, but is taken out by me. Andrews and I are taken back to town and then she is dropped, but comes to town with me in the back seat. And is she warm – God! I get her address and hope to return, but this damn posting signal may cock things up.

A magnificent bedroom, and a Canadian padre's bully beef for breakfast. The car is delayed due to a puncture, and we depart at 12.00, getting to Brussels Evere at 17.30, where I arrange to take off and fly home. But on running up the canopy it blows over a hedge and is broken, so I return to the Palace hotel for yet another night, returning here today on a Dakota lift at 06.45 – to find no posting signal – damn!!

15

June - September 1945

Air Movements Officer, SHAEF

The Hague
Holland

June 12th 1945

I PUSH OFF REGARDLESS of the posting signal after a small bottle (Scotch) party the night before, to which Burt Mann comes over from Group. We drive down in a jeep through the Ruhr, and it takes about 10 hours.

Not many occupation troops in evidence, and I see one coal mine working again. Many lorry loads of displaced persons pass, one with "Subjects of British Empire" chalked on it.

I stay two nights in the Palace hotel and fix the details of this job up with T of Rear. The second day, I meet Jonny Benbow, now a Lt Col, in SHAEF, looking after Indian POWs, and go on a bit of a party with him, though I do my usual vanishing trick at 11.30pm.

Next day, I drive to the Hague in a shockingly dirty 30 cwt truck which is governed down to about 30 mph. We arrive eventually, and I get a room at the Terminus hotel, where my office is to be, change, and go to the officers club. There I meet one John Hall, a F/L in Movements at T of Rear, plus one Lola Crowe, an attractive half Dutch driver for the Dutch Red Cross, and Jerry Pinder. We consume much Scotch and are joined by a Dutchman, one Bart de Schepper, to whose house we go for supper. I am the only sober one, Lola is sick and goes to bed, and I eventually collect them all in their jeep and see them on the way to Rotterdam.

Jerry has vanished and I find him asleep on the W/C seat. He gets up, apologises, and says that he was listening to the news!

Next day, W/C Mason in Air Component, SHAEF Mission, lends me a Utility, as I am supposed to have a car, in fact I am allotted one but it hasn't turned up. I lunch with Bart, then take him out to his house near Valkenburg airfield where I have to go. He takes me home for tea and I find that Betty, his wife, has produced a blonde and a brunette for inspection. I go off and change and take the blonde, Mary Wibort, out to dinner in the Officers Club. We try to dance at the Metropole but too damned crowded, and end

546

up smoking and necking in the Utility outside her hotel. I have a date for tonight but don't think I shall get anywhere, so I shall then have to give her up and go after Kieks again if I can find her. It's damn difficult.

June 13th 1945

QUITE A PLEASANT EVENING with young Mary, and I am told that in Holland one cannot sleep with a girl after knowing her only two days. I feel like asking "how long".

Next day I track down Kieks and make a date for 8pm. I go out to collect her, and we go to the dunes, but it is damn windy, so we go down an underground passage to the local Kommandant's room in a portion of the West Wall, where is a bed-less mattress and a chair. I set to work at once plus half a bottle of whisky, only to find myself up against principles – the one of 'husbands only'. I point out that she is not married, but no go. I return to bed a bit drunk on a quarter of a bottle of neat Scotch.

Yesterday I meet a US Colonel Mackolinger (is that his name?) who is sitting in the hotel lounge with a bottle of Scotch and another of Bourbon, a dame (Midge), and her husband, who is a flight lieutenant in the Dutch airforce and ADC to Queen Wilhelmina. I then meet an ENSA dame in trouble, and nearly finish my Scotch with her in my room, lending her my electric kettle to wash her hair.

I go and collect Mary but we find all the cinemas booked up, so sit in the Club and drink Scotch and then go and see her friend Yotja, whose mother is just out of Dachau. I see her home and kiss her in the car, and we all have a date for tomorrow – Saturday.

I have a room in the Terminus Hotel with a very comfortable bed, but no hot water. I have to feed in the SHAEF PWD (Psychological Warfare Division) Mess across the road, having fed at various places before. My office is in the hotel writing room

547

with two telephones, and a third on the way, and a staff of six, a 30 CWT lorry, and a utility that I have borrowed from the Air Component of the SHAEF mission. My job, not yet organised, will be to book people on aircraft to Croydon, and on the SHAEF Command squadron Austers to wherever they want. As for the rest, I am enjoying it, and provided I could find some nice girl to sleep with occasionally, I should feel content. However, no doubt I shall have to go – Transport Command may provide their own officer, or the Indian Army may catch me – Bah!

June 20th 1945

THE HAGUE

I HAVE A FEW MORE PARTIES with this Mary Wibort, and come to the conclusion, much to my annoyance, that I am making no progress, and that she is more or less the same with all. Hell! I kiss her goodnight in a fairly bad temper on Saturday night, and she looks at the sky as she says she thinks it will be a fine day tomorrow.

Thank God I can laugh – that damned gremlin again – I really must find something in this joint. All the airfield boys at Valkenburg reckon that they are fixed up.

I get a Mercedes from T.A.F. Main today, but the big end has gone, and it is practically useless. I get no exercise here, but feed quite well on American rations with SHAEF PWD.

June 23rd 1945

THE HAGUE

PARTIES, AND MORE PARTIES OF SORTS, and I get to bed every night I am here after midnight, last night being exceptional at 3.30am. I try my hand on the dames and no luck – Mary, I have had (up to here), some Quita dame who was warm and loved tickle and slap, and might be a good investment if she spoke any English, and was less like a furry mouse. Then I meet Louise Schuurmann! Dutch, in the A.T.A., and lived in the States a long time.

My No. 2 George Linton, turns up yesterday, so I am busy billeting and getting fed, Louise, who is here to look for her relations. I already have a date with Quita, so we make it four and go to the Club. Quita is sick, and we have to take her home, a little soberer, then the three of us adjourn to my room for rum and a bottle of wine. Louise is a bit tight already, George and I OK. We talk our heads off, Louise and I, after George has retired at 1 am, and early in the proceedings I am told she would hate to sleep with me.

We talk and talk and seem to have the same ideas on life, and end up in her room, a few along from mine, at 3.30, but nothing done. She does improve after being kissed a little, but that's all, and I retire to bed cursing that gremlin of mine.

People, parties, and drinks, but no damn luck with dames. Oh Louise – she would do for the lot of them, with her lovely accent and hard bitten expression, though only 24. In love with a married Yank, so that's that. Today I must take her to lunch at Betty's, and then I hope to Wasenaar to look for her friends – but she will probably have nothing to do with me.

June 27th 1945

THE HAGUE

I AM FALLING SLIGHTLY IN LOVE – or at least I think so. Louise stays two more days, and I take her out to see friends and an uncle in Wassenaar. Each evening, George and I and her have dinner and champagne in the Club, and reach varying degrees of intoxication.

The usual ending in or on my bed, 3.30, 1.30 and 2.30am, though I am not able to do anything, as she refuses, and the reasons are OK by me.

She has a charm and a certain type of character akin to mine, and even in the morning when I go to wake her up she looks and

549

smells good. "Earthy" is the expression she teaches me. I then, of all things, I go and cry when seeing her off on this morning's 'plane, which is a thing I do not remember doing before over any woman!! What is she? 24, Dutch, but lived in the States and Canada some 13 years except for four years in A.T.A. in England. (Air Transport Auxiliary).

With 2000 flying hours in on most types of aircraft, and a lovely Canadian accent, deep blue eyes, long curling eyelashes, a full shaped face and a bit furry all over! But she is getting out of A.T.A. and going back to the States, where her father is Consul-General in Chicago – and in love with some American, with a family.

July 2nd 1945

THE HAGUE

I NIP OVER TO ENGLAND to see the London Traffic Office and get a few tips, on Thursday 28th.

Louise is in Leicester, and rings me up about 4pm, so I hop on a train and reach Ratcliffe Hall, home of Sir Lindsay Everard, where all her A.T.A. pool live, at about 8.30pm. I have a damn nice bed, and we drink Scotch, and talk until about 1am.

Next morning she flies me down to White Waltham in the belly of a Barracuda, and I then hitch hike to London, arriving for Baffy's luncheon at Chandos at 1.20pm.

I go round to Wendy's for a bed, and get the whole flat as she is away to stay with J.J. for the weekend in Elstree. Louise is getting herself out of A.T.A., and I meet her at the American Red Cross in Chandos Street, and suggest that she comes and stays in the flat with me, which she does. We have dinner at the Brevet Club, and go back and drink some of Wendy's Madeira. She tells me she is in love with this American despite his family, so that's that.

Next day I do a few things, and she discovers that she cannot go back to him and America yet, as the US Embassy will not give her a visa, as they are getting out new rules and she is a Dutch

Louise Schuurmann

citizen. She is pretty damned depressed, and so am I, and after a few drinks and dinner at the Brevet with some friend of hers, we return home (meet Eric Milne and some of the boys in the Brevet Club). I get an awful fit of tears, which I never had before goddammit, and am talked to quite calmly by Louise, who points out that it will not work under the circumstances – agreed.

Yesterday I fly back from Hendon on the Dutch Dakota, and now feel a little better, though she still hurts a bit. God only knows what she must be feeling over this Yank – especially as she cannot now get over to see him! I call on her uncle in Wassenaar last night and leave some stuff – later going back for a rum and tea session, but her presence lurks there and I do not like it. I never told Monica that I was in town!

That trip in the Barracuda – sitting on piles of kit in Louise's dressing gown, in a slight loving haze.

July 6th 1945
THE HAGUE

I DECIDE TO TRY MY LUCK IN AMSTERDAM, and take myself there yesterday evening in the jeep. I arrive about 6.15pm and go to a Canadian officer's club, where I meet one be-medalled Major called Henry Druce[1], who I have seen in my office at the Hague. He has a spare dame, so I join up for drinks and dinner and dancing. He insists on playing hockey with a pen and two forks at dinner, and is threatened with assault by some Canadian officer.

My dame is called Nysha and has a laugh like a gargling bath club. I end up the evening talking to Druce's piece, one Wendy Weidemann, who is English with a Boche father, and find that she reads my character like a book in two hours. The jeep lights fail so she makes me a bed in a room with Martin, her brother, and Druce, all from the SAS. I get up at 6am to sneak out, but find that I am locked in – and even the back garden has no exit. Martin has to get up and let me go. Having slept none too well, am I tired!

Mary tells me to be myself and not to hunt around for women, as it is not in my nature – hell!

1 Major Henry Druce worked in Holland for MI6. In August 1944 he won a DSO at the head of an SAS team dropped in occupied France to support the French Resistance.

July 10th 1945
The Hague

Saturday night, George and I go out and visit the Wynbergs in Wassenaar, and get rather full of rum and a bit bored. Sunday I call at No. 2 int (V) sec's Mess at Wassenaar, and go out with Henry Druce, and some others, sailing. Sailing consists of lounging half naked on a smart cabin cruiser, taken over from the Germans, and drinking Bols, listening to the gramophone and doing a little swimming.

Mary, and Martin Weidemann, are there, but I do not get on particularly with any of the dames there. We land back at Varmont about 7.30 and I jeep home, change, and go to a party at the Hotel des Indes with one Charlie College – there is dancing, some rotten gin, a cabaret, and I retire slightly waterlogged at midnight. George sleeps out in Peter Hunt's flat, and the chambermaid has some caustic remarks to make about him.

Yesterday, my birthday, and we have some Scotch in the Club with Betty, Bart, Peter Hunt and Hoekstra, whose name is apparently "Apie". Then I have dinner with Bart and Betty, and go and call on some woman called Teddy, a friend of Apie's, who wants me to take her to Noordwijk on Wednesday night. I must get out of it, because she looks about 40. However, she has some English gin and Scotch, but we leave early and go to bed.

553

July 13th 1945

THE HAGUE

I HAVE HENRY DRUCE in to dinner at the Club, plus his dame, and an English girl who works in his outfit, one Iris Peake, such a beautiful blonde that it isn't true[1]. Once Anning, Lt Commander Philips and the Town Major and I were having lunch in the Club when she appeared with some guardsman, and we are practically put off our food!

Anyway, when I go out to Henry's for that boating party I see her there, and shake a limpid hand, though she doesn't come out on the party. So I tell Henry to bring her in, and much to my surprise he does. We then go to the Metropole and dance around, where she improves, being a little frigid it seems, and then back to my room for some beer.

The next day I go to this Teddy, Hoekstra's friend, with a half bottle of rum, and tell her that we cannot go to Noordwijk, as my jeep lights are U/S. She is livid, and makes all sorts of practical suggestions which I find great difficulty in turning down. We drink the rum and dance round the flat to three broken records, with pieces missing, and I eventually score a home base.

Next day I go out to Wassenaar to collect Iris and have dinner there, going to a cinema later – the Club where we encountered Leslie Wall, and then to his flat to brew tea. I take Iris home, and suggest tomorrow, but no good, so maybe I have 'had' her too. She goes out with a guardsman from Rotterdam, one George Broderick, and she seems a bit distant with me, so maybe she is in love with him – hell, but she's a beauty.

---

[1] *Iris Peake was an MI6 secretary, who had just finished an affair with a naval officer in MI6 called George Blake, who later was unmasked as a Russian spy. Iris Peake went on to become a lady in waiting to Princess Margaret in the 1950s.*

July 16th 1945

HENRY INVITES ME TO A PARTY out at Wassenaar, and the gallant Iris is there, and we dance around. I go out fairly tight, and get away about 2.30, before they start to break the joint up.

Yesterday I fly over in an Auster to wake them up, and Henry comes out onto his balcony to wave. After lunch I take Iris out to the beach near Wassenaar, and we swim amongst a host of jellyfish and lie on the beach in the sun and a miniature sandstorm.

She has a party that night so I do not see her, but I have met Lou at the previous night's show and have an introduction from him. I go round there about 7pm with a bottle of rum and a tin of tomato juice, and he has a bar in his house and a radiogram, and we have quite a party. I meet one Freddie, a red-headed dame who says she is divorced, and we get on damned well. I take her home eventually, and upstairs her husband is in bed – a second one that she had no mentioned. However, she says she will fix me up with one 'Luki', so I tentatively arrange to go round there tonight, though whether the fair Luki will be there I do not not know.

I do two Auster trips – dual of course, one with Apie Hoekstra, and we wander about over Wassenaar and Noordijk seeing a dump of V2s and a miniature submarine on the beach. George Linton has just come back from a weekend in the UK, and I shall hope to go some time this month, if we are still our own boss, and not under 18 SP at Valkenburg.

July 17th 1945

I GO ROUND TO SEE THE VAN BERGENS, and find some pongo Major called Mick already there. So Henry and I go out and collect another called Hanni – pronounced 'Honey' – a blonde whoa! However, this Mick guy is out to do his worst and to sleep in the house, so after some red and white liberated wine, and half a bottle of my rum I return to bed after an animated discussion on aircraft with Hans.

My sleep is disturbed by this dame and I feel a little shagged today, to say the least of it.

July 19th 1945

THE HAGUE

I ARRANGE TO TAKE THE GALLANT IRIS to Rotterdam, but she rings up and leaves a message that she is sick. I am out at Hilversum trying to get a spare wheel for the jeep, which I do, and am desolated.

So I have a few drinks at the Club, dinner with Betty and Bart, and am in bed by 9.30pm, but don't sleep particularly well.

Next evening I go round to the Van Bergens again, but they produce no women, and I sulkily consume a bottle of rum with them. The fair Luki shows up, also her fiance, one Robert Van Gudder who was at Harrow the same term as I.

Tonight I arrange myself a visit to Bill and Yvonne Wynberg, whether they like it or not, and tomorrow a return match with the Van Bergens, and only one bottle of rum left, so I don't quite know how I shall spin it out. The gallant Iris is elusive all week, though she has contracted to go a dance at the Valkenburg Mess on Saturday. However I can never get her alone at that sort of party, so that's that.

I hope to nip over to London next week, but if we go over to Transport Command and W/C Pippett, I suppose I shall have had it – as I shall any day now, when I get orders to return to the Indian Army.

July 23rd 1945

I HAVE ANOTHER SESSION with the Van Bergens and we go and call on one Ellen something, who speaks English with a strong American accent, and has a voice like Popeye. They had previously introduced me to one Tilly, who has a face like a Pekinese and not much nose.

On Friday or so I get a letter from Iris that she cannot come to this dance on Saturday, as a friend of hers is coming down from Germany to see her – presumably the Guardsman.

So on Saturday morning I go down to look at these two dames - Ellen and Tilly - with a view to taking one of them to the Valkenburg Mess dance on Saturday. Tilly looks shocking by daylight, so I escape after making some excuse about fixing up a tennis afternoon, and nip across the street to see this Ellen dame. She looks a bit grim too, but I coordinate her, and take her out in the jeep. Is she hot – whoa! We do not drink much, and spend a lot of time necking in long chairs, and my uniform now stinks of 'Je Reviens', though fortunately there don't seem to be much lipstick on it.

I put her home at 1.30 but am not invited in, so that's that.

Yesterday I play tennis out at Wassenaar, and then lie on a couch listening to Will Wynberg playing the guitar, and watching a swaying poplar through his window, with no cigarettes.

July 26th 1945

I NIP OVER TO TOWN ON A "CHARLIE", as some people call it, and am now in the Wings Club observing the election results.

Yesterday I went to a party at Ellen's, taking a bottle of rum with me, and there is a beautiful blonde there called Jane, and like the Daily Mirror's Jane too, though a bit young, and does not speak too much English – and wears glasses! Anyhow, I do a bit of cheek to cheek dancing, and get shivers all down my spine when she starts breathing down my starboard ear – quite unintentionally.

I am sort of barman, and dispense to all and sundry, getting to bed by 1am. Bart and Betty are there, demanding that their glasses be filled up, also Hans and Freddy, so I am well in. Anton too – with his car just swiped by the Military Police.

Today I sneak out to the airfield, and ought to return on Sunday, though I would like to stay until Monday – or would I?

I ring up Monica at her office, and am told rather curtly to ring later at 7.30pm, when she will be at home and packing, so it looks as though I have "had it" once more. What to do with the bottle of champagne that I bought her – also a pair of silk stockings for 125 cigarettes? I shall miss a damned good party on Saturday with Freddy and Henry.

I always enjoy coming in over the English coast, and looking down at houses and gardens and seafronts. I wish the "day would dawn" soon, or perhaps I am condemned to a bachelor's life.

I have got over Louise – and am afraid that if I ever collect someone, I shall then meet someone better later on, and wish I hadn't jumped first time. And become a second Johnny Benbow.

However, "press on irregardless" – as the expression goes....

July 28th 1945

London

I GO TO 10 CHARLES STREET and find that Louise is in, so we nip out for a quick one in the Brevet Club. Later we join Charlie Colledge in Tommy's Bar, some private joint in Dover Street, and consume Pimms. I then call up Monica, and am told to come round to her new address on Saturday, which is today. So we go on boozing and wander round the joints, and I go home with the idea of clearing my system of Louise, which I hope that I have.

Friday I go to Chandos to Baffy's and Colin Coote is there, and the spinach eating dame, and all very interesting. Later Bill appears in the Wings Club, also Keith McDiarmid and a beautiful WAAF in disguise, Eileen Hawkins. We have tea, then Bill and I go to the Berkeley to drink with the Neaves, of The Hague[1], then Shepheard's and on to the Brevet Club with Keith and the WAAF, and I get so waterlogged that I have to leave before closing time and stagger home to bed, chewing ovaltine tablets as I have had no dinner.

Today I book my passage home for tomorrow, and organise a tweed jacket and greyers (trousers), which I put on, and take Joan Linton, George's wife, out to beer and lunch. It's a bit difficult, as there seems to be a sort of barrier between us – God only knows why, but long silences etc. Roll on the day!

[1] *Airey Neave, who had escaped from Colditz, worked for MI9, and was later a Conservative politician assassinated by the IRA.*

July 31st 1945

THE HAGUE

I GO DOWN TO SEE MONICA, with the pair of silk stockings I bought her, and find that she is engaged, and going to be married for the third time! I am furious, so I don't mention the stockings, and retire to bed about 9.30pm, having to arrive at 05.30 to catch the a/c back.

London is strange at 6am, with a few people about who have obviously been up all night. At Croydon, Paddy Hynes and I steal into the Mess and have a surreptitious breakfast, and then off we go. It gets damn cold due to the air regulator being cold. I ring up Ellen when I get back, and take her out to dinner in the Officers

Club – she gets quite warm, and kisses me goodnight quite well
– Hell!

Yesterday I take a melon round to Hans and Freddie, and
the shoes that I got him in London, and then we later adjourn to
Ellen's, but I get damned bored, and leave at 10.30pm. Today is
raining, and I don't know what to do!

August 4th 1945
THE HAGUE

I AM SAILING IN KAAG WITH ELLEN, and then have dinner at
the Country Club at Varmont. I then get busy on her on a sort
of swing seat, but nothing doing that day. I also have a few parties
with Charlie Colledge and the two ENSA girls in the Hague and
Rotterdam, and I take them all sailing yesterday afternoon. The one
I have is blonde, and very bored, and called Norma.

Yesterday George and I have dinner with Lt Commander
Elliston at the naval Mess, and get to bed early, and not too full of
liquor for a change.

August 6th 1945
THE HAGUE

SATURDAY NIGHT I HAVE FREDDIE and Hans van Bergen to a few
drinks in the Club, and then we go round to Ellen's place, collect
her and go out to Meerunt. I meet a lot of people who I know,
including Gerard Dogger[1], and manage to get the lot away at about
12.30, having a fearfully dangerous jeep race with Henry Druce's
crowd on the autobahn on the way home.

I then drop the van Bergens, and take Ellen home. She has told
me all through the evening at various times that she has sent her
mother away for three days, and that I can come and stay the night.

She gets busy too in the jeep, whilst both my hands are tied to the steering wheel (making my race with Druce doubly dangerous), so we go upstairs and get busy on the sofa and eventually score a home base. She isn't too pleased afterwards, so I step out hurriedly and must now, I suppose, take her out again. I call her 'Popeye', as she has a shocking American gangster accent.

Yesterday I take Will Wolders out sailing on the Kaag, and we later have dinner in the Club. I see Ellen out of a window whilst I am changing, but fortunately she doesn't appear to have seen me. We then go to Till von somebody's birthday party. She is Henry's girlfriend, and Will and I have quite a good time. Under the influence of cognac and sugar she becomes quite cheerful, and much less shy - a lovely girl.

This is a shocking existence. A party of sorts - and different girls - every night, and no exercise, except walking around the town if George has the jeep. He did discover a squash court but I cannot get a game there. I haven't even time to read, except in the office, and then there is usually something going on there.

Will gives me a Dutch lesson yesterday on the boat, so I hope to master the pronunciation soon.

[1] *Dutch resistance fighter.*

August 20th 1945
THE HAGUE

I GET MESSAGES FROM BILL (Robinson) that he is calling in on his way from Kiel to Wimbledon, and he calls up from Apeldoorn, but never arrives.

Henri organises a party in Amsterdam on Saturday. We all collect at Ellen's and hang around, and finally set off, arriving at someone's flat about 10pm. I take one (one-eyed) "Chick" Rideal (S/L Eric Rideal), of the RAF Missing Research Enquiry Service, and we finally get back about 3.30am. I meet some girl Henri brought – one Lily Otto – and stick to her the whole evening, and sort of stroke her in the transport on the way home.

Someone brings us over three squash racquets and a ball, and George and I play last night, but he is not much good. If I can only find someone to play with. We later take Molly Cuypers to a beano at 12 L of C "A" Mess, where I do quite a line with another Tilly Van Dyke.

There are too many parties here. Tonight I have supper with Bart and Betty, and then hope to go and see the beautiful Lily, but I expect she will be already organised, or at any rate some'at is bound to go wrong.

Later: I go round to dinner at 7b Hertzog Straat and have soup, spaghetti with chillies, and a glass of cognac. Then I sneak along to see Lily at number 8 and find her out. I go to the Club, furious, and have two brandies, and then jeep round again at 9 to find her still out. Am I mad?

August 21st 1945

The Hague

I GO ROUND NEXT DAY and discover that Lily was at her mother's next door, but is not allowed out, as she must look after her child, her mother having gone on strike over it.

The Jap war finished a few days ago, and Basil Langton-Dodds invited George and I to a party in Varmont. George is too tired, so I take Henri and Freddie in his place, and some beautiful blonde they collect called Katie, with not much English and an angora doublet which moults, and which we sort of pluck whilst dancing, and stick to people on the dance floor. I have to take them home in the jeep with no headlights, and they insist on going to some place in Wassenaar which we cannot find – and eventually I get to bed about 3.30am.

Yesterday I have a good game of squash and feel the better for it, though it is damned difficult to find any players. Henri works in a jewellers, and I get a silver mounted cigarette holder on condition that I can get the jeweller a pipe – I hope from Brussels.

August 23rd 1945

The Hague

I GO TO A SHOCKING PARTY in Amsterdam with one Van Lighter. Two ENSA girls are supposed to be there, coming from Apeldoorn, but they do not turn up until midnight, during which time we have had nothing to drink since 9pm – I leave, very bored, and get home to bed at 4am, having great difficulty in finding my way out of Amsterdam, and also in keeping my eyes open during the drive back.

I play tennis yesterday out at Wassenaar, and later go by myself for a drink, but there's no party and am very pleased to get to bed.

August 26th 1945

The Hague

I GET A NEW OFFICER, one F/O Colyer-Commerford, who seems a bit odd. I take him out to Meerut and he gets tight, and is found running round in circles in the garden shouting "Dunford Wood". I stuff him in the back of someone's car and have them drop him at the Terminus (Hotel).

I meet an American-Dutch blonde out there called Louise Carriere, but she is heavily escorted by a Dutch airforce type, and we are not allowed to communicate much.

The other day I meet some F/L in the Club and take him and his sister, who turns out to be the notorious Helen, to Warmond. I dance around this Helen dame, who is exceedingly "hot", and even set her hair on fire at the bar whilst lighting someone's cigarette – but she is Henry Druce's woman, so the hell with her.

I am now at a loose end, as the glorious Tilly has departed to Amsterdam, and I reckon I have had her. I go and play tennis with people called Smalt at Wassenaar, who are damned good.

August 29th 1945

The Hague

George and I move into our new office in 33 De Plaats, and I take out some new dame called Sue Newall, who comes from Nebraska and works in the US Embassy, and get extremely tight one night at Warmond.

I drive back half asleep, and next day I give her dinner and take her to a tamasha[1] at the airfield, and

she is quite a good type, though a great prospect for me I don't think. Monday I go to a party of 12 L of C "B" Mess in "Corrida", and meet Helen and her brother (ACAF) in the Club beforehand, by chance, and am practically forced to take her too. We dance around most indecently, and then I take her to the office and up to the waiting rooms to try and telephone Henry. At least that is her idea – mine is quite different, but though she fiddles around, she is not having any, and I return to the party in disarray.

Yesterday I go out in the evening and play tennis with Henry Druce and have supper – returning home to an early night and a few pink gins with Richard Tull. I now come out in two rows of medals – Africa, Burma and France and Germany Stars, as well as my original three, and have a Defence medal to come.

The fair Lily departs with her child to Amsterdam, and promises to write to me when she is "receiving" there.

[1] *Urdu for grand show.*

September 3rd 1945

The Hague

I HAVE A MOST ENJOYABLE DAY'S SAILING with an old retired sea captain, and he navigates me round the Kaag. I then have a party at Meerut with Hymans, the Dutch press officer, and get off with some French actress he has with him.

Yesterday I have a game of squash, and then take Hans and Freddy to Amsterdam, when Van Ligten is throwing another party. Of course someone has to drop a bottle of Gordons Gin on the doorstep before we leave. Jock Toothill is there, and we do some good work on one Trat (pronounced Trout) Moltzer, an Austrian girl married to a Dutchman in Haarlem. We keep retiring with an odd bottle into corners, and later I go home with Jock, who is running a Canadian army leave centre, and he gives me a bed there at 2.30am.

At 7am I awake and set off for The Hague at 8am, and it is damned cold driving the jeep with only a shirt on.

George is posted to B.A.F.O. in Germany, so I shall be left with this chap Collyer-Commerford. We have a good party in Rotterdam to celebrate the departure of Herman Schricher to the UK. I have Sue and Louise there.

September 5th 1945

London

I ASK FOR A 72 (HOURS LEAVE) in London, but W/C Pippet says he cannot allow it, but if I get over on my own steam, then it's OK by him. So I arrange to be flown over and back by Auster. I came over on Monday, over Walchem and Calais to Dover, where we proceed to get lost, and eventually touch down at Fair Oaks near Staines, refuel, and fly on to Hendon.

Amsterdam in 1945

Here I get into trouble with the Customs officer over a parcel of stuff for George's wife, which I say is bulbs, a clock, and five pound notes which I do not mention. He grills me hard, and has me so nervous it's hardly true, then says "OK, see the currency officer" and I am free – let go! He had threatened to search me for jewellery etc.

I get a bed in the Wings Club, and take Louise Carriere out to the Brevet Club, 66 Grosvenor Club, and some club of hers. I get excited dancing with her, and she warms up a little, and we have quite a session on the stairs outside her flat afterwards, but nothing else, and I do not think there is anything there.

Next day I go and delve into BOAC for a job in the traffic department, and there is a chance of one at £300 – or about £100 overseas, after I am de-mobbed, which in point of fact means starting all over again.

That evening I go to Shepheards, and meet Ken Harkisson and have a few beers, and then I meet S/L "Horse" Evans from Habbaniya in the Brevet Club, get bored at 9.30pm, and return to the Wings Club, where I encounter Wilfred Van der Walle,

566

Hotel Terminus, The Hague

my Belgian friend, and we ride out on his motorcycle to the King George Club for some coffee.

Today I phone up Hendon about the Auster that was to bring me home and find it has not arrived, so I must go on a Dutch a/c to Valkenburg tomorrow, and it will be plain to all that I have been to the UK and I shall get into trouble. That's if the weather doesn't stop flying, in which case I shall have no bed.

This Louise Carriere would be extremely nice – my, my, but she is aged 20 and has old fashioned ideas, also hosts of boyfriends. We have lunch today at 3 Grosvenor Square, or Washington Square, or Eisenhower Plaats!

September 9th 1945

THE HAGUE

I TAKE LOUISE OUT AGAIN TO DINNER at the Brevet Club, where I meet Morley-Mower[1], who is, or was rather, Allan Haig's brother-in-law. We then go on to Chez Marcelle, and dance around in the usual fashion, and so home.

Next day I come over on the Dutch Military Air Service, as no one has turned up for me in an Auster, and hide on the airfield until the bus leaves for the Hague, so that no one shall see me.

[1] *Geoffrey Morley-Mower, author of Messerschmitt Roulette and Flying Blind.*

September 11th 1945
THE HAGUE

I GO OVER TO HEEMSTEEDE to see Trat but she is out, so I leave a message that I shall be back on Saturday, and drive home – 50 minutes jeeping.

Next night I take Sue Newall to a party at MRES, and then on to a dance at Schreveningen Casino, but she is still a bit stand-offish – I kiss her though.

Saturday I go to Heemstede with half a bottle of whisky, and we sit and talk and smoke until midnight, when I drive home. Nothing much doing, it seems, and so I arrange to go back to dinner on Monday. I go there and find one Yon Winser who was with her at that Amsterdam party, is living in the house, and has been since he was hidden there by the Underground in 1943 – presumably her lover – what a blow. However, I seem to make a little progress, and have arranged to take her to Meerut on Thursday, if nothing prevails in the meanwhile. She definitely has charm, despite her glasses and broken teeth, but this lodger is more than I can compete with!

The other day I decide to go for a walk on the beach, and call up Luki Dam, who says she is willing. We walk up and down, sit on a piece of driftwood, she snuggles around, so eventually I give her a kiss good and proper, as I cannot hold it any longer. The result is astounding, and she is hotter than anything I met in the Hague! But she is engaged to Robert Van Gudder, an Old Harrovian acquaintance of mine, and so that's that!

I see Lily Otto in the club – having told me she was going to Amsterdam and would write to me from there.

16

September 1945 - March 1946

RAF Hospital
Wroughton and Mongewell

UK

September 20th 1945

I FALL DOWN IN THE WORLD!

I take Trat to Meerut and we have a reasonable party, though she has a cold, and engages in a long session in Viennese with Bart, who later steals her away from dinner for a dance – much to my disgust.

The next day I arrange to take her with John Van Ligten to a party there, and I have a lot of difficulty in getting out of taking Henri and Freddy too, in fact I have to rope in Chuck with the 15 cwt to take them. I jeep off to Heemstede, and find Trat in bed with a cold. So we sit upstairs and consume a bottle of wine – of course John comes in and appears to own the place. I eventually take him off to the Amsterdam party where I entertain the guests (male) with my "Big Chief Boiler Kettle" story. At 11.30 I take John "home" – i.e. to Trat's house - where we have a cup of tea, borrow a book of Oscar Wilde and set off for home at 1.30am in pouring rain.

Going down the autobahn I notice I am doing about 40 mph, but my lights do not search far ahead, and all I can do is follow the centre white line. Suddenly something appears in sight but I haven't even time to brake, and I hit it full and square. It is the last of two small German tanks driven by Dutch drivers of the "Eclipse" scheme, which had run out of petrol and so just stopped on the road – no lights of course.

I bale out, bleeding from my nose, and find my right leg twisted inwards – the jeep horn full on, and much rain. Some civil policeman in a car picks me up and takes me to Valkenburg, where they give me a shot of Scotch and cocaine, and send me off to a military hospital in Rotterdam.

Next day I am x-rayed, and find my right hip is dislocated and the femur fractured. Chuck comes down, then goes back up to the Hague and brings me some kit, and a pukka "658" (a permission form for jeep transport), as the one I was using on the fateful night had his signature on it, forged by me. My hip is re-set, and I am put in a Thomas splint and packed off to Antwerp.

I have difficulty in sleeping on my back, and also in sitting on a bed pan, which has always been a hobby of mine. Next day I go to a hospital in Brussels, and yesterday am flown across to the UK.

I leave hospital at 12.45 for Evere and am put in the Dakota on my stretcher. It's 1.10 pm before we take off – hundreds of people get in and then off we go, arriving in Down Ampney[1] in 2.10 or so. Here I am carried into a long shed, my stretcher put on a couple of buckets, and I find myself next to a Pole from Italy. I am then given a cup of tea, a bottle, a cigarette, a newspaper, a "dinner" on a plate, a piece of chocolate and a wash, and a Red Cross dame comes round with a bag of toilet necessities and offers to send wires or telephone my next of kin – Heaven forbid!

Then off in another ambulance – my 7th – to Wroughton Hospital, where I now am, most depressed, as some Sgt bone shark has said it will all take about five months. So what to do with my kit in The Hague? I have just made a lying customs declaration to try and change 37 guilders, which I must get back and tear up, so I reckon that one way or the other, Joe Soap is in the SOUP!

[1] *RAF Down Ampney in Wiltshire.*

October 1st 1945

RAF HOSPITAL, WROUGHTON

I DON'T CHANGE MY GUILDERS, thinking it safer not to. I have now been here a fortnight, and Mama may be up next week. Sgt Lovell still has my fountain pen, so this is all I have *(he is writing in pencil).*

We are woken for washing at 6 am, and I then doze until breakfast at 8. Read the paper and write a letter until 12.30 lunch, then doze and a pipe until tea at 3.30, half a pint of beer and a cigarette at 6, and at 10.30 the ordeal of sleeping begins. Lately my foot has started to ache, so I have to be well doped to get any sleep at all. I have no appetite, and have trouble with my bowels.

I see that Golly Gilbert gets out from Malaya. I take up pipe smoking again – and try and arrange to get my kit sent across from The Hague. What next. *Quien sabe?*

October 21st 1945

RAF HOSPITAL, WROUGHTON

I AM STILL HERE, and with a 5 week moustache. My foot does not ache so much, and is strung up on a Balkan bed. Mama comes up, and brings my radio, but it is a bit sick after 10 years service. My kit arrives safely at the Wings Club.

Fernshaugh calls in to do the Court of Enquiry, and says the damage to the jeep is £100. Louise comes up one day, and stays 1-6pm, during which twice my bladder nearly bursts. I get a bottle of scotch from Tobermory, on Ma writing there.

Letters from Henri van Bergen, John van Ligten and Herman Hymans in The Hague and Amsterdam, but none from my office. Also one from Dicky Cuypers.

November 5th 1945

RAF HOSPITAL, WROUGHTON

STILL HANGING ON MY BALKAN BEAM. Time for some recollections of the Hague I feel.

I live in the Grand Hotel Terminus, room 110, with an extremely comfortable bed and a bathroom. The maids are efficient, and being well primed with chocolate, do all my darning etc. My room overlooks the station, and every morning, early, a crowd gathers to catch the train to Rotterdam and sometimes someone plays a guitar whilst waiting.

I mess across the road with the 11 P.W.S. team, and it is not much good when we change from U.S. to British rations. At the same time we lose our P.X. rations – the U.S. candy and cigarette racket. The office is originally in the hotel writing room, with a board of directors table and eight chairs to match, overlooking a patio with goldfish and an intermittent fountain. The telephone girl next door is full of curves.

At one period I organise lunch for passengers, before shipping them off by bus to 18 S.P. P&F section on the airfield, where they are manifested. Later we move into Muller's travel agency, Plaats 33, where we use about 3⁄4 of a long bar with a glass top, later cracked by Mr Sonderland's char lady. Mr S. retails train tickets over the other quarter of the bar.

We have our three telephones installed and a weighing machine, and do all the manifesting on the spot, having a waiting room upstairs with some fairly recent magazines presented by Micky, being surplus from her library. The afternoons I take off alternately, as our two air services – Croydon and Brussels, depart in the morning, and all that is left is bookings and our tame Dutch Auster squadron commanded by Captain Harry Niemhuis.

I go sailing occasionally at Varmont, where I go in one or two boats out on the Kaag, where the Dutch are accustomed to sail practically all the year round. Some have houseboats and live there. There is squash, which I play whenever I can, but find that I am not too good. All this of course is done by jeep. I go down to the beach too, before the West Wall, where there are anti-invasion stakes and occasionally some interesting flotsam and jetsam. Germans are removing mines up towards Nordwyk, and occasional explosions occur. We bathe sometimes, and I give some rifle instruction to two young lads in the Interior forces.

The evenings – Christ! – there is drinking and dinner at the Dyers restaurant, the Naafi 'Ambassadors' Club, where I am on the committee and latterly secretary, at little tables downstairs with lashings of Scotch - a double costs 60 cents. A piano and string band performs, its favourite being "Lily Marlene", and the violinist wanders from table to table playing to the pretty girls.

Then there's the Officers Country Club at Varmont, 20 minutes jeeping away and slightly drunk, where there is a horse shoe bar with high stools and a foot rail, a dance floor with a crooner, and dinner. Outside, the garden runs down to a canal, which runs into the Kaag, and there are swing seats a la summer with awnings above them.

And the people – my friends are: Bart and Betty Ijssel de Schepper, with a small house near the Plaats for 40 guilders a month, and who are friends with some Colonels in the Canadian army HQ in Hilversum, notably Col Leslie Chater.

Henri and Freddy Van Berger, whom I discover are not married, Louki who lives below them, and then a variety of women, some dumb, some beautiful, and some without any English – "Yonker", Katie, Lilly, Ellen with her U.S. accent, and many others whose names I have forgotten. At Wassenaar are some more, and also one or two messes belonging to semi-political intelligence units who never do much work. Major Henry Druce DSO bar, MC, Croix de Guerre etc, is one of them, and apparently mad as a hatter. The beautiful Iris Peake, is another.

I never ever get to bed before 12, and about once a week there is a bottle party of sorts at 69 Apollolaan in Amsterdam with John van Ligten, but latterly these are not so good. Here Jock Toothill and I meet the gallant Trat Moltzer. Occasionally I long for hills and jungles after months of pavements, but I am only here three months, and had arranged to have Dutch lessons when I had to leave so suddenly. I must not forget the U.S. Embassy girls...

What of the future? I come on the strength of 1 P.H.U. Innsworth[1], and when I am fit, about January I suppose, they will inform the Air Ministry that I am available for posting. If I can't pull a string so that someone asks for me, then God knows where I shall get to!

[1] *1 Personnel Holding Unit, formed at Innsworth in March 1945.*

December 6th 1945

St Ives

A CHAP FROM 283 SQUADRON comes in, and I hear that they have moved to Penang. I am let out on crutches for 14 days leave, and get on a train at Swindon in a compartment labelled "not for public use", and reach St Ives via St Erith. I stay at St Christopher's, a short crutch from the "Sloop" and Ma's flat, and I go to the "Sloop" on my first night.

Here I encounter Marika, now Mrs Roberts, who seems pleased to see me and escorts me home, even kissing me on my doorstep, but I haven't seen her since, so that's done me no good.

I can hear the sea at night. The sea here and the gulls always remind me of my first experience of St Ives, one of frustration over that Denise Bennett dame. I read Baffy's book "Family Homespun". I am put up for a Defence Medal and now have seven of the things.

A letter from Burt Mann, and he is only offered a four year extension of RAF service, so I might as well give it up and return to the Indian Army.[1]

[1] *Burt Mann was the only other surviving Indian army officer who had transferred to the RAF.*

December 10th 1945

RAF Hospital, Wroughton

I NEVER SEE MARIKA AGAIN, and spend most evenings in bed with a book. Eventually I am taken to look at Land's End and Cape Cornwall, but am not very impressed, and come up to London on Friday and stay at the Wings Club. Mike Jacobs, who is working in the United Pool of Artists, comes in, and I fill him up with gin, so that he has to retire in the middle of dinner, whilst I make a fairly reasonable pass at a blonde waitress called Mary, and I eventually have to see him to the front door and home.

Saturday I have lunch at the Cafe Royal with Mike and his fiancé Lena Barrie, but he is half an hour late, and we don't finish until 3pm and then dive into a news flick.

Louise takes me to the Wellington on Saturday night, but not a very successful party, though a lot of money goes down the drain. She sits with me for an hour at the Wings afterwards, but what can I do, though I am sure she is a waste of time, even if she wasn't going to the States next week.

Sunday I see McKilligan, from my Maungdaw flight and ex-Malaya, and have a few beers in the Wings Club with him, and we reminisce on Ambala days. Marnie Lowry comes to lunch and is then thrown out by the porter at 2.30pm, and I get on a train to Swindon.

Today I am told I need an X-ray, and will not be going to Loughborough, but to the other place, near Oxford – when? Christ.

December 19th 1945

RAF Hospital, Wroughton

I GET ONTO WALKING BETWEEN CRUTCHES, and tomorrow will get a pair of sticks. There is one Gus Sherrit here with a Ford 8, and Chris Arnell of 268 (Squadron) and myself go into Swindon several times. We get into the cinemas free for being crocks, and later go to the Kings Arms, The Bell or Goddards Arms to drink beer and get into conversation with the dames – not too successfully though.

Gus meets and fixes up a date with one of the ward WAAF orderlies. Three of us go in one night on six crutches, which looks a bit odd.

I ring up Daph when they suddenly want to turn me out, and she cannot have me until the 22nd, so I am in a bit of a quandary, until they change their minds.

I hear from Mhairi that she is going to marry a Russian. I see an 'Erk' in the reception office who has just come back from

Singapore, after drinking some local hooch which was reputedly brought across the Causeway by Chinese women in the tyres of their bicycles. 21 died, 2 are paralysed and he and another go blind.

I see a somewhat emotional U.S. film called "When You Went Away", which reduces me to tears – I always seem to get right into the mood of a film, and usually come out in a sort of daze afterwards.

December 31st 1945

Yorkshire

I LEAVE SWINDON ON A PAIR OF STICKS, and am met at Harrogate station by Jarvis Blayney, and have now been staying with them at Rutland House some ten days or so.

We have a party or two at Mrs Jacobs', with Mike and Freddie his fiancé, and Jarvis and I do a bit of drinking together, both at home and at the Red Lion, as well as at the Drovers Arms and the Chequers beyond Ripon. We also pay a visit to Scarscroft, and I get a glimpse of a local beauty called Judy Hare.

I go over to Bardsey where Grannie and Aunts Marion and Phyllis are installed, and discover that my great-grandfather was manager of Bramham Moor Stables for some 40 odd years. I also meet Aunt Molly and Jean in Harrogate for lunch, and later visit Aunt Hattie, in a nursing home with a drop of cancer.

Jarvis goes to his work in Batley every day, and I do a bit of walking in the morning, and then have lunch with Daph and Nancy at home. I seem to have got over the local infatuation of 18 months ago when I stayed with the Sproats at Rawdon.

Much fog, and I have a cold. I have a beer or two in the "Prospect Bar" during my morning excursions to Harrogate. I can walk fairly well without crutches, and get exceedingly drunk last Saturday on double Scotches, having exceeded my half dozen.

January 6th 1946

YORKSHIRE

WE GO TO THE RED LION FOR DINNER on New Year's Eve with Ronnie Hare, the beautiful Judy having cried off through a cold. Later to Mrs Jacobs' for the New Year, where I have a discussion on Burma, dates and what have you, with Ronnie at about 1.30am, only to discover we missed each other by two years. The rest of the week I walk about and go to a few cinemas, also over to Rawdon to see the Sproats and Betts.

I suffer from one or two bad attacks of my private gloom here, and I think I should have been better advised to go to St Ives, where there seems to be a bit of life all of a sudden over Christmas.

Tomorrow I shake off the fog of Harrogate from my moustache and go to be rehabilitated at Wallingford.

January 14th 1946

MONGEWELL PARK, WALLINGFORD

I GO DOWN TO MONGEWELL PARK, which is a millionaire's house and grounds near Wallingford, Berks. The Doc sees me and I throw away my sticks and do intensive P.T., swimming and bicycling. Gus Sheret is here, and we go into Henley one evening, and I meet some doctor and his erstwhile assistant.

Thursday I go to a Mess dance, and get hold of one Kay Beamish, a dental flight officer, and give her a kiss or two behind a screen in the billiard room. I meet up with Ellis and Briggs, with whom I was at Sandhurst, now a Wing commander.

On Friday Gus takes me to Uxbridge tube by road and I spend the weekend at the Wings Club. I ring up Wendy, and meet her and her "latest", one Derrick Llewelyn and a Patsy Westly, at the Cumberland Hotel, where we get large scotches by asking for brandies – some arrangement of Wendy's.

Then on to the Brevet Club, where I meet Mills (9 G.R.), one of my junior A.L.O.'s in 2 Sqn IAF., and from there to the Wellington and a night club called the "Silver Dollar". I am set back to the tune of £8 and get nowhere, on this Patsy job, though good to look at, and with long blond hair done up in a scarf like a Pekinese. She has a load on her mind, a Norwegian husband she doesn't want, and is extremely difficult to talk to, though she eventually has sufficient scotch to pour out all her troubles. I see her home, and suggest she comes to stay in Mayfair with me, but no go.

Bed at 4am, and next morning to Grindlays Bank to get some more money, and then to the India Office, where I had filled in a form for recruitment to the Burma Police (Class 1), but cannot produce my birth certificate to prove my age. He tracks down my 1936 Sandhurst entrance exams, papers and results, where the age qualifications are set out, and by a little calculation my age is proved. I then have lunch with Bill Robinson in the Wings Club, and afterwards take myself to see "Whilst the Sun Shines". Saturday evening I go drinking at a Mayfair bar, where I meet a South African Major and a G.I. who, whilst on temporary duty in the UK, get double my pay. I take the Major to the Brevet Club where I meet this Patsy again, get a bit drunk, and retire. I spend £2 on the way, and annoy the woman by attempting to kiss her.

In the Brevet Club on Friday I had met one Joan Anderson and arranged lunch on Sunday, but on calling her up she says she cannot come, but we fix up a date for next Friday – but quien sabe? So I take myself to see "Brief Encounter", then out to Uxbridge where Gus collects me at 7.30pm in his car. We stop in Henley for a few drinks, and then come on home. My leg is damn stiff after stopping exercises for a couple of days.

January 23rd 1946

I GO UP TO TOWN LAST WEEKEND with W/C Briggs in the car. He was in 1 Coy at RMC (Sandhurst), and I meet Joan Anderson in Mayfair for dinner and dance. Whilst out with Wendy and the Pekinese, I had met her in the Brevet Club and fixed up this date. I get on fairly well, and arrange to call her on Saturday afternoon, but get browned off and don't, going out instead to the Bristol Grill with Bill Robinson and two of his girlfriends – Daphne, and Majorie Wheldon the American, now in the U.N.O. Secretariat. I go to the India office, and some Brigadier thinks I should go back (to India), and that they will be unlikely to let me go to the Burma Police as I was thinking. I give Baffy lunch, and pour out my troubles to her, and she reckons the Indian Army is the best, as there is a pension.

On Monday (21st) I invite one of the physiotherapists out for a drink, Angela Elliott, and we drink in a couple of pubs in Wallingford. Since then I have spent all my time thinking of her, taking her to India etc, though I'm sure I don't know why, because all last week I had this Joan on the brain.

On Monday night my room mate, one F/L Young, excels himself by coming to bed stinking, and wetting the floor and fouling his counterpane.

Today I am taking Angela out to dinner, and expect to be chucked out of here next week as fit.

January 25th 1946

WE HAVE QUITE A SUCCESSFUL EVENING, Angela and I, and consequently I get no sleep until 3am through thinking of this and that. I had arranged to meet Barbara Paul in London this weekend, but I think it would be far better to meet Angela, so I ring up Barbara and say I am awfully sorry but I have gone and fallen in love with some girl and want to see her instead. She says it's alright, and "I hope you will be very happy". Which grates a bit on my ears, and I try and explain that I am not in that deep yet...

Last night I take Angela to "The George" but we seem a bit sticky, and I for one have difficulty making conversation. I burn my boats and write to my unit, now I.P.H.U. Innsworth, the India Office, and the Secretary for recruitment who dealt with my Burma Police effort, and hope to get my khaki uniform let out, if there is enough to let. I should be boarded soon[1,] but the M.O. is sick, so God knows how long it will take.

[1] *Medical Board to pass him as fit.*

January 28th 1946

I GO UP TO TOWN WITH GUS and then meet Angela at Paddington station. We drop her bag and go to Quaglinos, where we have a damn good evening.

Saturday to see "Sigh No More", and I get a table at Bagatelle for dinner, after a couple in my favourite bar, the "Mayfair". I don't think much of Bagatelle as the Scotch runs out, there's no room to dance etc.

Sunday we walk around Hyde Park, then to a film "Caesar and Cleopatra", and back to the Wings Club for dinner and then the 9.25 from Paddington.

I have given up trying to convince myself that I am not in love with her, and instead sometimes wonder how much it will hurt if she says "No". With no effort on my part we seem to click, and everything has seemed so natural without any of my usual evasions, prevarications, and what-have-you's when dealing with "dames". I am to be put out on Wednesday, and will go to town for a few

Angela Elliott

days, and then back here on Friday for a dance, and back home with Angela on Saturday for the weekend with her family. Oh – Hell!

February 2nd 1946
LONDON

WE GO OUT TO DINNER in "The Lamb" in Wallingford on Monday and Tuesday, and I leave for town on Wednesday. I go to the Air Ministry, and find out that my application for a permanent commission in the RAF has not been considered, so I decide to return to the Indian Army. I have one week's leave, and apparently no unit, so I see some chap who says go away until you hear from us, as having been given back to the India Office. I then go to the India Office, and find that I can claim only British lieutenant rates until I reach India.

I have a drink with Bernard Fergusson in Mayfair where I meet Pete Jennings, a W/C with more gongs than I have!

Yesterday I take Aunt Vivy to lunch and a cinema, and then visit Mrs Fraser for a very excellent dinner in her flat, and a discussion of Ma's finances. Today I am off to Baffy's lunch party, and then down to Mongewell.

February 7th 1946
STOKENCHURCH

I GO TO BAFFY'S LUNCH AT CHANDOS, where Bernard Fergusson is holding forth and one Anne Balfour, her niece. Then down to Mongewell Park where I meet Angela for the dance. Her parents come over, but I didn't feel too good about things, and retire to bed somewhat confused.

Saturday she brings me over to her home in Stokenchurch, and after lunch I take her for a walk, determined to say my piece, but still not feeling as though I was floating on a cloud. Rather the reverse, as though an abyss was at my feet. With some difficulty I spill the beans, with the rider that I don't feel as happy as I should. She says she hasn't known me very long, and we decide that I should take her away for another week, on approval, down to St Ives.

Her parents, she tells, and they soon overtake us on the fairway, and are practically putting on the green before we have driven off the tee! I have a session in the library with Dr Elliott, and deny any insanity etc in my family, and say I can keep her on my pay, without feeling inclined to go into various financial difficulties that may well arise.

Saturday night we rather bill and coo on the sofa until 1am, and on Sunday we drive over to Mongewell to try and get A. off for a week.

Today I drive her to work, in a 1933 Morris 8, the first time I have driven a car in the UK since 1937, and am going up to town shortly, hoping to meet her this evening, and go down to St Ives tomorrow. I ring up Ma, who didn't sound particularly enthusiastic – so we shall see.

February 10th 1946

St Ives

I take Angela down to St Ives, where Ma has arranged for her a small flat near the Quarterdeck. Ma seems to get on with her extremely well as day succeeds day. I get a bad attack of stage funk on the train, and retire to bed the first night in a state of extreme gloom, which is however dispelled in the morning when I go and collect A. for breakfast. I still do not feel somehow as I imagined that I should feel, but I seem to have been caught out in a somewhat similar fashion before.

The Air Ministry gave me another week's leave, and another warrant to St Ives, after which I shall presumably report to 1 P.H.U. Innsworth to await news of my fate.

Let there be no more gloom.

February 18th 1946

I TAKE A. OVER TO PENZANCE on Friday to try and get her an engagement ring, but the shops are shut, and we come home, and Ma produces a bottle of champagne and a signet ring left me by Lady F.B., which A. likes and wears in lieu of the proper thing.

We go to Tregenna on Saturday, but I'm not in a dancing mood, and she eventually leaves on Sunday, laden down with gold chains and presents, like a savage. I do some heavy reorganisation of my kit, and today go to Redruth to get photographed. Tomorrow I go up to town and hope to stay at the Wings Club. A and I climb up to the top of the hill behind Tregenna and have a kiss or two at the base of some granite monument there.

I well remember her standing by the mantlepiece in the flat she stayed in, "Cat View", saying that if I don't want her, she will go back to the Unit and try and forget etc.

I purposely get into some compartment on the St Ives train today where there is no blonde! A letter from A's father, saying he has fixed up with me to see A.V.M. Sir Alan Lees at the Air Ministry with regard to my application to transfer to the RAF, my previous one having apparently been lost, and not turned down as I had thought. I don't know – India is going to be grim for me now, both politically and professionally.

I arrange to continue Ma's £100 p.a. on condition that she leaves me her £3 a week, and can only hope it won't be too difficult. Or that she... I can't write it!!!

February 22nd 1946

I SPEND THE WEEKEND at Stokenchurch, helping organise the wedding at 14.30 hrs on March 12th. A. has flu and toothache, but goes back to work Monday morning, driven by me. I also meet Tony[1], and lots of old hags, and get a lift up to the Wings Club with some M.A.R. type on Tuesday. I meet Burt Mann and Bill Robinson, and we have a minor party with his current girlfriend Daphne Lyall Grant.

Today I go to the Air Ministry and find my case is still pending, so I rush it through a couple of departments with some WAAF officer, and a civil servant then telephones the India Office, and I shall go and see them tomorrow. I get two fivers from the Sproats, and two guineas from Susan Fraser, who can ill afford it. My kit will be limited to 4 cwt, which it probably exceeds, and I shall have to try and get a couple of boxes crated. I want to go down to St Ives in the meantime, and Ma wants to come up, so God knows what will happen.

I get pulled up in Piccadilly by a F/Lt Provost, who stops his car, gets out, and says "Excuse me, do you mind taking your hand out of your pocket when you walk down the street." I have one in my raincoat pocket!

I meet Clapham, a Lt Colonel, in the street, who commiserates me on my future rank!

[1] *Angela's brother, Tony Keable-Elliott.*

February 25th 1946
STOKENCHURCH

I ARRIVE FOR ANOTHER WEEKEND at Stokenchurch after an evening's drinking with Tony Keable-Elliott down in the London Bridge area, where the scotch is 1/4 a shot.

I go riding with A. but don't seem able to grip with any great strength. We ride through some woods, and I have to take up a couple of fence posts to get through into various fields. We have lunch in Henley with her grandmother, known as "Wuffy", who is

588

a bit deaf, so I leave the talking to A., putting in a few topical asides myself in a voice that she does not hear.

The odd cheque rolls in, and today we go to Oxford where I find a suitable zircon ring – £35 – which A. seems to like.

March 2nd 1946
St Ives

I SPEND A COUPLE OF DAYS IN TOWN with A. and then come down to St Ives. We go to Cinderella, and see her friend Peggy Murdoch in her dressing rooms where the fairy godma displays a lot of brown powdered flesh. Next day we go down to Kew Gardens, where I have a sudden longing for the Wynnaard near the Nilgiris, and then have drinks with Cecil and Vera Williams and their Ma at the Normandie, and later dinner at the Bristol Grill, where I dance around with A. with a little more zest than the last time in the Tregenna. Perhaps it was the music.

An O.H. (Old Harrovian) at the local box factory in St Ives is going to fix up my trunks in crates, and then I have to pray that the weight is under 4 cwt, or I shall have to reshuffle everything again. We meet Bunny Stone in the Sloop, and are to go drinking with him tonight.

Ma unpacks all sorts of silver and gives us a little! I get to thinking of India last night, and God knows what I shall do. Start off again as a Coy officer, knowing nothing?

17

March - April 1946

A Wedding and Farewell

UK

March 9th 1946

I COME UP TO TOWN and find that I am out of the RAF on March
1st. A chap called Cam gives me 14 days leave at the India Office,
but later increases it to 21 days, as the wedding is on 12th March,
and there is a draft sailing on the 15th. I sell my blue uniform to
Moss Bros for £2, and my raincoat for 30/-, and put on my old
Sandhurst superfine barathea[1], enlarged somewhat, and not so well
at the back, by "Flights".

I go out to christen it, and meet Ronald Deakin, a Major R.A.,
and we have quite a session at various bars, including the Brevet
Club, where he becomes a member. He later takes me home to his
flat where I have a couple more scotches, and suddenly realise I
have had it and go out and am sick, fortunately in the right spot.
He then drives me home to Nuffield House. Next day I come home
straight to Stokenchurch, and Ma arrives a couple of days ago, and
it's damned cold, and she is definitely off her best form.

Yesterday I high-tail it to Moss Bros and hire a sword[2], and
meet Bernard Fergusson and Brigadier Sanders-Jacobs there. I
appears that I have to make a speech, which will be difficult, as I
shall be overpowered by the other side – few DW supporters being
present. It all doesn't seem quite right, and yet it does!

[1] A type of super soft material.
[2] Colin lost his Sandhurst sword at some point during the war, and incredibly it
turned up 80 years later during Covid in a flea market in Vienna, identified as
belonging to Colin by its Wilkinson sword serial number.

March 12th 1946

BILL ROBINSON AND I are staying at Hambledon, preparing for a
wedding, my own, at which he is best man. We spend the morning

polishing Sam Brownes and swords. Old Hume sends two table napkin rings. John and Betts[1] give a sort of party in our honour on Saturday with some very good rum punch, where I meet Mike Chates, O.H.

594

Colin's best man Bill Robinson follows behind the happy couple.

A. and I have a puncture on the way, and I have to change the wheel. I cause a sensation by walking home from High Wycombe yesterday, and spend the afternoon writing letters. Last night Tony, John, Bill and I finish the last of the rum punch and some cocktail sitting in the dining room on hard chairs before an electric fire, and hold forth on life, and soldiering, in general.

[1] *Angela's elder brother John Elliott and his wife.*

March 18th 1946

BRIGHTON

I GET MARRIED by the ex-Bishop of Singapore, and everything goes O.K., except that I sit on my hat and try to put the ring on the wrong finger. Bill and I discover that we can't raise the necessary[1], after the Verger has presented the bill, but fortunately J.J. is at hand, and passes £10 over the pews.

At the reception I stand on my sword and shake a lot of hands and try and pop down a lot of drinks as well. One old buffer says "Nice to see an officer properly dressed again – with a sword." I produce my speech, already prepared, which seems to go O.K., and we later depart in the Morris 8 for the Woolpack Inn, Elstead, Surrey.

At the wedding I remember Aunts Babs and Vivy, J.J., Peggy, Gigs, Wendy, Mike Jacobs and Freddie, Mike Lowry, "Stew" and Anderson from Roland Gardens, and Mrs Steele Smith. Mike presents me with a cheque for £15! Also Ronald Deakin and Cecil Williams, who carries out one of the bridesmaids, Mary Haines, the other being her sister Vera.

I am reduced to tears in the Vestry, and forget to kiss A.

We go down to Brighton and lunch at the Old Ship, dine at the Crown at Chiddingfold, and yesterday morning I dress up and we go and visit the R.M.C. (Sandhurst). It is much the same, with the same 'bluebottles', but damned cold. I teach A. cribbage, and we walk around the surrounding country.

[1] *The Church of England marriage fee.*

March 31st 1946
STOKENCHURCH

WE SPEND A COUPLE OF DAYS in Brighton and then return home, and we ride a little and go out drinking here and there. I have a very good ride by myself along the Icknield Way, and see so many rabbits that I decide to unpack my .22.

We then go up to town for a few days, and stay in the Dominions Hotel. We see aunts B. and V., Mama, and Bill Robinson, and go to the theatre and Ciro's with the Broomes, who are local residents and rolling in the stuff.

I go to the India Office and find that I shall only get four days notice to sail, and that A. will be unable to come until I can get her accommodation. I also see one Lt Col. Owens, 1/8 G.R., in G1 Training, who advises me to write to the regimental centre and ask for a course when I get back, and set to work and start at the beginning again.

We later return to Stokenchurch, plus rifle, and Tony and I beat around Beacon Hill yesterday. I miss one rabbit, but there are plenty there. I say farewell to Mama at Marylebone station. I have done no work for six months and it is time I did.

April 7th 1946
STOKENCHURCH

I GO OUT SHOOTING WITH A. and get a rabbit and a grey squirrel. We also have a sort of family ride and I go over three jumps. The second one I do badly and come off, the first time ever in my life. I hurt my shoulder and go in to Oxford for an x- ray – it is OK and recovers after a bit of massage.

Plenty of sun here, and I try and learn up a little Urdu, not very successfully. I get orders to report to the London Assembly Centre, Great Central Hotel, on 12th April at 4pm, and go up to town to see about my baggage. I have just over the prescribed 4 cwt and I want to put it all in the luggage room, which is not allowed, so will hope for the best. I insure it, and find that I shall be a bit short of money.

Yesterday we go to the Old Berkeley Point to Point at Kemble, but I am unable to pick a winner. It's about time I got on with some work again.

April 19th 1946

STOKENCHURCH

ON 11TH I GET A WIRE POSTPONING MY REPORT until 20th and I am annoyed. I go up to London the next day and find that I am on a draft leaving on "Britannic" ex Liverpool about 25th, so A. and I are going up to town tomorrow. We have arranged a small party tomorrow night.

We walk and ride a bit here, and I knock off a couple more rabbits. My first English shooting since 1938, and very nice round here, as one can practically sunbathe. I get an urge for Scotland, and Tiree[1], but God only knows when I shall get there.

A. thinks she is having a baby, which may well postpone her voyage to India – I hope not. I get 2nd Lt Indian Army rates of pay, about £50, having sent a postcard to the India Office saying I am living on air and good literature – they pay me by return!

I get an urge to do some work again, as I have a lot to make up. At present I am wandering around with as many medals as a Lt Col at least! Follow that star...

[1] *Where Colin was brought up.*

April 22nd 1946

WE COME UP TO TOWN and stay at the Majestic Hotel in Cromwell Road. I go to the Great Central Hotel and meet Jerry Philips, 10 Baluchis, Donald Gorden, 7 Jajputs, and Macdowall, now a Lt Col working at the India Office. The outlook appears a bit depressing in India, and no word of when we sail.

I report there at 10.30 and 5pm every day. Saturday we have a party at Quaglinos. Mike Jacobs and Freddie, Bill and Daphne Lyell-Grant, Bob his brother, and dame, and the Osbornes, which is not too bad, and I get quite a lot of financial support – from A. too!

Sunday we go down to Sutton to the Williams' and then have dinner with Mrs Fraser. Bill has got himself engaged to Daphne and we are going to have a party tonight. I shall be glad to get away at last, but do not see what the future holds.

I landed on 25th two years ago. Little did I know!

April 27th 1946

A. AND I HAVE A DRINK with Jerry Philips in my favourite bar, the Mayfair, and then we have dinner with Bill and Daphne at Manetta's, where I get a bit weary at 11.30 or so. We see Mary Churchill[1], who recognises A. with whom she was at school, and A. says "Yes, you are Mary – Mary?"

Next day we say farewell in the entrance to Marylebone underground in a flood of tears, and A. makes straight for the up escalator.

[1] *Winston Churchill's daughter.*

Angela at Flashman's Hotel in Rawalpindi, where she was finally reunited with her new husband.

Postscript

A Passage to India

By Angela Dunford Wood

IT HAD BEEN SNOWING since before Christmas, and now it was early March 1947, and the weather had not changed. Snow was banked unevenly each side of the roads, like petrified clouds. The white fields lay stunned and silent. I was tucked into the back seat of the car with a rug and hot water bottle on my lap. Cars didn't have heaters then. Beside me was my 3-month old daughter, Cynthia, in a carry-cot covered by a blanket, together with my mother.

We set off at 8am to drive to London from my parents' home in Buckinghamshire for me to catch the train to Liverpool. My father sat in front, and a friend drove the car carefully along the icy road.

I shivered as I looked out of the window, with a mixture of emotions, partly because of the bleak outlook, but also from apprehension about the journey I was about to undertake to India with Cynthia.

My thoughts went back to early 1946. It had all happened so quickly. Colin and I were out for a walk during a week-end visit to my parent's home. We were resting on a log in the wood after a steep climb up the hill when he suddenly turned to me and said:

"The time has come, the walrus said, to speak of many things."

Of course I knew this quotation, but what on earth————? I looked at him blankly, and he continued without more ado:

"Will you marry me?"

I was dumbfounded. No preliminaries, not even a kiss or a cuddle —–I ask you!

"I haven't known you very long," I said shakily.

True, we'd been going out together since I'd met him just after Christmas, but this was only a few weeks later, and we'd never more than held hands, and had the odd kiss, and danced together.

"Well you'd better make your mind up soon, because I'm due to join my regiment in India soon."

I told him I'd think about it. We did have a kiss then, before racing down the hill and back to my parent's home. There must have been some magic in the air, because within a few days while Colin was staying I got to know him better and realised I did love him and wanted to marry him. It was like a dream, I couldn't believe this was really happening, but somehow I knew this was the right decision, and I felt more certain every day.

So it was like a whirlwind; we got engaged on 8 February, and married on 12 March from my home. After a brief honeymoon we returned to my parent's home where we stayed for several weeks before Colin sailed for India. I couldn't go with him as wives had to wait their turn before being allocated a passage on a troopship, according to the length of time of separation from their husbands.

Before he left, I realised I was pregnant and I wasn't offered a passage for several months. I was advised by my doctor not to travel until 3 months after I'd had the baby, so I decided to stay with my parents until it was time to go. They were very caring, and looked after me with love.

Now it was nearly a year later, and I was about to be reunited with this man I'd known only briefly, with his daughter in my arms.

I had feelings of excitement, anticipation, and insecurity. What if I didn't like Colin after all this time? It was too late to think about this now.

It took several hours of slow, careful driving, with a few stops on the way, before we reached Euston station and located the waiting train, which had several feet of snow on the roof.

The platform was crowded with troops loaded with kit-bags, and civilian passengers and their friends and relatives who had come to see them off. The air was thick with smoke and frosty breath from the mouths of the noisy mass of humanity with their farewell messages. As I boarded the train, I said a tearful goodbye to my parents. I didn't know if I would ever see them again. I expected to be in India for several years.

The train journey to Liverpool seemed endless. It was very cold in the carriage, and I noticed a drip falling regularly onto Cynthia's blanket from the snow on the roof above, and hastily moved her carry-cot a few inches, as far as our cramped conditions would allow.

The stevedores who were supposed to load the luggage onto the troopship Georgic, had all gone home as it was late. The soldiers coming off the train had to heave the trunks and baggage into the ship's hold, rather roughly.

We were herded on board and allotted our cabins. I couldn't believe my eyes when I saw where I was to sleep. I had a bunk in an 18-berth cabin, with a string cot attached to it. The cabin was like a hospital ward with bunks close together along each side, some with cots attached like mine. We were all wives, some with children or babies. It was very spartan; the only porthole was blocked by a life-raft fixed over it outside. The one wash-basin was inaccessible, and we all had to share a communal wash-room with basins side by side, and the only privacy was in the lavatory.

After changing and feeding Cynthia, which was last done on the train, I collapsed on my bunk and slept.

Next day, we were told where and when to get breakfast, and I had a look out on deck. It was bare apart from lifeboats and other equipment, and there were park benches fixed to the deck at intervals. They had just been painted dark brown and were still sticky to touch. It was very discouraging. There was hardly any room to move in our cabin, and we were told that the Captain made an inspection every day at 10am, when we were all to be out of the cabin. I ignored this instruction, as I said I had to feed my baby at this time. I sat on my bunk breastfeeding Cynthia when the Captain came round, and I looked at him defiantly. He went away after a cursory glance round the cabin.

I had to bath the baby and later wash her nappies in a tin washing-up bowl which someone at home had wisely suggested might be useful, and that proved invaluable.

There was a very basic lounge at the end of which was a notice board on the wall showing the ship's route and daily progress, and also a daily news bulletin which made depressing reading. India seemed to be in turmoil, especially in the Punjab, which was my destination. My husband had written before I left home to say that he would meet me when the ship docked in Bombay.

However, 10 days later, when we got to Port Said where some of the troops disembarked, there was a message from him saying he might not be able to meet me, as he was engaged in quelling the riots which had broken out. That was a daunting prospect.

It became very hot and stifling in the cabin, which smelt of stale sweat and babies' nappies. We didn't have disposable ones in those days. On deck the atmosphere was even worse. The heat wafted, stinking of dirt and dust, spices and dung, and the noise was deafening with traders and the crowds ashore.

Some tradesmen were allowed on board to sell materials and trinkets, and men in djellabas (loose cotton robes, which most of the Indians wore) called gully-gully men performed conjuring tricks for the passengers left on board.

When we left port, I was transferred to another cabin, luckily much more spacious, and occupied by just one other woman, an Indian lady who was very pleasant and friendly. She showed me how to wear a sari, and I envied her colourful ones and determined to buy one for myself one day. It became even hotter as we sailed through the Red Sea and many people chose to sleep on deck, with men on one side and women on the other. I joined them with Cynthia, and it gave us a bit of relief.

One day I read on the bulletin news: 'Riots in the Punjab, Murree in flames'. This was where I was going. My heart sank, and I began to wonder whether I should have stayed at home. As we approached Bombay we had to line up and were asked by an official what our destination was. I said 'Rawalpindi' which was where my husband had arranged for us to break our journey before driving up into the hills. My luggage and papers were all marked Bombay, which was where I was expecting Colin to meet us. I just hoped he'd be there. The voyage had taken 3 weeks.

When the ship docked, the wives and families all lined the deck, trying to spot their husbands waiting for them on the quayside. I dressed Cynthia in her prettiest dress, and made myself look presentable, and waited on deck in anxious anticipation, with the others. I was aware of the heat, and the even more pungent spicy, dusty smells than I'd experienced in Port Said. The noise of the crowd ashore, mingled with the excited cries of those on deck, were deafening.

Wives called out 'There he is, I've seen him!' waving frantically and jumping up and down. I waited and waited – in vain. No husband.

Eventually I was summoned to speak to a man from Grindlays Bank with a letter from Colin enclosing some money, saying he was sorry not to be able to meet me, and suggesting I find an hotel in Bombay, and book myself a passage on the Frontier Mail, which was a train running every few days to Rawalpindi, a 48-hour journey. I felt quite unprepared in every way, to make the arrangements myself, not knowing the country or its language or customs, and with a fractious baby and all my luggage to contend with.

I was lucky to be befriended by a very kind and capable colonel's wife on board, who took pity on me and suggested I should ask to be able to remain on board until the ship turned round for the return journey. She contacted her brother-in-law who was a director of the Indian railways, and he had a compartment reserved for me in two days' time.

This was a great relief, and I found there was another wife who was also staying on board. She had sprained her ankle badly, and had to rest up for two days. She was going to Lahore, which was on the same route as my train, so we travelled together until she left the train there. I still had some way to go, and I was transferred into a 4-berth cabin with just one Indian lady. It was reasonably comfortable, but hot and stuffy and if the windows were opened, a shower of smuts was blown in from the engine, and it was even hotter. We bought food from the vendors at the stations at which we stopped on the way, and I had to ask for boiling water for drinks for Cynthia between feeds. After two nights and two days we reached Rawalpindi, and I left the train with Cynthia in her carry-cot, to be met by an army sergeant. He saluted smartly and asked:

'*Excuse me madam, are you Mrs Dunford Wood?*'

I was so thankful that someone knew who I was, that I almost embraced him. He busied himself seeing to my luggage, and I asked him where my husband was.

'*The colonel isn't able to come today, as he's occupied with the rest of the company quelling the riots.*'

'*But what about my husband?*' I persisted.

The sergeant explained that my husband had been appointed temporary lieutenant-colonel, as one of his senior officers was on leave and the other one had been promoted, and Colin was the next in seniority although he was only a lieutenant!

From then on things went smoothly. I was driven with the baby and all the luggage in an army staff car to an hotel, and shown to a self-contained chalet in the green, spacious grounds of Flashman's Hotel in Rawalpindi. It was a calm haven after the noise and bustle of the street on the way there, which was a cacophony of screeching horns and street vendors. There were cattle wandering along the middle of the road in some places, and pedestrians pushing carts, and wobbling cyclists careless of other traffic.

Once we'd arrived I took stock of my new surroundings, and as if by magic, an ayah arrived for me, and a bearer, who took care of all my needs. The ayah spoke English, and was a Christian, and had been engaged for me by friends of Colin's. She competently took over the duties with Cynthia, and the bearer sorted out the luggage. We stayed in that chalet for two days, and I took my meals in the main building of the hotel. Then, suddenly, Colin appeared at the door of my chalet. There he was, tired but tall, bronzed and handsome. All my bells started ringing. I was holding Cynthia at the time: for a moment we just looked at each other, then I thrust the baby into the ayah's arms and rushed to embrace Colin.

At last my troubles were over.

Afterword

Colin in 1947, after his return to the Indian Army

Although Colin started these diaries as an army officer, first with the Leicesters and subsequently with the Indian Army, the bulk of his war was spent with the RAF. In total, he racked up over 850 hours as a pilot, which included over 150 operational sorties and combat missions, for which he was awarded the DFC, covering four operational theatres of war. The list of plane types he flew ran to over 50, but the bulk of his flying was done in Audaxes, Lysanders, the Hurricane 11B and the Spitfire XIV.

When he returned to the Indian Army in 1946, incredibly he had to restart from where he had left off - as a 2nd Lieutenant - because the Indian Army did not recognise RAF ranks! Then Partition came, and once again he was repatriated to the UK in 1947.

Unfortunately, he was late to the party by that time, and there were not many jobs available in the regular army, which was rapidly being slimmed down. The best he could find was a job with the Royal Army Service Corps (later to become the Royal Corps of Transport), looking after water transport.

At the time, he must have been a strange sight in uniform - an army Captain with RAF wings and the medals of a Brigadier! Subsequently, he spent many happy years teaching young army cadets to sail in requisitioned 1930s yachts that used to belong to the Luftwaffe.

His last operational tours of duty were to Christmas Island as part of Operation Grapple in the 1950s, to work on the atomic weapon tests, and to Borneo in the counter-insurgency operation of the early 1960s.

He reached the rank of Lt Colonel, and died while still in the army, in 1971.

of smoke, and tracer comes up past me from both sides. I [...]
skid and turn and climb, and feel a little more comfor[...]
4500', but still no cloud. Eventually I get clear an[...]
Today I see the pictures — perfect and congratulations [...]
sides. There is one car, 16 HGT, one flak gun, an e[...]
position — one hun getting off her bicycle, two men r[...]
from the horse & cart they are leading, and many other [...]
some cool and collected, others with guilty consciences. [...]
Maitland, the C.O. goes out to do a further p[...]
job and gets shot down. So it looks as though Is hall [...]
some more — and probably follow him too — as [...]
well shaken up in that area and on the qui vive

March 24th

The forward facing jobs are now postponed I can celle[...]
god. Hamish Selkirk finishes his tour and there is the [...]
party with "B" flight drunks very prominent. I get a[...]
and have my tie chewed off twice and bruise a ri[...]
a chair during a fall. It puts me off flying for two [...]
During one mêlée I grab Johnny Young by [...]
of his pants and he jumps around screaming [...]
calf in hot brine. Later he tells me that [...]

a grip on his piles! I go down to Oysterwich and visi
Griffiths, Ma's Canadian friend of Tregenna days a
me a meal and quite some hooch. He is Adm
4 Can. Arm. Div. I get two letters from Monica, w
very nice bits in them! I am flight commander
as Alan C-Mogg is acting C.O. and I am enjoyi
with the first job of work for over 12 months! T.
allies attack across the Rhine. Nick Bowen &
anti-flak patrol between Weesel and Bocholt
and spot the gun flashes and get the "cabrank"
on to them. There is masses of 88.8 40 m/m ab
navy a flash do I see, and we reckon they are us
flashless ammunition. We are expecting to see
and at 100.0hrs I see them just as Nick calls up
Tattoo", our agreed call. We go and watch and
photographs but due to the haze they are not up.
The first drop seems unopposed, but the second come
a hail of 40mm flak. The leading Dakota, catc
but continues his run, turn, and then they / the
bail out. I see about 6 Dakotas burning, 2
crash, one puts out it fire, in an engine, and 1 j.

An excerpt from Colin's diary for March 1945, with the corresponding log book entries on the following page.

613

| YEAR | | AIRCRAFT | | PILOT, OR | 2ND PILOT, PU |
MONTH	DATE	Type	No.	1ST PILOT	OR PASSENGE
MARCH	6TH	DAKOTA	PK113	W/O BOOST	SELF
FBRCH	8TH	SPITFIRE XIV	RM712	SELF	SOLO
MARCH	9TH	SPITFIRE XIV	RM712	SELF	SOLO
MARCH	10TH	SPITFIRE XIV	RN113	SELF	SOLO
MARCH	11TH	SPITFIRE XIV	RM871	SELF	SOLO
MARCH	11TH	SPITFIRE XIV	RM812	SELF	SOLO
MARCH	13TH	SPITFIRE XIV	RM800	SELF	SOLO
MARCH	14TH	SPITFIRE XIV	RM800	SELF	SOLO
MARCH	14TH	SPITFIRE XIV	RM795	SELF	SOLO
MARCH	15TH	SPITFIRE XIV	RM812	SELF	SOLO
MARCH	17TH	SPITFIRE XIV	RM812	SELF	SOLO
MARCH	19TH	SPITFIRE XIV	RM920	SELF	SOLO
MARCH	23RD	SPITFIRE XIV	AM712	SELF	SOLO
MARCH	24TH	SPITFIRE XIV	RM901	SELF	SOLO
MARCH	24TH	SPITFIRE XIV	RM703	SELF	SOLO
MARCH	25TH	SPITFIRE XIV	RM825	SELF	SOLO
MARCH	27TH	SPITFIRE XIV	RM872	SELF	SOLO
MARCH	28TH	SPITFIRE XIV	RM920	SELF	SOLO
MARCH	31ST	SPITFIRE XIV	RM825	SELF	SOLO
			TOTAL	FLYING TIMES	
C.J. Dunford Wood F/L				MARCH 1945	
O.C. "B" FLIGHT No 2sqn R.A.F.				HOLLAND	
APRIL	1ST	SPITFIRE XIV	RM795	SELF	SOLO

GRAND TOTAL [Cols. (1) to (10)
.........805.........Hrs.........55.........Mins

DUTY	SINGLE-ENGINE AIRCRAFT				
(& RESULTS AND REMARKS)	DAY		NIGHT		DUAL
	DUAL	PILOT	DUAL	PILOT	
	(1)	(2)	(3)	(4)	(5)
TOTALS BROUGHT FORWARD	104.05	664.50	7.25	10.15	
— GILZE RIJEN					
JEN — MILL		.20			
GORINCHEM and LEIDEN MILL		1.05			
ERTICAL OBLIQUES BRIDGES NEAR 11TH ARM. DIV.		1.05			
/R WESEL–DINSLAKEN– CONTACT/R		.55			
AC/R RETURNED BAD WEATHER		.20			
ST — CAMERA FAILURE		.25			
AC/R ARNHEM–APELDOORN MUNSTER		.55			
TAC/R RRETURNED ENGINE ROUGH		.10			
C/R UTRECHT–GOUDA– GORINCHEM		.55			
14" FORWARD FACING WEHL & HEERENBERG–KILDER 500'		.30			
4" FORWARD FACING OBLIQUES		.40			
/R UTRECHT–GOUDA– GORINCHEM		1.00			
R UTRECHT–GOUDA– GORINCHEM "No 2" LANDING IN DIERSFORDTER WALD		.55			
I–FLAK RECCE DURING 6TH AIRBORNE DIV.		1.05			
R EMMERICH–ZUTPHEN –DEVENTER BOSCH		.55			
ARTY/R GUNS IN STOKKAMMOR "No 2"		1.00			
R SCHOUWEN–ROTTERDAM–THE HAGUE – STADTLOHNE		1.20			
NEEDE–AALTEN–GROENLO –AHAUS		.55			
WAGENINGEN –ZALTBOMMEL		1.00			
C/R UTRECHT–AMERSFOORT —					
		14.25			
15		13.10			
–WAGENINGEN –ZALTBOMMEL 500–1000 AC/R MISSION UTRECHT–AMERSFOORT–		.40			
TOTALS CARRIED FORWARD	104.05	679.55	7.25	10.15	
	(1)	(2)	(3)	(4)	(5)

About the Editor

James Dunford Wood has worked in the film industry, in e-commerce, and as a publisher, travel writer and author. For advance news of James's new books, visit at jdwoodbooks.com

Also by James

The Big Little War

For wider context on The Battle of Habbaniya, based on these diaries, read James's history 'The Big Little War'. This is the incredible true story of how a handful of RAF trainee pilots, of whom Colin was one, and their instructors, in antiquated biplanes, defeated the Iraqi army and the Luftwaffe, to save Britain's Middle East empire. See the diary entries for April and May 1941.

Glossary

The diaries are full of acronyms, abbreviations, military names and words in Hindi, Urdu and Pashto. Below is a list of the most common:

- *'P' staff - personnel department.*
- *2/13 G.R. – 2nd battalion, 13th Gurkha Rifles etc.*
- *56th - 2nd Bn, 13th Frontier Force Rifles (Colin's former unit).*
- *AILO - Air Intelligence Liaison Officer.*
- *AMO - Air Ministry Order.*
- *APM - Assistant Provost Marshal (military police).*
- *ATS - Advanced (flying) training school*
- *AVG - American Volunteer Group, the 'Flying Tigers'.*
- *B.F.F. - Burmese Frontier Force.*
- *B.O. – British Officer.*
- *B.O.R. - British other ranks.*
- *Babu – Indian orderly.*
- *Badmash – bad man.*
- *Balbo - a big formation of aircraft.*
- *Bandobust - Hindi word meaning an arrangement made to deal with something.*
- *Bde – Brigade – typically 2-5 Battalions, c. 5000 soldiers.*
- *Bn – Battalion, 800-1200 soldiers.*
- *Bearer - an officer's personal servant, paid for by the officer.*
- *B.O. – British Officer.*
- *Bisley - Blenheim aircraft.*
- *Bn – Battalion, 800-1200 soldiers.*
- *Board - Medical Board, meaning assessment.*
- *Bully - bully beef rations.*
- *C.O. – Commanding officer.*
- *Chankider - nightwatchman or guard.*
- *Chapao - night raid.*

- *Chaplies – leg protectors at ankle height, also Indian sandals.*
- *Chaprasi - office boy or junior.*
- *Charpoy – boy servant.*
- *Chattai - natural roof or flooring, made from rushes.*
- *Chokra - a boy employed as a servant.*
- *Chota peg - a measure of spirits, usually whisky.*
- *Column – a Battalion size expedition, large sortie.*
- *Column – an Battalion size expedition, large sortie.*
- *Coy – Company – a unit of 100-200 soldiers.*
- *CR42 - Italian Air Force Fiat Falcon, single seater fighter.*
- *D.S.P. - Deputy Superintendent of Police.*
- *Dogras – Indian troops, like Gurkhas (the Nepali equivalent).*
- *Dushman – a local tribesman.*
- *D.V. – Deo volente for God willing.*
- *Dhobi or dhobie – an Indian washerman or woman.*
- *ERK - Lowest rank RAF groundcrew.*
- *F/R - Fleet Air Arm Reconnaissance.*
- *Fils - lowest denomination of Iraqi money.*
- *G.R. - Ground reconnaissance.*
- *G2 - general staff officer, responsible for intelligence.*
- *G3 - general staff officer, responsible for ops and training.*
- *Gasht - trek, expedition on foot.*
- *Group - an RAF organisation made up of operational, administrative and training units.*
- *GSLO - General Staff Liaison Officer.*
- *GSO - General staff officer.*
- *Havildar - Indian Army sergeant.*
- *Hurry - Hurricane aircraft.*
- *I.A.F. - Indian Air Force.*
- *I.O. – Indian officer.*
- *I.O.R. – Indian other ranks.*
- *Jhil - a small lake.*
- *Kaccha - Hindi for raw or basic.*

- *Khasadar – locally raised militia.*
- *Khel - Wazir village or clan.*
- *Khud - a ravine.*
- *Lashkar – rebel, insurgent or group of them.*
- *Levies - Assyrian militia serving as RAF guards in Iraq.*
- *ME109 - Luftwaffe Messerschmitt Bf 109 fighter.*
- *Link trainer - a flight simulator.*
- *Lizzie - Lysander aircraft*
- *M.G. – machine gun.*
- *M.O. - medical officer.*
- *M.T. - motor transport.*
- *ME110 - Luftwaffe Messerschmitt Bf 110 fighter-bomber.*
- *Munshi - a secretary, or language teacher, or wise man.*
- *NCO - non-commissioned officer.*
- *Nullah – stream, dry river bed, gully.*
- *P.A. – Political administrator or agent (like local governor).*
- *Pani - water.*
- *P.O. - pilot officer.*
- *P.R.U. - Photographic Reconnaissance Unit.*
- *P.W.D. - Public Works Department.*
- *Pani - water. (Nimbu pani - lemonade).*
- *Penguin - senior officer.*
- *Picquet – forward observation post.*
- *R.A. – Royal Artillery.*
- *Pongo - the name given to soldiers by the RAF.*
- *Prayers - senior staff meeting.*
- *Prune - a hapless, novice pilot.*
- *Queen Sabe - who knows?*
- *R.P. – Reconnaissance Patrol.*
- *R.T.R. – Ready to Return, less often Royal Tank Regiment.*
- *R.U.R. – Royal Ulster Rifles.*
- *Rajputs – 7th Rajput Regiment.*
- *RASC / ASC - (Royal) Army Service Corps*
- *Razcol – Waziristan campaign army, named after Razmak.*

- *RIASC – Royal Indian Army Service Corps.*
- *RMC - Royal Military College, Sandhurst.*
- *Rs - rupees.*
- *RSM – Regimental Sergeant Major.*
- *S.M.O. - senior medical officer.*
- *Sangar – defensive position, normally sandbagged.*
- *SASO - Senior Air Staff Officer.*
- *Satellite - Satellite Landing Ground.*
- *Scouts – locally raised militia.*
- *Shikara - guide, hunter.*
- *Shikari - lake boat.*
- *Tac/R - tactical reconnaissance.*
- *U/S - unserviceable.*
- *Ulia – Unit liaison officer.*
- *V.B. – Vickers-Berthier light machine gun.*
- *WAC - Women's army corps.*
- *Wimpey - Wellington bomber.*
- *Wing - an RAF Unit made up of several Squadrons.*

Milton Keynes UK
Ingram Content Group UK Ltd.
UKHW012104171123
432796UK00003B/37